The Strengths Model

The Strengths Model

Case Management with People with
Psychiatric Disabilities

Second Edition

Charles A. Rapp

Richard J. Goscha

OXFORD
UNIVERSITY PRESS
2006

OXFORD
UNIVERSITY PRESS

Oxford University Press, Inc., publishes works that further
Oxford University's objective of excellence
in research, scholarship, and education.

Oxford   New York
Auckland   Cape Town   Dar es Salaam   Hong Kong   Karachi
Kuala Lumpur   Madrid   Melbourne   Mexico City   Nairobi
New Delhi   Shanghai   Taipei   Toronto

With offices in
Argentina   Austria   Brazil   Chile   Czech Republic   France   Greece
Guatemala   Hungary   Italy   Japan   Poland   Portugal   Singapore
South Korea   Switzerland   Thailand   Turkey   Ukraine   Vietnam

Published by Oxford University Press, Inc.
198 Madison Avenue, New York, New York 10016

www.oup.com

Oxford is a registered trademark of Oxford University Press

Library of Congress Cataloging-in-Publication Data

Rapp, Charles A.
The strengths model : case management with people with psychiatric disabilities /
Charles A. Rapp, Richard J. Goscha.
p.   cm.
Summary: "Second edition grounds the strengths model of case management within the
recovery paradigm and details evidence-based guidelines for practice. Describes the
conceptual underpinnings, theory, empirical support, principles, and practice methods that
comprise the strengths model of case management"—Provided by publisher.
ISBN-13 978-0-19-518285-9
ISBN 0-19-518285-5
1. Psychiatric social work—United States.   2. Social case work—United States—
Methodology.   3. Mentally ill—Rehabilitation—United States.   I. Goscha, Richard J.
II. Title.
HV690.U6R36 2006
362.2′0425—dc22   2005029425

1 3 5 7 9 8 6 4 2

Printed in the United States of America
on acid-free paper

For my sons, Justin and Devin,
and
Linda, my wife, who also is the best strengths
practitioner I have known.
Thank you for all you have given me.
Charles A. Rapp

To my wife Shelly, and my children Bayley,
Brendan, Callie, and Kelsey,
You are my passion for life and the inspiration
behind everything I do.
Thank you for all your love, support, and patience.
Richard J. Goscha

Foreword

When I was still a teenager, I was admitted for a second time to a psychiatric institution. Although it was the same unit, with the same staff who had been there during my first admission, there was something different about the way they treated me that second time around. In retrospect, I now understand that on my second admission, the staff had lost hope for me. In their eyes, I was no longer one of the ones who might leave the hospital and never return. I had returned, and I was now counted among the recidivists.

Even the new diagnosis I was given reflected the hopelessness surrounding me: Chronic Undifferentiated Schizophrenia. Perhaps that's why I felt a deep urgency to mobilize all the energy I could muster to get myself out of that place as quickly as possible. Perhaps I was afraid if I fell into the depths of the hopelessness mirrored in their eyes, I might never leave and would be lost forever. In order to avoid that fate, I focused on one thing—getting back to school. More specifically, I insisted I had to be discharged on a Wednesday morning, so I could make it back to my evening English Composition II course at the local community college.

It took three weeks, and all the strength I had, but, finally, there I stood on a bright April morning, discharged, standing on the steps of the mental hospital, with my suitcase in hand. On the outside, I must have looked pretty ragged and worn. There were dark circles under my eyes. My hands trembled, and my skin was the pasty white mask that high doses of haloperidol can create. But by six o'clock that evening, I was sitting in my college course, with my notebook open. I tell you this was a triumph! Yes, I was so drugged that I was nodding in and out of a stupor, but I remained upright at that desk. Yes, my hands were trembling but I was holding that pen. Yes, my eyes were glazed but I stared straight ahead and focused on that teacher. Yes, my vision was blurred but I tried with all my might to listen to the lecture. From where I sat, this was a moment of triumph. I felt like I had just climbed Mt. Everest, standing upright in the thin air with arms raised, my spirit enduring like brightly colored Buddhist prayer flags against the white snow.

At the midpoint of the class, it was customary to take a coffee break. As the other students filed out, the professor approached me. I liked him and smiled as he came over. I thought he would be happy to see me and would say he was glad I was back in class. Instead, he bent toward me and said, "Pat, you look awful. Why don't you just go home tonight, and we'll see you next week." Something in me collapsed at that moment. I felt my spirit breaking. Didn't he know how hard I had worked to get to class that night? Why couldn't he see how strong I was? Why was he focusing on what was wrong with me, instead of celebrating my achievement? I dragged myself home and gave up. I sat on the couch, smoking cigarettes and staring at the nicotine-stained wall in front of me for the next nine months.

I do not fault that professor. I believe he thought he was being helpful. But his help was not helpful, for two reasons. First, he thought he knew what I needed and prescribed his help without my input. He did not understand that in order for help to be helpful, it must be cocreated in a partnership between a person asking for help and a person offering to help. Secondly, the professor focused on what was wrong with me and failed to see the strength in my vulnerability. He probably thought strength and vulnerability were mutually exclusive. He did not understand that in and through my vulnerability, I had found the strength to get discharged from a mental institution and then make it to class that same day.

My experience occurred in a school setting, but the same sort of thing also happens over and over again in mental health practice. With the best of intentions, staff focus on our deficits, fail to discern our strengths, and prescribe help that is unhelpful. "You should try a volunteer job because you are not ready for work." "We recommend group home placement because you are not high functioning enough to live in your own apartment." "Avoid stress and stay on medications for the rest of your life." In economic and in human terms, the cost of this deficits approach is high. Because of it, too many people receiving services in the nation's mental health system have put their dreams, hopes and aspirations on hold and are living marginal lives in handicaptivity.

The Strengths Model described in this book represents a powerful antidote to the high cost of the deficits approach. In this model, strength is not constructed as some superheroic state of invulnerability. Rather, we learn that even when people present with obvious vulnerabilities, they also have strengths. Their strengths are in their passions, in their skills, in their interests, in their relationships, and in their environments. If mental health practitioners look for strengths, they will find them. After strengths have been identified, the practitioner and the service user can begin to cocreate help that is helpful. Help that is helpful focuses on the service user's strengths and finds niches in the environment where those strengths can be used and valued. A farmer diagnosed with schizophrenia begins to farm again. A man who can't hold a job does so to buy the motorcycle he has always wanted. A woman with major depression who is too lonely begins to teach her granddaughter to crochet, and loneliness recedes to the background as visits from her family become more frequent. And then, the authors tell us, a remarkable thing happens. A "radiating effect" occurs. It's as if by focusing on a single strength, the strong part of the self begins to radiate outward, building a new life of meaning and purpose.

There is strength in vulnerability. This book teaches us that. In practical terms, it teaches us the concrete skills necessary for working with clients in real world settings from a strengths' orientation. Additionally, empirical evidence is provided demonstrating that the Strengths Model is not just a good idea, but an effective intervention as well. The application of the Strengths Model makes a positive difference in the lives of real people in real world settings. Let's use it!

Patricia Deegan

Foreword to the First Edition

In the fall of 1982, as a part of my M.S.W. practicum requirements, I was assigned to a special project at the Bert Nash Mental Health Center in Lawrence, Kansas. I was still working full time at the Menninger Foundation Children's Residential Treatment program, a job I had held since earning my Bachelor's Degree in Social Work. This new project was headed by a doctoral candidate, Ronna Chamberlain, and featured an outreach case-management project serving those we then called the chronically mentally ill. In this project, we were to visit people in their homes, assist them with the problems of living they faced, and help them reach their goals by focusing on personal and environmental strengths.

I could not have been operating in more contrasting worlds. In my job, I was spending a considerable amount of time in a hospital setting, operating from a psychodynamic orientation, with great emphasis placed on accurate diagnosis and treatment. In my educational experience, we were operating freely in the community and we were intentionally not told the diagnosis of those with whom we worked. At first, I and others found the work a bit confusing. The professionals who surrounded us had a more sophisticated lexicon to describe their work, and there was a great deal of concern about very lofty issues like professional boundaries, creating false expectations among "the patients," and such.

Yet, as the project expanded to other sites, it became clear that consumers were accomplishing things that certainly were unexpected. First, they were staying out of the hospital despite the fact that many were referred with the stated belief that it was only a matter of days before another hospitalization would be necessary. Beyond this, consumers and case managers began talking about finding jobs, making friends, and living independently. Interestingly, when case managers brought these goals to treatment team meetings, they were met with a wide range of reactions, from amazement to ridicule, but most often we were subjected to a lecture about our naiveté and the true nature of serious mental disorders.

The work itself was hard but fun for many of us, but utterly distasteful to others. This has not changed. For those of us who enjoyed the work, there was a real sense of being a mental health maverick, and this created a sense of purpose. You spoke so differently about these folks than did other staff. You seemed to know so much more about their lives and what they still dreamed for. I remember an early attempt to learn from the consumers about case management: what they saw as helpful or not helpful. It seems funny to look back now and recall that we were a bit disappointed by the early returns. The consumers said that they appreciated that the case manager helped them rearrange furniture, structure their day, or cooked a meal with them. They didn't discuss feeling empowered, or how completing the strengths assessment improved their self-esteem. Yet, they were taking more control over their life and they did seem to feel better about themselves.

Herein lies the dilemma that case managers so often face. Case management is so practical that some, even case managers themselves, devalue the importance of it. We know now from consumers that the fact that the service operates where the rubber meets the road is why it matters so much to them. The power lies in the practicality.

By focusing on real-life goals in real-life settings, strengths-based case management predated by 15 years the current interest in recovery as a mission of our work. Implementing the strengths model elevates the consumer from a passive recipient of services to the director of the process. It affirms the person not as a patient, or client, or even a consumer but instead as a citizen. Case managers working from the strengths model help others reclaim full citizenship, replete with all the rights and responsibilities that come with citizenship. Case managers also challenge our communities to move beyond the segregation impulse to embrace instead those who face serious challenges and to allow them to make their contribution to the human enterprise.

In the early days, little time was spent considering the power and potential of the strengths perspective in other realms of social work practice. Instead, work began with professionals and officials in other states to understand and implement case management in mental health. This would require plodding through predictable skepticism and scorn, but slowly but surely the model took hold. This effort has never lost steam. Training and technical assistance have occurred in over 40 states in the United States and internationally. This fact alone makes this one of the most eagerly awaited books in our field. Charlie Rapp and others have been just too busy to write it all down until now.

The concepts and principles that underpin the strengths model have stood the test of time. This model is based on humanism and pragmatism—a wonderful combination. The growth of case management and other helping modalities in mental health has had an enormous impact on the field. Today, state hospital roles are shrinking, hospitalizations are of shorter duration, and we have not only specialized housing and work programs but we have consumers running such programs. Better still, we have consumers living and working in normalized settings, drawing on the supports of friends and, at times, professionals. The technology has changed but is still centered on a person who listens, cares, and helps people with the practical issues they face in daily life. We call these people case managers.

There is great danger in reading this book too narrowly. The power of this method of helping is only underscored when one considers that the successes recorded here were with those considered among the most disabled, the most impaired, and those least likely to approach normalization. This model suggests that individuals and communities have strengths that can be called forth, expanded, and matched to help people reach their potential. These same processes can help all of us lead successful and satisfying lives.

There is also danger that readers will dismiss this work as simply good social work practice—the way, in fact, most professionals operate on a day-by-day basis. To embrace the strengths perspective requires that all aspects of practice must be examined and challenged. This text makes clear that all key phases of social work practice, from engagement and assessment to the evaluation of outcome, look different when the strengths perspective is employed.

There were precursors to this work, of course, such as White's pioneering work on competence and Maluccio's application of the principles of competence in social work practice. However, the interest in strengths-based practice models, particularly in case management, has led to applications in alcohol and drug treatment, public assistance programs, older adults, and children. Indeed, the strengths perspective has reenergized all facets of social work including direct practice, public policy, and research. Accordingly, the principles and methods in this book have wide application on the streets and in the classroom.

W. Patrick Sullivan, Ph.D.
Professor
Indiana University
School of Social Work

Preface

In the eight years since the publication of the first edition, the recovery movement has risen to prominence internationally. Parallel to this and perhaps in part due to it, the practice and intellectual energy devoted to strengths-based practice have grown exponentially. Books have been published, conferences are held, articles written, and university courses are focused on or at least include attention to strengths-based practice. Strengths-based practices are increasingly being adopted by mental health agencies and other fields of practice. A redesign of case management and other services, sometimes quite dramatic, has occurred in New Zealand, Japan, England, and Canada. Ironically, perhaps most suggestive of its rising status and credibility has been the presence of critiques of the model in scholarly journals.

Although this increase in activity is welcome, there is danger lurking. The term "strengths" as applied to mental health and other human services resonates with many people and conjures up positive images of our clients and our work. The currency of the word is such that it is being applied with great casualness. Some believe that just treating clients with respect and courtesy means you are strengths oriented. Others think that if we add a few lines on "client strengths" to an assessment form, we are now implementing the strengths model. Placing a thin patina of strengths on traditional approaches and labeling the approach "strengths" is nothing more than old wine in a new bottles. It runs the risk of weakening the future development and creditability of strengths case management and strengths-based practices in general.

The strengths model is not just a philosophy or perspective, although it is that. It is rather a set of values and principles, a theory of practice, and explicit and rigorous practice methods that have been developed and refined over the last 25 years. The empirical testing of the case management model has shown consistent results that are superior to traditional approaches to serving people with severe psychiatric disabilities.

Having said this, much work is yet to be done. Too often, achievement and the quality of life of people with psychiatric disabilities remain inadequate. Unemployment is between 70 and 80%, loneliness dominates many lives, much of their time is spent segregated from "nonclients", poverty places a pall on their being, and options are severely constricted. Even though the strengths model is not a panacea for this oppressive situation, it has demonstrated its ability to make a positive difference in the lives of people we are privileged to serve.

This book is primarily a practice text. It is the first attempt to translate systematically the ideas and conceptions about the Strengths Model into a set of empirically derived practices. While the first three chapters are more conceptual in nature and chapter 8 discusses the organizational and managerial context for practice, the central focus of the book is strengths model practice: engagement, strengths assessment, personal planning, and resource acquisition. This edition of the book includes more vignettes than the previous edition to make the practice "come alive" for the reader. There are more strengths model tools or what one colleague calls "navigational aids" to foster the skillful implementation of the methods. There is an expanded section on recovery and its relationship to strengths-based practice. Reflective of the growing international interest the model, there is more material from other countries. Because the strengths model is still in its infancy, much has been learned about the methods that comprise the approach. This volume includes that which we have learned.

Given this purpose and feedback received from a wide variety of people, we have come to believe that this text has relevance for multiple audiences. For social work students (B.S.W. and M.S.W.), the book should be directly applicable for any classes devoted to case management or mental health practice. It has been used as supplement to undergraduate or graduate social work practice classes. Some universities have begun elective courses on the strengths model. For these courses, the fit seems to approach the ideal. We have also been told that the book would also have relevance in some university curricula in psychology, nursing, psychiatry, vocational rehabilitation, and occupational therapy.

The book was also written with current mental health professionals in mind. Case managers should find this volume directly relevant to their practice. Team leaders, supervisors, and administrators will benefit from the detailed explanation of the methods as well as the chapter on creating a supportive case-management organizational context. The behavioral listings of strengths-oriented practices following each of the practice chapters and the fidelity instrument (chapter 8) are currently being used by quality assurance personnel. For people responsible for staff development and training, the book should provide a blueprint for organizing and implementing training for case managers.

The authorship of this book camouflages the fact that no book owes more to more people than this one does. The book started in 1982 when the University of Kansas School of Social Welfare was awarded a $10,000 contract to provide case management services to a group of people, referred to, then, as "chronically mentally ill." With good fortune that only could have come from a higher being, Ronna

Chamberlain, a new Ph.D. student, was assigned to me (Charlie) as a research assistant to design and mount this project. We identified the desired client outcomes (e.g., community tenure, independent living, work, leisure time activities) and were befuddled by how existing case-management approaches with their emphasis on linking clients to formal mental health services would be able to achieve them. Discarding the current approaches, we began identifying the elements of practice that we thought would make sense. The notion of individual and community strengths was central to this initial formulation. We selected four students who were then assigned to the project to meet their field practicum requirements for their B.S.W. or M.S.W. degrees. Ronna acted as their supervisor and field instructor.

We evaluated the work as best we could. Given that the intervention was new and quickly put together, that we were using inexperienced students to actually deliver the service, that the host agency was not always supportive of our efforts, and that very few approaches with this population had demonstrated success, we were at best hopeful that the data would show some areas of success and provide direction for improvement. We found, much to our surprise, that on 19 of the 22 indicators we assessed, the results were positive (Rapp & Chamberlain, 1985). We could not really believe it, but the next year we mounted three other projects in three different mental health centers. Matt Modrcin, Dick Wintersteen, and Jim Hanson joined the team. Refinements were made in the approach, the evaluation was made more rigorous, and once again, positive results were found. Based on this work, we put together a training manual.

By the mid-1980s, case management was becoming the centerpiece of community support services and states were devoting considerable effort to developing case management "systems." We were asked to provide consultation and training in Kansas and several other states. It was at this time that we became acutely aware that this "strengths approach" was a dramatic shift from the past. In a typical group of trainees, it seemed half the people said they were already doing it, and the other half said we were crazy for thinking it. We wish we had been smart enough at the time to let them battle it out instead of trying to convince each half that they were wrong. To be fair, even in the earliest training groups, there were always a few people for whom the approach resonated. It put into words and methods what their own practice sensed was right. These people became the "champions" of the strengths approach.

By the late 1980s, the strengths approach was benefiting from the attention of an increasing number of faculty members and Ph.D. students at the School of Social Work. Liane Davis and Sue Pearlmutter applied the model to AFDC recipients of benefits from the Aid to Families with Dependent Children Act in the Job Opportunities and Basic Skills Training (JOBS) program, Becky Fast applied it to work with the elderly in long-term care, Dennis Saleebey sought to tailor the model to an approach to community development, John Poertner applied it to work with youth and families, and Rosemary Chapin sought application of strengths to social policy analysis and development. Ann Weick, Jim Taylor, and Dennis Saleebey applied their intellectual energy to developing a richer conceptual understanding of the model. In 1993, as part of the Council on Social Work Education (CSWE) reaccredition study, the School adapted the strengths perspective as one of its guiding curriculum themes. It is rare in social work and other disciplines for a whole school to be so identified with a particular innovation. To be a part of such an experience is a source of great pride and joy.

So, the "we" is the faculty and Ph. D. students of the Kansas University School of Social Welfare. The "we" is also the myriad people in practice and administration who based their practice on the model who were able to show us where further work was needed but whose work gave the model a credibility it would never have achieved if relegated to academics. Among the "we" we are indebted to are Leslie Young, Estelle Richman, Kevin Bomhoff, Marti Knisely, Tom Wernert, Martha Hodge, Linda Carlson, Diane Asher, and Diane McDiarmid. More recently, Barbara Anderson of Te Korowai Aroha (TKA) in Auckland, New Zealand and Paul Liddy of Timaru, New Zealand, have inspired us and educated us about how the strengths model can revolutionize a system of care.

The "we" also includes those people, many from other universities, whose work has mightily influenced the approach. This includes Julian Rappaport, Steve Rose, Bob Drake, Gary Bond, Debbie Becker, Priscilla Ridgway, Richard Rapp, Pat Deegan, Paul Carling, and Steve Huff. Dr. Deegan has honored us with her Forward to this edition. Dr. Drake has graciously written the afterword for this second edition. From across the seas, we have learned much from Dr. Peter Ryan of Middlesex University in England, and Dr. Hideki Tanaka from Nagasaki Wesleyan University in Japan.

There are two special "we's." The first and foremost is Ronna Chamberlain. Her ideas at the start and throughout its development comprised the core ideas of the strengths model. Because she does not like to write, although she does it well, or speak publicly, although she is quite articulate, her contribution is hidden from most people. Without her, this book would not exist.

The second special "we" is Pat Sullivan, currently Professor of Social Work at Indiana University, and the former Director of Mental Health for the State of Indiana. Pat was a student case manager in our first project in 1982, was a supervisor of one of our special student units, supervised the supervisors of other projects, helped design the early training, was a trainer, ran a community support program (CSS) based on the strengths model, and provided technical assistance to CSS programs trying to implement the strengths model. He extended the model to work with substance abusers and employment assistance programs. Pat has done more to conceive of and articulate the role of environment in the strengths model than anyone else. We were honored that Pat agreed to write the foreword for the first edition of the book. In a sense, the circle has been completed.

We would like to express appreciation to Orlena Carr for typing, retyping, retyping, and retyping the manuscript over the last year.

A Few Comments on Language

In this book, we have used various terms to refer to people with psychiatric disabilities. Occasionally we used the term "consumer," which had currency in the 1990s as the preferred term but is now losing favor. Often we use "client." Whenever possible we have tried to just use "people" or "person" unless the context of the text demanded making a distinction between the person receiving services and other individuals or groups of people. Please understand, the use of each term is a rhetorical convenience. We find no term that separates people with psychiatric disabilities from the rest of society to be acceptable. The entire strengths approach is about personhood, not patienthood or clienthood or even consumerhood. People's courage, resilience, and, yes, their strengths in the face of distressing symptoms, disabling conditions and an often unresponsive and oppressive society have taught us more about being human than anything else.

We also use the term "case management" in this text. We acknowledge that this term is considered pejorative to many persons with psychiatric disabilities. People with psychiatric disabilities are not "cases" and they do not need to be "managed." A more accurate reflection of what this service entails is that it is the services that are managed to help people reach their goals and recover their lives. We use this term for this particular service only because it is the most widely recognized in the field at the current time. Our goal is to change people's approach to practice, not just the term. This book is written for multiple audiences and our hope is that people within systems who currently provide "case management" services will read this book and use it to move their systems toward being recovery oriented.

During the writing of the text, we experimented with terms such as "recovery coordinator," "life coach," "recovery guide," and "recovery consultant." Each of these terms, we feel are far superior to "case manager." We hope that people will continue to advocate for replacing this term with one that more reflects recovery. Until a more appropriate title becomes globally recognized, the term should be used with sensitivity to the negative connotations it carries.

So we end this preface with a favor to ask of the reader. If any of the terms used in this book have negative connotations to you, or even if they do not, don't just read "client" or "consumer," but think Alice, Joe, Joan, Bill, or some other name. We refer to people, just like you and me who are striving for the same things we are, who are both flawed and flawless, who have struggles and difficulties, who valiantly fight every day, and can experience joy and passion for life. In other words, they are you and me.

Acknowledgments

The section in chapter 1 headed "The Dominance of Deficits" has been reprinted from Ann Weick, Charles A. Rapp, W. Patrick Sullivan, & Walter Kisthardt, (1989), A strengths perspective for social work practice, *Social Work, 89,* 350–352.

Much of the section in chapter 1 under the heading "Ecological Perspective" is taken from James Taylor (1997), "Niches and practice: Extending the ecological perspective," with permission. In D. Saleebey (Ed.), *The strengths perspective in social work practice,* 2nd Ed. New York: Longman.

The description of entrapping and enabling niches in chapter 2 is from James Taylor (1997), "Niches and practice: Extending the ecological perspective," with permission. In D. Saleebey (Ed.), *The strengths perspective in social work practice,* 2nd Ed. New York: Longman.

The section entitled "The dimensions of resources: The four As" in chapter 7 has been excerpted from Walter Kisthardt and Charles A. Rapp (1992), "Bridging the gap between principles and practice," with permission. In S. Rose (Ed.), *Case management and social work practice.* New York: Longman.]

Figure 7.1 has been reprinted with permission from W. B. Davidson and C. A. Rapp (1976), Child advocacy in the justice system, *Social Work, 21,* 225–232.

Portions of chapter 8 ("Traditional Management Practice" through the material discussing "The Case of Estelle Richman") has been adapted from Charles A. Rapp (1993), Client-centered performance management for rehabilitation and mental health services, in Robert W. Flexer and Phyllis L. Solomon (Eds.), *Psychiatric rehabilitation in practice,* with permission from Andover Medical Publishers.

Contents

The Strengths Model

CHAPTER ONE

History, Critique, and Useful Conceptions: Toward a Strengths Paradigm

THE STRENGTHS MODEL REPRESENTS a paradigm shift in mental health, social work, and other helping professions. A paradigm is a model or way of perceiving the world and solving problems. The current paradigm, which has continued for over a century, has been found wanting. The lives of people with psychiatric disabilities continue to be marked by poverty, loneliness, limited opportunities for achievement, discrimination, and oppression. As Saleebey (1996) writes:

> The impetus, in part, for the evolution of a more strengths-based review of practice, comes from the awareness that our culture and the helping professions are saturated with an approach to understanding the human condition obsessed with individual, family, and community pathology, deficit, problem, abnormality, victimization, and disorder. (p. 1)

This chapter sketches the context within which the strengths model evolved. We first describe and critique the paradigm that has dominated mental health practice for the last century. We then turn to ideas and conceptions that have been useful in developing the strengths perspective.

Social Processes and Sensitizing Viewpoints

People with psychiatric disabilities continue to be oppressed by the society in which they live, and this oppression is often reinforced by the practices of the professionals responsible for helping them. This is rarely done intentionally or with malevolence but, rather, is elicited by compassion and caring. Because the oppression is dressed up in the clothes of compassion, it is difficult to identify, to understand in its underlying dynamics, and to develop alternative approaches to it.

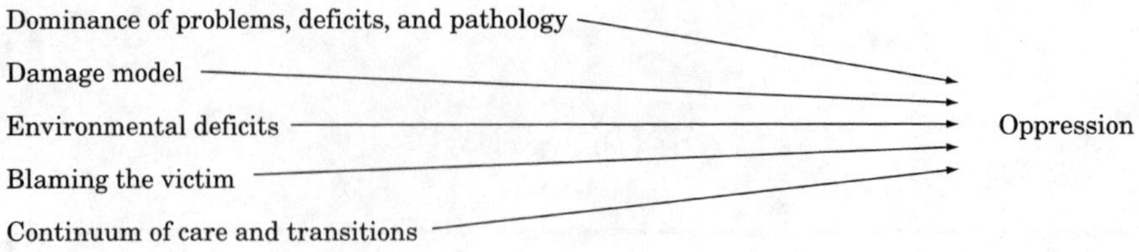

Dominance of problems, deficits, and pathology

Damage model

Environmental deficits   Oppression

Blaming the victim

Continuum of care and transitions

Figure 1.1 Social processes and practices contributing to oppression

This section seeks to describe those social processes and professional practices that contribute to the oppression. Figure 1.1 depicts the key elements of the current dominant paradigm.

The Dominance of Deficits

Dichotomies pervade human life. In trying to cope with complex realities, human societies have created stark divisions between the good and the bad, the safe and the unsafe, the friend and the enemy. It is a curious fact that greater attention invariably is paid to the negative poles of the dichotomy: to the bad, the unsafe, the enemy. This pull toward the negative aspects of life has given a peculiar shape to human endeavors and has, in the case of social work and other helping professions, created a profound tilt toward the pathological. Because of the subtle ways in which this bias is expressed, its contours and consequences must be examined to set the stage for a different perspective. The strengths perspective is an alternative to a preoccupation with negative aspects of people and society and a more apt expression of some of the deepest values of social work.

Tracing the Roots

Social work is not unique in its focus on the pathological. Throughout history, cultures have been preoccupied with naming and conquering outsiders and waging battles against the enemy in people's souls. Judeo-Christian heritage has given rise to a clear sense of human frailty through its concept of sin and has used that concept to limit or punish those thought to transgress moral norms.

Social work's origins are in the concept of moral deficiency. The Age of Enlightenment created the philosophical backdrop against which to consider in a new way the plight of the less fortunate; but, given the economic environment in the 1800s and the religious convictions of those in the so-called charity organization society, the strategy was one of moral conversion. Poverty was attributed to drunkenness, intemperance, ignorance, and lack of moral will (Axinn & Levin, 1975, pp. 89–94). Change was to come about not through provision of monetary assistance but through persuasion and friendly influence. The emphasis on human failings as the cause of difficulties established a conceptual thread with strands that are still found in practice today.

The focus on moral frailty went through an evolution that both softened and disguised its presence. Soon after the turn of the previous century, social workers began calling for a more professional approach to the work of helping people (Leiby, 1978, p. 181). The adoption of the empirical method used in the natural sciences was the stimulus for the social sciences and for the emerging professions to define themselves not as crafts or philanthropic efforts but as organized disciplined sciences (Leiby, 1978, p. 348). Mary Richmond was one of the earliest proponents of using a logical evidence-based method for helping (Goldstein, 1943, p. 29). Through her and others' efforts, increasing attention was paid to defining the problems in people's lives so that a rational, rather than a moralistic, strategy of intervention could be pursued.

The development of this formulation of professional practice was intersected in the 1930s by increasing interest in psychoanalytic theory as the theoretical structure for defining individuals' problems (Smalley, 1967, pp. ix–x). But the cost of this affiliation with psychoanalytic theory and its derivatives was an ever more sophisticated connection with human weakness as the critical variable in understanding human problems.

These weaknesses became reified with the language of pathology. A complicated clinical nomenclature grew up as a descriptive edifice for these new psychological insights. The art of clinical diagnosis was born—an art far more complicated than Richmond's logical steps to assessment. In keeping with the scientific belief that a cause must be found before a result could be achieved, attention was paid to all individual behaviors that signified a diagnostic category. After a diagnosis was established, treatment could proceed. In this process, every category of clinical diagnosis focuses on a human lack or weakness, ranging from the relatively benign to the severe.

Recent Directions

The profession has not been oblivious to the importance of recognizing individual strengths in practice encounters. Indeed, in 1958, the Commission on Social Work Practice included as a main objective of the field to "seek out, identify, and strengthen the maximum potential in individuals, groups and communities" (Bartlett, 1958, p. 6). Later writers, such as Hepworth and Larsen (1986), Shulman (1979), and Germain and Gitterman (1980), have given attention to the danger of focusing narrowly on individual pathology while ignoring strengths.

However, a subtle and elusive focus on individual or environmental deficits and personal or social problems remains in recent frameworks. The "ecological perspective" of social work practice, a model developed by Germain and Gitterman (1980), illustrates this point.

Germain and Gitterman (1980) built on the social work tradition of focusing on the interface between person and environment, introduced ecological concepts such as adaptation, and suggested that attention should be focused on the transactions that occur between people and their environments. They contended that it is in these complex transactions between a person and the environment that "upsets in the usual adaptive balance or goodness-of-fit often emerge" (Germain &

Gitterman, p. 7). These "upsets," from their point of view, often are the result of "the stress generated by discrepancies between needs and capacities on one hand and the environmental qualities on the other" (Germain & Gitterman, p. 7). In short, it is either the characteristics of the individual or of the environment that create the problem. Emphasis thus rests on the ability to assess adequately the nature of the problem. Although Germain and Gitterman acknowledged the importance of "engaging positive forces in the person and the environment," the goal is to reduce "negative transactional features" (Germain & Gitterman, p. 19). In a subtle way, negative aspects still dominate this view.

A focus on the adequate assessment and diagnosis of the "problem" has deep roots in the profession and remains a central tenet of modern practice tests. For example, Compton and Galaway (1984) saw the focus of social work as "using a problem-solving focus to resolve problems in the person-situation interaction . . ." (p. 12). Hepworth and Larsen (1986), who devoted an admirable amount of attention to the identification and use of strengths, also considered the problem-solving process as essential to social work practice and promoted the importance of "assessing human problems and locating and developing or utilizing appropriate resources systems" (p. 23).

Problem-solving models are closely tied to the notion of intervention. As Compton and Galaway (1984) described it, "Intervention refers to deliberate, planned actions undertaken by the client and the worker to resolve a problem" (p. 11). Although writers such as Shulman (1979) sense the need to identify the strengths of both the individual and the environment, the focus of intervention is on the "blocks in the individual—social engagement" (p. 9). Read closely, these views all suggest that accurate diagnosis or assessment of a problem lead naturally to the selection of particular "interventions" that, it is to be hoped, disrupt the natural course of individual or social difficulty. The difficulty or problem is seen as the linchpin for assessment and action.

Charles Cowger (1992) claims that virtually all our professional attention and assessment protocols are focused on deficits of the individual or environment. He developed a grid to group the approaches:

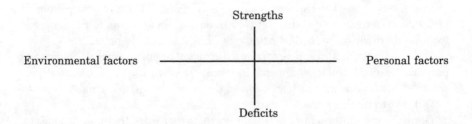

He suggests, "A new theoretical interest in how environmental factors affect practice has been increasingly evident in the literature since the early 1970's. However, like renewed interest in client strengths, this interest has not been fully realized in actual practice because practice guidelines and specific practice knowledge have lagged" (p. 142–143).

Maluccio (1979) found that social workers underestimated client strengths and had more negative perceptions of clients than clients had of themselves. "Social workers persist in formulating assessments that focus almost exclusively on the pathology and dysfunction of clients—despite the time honored social work plat-itude that social workers work with strengths, not weaknesses" (Hepworth & Larson, 1982). As Cowger (1992) states, "a library search for assessment tools that include client strengths is a particularly unrewarding experience" (p. 140).

The Problem With Problem Focus

Attention to people's inability to cope is a central expression of the prevailing per-spectives on helping. Approaches differ in the way the problem is defined, but vir-tually all schools of therapeutic thought maintain the belief that people need help because they have a problem—a problem that in some way sets them apart from others who are thought not to have that problem. The terminology, "having a prob-lem" suggests that problems belong to or inhere in people and, in some way, ex-press an important fact about who they are. The existence of the problem provides the rationale for the existence of professional helpers. In an extreme form, it cre-ates a view of professional helping that has a hidden logic and questionable results.

Concern about establishing the precise cause of a problem ensnares social work-ers in a strategy for dealing with the problem in those terms. If it is determined that a person's difficulties are linked to family dynamics in early childhood, then the approach "teaches" the person this view of the problem and justifies the at-tention on understanding these formative relationships. If the cause of family prob-lems is thought to be patterns of communication, then the approaches will train the family in new communication skills. No matter what the cause, there will be some strategy to teach the clients the nature of their problems and the particular route to recovery.

Using Gregory Bateson's (1972) work, Watzlawick, Weakland, and Fisch (1974, p. 39) analyzed this approach in relation to alcoholism. They showed that the view of the problem is carried into the solution. If alcoholism is defined as a disease in-volving excessive alcohol consumption, then the therapeutic approach must be cen-tered on abstinence. Getting a person with an alcohol abuse problem to stop drink-ing is the first step in recovery. In this way, alcohol is both the center of the problem and the treatment. Even when someone is successfully sober for long periods of time, alcohol remains a central concern of his or her life. The image of the bottle is as prevalent in sobriety as in drunkenness.

When the cause of a problem is defined, the problem exists in a new way. The process of naming something heretofore unnamed creates it as a reality toward which therapeutic effort must be directed. Instead of the vague unease or intense discomfort a person in her or his situation experiences, the source of the difficulty is identified and feelings are focused on it. It is named—a process that carries with it a magical quality because it makes something comprehensible that had been puz-zling, frightening, and mysterious. The sense of control that often comes with naming provides a sense of initial relief. The unknown has been categorized and labeled. By making the problem subject to rational processes, the person in the grip of the difficulty sees that it has some shape and can be contended with. The power of the professional comes from naming the problem and from having in mind a strategy for overcoming the difficulty.

This process of naming occurs using a language that belongs to the professional, not the client. Diagnostic categories establish classes of conditions with which a client is matched. To accomplish this match, a clinician must look for broad commonalities rather than idiosyncratic characteristics. The client's situation must be made to fit predetermined categories and those categories are not ones that the client would devise as an adequate description of his or her situation. To categorize someone as depressed provides only the most global assessment. It does not reveal the meaning of that person's struggle nor the strengths that lie hidden in that person's story.

Problem-based assessments encourage individualistic rather than social-environmental explanations of human problems. Although it generally is understood that people live in complex social milieus that dramatically affect them, assessment rarely takes into account larger social variables. Even when long-term conditions, such as poverty, are seen to severely limit people's ability to manage their lives, attention often is concentrated exclusively on efforts to change the behavior of those affected. The difficulty in changing social conditions deters helpers from keeping those factors in the picture and results in a view of people as the cause of their own problems.

The problem, deficit orientation, sets up other barriers for clients. One manifestation occurs frequently in residential treatment programs. Deficiencies in behavioral skills are identified in the initial assessment, and a treatment plan is devised to teach these skills. When the person demonstrates these skills, the staff is inclined to count it as a successful intervention. However, success is marred by other so-called dysfunctional behaviors that are observed and the strategy of correcting them is similarly programmed. This pattern may be repeated numerous times, turning what was expected to be a three-month stay into several years of treatment. The focus on problem behaviors develops a life of its own and is paradoxically reinforced by the fact that the residential environment in itself creates "problematic" behavior. Although a focus on such behavior may temporarily alleviate its expression, there is no evidence that the results of such residential intervention will carry into the person's life after release from the program. Gearing treatment goals to problem behaviors ensures that there will be a never-ending requirement for continued intervention and little sense of success.

Finally, the activity of searching out the problem creates the illusion that there is an identifiable solution or remedy for it. Underlying the problem approach is the belief that an accurate naming of the problem will necessarily lead to an appropriate intervention. Although that belief may occasionally be justified, the daily practice experience is far less precise. Many professionals find that naming a situation provides no clues about how best to proceed—and that the real clues emerge from the continuing and ever-changing interaction with clients who are in the situation. In addition, the very act of diagnosing the problem may add a new layer of problem that complicates notions about a clear course of treatment.

The focus on the problem and the process of defining it established the contours of much of what is identified as helping. Three dynamics are clear: (1) the problem invariably is seen as a lack or inability in the person affected, (2) the nature of the problem is defined by the professional, and (3) treatment is directed toward overcoming the deficiency at the heart of the problem. This triumvirate helps ensure that the helping encounter remains like one conducted in an emergency room, where wounded people come to be patched up.

The Damage Model

One manifestation of the deficit orientation is described by Wolin and Wolin (1993) as the damage model. Based on their work with "survivors of troubled families," they describe the damage model as resembling the germ theory of disease:

> Troubled families are seen as toxic agents, like bacteria or viruses, and the survivors are regarded as victims of their parent's poisonous secretions. Children, according to the Damage Model, are vulnerable, helpless and locked into the family. The best survivors can do is to cope or contain the family's harmful influence at considerable cost to themselves. (p. 13)

It is easy to replace "troubled families" with "people with psychiatric disabilities" and see that the same dynamic currently dominates the care, treatment, and expectations of the people receiving services.

The authors describe the damage model as "half of a treatment" that:

1. offers few clues about how survivors could build and maintain loving relationships with other adults, function as effective members of the community, raise children . . .
2. solidifies an image of themselves as helpless in the past, which then becomes the basis for fault-finding and continued helplessness in the present . . .
3. the premise that family troubles inevitably repeat themselves from one generation to the next, coupled with the model's omission of resilience, does as much to frighten survivors as it does to help them. (pp. 14–15)

Environmental Deficits

The preoccupation with deficits has also colored our view of environments and communities. We talk of needy, impoverished, and pathological communities. We lament the presence of stigma and discrimination. We complain that the community lacks the resources to build a good life for people with psychiatric disabilities and that the service system lacks resources to provide assistance to people's recovery.

Rather than attributing the cause to individual deficits, deviance is seen as a result of pathological subcultures or social forces. Therefore, the failure of people with psychiatric disabilities to be employed is attributed to discrimination, local unemployment rates, failure by employers to make reasonable accommodations, or the nature of the capitalist economic system.

The toxicity of the environment has been a dominant theme in mental health. The growth of asylums in the nineteenth century was viewed as replacing the chaos of urban life and unhealthy social conditions with new therapeutic environments located in less stressful rural environments (Rothman, 1971). There was a wide agreement among sociologists throughout the first half of the twentieth century that urban life was linked to mental illness (Faris & Dunham, 1939; Park, 1952; Wirth, 1964; Hollingshead & Redlich, 1958). As Burgess (1939) wrote "definitely and unmistakably the incidence of the chief psychoses are related to the organization of the city" (p. ix). The need for replacement environments was implicit in the growing stature of "therapeutic community" and "milieu therapy" in hospital programming during the 1940s and 1950s.

The community mental health movement and the failure of deinstitutionalization placed renewed focus on the poor social conditions these former hospital patients were now living in. The solution was to develop a network of new professionally operated community support services (Turner, 1977). Unfortunately, these new programs followed the blueprint of the state hospital system:

> By developing segregated housing programs, therapy, and recreational groups, and by relying on sheltered employment opportunities, the state hospital, in effect, has been replicated in the community. As a result, thousands of mentally ill individuals are living in prophylactic environments, systematically and silently excluded from natural community processes. (Sullivan, 1992, p. 152)

Social policies are viewed as societal responses to social problems (Chambers, 1993; Jansson, 1990; Chapin, 1995). One result has been that "low income urban neighborhoods are now environments of service where behaviors are affected because residents come to believe that their well-being depends on being a client (Kretzmann & McKnight, 1993, p. 2). Services, at best, ensure survival but significant improvements in quality of life can only be achieved by exploiting community capacities (Kretzmann & McKnight, 1993).

Blaming the Victim

The preoccupation with deficits, needs, weaknesses, and pathology when viewing individuals or environments has led to "blaming the victim." In the words of Ryan (1974):

> The formula for action becomes extraordinarily simple: Change the victim. All this happens so smoothly that it seems downright rational. First, identify a social problem. Secondly, study those affected by the problem and discover

in what ways they are different from the rest of us as a consequence of deprivation and injustice. Third, define the difference as the cause of the social problem itself. Finally, of course, assign a government bureaucrat to invent a humanitarian action program to correct the differences. (p. 8)

The perniciousness is increased because this line of reasoning is always cloaked in humanitarian language. Of course, psychiatric disability can have a significant impact on a person's entire life. But the solution for such people is to train them, to protect them, to change them. The same solution occurs if the focus is on the uncaring or toxic community. As Rappaport (1977) writes, "The genetic and the environmental victim-blaming strategies are functionally equivalent" (p. 118).

A necessary component of victim blaming is labeling. After differences between one group and the rest are specified, then a name is given to this "different group." Because the perceived difference is always based on deviations from the norm, the label quickly assumes a negative connotation or meaning. An "outgroup" is thus created, people assigned a degraded social identity. At its full flowering, the members of the group not only are assigned a degraded social identity but become that social identity.

People with psychiatric disabilities, although this is changing, have been referred to by their diagnosis, "He's a schizophrenic" or "borderline," or by their social service status, "She is a patient." The disability is only one part of the person's being, yet the person's identity is seen as being best described and explained by the disability. Sue Estroff (1989) has documented how that "sick" identity then becomes the self-definition of the person. With it comes the baggage of helplessness and weakness.

Labeling has another detrimental effect. Labeling groups leads to muting of perceived within-group differences. As a consequence, programming becomes generic; everybody so labeled needs about the same amount of the same thing. The continuing tendency, for example, is to recommend social skills training for all people with a psychiatric disability; so that many treatment plans continue to look alike. The deindividualization of people with psychiatric disabilities not only reduces the effectiveness of interventions but dehumanizes people.

Continuum of Care and Transition

The mental health system has long been based on a continuum-of-care perspective. This orientation is underpinned by the notion that the ideal service system would have various services at varying levels of intensity available to people who, depending on the severity of their "illness" or "social dysfunction," would then receive the appropriate level of service. Although having diverse services is important, this perspective unfortunately has been used in ways that have been destructive to people. The first way has been to view the continuum as the logical progression that *all* people with psychiatric disabilities *must* go through. For example, a person who wants to live in his or her own apartment or house must first demonstrate success in other more restrictive living arrangements (e.g., residential care facility, board and care, transitional living program). A person who wants to work as an accountant must first complete vocational testing, prevocational skills classes, a transitional job slot, or some other intervening status.

Absurd but true anecdote: A young man with a psychiatric disability was enrolled in two university classes and had a part-time job. The mental health center staff was concerned that this level of activity would prevent the person's participation in the partial hospital program and sought to convince (it bordered on coercion) the person to drop either the classes or the job. During a staffing, it was suggested that the partial hospital activity that was most important for the person to complete was a "How to get a Volunteer Position" class.

Transitions are difficult for all people: moving, divorce or dissolution of a relationship, a loved one's dying, a new job, going from school to work, homemaker transitioning to outside work, being childless to having children, or many other critical situations. Even those transitions that are eagerly awaited and exciting have elements of anxiety, adjustment, and stress. Other transitions are painful and elicit fear. Despite the difficulty of transitions, the mental health system has increased the number of transitions that a person needs to traverse. These increase stress, can exacerbate distressing symptoms, and may lead to a person's becoming completely overwhelmed. For many people, they never seem to be able to complete all the "necessary" steps after languishing in one status or recycling through repeated attempts.

A second consequence of the continuum-of-care and transition perspective is that limited funds are often allocated to the most intense level of services. Psychiatric hospitals still consume a significant portion of all mental health expenditures. Residential care facilities, transitional housing, and nursing homes for mental health consume a large portion of limited funds. There are therefore few funds remaining for tenant-based assistance (e.g., rent subsidies), case management, or attendant care services that might be helpful to people living in places of their choice in the community. Funding allocated to the array of prevocational and sheltered employment programs means that the funds are not available for working with employers to create or maintain competitive jobs. The result is that the needed supports for a "normal" life are not present, trapping people within the mental health system.

Oppression

Deficit orientations toward individuals and environments, labeling, and blaming the victim are part of the social processes that have oppressed people with psychiatric disabilities. To oppress is defined as "to crush, burden, or trample down by or as if by the abuse of power or authority" (Webster, 1976). Bulhan (1985) suggests that "All situations of oppression violate one's space, time, energy, mobility, bonding, and identity" (p. 124).

The male slave was allowed no physical space which he could call his own. The female same had even less claim to space than the male slaves. Even her body was someone else's property. Commonly ignored is how this expropriation of one's body entailed even more dire consequences for female slaves. The waking hours of the slave were also expropriated for life without his or her consent. The slave labored in the field and in the kitchen for the gain and comfort of the master. The slave's mobility was curbed and he or she was never permitted to venture beyond a designated parameter without a "pass." The slave's bonding with others, even the natural relation between mother and child, was violated and eroded. (p. 124)

Although perhaps not so blatant, the situation of people with psychiatric disabilities has parallels. It is not difficult to view psychiatric hospitals as violating a person's space, time, energy, mobility, bonding, and identity. It is perhaps less obvious but no less true for the person living in the "community." Many people with psychiatric disabilities have little space they can call their own. Those living in congregate facilities (e.g., group homes, residential care facilities) have little of their own space and even that space is often invaded by other clients and staff. People living in apartments are better off but are still renting. Home ownership is rarely a possibility. Privacy and control of space are virtually impossible in day programs, which still dominate much of community care. The recent data concerning psychical and sexual abuse of people with psychiatric disabilities suggest that their lives, like that of a slave, contain histories of even their bodies being treated as someone else's property (Rose, Peabody, & Stratigeas, 1991; Bryer, Nelson, Miller, & Kroe, 1987; Jacobson & Richardson, 1987; Rose, 1991).

Time, like space, has been expropriated. The so-called need of people with psychiatric disabilities for "structure" has led to treatment plans and services that dictate a person's use of time. Day treatment and partial hospital programs, in particular, contain hour-by-hour activities to which people are assigned. Failure to follow this schedule is often interpreted as "resistance to treatment" by the involved professionals.

A person's energy is devoted, not to creating a better life, but to conforming to dictates of professional staff and sometimes families. Many people with psychiatric disabilities are stuck in that stage of oppression called "capitulation" by Bulhan (1985), where energy is spent assimilating into the culture.

Mobility is constrained by the rules of congregate facilities (the most obvious being the psychiatric hospital), lack of car ownership, inadequate public transportation, or reliance on mental health worker's transportation. State policies often place barriers to people moving between service catchment areas or actually restrict choice of service providers.

Relationship, or what Bulhan (1985) calls "bonding," is also restricted. Because most of their time is spent in the company of other clients and staff, people with psychiatric disabilities have their social world constricted. Staff need to keep "professional distance." Many living arrangements are single gender. Apartment roommates of different genders are usually discouraged. Strict rules of conduct in day programs discourage displays of affection. The courts' determinations, combined with the lack of supports provided by human service agencies, often lead to children whose parents are diagnosed with a psychiatric disability being removed from their parents' custody. It was not too long ago that sterilization was considered a desirable alternative for women with a psychiatric disability.

As has been discussed earlier in this chapter, oppression shapes self-identity of the person. People internalize the negative images thrust on them by their oppressors. They lose their identity as people, as women or men, as members of a racial, ethnic, or cultural group; instead they become "the schizophrenic," "the client," or "damaged goods." Many develop a "victim complex" whereby all actions and communications are viewed as further assaults or indications of their victim status (Bulhan, 1985). As Estroff (1989) describes:

> Having schizophrenia includes not only the experience of profound cognition and emotional upheaval, it results in a transformation of self as known inwardly, and of person or identity as known outwardly by others. Schizophrenia, like epilepsy or hemophilia, is an "I am illness," one that is joined with social identity, and perhaps inner self, in language and terms of reference. (p. 189)

One's identity is shaped by the interaction between the individual and the environment, the oppressors and the oppressed, which Crapanzano (1982) calls a "conspiracy of understanding" (p. 192). It is this conspiracy that defines who we are, which categories we belong to,and which labels are given and received.

The two worlds, client and professional, created by the oppression is captured by Paul Carling's (1995) reflection of his early mental health experience:

> I found myself spending more and more time with ex-patients, trying to learn what having a psychiatric disability was about from their perspective. Almost immediately, I began hearing about civil rights and involuntary treatment; the learned helplessness that so many services seemed to induce; the violations of personal dignity and choice; and the profound pessimism about ever being accepted as an equal. These issues were very different from typical professional concerns, and in fact there was surprisingly little discussion of them within professional circles. Thus, at an early stage of my career, it became completely obvious that I had to learn about two worlds: the professional world and the client world. These worlds seemed to overlap only rarely, since the power differences between those who inhabited them were so great. In fact, what I seemed to be seeing was a pervasive charade in which clients often framed their responses to professionals—and even their own internal experiences—in the professionals' terms, in order to retain access to the resources that the professional controlled. (p. 11)

People with psychiatric disabilities continue to be oppressed. Their space, time, energy, mobility, bonding, and identity are constantly being violated and assaulted. Fanon (1968) states that the first thing the oppressed learn is to "stay in your place" (p. 52). Your world is constricted and your personhood is constricted. Do not go beyond the limits. Limit your dreams or relegate them to the hereafter.

Useful Conceptions for Strengths-Based Practice:
The Recovery Imperative

Mental health services must become more recovery-oriented or else we will continue this cycle of oppression toward people with psychiatric disabilities. Recovery should move us away from "disease" and "deficits" and move us toward human potential and well-being. It should move us out into the community rather than withdrawing from it, seeing possibilities rather than only barriers. A focus on recovery should enhance the uniqueness of each person before us.

Although there are no universally recognized definitions of recovery, the following from Patricia Deegan (1988) is used for our purposes:

> Recovery is a process, a way of life, an attitude, and a way of approaching the days' challenges. It is not a perfectly linear process. At times our course is erratic and we falter, slide back, regroup and start again. . . . The need is to meet the challenge of the disability and to re-establish a new and valued sense of integrity and purpose within and beyond the limits of the disability; the aspiration is to live, work, and love in a community in which one makes a significant contribution. (p. 15)

Deegan's definition suggests that recovery is both a process and an outcome.

What Recovery Does Not Mean

Recovery does not mean that a person will no longer experience symptoms. More than having or not having psychiatric symptoms, recovery is about how a person lives life in the midst of experiencing symptoms, facing stigma or trauma, and other setbacks. Similarly, just because someone may be having major struggles does not mean they are not recovering. Is there anyone who is free from struggle? Life in itself can be a struggle. What we often do is begin to confuse the boundaries between daily life struggles and the symptoms people experience. Every struggle then is often interpreted by both professionals and clients themselves as being a symptom of their "mental illness." Recovery means that we stop pathologizing daily life struggles and focus instead on how we can better navigate through life's difficulties to help people achieve what they desire.

Recovery does not mean that a person will no longer use mental health services. As people progress in their recovery they may very well still use mental health services, but they may use them less frequently, and they may use them more actively. Recovery does not mean a person will not use medications. A person may still be taking medication but possibly taking a smaller dose and supplementing medications with other strategies. Many people see medications as a valuable part of their recovery, but others see it as an obstacle, especially considering adverse effects that people experience. Pat Deegan (1989) encourages a change of language from "I take medication" to "I use medication" to help me achieve what is important to me in life. In recovery, people become active participants in their own well being rather than passive recipients of mental health services.

Recovery does not necessarily mean a person will be completely independent in meeting all of his or her needs. No person is "perfectly independent"; we are all interdependent. Recovery will be different for different individuals. One person may move from not working at all to working full time. Another may move from sitting on the couch all day watching TV to doing volunteer work or engaging in leisure activities with friends.

Recovery as a Process

As a process, recovery is a complex and nonlinear evolution that Ridgway (2001) describes as being comprised of a series of journeys including:

- reawakening of hope after despair
- breaking through denial and achieving understanding and acceptance
- moving from withdrawal to engagement and active participation in life
- active coping rather than passive adjustment
- no longer viewing oneself as primarily a person with a psychiatric disorder and reclaiming a positive sense of self
- moving from alienation to a sense of meaning and purpose

The journey involves recreating a sense of self, responsibility for self-care, and a life beyond the mental health system. Recovery is not accomplished alone but requires support and partnership (Ridgway, 2001).

The last 20 years have witnessed a dramatic increase in published first-person accounts of the experience of psychiatric disability and recovery. Recovery refers to "a deeply personal, unique process of changing one's attitudes, values, feelings, goals, skills and/or roles. It is a way of living a satisfying, hopeful, and contributing life even with limitations caused by illness" (Anthony, 1994, pp. 559–560). Recovery does not mean that symptoms disappear but, rather, that despite the symptoms life can go on. Although the experience of psychiatric disability and recovery is unique to each person, certain common elements can be discerned from the first-person accounts.

One critical element of recovery is the person recovering or reclaiming her or his sense of self. Estroff (1989) found that people with psychiatric disabilities often lose their "selves" when being diagnosed with a mental illness. People begin to see themselves as the "illness," rather than experiencing psychiatric symptoms as being only one aspect of their life. In recovery, people begin to see that what defines them as a person is much more than the symptoms they experience or the diagnosis they are labeled with.

> The key for me to do this, I think, was to learn for the first time what schizophrenia was and what its different symptoms were; to develop a vocabulary to restructure the shattered jigsaw puzzle of my life. (Stanley, 1992, p. 25)

> We can overcome the stigma, prejudice, discrimination, and rejection we have experienced and reclaim our personal validity, our dignity as individu-

als, and our autonomy. To do this, we must change the image of who we are and who we can become, first for ourselves and then for the public. (Leete, 1989, p. 200)

It seems that there is a correspondence between the separation of the "illness" and self, and increased attention to self-managing symptoms that are distressing or disabling for the person (Strauss, 1989).

A second theme is the need for personal control. When experiencing distressing symptoms, overwhelming life situations, and disabling social responses, people often lose a sense of control in their lives. People with psychiatric disabilities often feel "alienated and rejected, vulnerable and powerless, discounted and defeated" (Leete, 1993, p. 125).

> Recovery appears to be related to having control over one's life, having choices. . . . In contrast, involuntary treatment appears to leave individuals feeling hopeless, helpless, and believing they will never recover. (Blanch & Parrish, 1993)

> I needed to be in charge of my own changes. . . . I lived alone and I have chosen pictures and colors and little touches that make it feel like my very good, safe place. I work part time in a floral shop and I have acquired a relatively new car. I do my own laundry. Food is there if I cook it, and the house is as clean as I make it. I'm my own boss in other people's eyes. (Reilly, 1992, p. 20)

> Ultimately it is the consumer alone who decides what is helpful in overcoming the tremendous suffering of mental illness. (Scheie-Lurie, 1992, p. 36)

> To overcome these negative feelings and our resulting sense of impotence, empowerment is crucial, giving us the strength and confidence to individually and collectively make choices and control our own lives. . . . I find my vulnerability to stress, anxiety, and accompanying symptoms decreases as I gain more control over my own life. (Leete, 1989, p. 198)

As Anthony (1994) states: "Critical to recovery is regaining the belief that there are options from which one can choose—a belief perhaps even more important to recovery than the particular option one initially chooses" (p. 565).

A third critical ingredient seems to be purpose. The experience of psychiatric disability is often one of: "I have nothing to live for, no drive but to just exist. . . . Sometimes I sleep 12 to 14 hours because there's nothing else to do. No zest" (Stanley, 1992, p. 25).

> And so I took my dream off the backburner and claimed as my personal goals, understanding, writing and doing something to help others who were afflicted. Doing so was neither grandiose or magnanimous. It was survival. (Keil, 1992, p. 6).

One short term goal was to further myself educationally, and I took buses to get to college. (Reilly, 1992, p. 20)

You can live through any kind of a situation, if you find a reason for living through it. We survivors were daily living through impossible situations precisely by finding reasons for living. (Fergerson, 1992, p. 30)

With Mark's death, I was snapped into a new awareness that resulted in my not only caring about others, but having a cause worth fighting for. (Risser, 1992, p. 39)

A fourth theme of recovery seems to be some early sense of achievement or assuming some responsible role. The experience of psychiatric disability is often one of "I was a failure" (Fergeson, 1992, p. 29).

I learned to find pleasure in the daily-ness of life. I looked with pride on the way my children were growing. I was working part-time, and I had learned so very much about the unexpected. (Keil, 1992, p. 6)

It seems that I'm now in the role of helper and enabler—not clients. (Glater, 1992, p. 22)

Another person who once described herself wrote:

I'm Donna Fergeson, 38 years old, and, for being betwixt and between emotional tides, I usually do very well. I'm currently going to school for an A.S. in Word Processing (I have an A.A. in Psychology, a Certificate as a Paraprofessional in Social Work, and am a Certified Respiratory Therapy Technician). I've worked about 8 years, and been on Social Security Disability before I worked and when I had to stop due to my illness. I go to school, see my friends, enjoy my job, and want to write a book, a personal account of living with Borderline Personality Disorder. I'm usually happy. (Fergeson, 1992, p. 30)

The most common types of achievement included in first-person accounts are helping others (often peers), work or vocational involvement, and hobbies or arts. Work, in particular, is commonly identified by people as both a goal and a force in recovery (Arns & Linney, 1993; Sullivan, 1994a).

A fifth element in recovery is the presence of (at least) one person. Although recovery is highly personal, most first-person accounts point to the presence of a friend, a professional, a family member, a teacher, self-help groups, or at times the staff of a particular program that helps trigger and sustain the recovery process. This element parallels one of the seven resiliencies, relationship, identified by Wolin and Wolin (1993). The experience of psychiatric disability is sometimes one of "I was frightened and alone" (Glater, 1992, p. 22).

Residents were accepted and always treated with respect, and thereby we clients gained in self-respect. (Leete, 1993, p. 120)

. . . My expectations were of basket weaving and sheltered workshops. I'd had that dull stuff foisted on me before . . . a vocational counselor saw my potential and suggested that I look into music therapy as a career. (Glater, 1992, p. 22)

At critical turns along the road, I was blessed with helpers (professional and others) who encouraged me to trust my own ability to make valid choices for my life and recovery. (Scheie-Lurie, 1992, p. 36)

It is clear to me now that a supportive, accepting, and loving relationship with others—my interpersonal environment—has been the key element in my recovery from this major mental illness. (Leete, 1993, p. 114)

It is difficult to find a first-person account that does not attribute relationships as a critical ingredient to recovery (Sullivan, 1994a; Deegan, 1988; Leete, 1988; Hatfield & Lefley, 1993). The characteristics of those relationships are discussed in chapter 3.

The Roots of Oppression: The Berlin Wall of Recovery

Recovery requires overcoming the despair, withdrawal, alienation, and loneliness that derive from two sources. First, people can become overwhelmed by distressing or disabling symptoms. It is an experience of profound emotional and cognitive upheaval. The medical treatment for many symptoms involves powerful drugs, all of which have side-effects that range from merely unpleasant to iatrogenic. These drugs are capable of creating an almost "zombie-like" state. Extreme emotional states like those caused by psychiatric distress cause great fatigue and exhaustion. The emotional trauma caused by a significant loss in one's life (e.g., death of a loved one, severing of an important relationship) that many people experience often contributes to a state of severe weariness. The exhaustion and constant fatigue caused by psychiatric distress are considerable. The drugs can also obstruct a person's use of "personal medicine". Personal medicine is an umbrella concept comprising those "activities that give meaning and purpose to life, and that serve to raise self-esteem, decrease symptoms, and avoid unwanted outcomes such as hospitalization" (Deegan, 2005). These nonpharmaceutical medicines could include work, exercise, being a good mother, being in a singing group, or any other fulfilling acitivity. Second, recovery is a fight against the forces in society and the system of care that society has established. These systems have been experienced as oppressive, creating and reinforcing the despair and alienation through violation of a person's space, time, energy, mobility, bonding, and ultimately their identity (see section on oppression).

There are five factors that contribute to and manifest the oppressive life people with psychiatric disabilities inhabit: mentalism, poverty, fear, professional practice, and the structure of the mental health service system (see Figure 1.2). The first factor, mentalism, is a force every bit as powerful as racism, sexism, and ageism. Like all "isms", this one derives from a thought process by which we attribute behavior or social situations to the overt differences between people (e.g., race, gender).

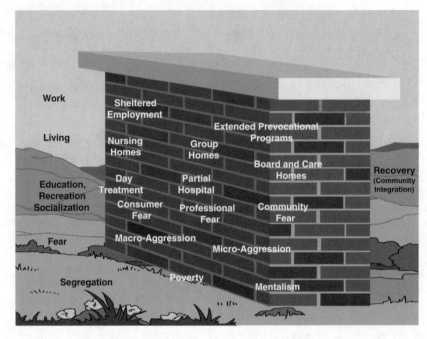

Figure 1.2 Berlin Wall of recovery

Mentalism refers to the tendency (i.e., compulsion) to attribute and explain most of the behavior of people with psychiatric disabilities as a function of the "illness" (Chamberlin, 1978; Deegan, 1992). In every day practice, such divergent behavior as passivity/apathy and hostility/aggression; poor hygiene and unemployment; and failure to comply with treatment and social isolation are implicitly or explicitly attributed to mental illnesses. The reasoning is similar to "blaming the victim" (Ryan, 1971).

This explanation is convenient and at times plausible but its effect is to replace a human being with an illness, much like skin color replaces humanness in the case of racism, and obscures the fact that the behavior is as much or more a function of an oppressive social situation. It thereby blinds us to ways we can help and support the people we serve.

A second factor is poverty. Most people with psychiatric disabilities are living entirely because of government assistance. Poverty means inadequate housing, reduced mobility, and limited opportunities for recreation, education, relationships, and employment. The hope-damaging effects of poverty contribute to lethargy and alienation.

A third factor is fear. People with psychiatric disabilities often live in fear, lacking confidence and self-efficacy. The niches they have been relegated to have not allowed them to achieve their goals. Attribution of "failure" often is directed to personal deficiency of a generalized and enduring nature: "I'm weak," "I'm sick." Fear also relates to professionals who fear exacerbation of symptoms, relapse, and failure. Laypeople fear physical harm and awkward interactions. The confluence of "fears" leads to a situation of low expectations, attempts to "protect" people, and segregation.

The fourth factor concerns the nature of our professional practice. People with psychiatric disabilities confront a life replete with macro- and microaggressions against the human spirit (Pierce, 1970). Macroaggressions include the use of restraints and isolation rooms, or being forced into a police car to transport the patient to the hospital or jail, or the use of payeeships. These are similar to the methods used by repressive governments to break the spirit of political dissidents. Microaggression refers to the messages conveyed in the myriad interactions people receiving services have with providers and others. In so many ways, the mental health system has institutionalized low expectations and blame for failure. Although microaggressions are more subtle than macroaggressions, they are as powerful and pernicious in breaking the human spirit.

The fifth factor concerns the structure designed, funded, and operated by the mental health system that force people into entrapped niches (Taylor, 1997) and prevent achievement and true community integration. Examples include sheltered workshops and extended prevocational programs as a surrogate for work; nursing home, group homes, and board-and-care homes as a replacement for your own apartment or house; partial hospital, day treatment, and some psychosocial programs as a forced alternative for places to recreate, socialize, and be educated. These structures are caused by, reflect, and reinforce the other four factors of mentalism, poverty, fear, and spirit-breaking aggressions.

Recovery Happens

Schizophrenia and other psychiatric disabilities have been viewed as chronic and degenerative diseases. Mental health professionals routinely predict poor prognosis, a downwardly spiraling course and poor outcomes. People are assumed to be permanently disabled.

The research evidence suggests that this belief is in error. There are seven longitudinal research studies that have followed large numbers of people with psychiatric disabilities for up to 35 years. The studies from Europe, Japan, and the United States find that 46 to 68% of the people achieved significant improvement and recovery (Bleuler, 1978; Ciompi & Miller, 1976; DeSisto et al., 1995a, 1995b; Harding et al., 1987a, 1987b; Huber, Gross, & Schuttler, 1975; Ogawa et al., 1987; Tsuang et al., 1979). Table 1.1 summarizes these studies.

DeSisto et al. (1995a; 1995b) matched people with psychiatric disabilities from Vermont and Maine by age, gender, diagnosis, length of hospitalization, and several contextual variables (e.g., catchment area characteristics, use of diagnostic tools). Recovery rates for Vermonters was 68%, for Mainers, 49%. Harding (1999) attributes the differences to the difference between the two states' mental health systems. Although Maine's system at the time focused on maintenance, stabilization, and entitlements, Vermont's model of care emphasized rehabilitation, self-sufficiency, and community integration. It is noteworthy that even in Maine's

TABLE 1.1 Long-Term Studies Involving People with Psychiatric Disabilities

Study (Study leader, location of study)	Sample Size	Average Length In Years	Clients Who Recovered and/or Significantly Improved (%)
M. Bleuler (1978) Burgholzi, Zurich, Switzerland	208	23	53–68
Huber, et al. (1975) Germany	502	22	57
Ciompi & Muller (1976) Lausanne, Switzerland	289	37	53
Tsuang et al. (1979) Iowa 500	186	35	46
Harding et al. (1987) Vermont	269	32	62–68
Ogawa et al. (1987) Japan	140	22.5	57
DeSisto et al. (1995a, 1995b) Maine	269	35	49

Total number of people in studies: 1,863
Average length of time sample was followed: 29.5
Average percentage of people who recovered or improved significantly: 55.4% (1,132)

system of care, 49% of people with psychiatric disabilities still recovered or significantly improved.

The Vermonters were also asked about what really made a difference in their lives. The most prevalently mentioned factors were decent food and clothing, people to be with, a way to be productive, a way to manage symptoms and systems, individualized treatment and case management. Case management was the only service mentioned in the top ten factors that made a positive difference.

Evidence beyond these longitudinal studies can be found in the thousands of first-person accounts of recovery. These narratives resound with courage, resilience, and achievement. Although any one story is inspiring, taken as a whole, they provide powerful evidence that recovery occurs.

Recovery as Outcome: Psychological States

Recovery as an outcome is a state of being to aspire to. It is composed of two components. The first concerns an individual's self-perceptions and psychological states. This includes hopefulness, self-efficacy, self-esteem, feelings of loneliness, and empowerment. The second component closely resembles community integration (Bond, Salyers, Rollins, Rapp, & Zipple, 2004). In short, people should have the opportunity to live in a place they call home, work at a job that brings satisfaction and income, have rich social networks, and have means available for contributing to others. It also means avoiding the often spirit-breaking experiences of forced hospitalization, homelessness, or incarceration.

Hope

The presence of hope is the most prevalently mentioned correlate of recovery. Hope resounds through the hundreds of first-person accounts of recovery. Pat Deegan's (1988) poignant reflections of her recovery places hope at its core. As she writes:

> When one lives without hope, (when one has given up), the willingness to "do" is paralyzed as well. (p. 13)

> Hope is crucial to recovery, for our despair disables us more than our disease ever could. (Leete, 1993, p. 122)

> My mood changed—I was happy and hopeful once again. (Fergeson, 1992, p. 29)

> I find myself being a role model for other clients and am only a bit uncomfortable with this. For the first time, I begin to feel real hope. (Grimmer, 1992, p. 28)

> Success will never be realized if it cannot be imagined. (Leete, 1993, p. 126)

Snyder (1994) defines hope as "the sum of the mental willpower and waypower that you have for your goals" (p. 5). "Goals are the objects, experiences or outcomes that we imagine and desire in our minds . . . it is something we want to obtain or attain" (p. 5). "Mental willpower is the mental energy . . . the reservoir of determination and commitment that we can call on to help move us in the direction of the goal . . . it is made up of thoughts such as I can, I'll try, I'm ready to do this, and I've got what it takes" (p. 6). "Waypower reflects the mental plans or roadmaps that guide hopeful thought . . . a mental capacity we can call on to find one or more effective ways to reach our goals" (p. 8). In short, a hopeful person has goals, the desire or confidence, and a plan for achieving that goal. In contrast, the more prevalent experience of people with psychiatric disabilities is described by Patricia Deegan (1996):

> Giving up was not a problem. It was a solution because it protected me from wanting anything: If I didn't want anything, then it couldn't be taken away. If I didn't try, then I wouldn't have to undergo another failure. If I didn't care, then nothing could hurt me again. My heart became hardened. (p. 93)

The research suggests that high-hope persons have "a greater number of goals, have more difficult goals, have more success at achieving their goals, have more success at achieving their goals, have greater happiness and less distress, have superior coping skills, recover better from physical injury, and report less burnout at work . . . and this is true even when controlling for intelligence, optimism and other motives and emotions" (Snyder, 1994, p. 24).

Many times it is difficult to envision a person recovering his or her life, especially if the person has been in the system for a long time and clinicians have not seen any significant progress. The following story shows how a recovery-oriented case manager must persevere and must sometimes carry hope for people even when they cannot carry it for themselves.

> When I was doing case management I worked with an individual named James for a six year period of time. During this time James would go in and out of the hospital on a fairly regular basis; either to the inpatient psychiatric unit or inpatient addiction treatment services. Not only did James hear voices that he found distressing, but he also had a poly-substance chemical dependency. During the six years I worked with him, there was very little progress made. When he was not in the hospital, it was a major effort just to keep him safe. James was kicked out of every shelter in town; he was robbed several times on the street. We would get him into housing, and then James would lose housing. It seemed that each week we went from one crisis to the other.
>
> One day, James and I were sitting along the riverbank after a weekend relapse. Not really knowing what to say, but wanting to hang in there with him, I asked what even kept him going with all that he went through in life. He looked over at me and said that he had a vision that one day he hoped he might have a relationship again with his daughter.
>
> Eight years prior to this date, James was newly married with a baby and had started his second semester of college. This quickly unwound for him as voices he had heard since being a teenager became overwhelming and he could no longer concentrate in school. Life at home was tense and his wife left him and took their daughter with her. James' drug and alcohol use increased and within that year he was homeless.
>
> While little seemed to change with James from that day along the riverbank, what we talked about did change. I started asking him more about his daughter and he would light up when he would talk about her.
>
> One day James just disappeared. It wasn't out of the ordinary for him to leave town for a few months at a time, but this time, he didn't come back. He didn't return again to our program until five years later and I was now director of the program. When I saw James, his entire appearance had changed. He told me he had moved to Iowa where his ex-wife lived, had been sober and clean for 18 months, had a part-time job and had established a relationship with his daughter again.

James was asked what made the difference for him. What precipitated the change? He stated that two things were important to him.

One was the vision he had of his daughter. James had heard every reason imaginable as to why he should give up drugs and alcohol, but for him none of those reasons held any value for him. Yet the internal motivation to establish a relationship with his daughter was significant enough for him to keep going and was used to gain personal strength to begin his recovery journey. Another important aspect of James's recovery that he mentioned was that we hung in there with him even when he had lost hope and confidence in himself. We call this "carrying hope for people when they can't carry it for themselves." Carrying hope for people is an important aspect of recovery-oriented services, because many of the people we work with often lose hope in being able to have a positive impact on their current situation in life. Our ability to carry hope for people stems largely from our belief in the potential for people to recover, reclaim, or transform their lives. If we believe that recovery is possible, even if the people cannot see it for themselves, we will hang in there with people and maintain a posture of patience while keeping our creative energies open.

Because hope seems to be related to achievement, its relevance for a strengths perspective and intervention is important. Interventions need to be goal oriented and assistance must be provided to help people set goals. Interventions should help build a person's mental willpower through confidence-building interactions and activities. Interventions should assist people in developing step-by-step plans for achieving their goals.

Resilience

Although a consensual definition of resilience has not emerged, Ridgway's (2000) view seems sensible. In general, resilience is demonstrated in the ability to remain flexible and experience positive adaptation even when one's life circumstances are rife with stressors and strains. Resilience is evidenced by the ability to resist, withstand, cope with or rebound from stressful life events and find or maintain the ability to function relatively well despite exposure to risks that tend to reduce the likelihood of social, physical, or emotional well-being or increase susceptibility to physical and mental distress. When people evidence resilience, they are able to stay on, or return to, trajectories of positive human development, even while strong forces are at play that throw many people off course. (p. 8)

There is an increasing body of literature contradicting the dominant beliefs of developmental theories, the deficit orientations, and victim blaming. It is based on research that shows that most people (mainly children) who grew up under the most horrifying conditions have managed to become successful. This includes studies of children who were raised in harsh and punitive institutions (Goldstein, 1992), children of parents with substance abuse problems (Wolin & Wolin, 1993), children who were abused (Kaufman & Zigler, 1987), children in poverty defined as "at risk" (Werner & Smith, 1982, 1992), and children with parents with psychiatric disabilities (Bleuler, 1978). The Vermont longitudinal research on people with psychiatric disabilities indicates that most became woven into the fabric of community life (Harding, Brooks et al., 1987a, 1987b; Harding, Zubin, & Strauss, 1987). The evidence is that these people developed into fine human beings who worked well, played well, and loved well and that many thrived.

Wolin and Wolin (1993) identified seven resiliencies: insight, independence, relationships, initiative, creativity, humor, and morality. They indicate that it is these seven attributes that develop from adversity and allow and explain a person's ability to overcome. Of particular importance to intervention is the relationship. As the authors describe:

Relationships are intimate and fulfilling ties to other people. Proof that you can love and be loved, relationships are a direct compensation for the affirmation that troubled families deny their children. Early on, resilient children search out love by connecting or attracting the attention of available adults. Though the pleasures of connections are fleeting and often less than ideal, these early contacts seem enough to give resilient survivors a sense of their own appeal. Infused with confidence, they later branch out into active recruiting—enlisting a friend, neighbor, teacher, policeman, or minister as a parent substitute. Over time, recruiting rounds out to attaching, an ability to form and to keep mutually gratifying relationships. Attaching involves a balanced give and take and a mature regard for the well-being of others as well as oneself. (p. 111)

Our professional relationships need to convey a sense of caring and respect. We need to act as "mirrors" reflecting the person's sense of worth, strengths, capacities, and attractions.

This literature suggests that most, if not all, humans have a capacity for overcoming the harshest of experiences and most actually do. For recovery-oriented work, we must replace the imagery of deficits and pathology with the imagery of strengths and resilience. Assessment must include the uncovering and description of these for each individual. Given the importance of at least one key relationship, professionals and other helpers should seek to create and nurture such relationships between the people we serve and others in the community.

Empowerment

The last 20 years have witnessed considerable scholarly and practice activity focused on empowerment as a central construct of mental health and social work. The concept is discussed both as a process and as an end or goal or state. In the strengths model, empowerment is used as a state that people aspire to and that clients and professionals collaborate in achieving. The strengths model, itself, is a set of methods and perspectives that embodies the process. Therefore, empowerment will be described here in terms of a desired state. Despite the diversity of conceptions, theory, and methods, options and power seem to be two prevalent elements. Each of these elements has an objective reality and a subjective reality that influence empowerment. The interplay of elements and the two realities help define the components of empowerment:

	Objective Reality	**Subjective Reality**
Options	Choices or options	Perception of choices
Power	Authority	Confidence

To "be empowered," a person or group requires an environment that provides options and ascribes authority to the person to choose. One can hypothesize that the more options actually available to a person, the greater the contribution to that person's empowerment will be. Authority refers to the person's actual power to select from the options. For example, many people with psychiatric disabilities do not have the authority to decide when they will be discharged from the hospital or group home or nursing home. That power has been granted to mental health personnel.

Empowerment is also affected by the subjective reality of the person. A person could have many options, but their perception of the options is much more limited. For example, a person who likes to dance may have a score of options available but is aware of only one or two options. Most people are not aware of all the options available. For people with psychiatric disabilities whose lives have been sheltered and segregated, a limited view of options is even more pronounced.

Power is part authority and part confidence or perception of authority. A person can have the formal authority to make a choice or decision but may perceive they do not have that authority or they do not have the confidence to select. For example, in most mental health systems, the client has the authority to decide where they will live and what services they will receive. The perception or subjective reality of many clients, however, is that the authority is vested in mental health personnel. Sometimes people lack the confidence to choose or to act on the options available. In these situations, a person may have the authority to choose and act (e.g., for apply and acquire a job) but, lacking in confidence, decides that is not an option and settles for a sheltered job at the mental health center.

The last element of empowerment is action. Most treatises on empowerment suggest that action by the person is indispensable. As Kieffer (1984) states, "empowerment is not a commodity to be acquired, but a transforming process constructed through action" (p. 27). As will be seen in the remainder of the book, the strengths model is designed to increase each of these components: choices or options, authority, perception of choices, and confidence, and facilitate action.

Recovery as Outcome: Integration, Normalization, and Citizenship

Integration is the "incorporation into society or an organization on the basis of common and equal membership of individuals differing in some group characteristic" (Webster's Third New International Dictionary, 1976). Simply, people with psychiatric disabilities should have equal membership or citizenship in the human collective. All people are different. The presence of a psychiatric disability should not exclude such membership. There are four dimensions of "equal membership": resources, options and opportunity, choice, and location.

1. Equal membership requires equal access to societal or environmental resources.
2. Equal membership requires equal access to options and opportunities.

3. Equal membership requires the equal power of individuals to choose from the array of options and direct their own lives; they have the same rights as others.
4. Equal membership requires that the "location of life," where people live, work, play, and pray, is the same as where others do so.

Equal membership or integration "entails helping people to move out of patient roles, treatment centers, segregated housing arrangements and work enclosures, and enabling them to move toward independence, illness self-management, and normal adult roles in community settings" (Bond, Salyers, Rollins, Rapp, & Zipple, 2004, p. 570). Community integration implies normalization (Wolfensberger & Tullman, 1982). Normalization is the circumstance in which individuals with disabilities live, work, play, and lead their daily lives without distinction from and with the same opportunities as individuals without disabilities.

It should be clear by now that integration is but a faint hope for many of people with psychiatric disabilities. Many live in poverty, their options for life are constricted, and their power to choose is constrained by society and professionals. The result is that much of their lives are lived in locations separated from the rest.

Charlene Syx (1995), a person with a psychiatric disability who has achieved a high level of recovery, writes:

> For in a good faith effort to help, Archway and other mental health providers ensconce people in a protective bubble, shielding them from their community and ultimately from their future. Had I been encased in that bubble, I can't help but wonder if I, too, would now be trapped, working in the clerical unit or running for clubhouse president. (p. 83)

She urges a new system that replaces segregation with true community integration, that emphasizes change and movement not utilization, that uses resources as a means to access the real thing: "instead of purchasing buildings for people to gather in, we should help people make links in the community. Instead of buying vans, we should provide stipends for use of public transportation. And instead of being everything to everyone, we should help people develop real relationships" (p. 85).

Sullivan (1994b) has argued that higher recovery rates for people with psychiatric disabilities in third world countries is partly a function of more accessible meaningful social roles (e.g., work, family) and niches provided by the societies. If we truly adhered to client self-determination, integration would be the norm, not the exception.

As Patricia Deegan (1996) writes:

> The goal of recovery is not to get mainstreamed. We don't want to be mainstreamed. We say let the mainstream become a wide stream that has room for all of us and leaves no one stranded. (p. 92)

Ecological Perspective

Ecology is the biological science that studies the relationship between organisms and their environment (Grinnell, 1917; Elton, 1927). Carel Germain (1991) used ecology as a metaphor to better understand the ways "people and environments influence, change, and sometimes shape each other." (p. 16)

Biologists define an "ecological niche" as "the environmental habitat of a population or species, including the resources it utilizes and its association with other organisms" (Strickberger, 1990, p. 518). By this definition, a niche exists as something in the environment. Its description requires details about the place and conditions where the species is found, the resources that allow a species population to maintain itself over time, and the relationships of that species with other species.

This biological definition needs revision if we are to describe niches in human social systems. One biological species inhabits at most a few niches over a lifetime, but we want a concept that allows us to describe an infinite variety of social niches filled by a single species, *Homo sapiens*. Unlike an ecosystem, a social system contains symbols, meanings, and social forms. For these and other reasons, the biologist's "ecological niche" at best provides a framework, an analogue, for the concept needed by the helping professions.

The idea of "species" is central to the notion of ecological niche. Species inhabit a niche. Is there anything equivalent to "species" for "social niches"? In talking about niches in the social world, it seems natural to refer to different categories of people. Instead of bay-breasted warblers and myrtle warblers, we have niches filled by "artists" and "welders" and "college professors"—all with their own environmental habitats and their typical resources. Thus by analogy, we replace "species" with "social categories." "Species" of people are commonly found in association with other categories of people: students with teachers, physicians with patients, politicians with lobbyists, and other situations. Such associations help define the niche.

The idea of "habitat" includes the "place and conditions in which an organism normally lives" (Strickberger, 1990). Places are easily described: they include residences, stores, shopping malls, bars, and restaurants. The term "community" captures some of this, as does the idea of "settings" in Roger Barker's (1968) ecological psychology.

The idea of "resource" is a bit more complicated. For an animal, a "resource" may be an optimal temperature range, the presence (or absence) of water, the availability of food or prey, the presence of soil suited for burrowing—the list can be long, but it generally will refer to tangible things. For humans, tangible resources are mainly acquired by money or barter, so for our culture and time we include "money" and access to sources of money (e.g., jobs, transfer payments, investments) as resources, and this has no analogue in animal kingdom.

Other resources are also symbolic, since human beings are social and information—using animals, and they need such social and symbolic things as intimacy, specialized knowledge, a sense of direction and structure in life, conviviality, consensus on social reality, and reciprocal ties of mutual aid. These aspects of human niche have no parallel in biological ecology.

Kelly and associates (Trickett, Kelly, & Todd. 1972; Mills & Kelly 1972) have suggested three principles of a human ecology model: First is the principle of interdependence whereby a change in one part of the ecosystem in turn alters the relationship among other elements. This suggests that interventions need not be limited to the individual level of analysis but, rather, efforts to change can be contemplated at family, small group, community, or institutional levels.

Second is the principle of cycling resources, which refers to the distribution of resources within an ecosystem. This principle implies that intervention needs to include identification of resources and strengths and their redistribution on behalf of a client or client group.

Third is the principle of adaptation where environments and people change to accommodate each other. It places emphasis on different environments requiring different adaptive skills or behaviors than other environments. Intervention, therefore, can profitably be focused on "helping the client cope" (the dominant current strategy) or to find or create niches in which a client's current repertoire of skills, talents, and behavior are already valued by a particular environment.

In the next chapter, the application of this ecological perspective to the strengths model are described (see section on "Niche").

Community (Environmental) Strengths

In contrast to the "deficit of the environment" perspective described earlier, a community of environmental strengths orientation is emerging. Most of the writing has derived from work with low-income and/or minority neighborhoods. Yet the precepts are relevant to the viewing of any geographic entity that we may term "community." As Kretzmann and McKnight (1993) state: " . . . wherever there are effective community development efforts, those efforts are based upon an understanding, or map, of the communities' assets, capabilities, and abilities" (p.5).

The first precept is that each community possesses a unique configuration of capacities, skills, and assets. These strengths are embodied in the individuals, families or households, networks, and associations and institutions that comprise that community. The second precept is that all communities, no matter how poor or rich, how rural or urban, how racially or ethnically diverse, how old or young, have a wealth of strengths. The third precept is that after being identified, these community strengths can be mobilized to build better lives for the people we serve.

Rather than seeing the community as toxic or too demanding for people with psychiatric disabilities, the environmental strengths position argues that each community is almost unlimited in the resources and opportunities available (Sullivan, 1992). In another article, Sullivan (1989) provides an example:

Many urban areas hire recreational therapists to develop recreation programs and provide clients with a variety of opportunities to participate in active leisure-time activities. While recreation therapists clearly serve a valuable function in these programs, most rural programs do not have the luxury of hiring this type of staff person. Yet nearly every community has a gymnasium. In many small communities one can find exercise classes, and even aerobic instruction. Softball teams and leagues can be found everywhere. We must resist ideas that clients must engage in segregated activities. While the client may need help in making initial contacts and periodic support through-out the experience of engaging in community recreational activities, success is possible. Key personnel are also available to provide support for clients. High schools employ physical education instructors. Local athletes may be willing to help. All of these resources can be used to develop a good recre-ation program. (p. 22)

By placing a premium on the identification and use of community assets, the resources available to people with psychiatric disabilities dramatically expand. At the same time, true community integration is fostered. Our attempts to "fix" in-dividuals and communities have a dismal record. Perhaps, instead of such fixing, we should devote ourselves to the exacerbation of strengths of individuals and com-munities. The questions and interventions become altered: "What resources exist and how can they be bolstered?" rather than "What is the deficit to be fixed?"

The Interaction of Psychological and Environmental Outcomes and Case Management

Recovery as an outcome involves achieving particular psychological states and a degree of community integration. In life, the two are closely entwined. An increased sense of hope can contribute to having more friends or pursuing a job. Increased confidence may lead to enrolling in school. Similarly, obtaining a job may lead in-creased feelings of self-efficacy and empowerment. Having an enjoyable date may buoy one's self-esteem.

It is not only important to understand what recovery is and what it is not, but how recovery may unfold over a person's life. The dark line represented in Figure 1.3 could represent anyone's life, the high points representing those peak

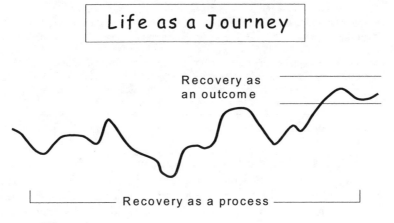

Figure 1.3 Life as a journey

TABLE 1.2 Recovery-Oriented Practice*

Recovery-Oriented Practice	Nonrecovery Practice
1. **Hope is communicated** at every level of service delivery system.	There is little communication of hope.
2. The **relationship** between the service provider and participant is **based on compassion, understanding, and knowing each other as unique individuals** and is the basis for good work to happen.	Controlling, caring for, and protecting people is the basis of the work.
3. There are **high expectations for recovery** and it is considered the outcome of service.	Stabilization is the expected outcome of service.
4. **Work with people is purposeful and designed to assist people in *their* growth and recovery toward their dreams, desires and goals.** The primary mechanism that drives this process is with proactive, planned contact using written goals and steps toward achieving goals.	Work with people lacks direction and is crisis-oriented. There is little or no use of planned purposeful contact. Written goal planning, not used; goals are driven by service delivery or service providers.
5. **Self-care, self-management, and education are emphasized.** People are supported in becoming experts of their own self-care. People are educated about medications, self-help, coping strategies, and symptom management. Information is openly shared and consumers have access to information.	Compliance is desired. Professionals are seen as knowing what is best for consumers. Information is withheld on the basis that consumers do not understand or will not make good use of it.
6. **Community integration** is the central focus of practice. This includes: normal, integrated housing, real work experiences, and work that is meaningful to the individual, linking to members of community, social and recreational activities with lessemphasis on mental health programming and groups.	There is an emphasis on use of mental health programs for work (e.g., sheltered work, prevocational work units, and classes), social and recreational endeavors (psychosocial groups).
7. People are **supported to take risks** (failure is part of growth of individuals).	Protection and emotional safety are of primary concern.
8. **People receiving services are involved at *every level* of decision making** and directors of their own care: as directing the goal planning process, directing the amount and type of services, and directing program planning and policy-making.	Professionals reserve decision-making power and know what is best for consumers.
9. **Peer support and mutual self-help are encouraged and valued.**	Peer support and mutual self-help is not talked about or supported by service providers.
10. **Staff anticipate crisis and do precrisis and crisis planning** with consumers.	Staff does not spend time on health and wellness or wellness planning and therefore spend much time tending to crisis.

*Adapted from Pat Deegan

moments in life when a person feels hopeful and in control of their life, and the low points represent those valley moments where a person may feel overwhelmed with life and lack hope. If this line represented the life of a person who experiences psychiatric symptoms that are distressing or disabling, when would they typically come into contact with the mental health system? At the low points. Our view of people can sometimes become limited by the system we are a part of because when they become well they often leave the system. Think about people who work at a state hospital or work in nursing homes. They typically only see people when they are in these valley points. They never get to hear about what happens afterward, especially if the person is recovering. This tends to shape how they perceive psychiatric disability and the capacity of people to recover. The same thing can happen in community support services.

To understand recovery we must take a broader perspective. First, we must try to understand who this person was before coming for services. What were their dreams, interests, and aspirations? Who were this person's supports? What were significant experiences for this person in life? We are looking for what is it that this person brings into the helping relationship. Basically we are looking for their strengths. We must also ask ourselves what we believe about this person's future. Do we believe that they have the ability to recovery, reclaim, or transform their life? What we believe about people will have an impact on the way we interact with them and will shape the nature of the helping relationship.

For the strengths-model case manager, recovery is the vision to be held for each of the people we serve. The lack of such a vision leads to case management practice that is be preoccupied with maintenance rather than growth and achievement. Without the hopeful vision of recovery, practice becomes reactive rather than purposeful and proactive. The recovery vision means that every contact with a person can be an opportunity for building hope, increasing confidence, and taking steps to create a better life. The recovery vision becomes the engine of our strengths-based practice. Table 1.2 contrasts recovery-oriented practice with non-recovery-oriented practice. As you progress through this volume, you will see how strengths-based practice parallels recovery-based practice and how the two enrich each other.

A Beginning Theory of Strengths

THIS CHAPTER PRESENTS a formulation of the theory of strengths and reviews the research results on the model. This chapter acts as the backdrop to the practice methods.

The strengths model posits that all people have goals, talents, and confidence. Also, all environments contain resources, people, and opportunities. But our usual perceptions of these are limited, modest, dysfunctional, rife with considerations of barriers and pathology, and these pale in comparison to the deficits. Both can be "objectively" true.

Theory is perceptual. By its very nature, theory seeks to explain a phenomenon by identifying the elements that contribute to the phenomenon and the interrelationship of these components parts. Theory, therefore, seeks to exclude those parts of life that are judged to be of no importance or lesser importance. This represents a a perspective. A theory is at best a "slice of life" or representation of life, rather than life itself.

The strengths model then is about providing a new perception. It allows us to see possibilities rather than problems, options rather than constraints, wellness rather than sickness. And after being seen, achievement can occur. As long as we stay in the muck and mire of deficits, we cannot achieve. Until we throw off the yoke of the "conspiracy of understanding" centered on deficits, we cannot effectively help. The stories of recovery powerfully resound with this kind of turning point.

A Theory of Strengths

Desired Outcome

The theory of strengths is a practice modality that seeks to define those factors affecting a person's life and the methods by which these can be altered. The theory

---

Desired Outcome

Quality of life

Achievement

Sense of competency

Life satisfaction

Empowerment

Figure 2.1 Desired outcome

must therefore begin at defining the relevant elements of a person's life; the desired outcomes (Figure 2.1).

At the core, the desired outcomes are those achievements of people based on the goals they set for themselves. Although these are highly individualized, the goals do seem to group themselves into a decent place to live, employment and/or opportunity to contribute, education, friends, and recreational outlets. In other words, people with psychiatric disabilities desire the same things that any other person wants. In addition, because people with psychiatric disabilities often experience psychiatric distress, they desire a lessening of this distress and avoidance of psychiatric hospitalization. Like other people, they want choices and the power to choose options. Together, these outcomes comprise the quality of one's life.

These outcomes are achievement or growth oriented. Clients do not speak often of adaptation, coping, or compliance as desired outcomes. Neither do they often conceive of their aspirations as learning skills unless it concerns a specific technical skill affiliated with a particular job or task. They rather speak of jobs, degrees, friends, apartments, and fun. Skills may be an interim goal, but they are rarely seen as an outcome in itself.

For the purposes of building a theory of strengths, reduced symptomatology poses some unique dilemmas. First-person accounts of recovery suggest the following:

1. The nature of psychiatric disability is such that total elimination of symptoms is rarely possible.
2. People who are recovering experience a similar roller-coaster pattern of symptom exacerbation but the frequency, duration, and severity of the episodes is often reduced.
3. People who experience symptoms can often still work, play, and live full lives in the community.

Helping clients (who desire it) live healthy lives, identifying helpful wellness strategies, and helping people identify early warning signs of psychiatric distress are all worthwhile activities. Perhaps the single most influential focus on reducing symptoms is to help people build a life that is satisfying and fulfilling.

Niches

Proposition: The quality of niches people inhabit determines their
achievement and quality of life.

The quality of life, achievements, the outcomes of a person's life, are determined
by the qualities of the niches within which a person lives. A niche is "the environmental habitat of a person or category of persons" (Taylor, 1997). People live in a
variety of habitats corresponding to different life domains: home or living arrangement, work, education, recreation, spiritual, etc. (Figure 2.2). Taylor (1997) goes
on to describe the basic feature of these habitats:

> The habitat conditions include the kinds of communities, settings, and domi-
> ciles in which these persons are usually found, the sources and levels of in-
> come available to these persons, the social resources and supports typically
> used by those persons, and the other categories of people commonly found
> in association with those persons.

The concept of niche can be a unifying element in case-management practice because it attends to both individual and environmental factors. As Brower (1988)
asserts, "It makes no sense to think of individuals separate from their immediate
environments, or to think of environments separate from the individuals who inhabit them" (p. 413).

There are two types of niches at the extreme: entrapping and enabling. Most
niches, however, tend to lay somewhere between these two extremes and contain elements of both. Entrapping niches can be seen as having the following characteristics:

- Entrapping niches are highly stigmatized; people caught in them are
  commonly treated as outcasts.
- People caught in an entrapping niche tend to "turn to their own kind"
  for association, so that their social world becomes restricted and limited.
- People caught in an entrapping niche are totally defined by their social
  category. The possibility that they may have aspirations and attributes
  apart from their category is not ordinarily considered. To outsiders, the
  person is "just" a bag lady, a junky, an excon, a schizophrenic . . . and
  nothing else.
- In the entrapping niche, there are no graduations of reward and status.
  One cannot be certified as a Master Bag Lady, or work up to the position
  of Head Parolee. Thus, there are few expectations of personal progress
  within such niches.
- In the entrapping niche, there are few incentives to set realistic longer
  term goals, or to work toward such goals.
- In the entrapping niche there is little reality feedback; that is, there are
  few natural processes that lead people to recognize and correct their own
  unrealistic perceptions or interpretations.

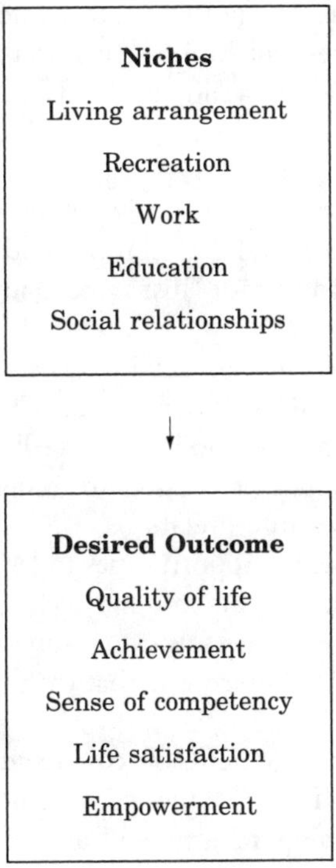

Figure 2.2 Niches, desired outcome

- In the entrapping niche, there is little chance to learn the skills and
  expectations that would facilitate escape. Especially this is so when
  the entrapping niche is free from the usual norms of work and self
  discipline, and no demands arise for clear structuring of time and effort.
- In the entrapping niche, economic resources are sparse. This in itself
  may lead to unproductive stress and may cause some people to seek
  reinstitutionalization for economic reasons.

Entrapping niches are often reserved for those at the margins of social life, like people with psychiatric disabilities. Once isolated in such niches, the availability of resources or mechanisms for escape are scarce. In fact, social, political, and professional processes are in place which make escape virtually impossible.

"The net result is social isolation defined in this context as the lack of contact or of sustained interaction with individuals and institutions that represent mainstream society" (Wilson, 1987, p 60). Wilson goes on to say that social isolation, not other factors, is the major determinant of unemployment and underemployment. The entrapment niche does not easily allow its walls to be penetrated.

In contrast, enabling niches are more likely to produce the life benefits described earlier. Enabling niches have the following characteristics:

- People in enabling niches are not stigmatized, not treated as outcasts.
- People in enabling niches will tend to "turn to their own kind" for association, support, and self-validation. But often the niche gives them access to others who bring a different perspective, so that their social world becomes less restricted.
- People in enabling niches are not totally defined by their social category; they are accepted as having valid aspirations and attributes apart from their category. The person is not "just" a bag lady, a junkie, an ex-con, or a schizophrenic.
- In the enabling niche, there are many incentives to set realistic longer term goals for oneself, and to work toward such goals.
- In the enabling niche, there is good reality feedback; that is, there are many natural processes that lead people to recognize and correct unrealistic perceptions or interpretations.
- The enabling niche provides opportunities to learn the skills and expectations that aid movements to other niches. Especially is this so when the enabling niche pushes toward reasonable work habits and reasonable self-discipline, and expects that the use of time be clearly structured.
- In the enabling niche, economic resources are adequate, and competence and quality are rewarded. This reduces economic stress, and creates strong motives for avoiding institutionalization.

The strengths model posits that creating enabling niches should be the major focus of work.

There is good reason to believe that the niches available to people with psychiatric disability influence the recovery process and their quality of life. In fact, Sullivan (1994b) has argued that higher recovery rates for people with psychiatric disability in developing nations is attributable to better access to enabling niches such as work. Sullivan (1994b) attempted to categorize niches for people with psychiatric disability based on enabling or entrapping, and natural or created (Table 2.1). In the strengths model, most work occurs in the two enabling niche cells.

Enabling niches closely correspond to concepts such as normalization and community integration. Each of these concepts suggests that marginalized people would be "better off" to the degree to which they can be woven into the fabric of normal everyday life. As can be seen by Sullivan's matrix, however, many of our attempts to assist people with psychiatric disability have reinforced their segregation through sheltered workshops, group residences, and congregate day programs.

The concept of niche forces us to think beyond "social location" to "social relations" (Rose & Black, 1985). The history of mental health has been based on simplistic notions of "community" and "integration." The radical downsizing of state psychiatric hospitals beginning in the mid-1950s was replaced by having people moving to nursing homes or being discharged into urban ghettos. As Talbott (1979)

TABLE 2.1 Natural and Created Niches

	Natural	Created
Entrapping niche	Natural exclusionary processes	Institutionalization
	Stigma	Psychiatric hospitalization
	Labeling	Sheltered workshops
	Homelessness	Group/board & care homes
	Poverty	Partial hospitalization/day treatment
	Unemployment	
Enabling niche	Natural inclusionary processes	Normalization
	Work opportunities	Supported Employment
	Recreation opportunities	Supported Housing
	Family involvement	Supported Education
	Affiliation With Community	Consumer Programming
		Self-Help

stated: "the chronic mentally ill patient [sic][has] had his locus of living and care transferred from a single lousy institution to multiple wretched ones" (p 622). They lived in inadequate housing, did not work, and interacted with people similarly situated. They moved from one location to another; from one entrapping niche to another. Their quality of life, in many respects, was no better and perhaps worse than they had known in the hospital. Yet, they were said to be living in the "community."

There are many people with psychiatric disabilities who live with others with similar disabilities, spend their days in day treatment programs, find any recreation with other clients, and if they work, do so in a sheltered enclave. Their lives are dominated by other clients and mental health professionals. They are *in* the community (social location) but still not *of* the community (social relations). In only the most nominal sense can they be thought of as achieving "community integration." This segregation reinforces stigma and discrimination, and the devaluing of people with psychiatric disabilities.

Entrapping niches created by society to care for people with psychiatric disabilities reduce access to resources, valued social roles, and status and rewards. They tend to reduce individual choice and self care, and increase feelings of dependency (Rappaport, 1985). These created niches are based on compensating for the deficits, pathologies and problems of people with psychiatric disabilities. This then becomes apart of a person's self-definition. They are their "illness" or problem rather than the psychiatric distress they experience being only one (small) part of them. Professionals often treat the person as a diagnosis. Failure to treat individuals as human beings with mutual respect has frequently resulted in the deterioration of their social behavior. Either because of this or in addition to this, programs like partial hospitalization/day treatment and sheltered workshops have failed to improve levels of client outcomes.

The factors that contribute to the quality of a person's niches emanate from two sources: the individual and the environment. We now turn to these factors.

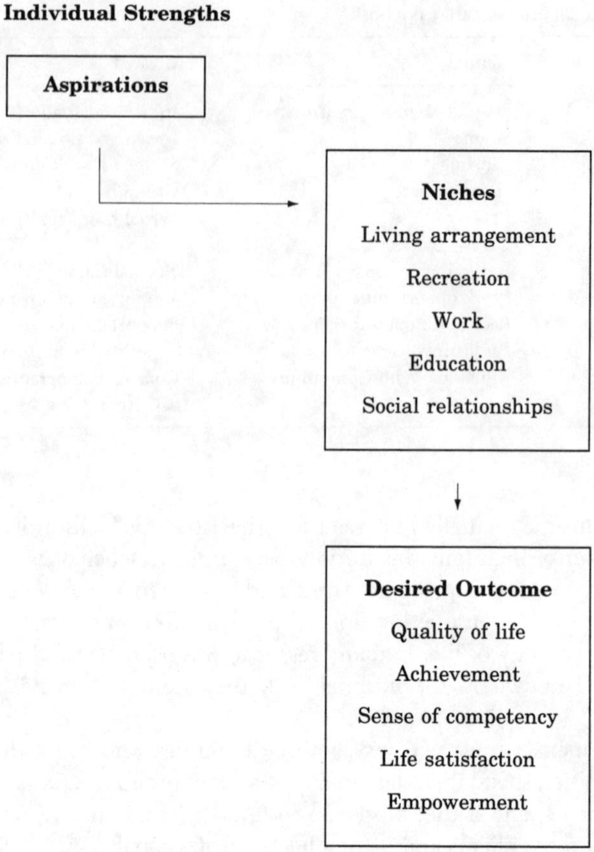

Individual Strengths

Aspirations

Niches
Living arrangement
Recreation
Work
Education
Social relationships

Desired Outcome
Quality of life
Achievement
Sense of competency
Life satisfaction
Empowerment

Figure 2.3 Individual strengths, aspirations

Individual Strength: Aspirations

Proposition: People who are successful in living have goals and dreams.

The strengths theory places a premium on human beings as "purposeful organisms." People have desires, goals, ambitions, hopes, and dreams. We have a driving motivation to be competent and to influence our world (White, 1959); we seek to achieve (McClelland, Atkinson, Clark, & Lowell, 1953). "Goals are any objects, experiences, or outcomes that we imagine and desire in our minds" (Snyder, 1994, p. 5). People who are successful in living, first and foremost, have goals of some consequence (Figure 2.3).

For many people with psychiatric disabilities, their lives since experiencing psychiatric symptoms and societal reaction to them, have been marked by pain and distress, disappointment and failure, and overwhelming messages of what they cannot do. As with other oppressed people, their aspirations often are few and nonspecific. For so many, they have lost their dreams or have diminished them to the most modest levels.

Professional helping often further restrains goal setting and achievement. For example, most professional helping methods begin with an exploration and definition of the client's problem (Cowger, 1992; Weick et al., 1989). The professional seeks to help the person solve that problem. Solving problems can be viewed as achievements but too often solving problems at best return a person to her or his previous state of equilibrium. Social work in particular has emphasized "coping," which is defined as: "to maintain a contest on even terms; to find necessary expedients to overcome problems" (Webster's Third New International Dictionary, 1976).

The outcomes of concern in the strengths model are quality of life, life satisfaction, achievement, among other factors. Solving problems is therefore seen as an occasionally necessary step toward these ends but still not sufficient. Successful resolution of a problem is not an end in itself. The strengths model is more concerned with achievement than with solving problems; with thriving more than just surviving; with dreaming and hoping rather than just coping, and with triumph instead of just trauma. For this to happen, people need goals, dreams, and aspirations.

Individual Strength: Competencies

Proposition: People who are successful in living use their strengths to attain their aspirations.

Competencies include skills, abilities, aptitudes, proficiencies, knowledge, faculties, and talents. "Continuing growth occurs through the recognition and development of strengths" (Weick et al., 1989, p. 353).

All people possess a wide range of talents, abilities, capacities, skills, resources, and aspirations (Figure 2.4). No matter how little or how much may be expressed at one time, a belief in human potential is tied to the notion that people have untapped undetermined reservoirs of mental, physical, emotional, social, and spiritual abilities that can be expressed. The presence of this capacity for continued growth and heightened well-being means that people must be accorded the respect that this power deserves. This capacity acknowledges both the being and the becoming aspects of life.

In the midst of a recognition of capacity for growth is the simultaneous recognition that no person perfectly expresses this capacity on all or even most of the planes of development during his or her lifetime. A few rare individuals may show high levels of artistic, spiritual, or intellectual development, but for most people, the evidence of life shows far more modest results. In a strengths perspective, a conscious choice is made to attend exclusively to those aspects of a person's life that reflect the gains made, however modest they may be judged (Weick et al., 1989, 352–353).

For so many people with psychiatric disabilities, their talents and abilities go unrecognized by themselves, acquaintances, family, and professionals. In fact, al-

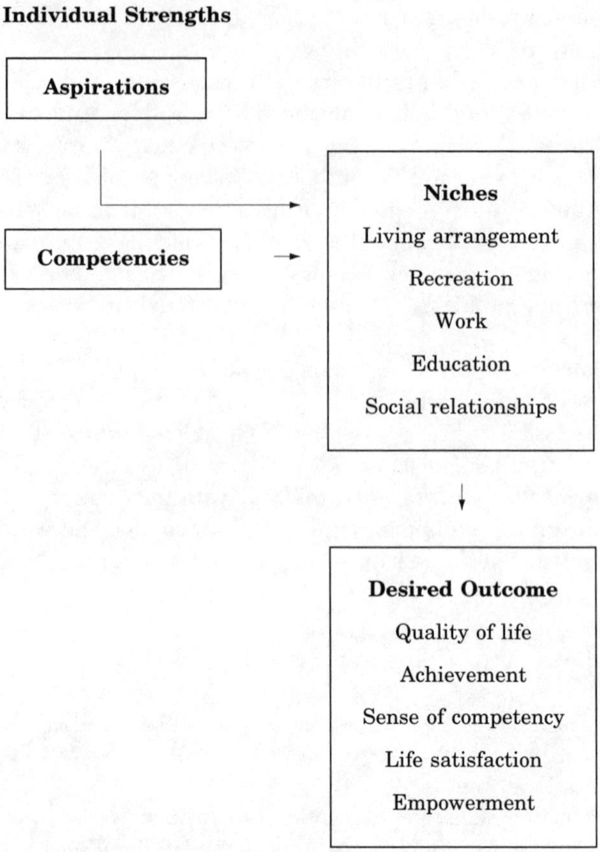

Individual Strengths

```
┌──────────────────┐
│   Aspirations    │
└──────────────────┘
         │
         │                    ┌────────────────────────┐
         └──────────────►     │        Niches          │
                              │                        │
┌──────────────────┐         │  Living arrangement    │
│   Competencies   │  ─►     │      Recreation        │
└──────────────────┘         │         Work           │
                              │       Education        │
                              │  Social relationships  │
                              └────────────────────────┘
                                         │
                                         ▼
                              ┌────────────────────────┐
                              │    Desired Outcome     │
                              │     Quality of life    │
                              │      Achievement       │
                              │  Sense of competency   │
                              │    Life satisfaction   │
                              │      Empowerment       │
                              └────────────────────────┘
```

Figure 2.4 Aspirations, competencies

most all helping methods are explicitly focused on uncovering the person's deficits, weaknesses, problems, and pathology. As Rose and Black (1985), have pointed out, many clients have developed their survival skills that are the opposite of the skills needed to achieve. For example, the skills and behaviors that make for a "good" patient or client often fall under the rubric of "compliance." Yet compliant behaviors are rarely associated with achievement or growth, which often involves some risks.

One strength of all people is their capacity to determine what is best for them (Weick & Pope, 1988).

This long-honored social work value recognizes that people have an inner wisdom about what they need and that ultimately, people make choices based on their own best sense of what will meet that need. Those who hold a strengths perspective assume that this inner wisdom can be brought into more conscious use by helping people recognize this capacity and the positive power it can have in their lives (Weick et. al., 1989, p. 353).

While most of our society, lay and professional, is mired in a deficit or problem orientation, there are interesting developments that further support a strengths
orientation. The most notable is the work of Wolin and Wolin (1993) on resiliency
and the development of the challenge model. They found that the vast majority of
children who grow up in abusive, troubled, and neglecting families not only survive but many thrive. These findings are echoed by the work of Goldstein (1992)
and Werner and Smith (1982; 1992).

The challenge model disputes the assumption that only damage comes from a
troubled family life which inevitably leads one to lifelong suffering. The challenge
model validates the pain that occurs from a troubled childhood, while recognizing
that resiliencies develop even against all odds. This framework for helping understands that trauma and triumph are forces that interplay with each other in managing an adverse childhood.

Individual Strength: Confidence

Proposition: People who are successful in living have the confidence to take the
next step toward their goal.

Related to the concept of confidence are power, influence, belief in oneself, and
self-efficacy. A person's behavior is selected based on the desired end (goal) and
abilities (competencies) but this is mediated by a person's perception of successfully behaving. There are many things people want to do and can do, but do not
do because they lack the confidence. (Figure 2.5).

Confidence resides at two levels. At the first level, confidence refers to the perceived ability of oneself to perform a certain task or set of behaviors. Can I cook
lasagna? Can I interview for that job? This level is specific to the situation and task.
A person can be confident in buying groceries but fearful of asking for a date. At
a second level, confidence is a generalized sense of oneself that each person brings
to different situations. Some people are just more confident when approaching any
task whereas others perceive themselves as being generally inept. This second level
has some similarity to "learned helplessness" (Peterson, Maier, & Seligman, 1993).

Even though it is wrong and dangerous to stereotype people with severe psychiatric disability, two characteristics seem pervasive: they often live in poverty and
live lives filled with fear. Fear often dominates their lives. The niches they have
been relegated to have not allowed them to achieve. Attribution of these "failures"
often is directed to personal deficiencies of generalized and enduring nature: "I'm
weak"; "I'm sick", and other classifications. Anxiety, dependency, depression, fu-
tility, and apathy result.

Professional services tend to reinforce these feelings of inadequacy. The focus
is on what is wrong with person and what they "have to" or "should" do differently. This blaming the victim (Ryan, 1971) message finds easy acceptance by people who already lack confidence and belief in themselves. Even if this were not true,
just the coming for help is often perceived as admitting to the person's failure
(Rappaport, 1985).

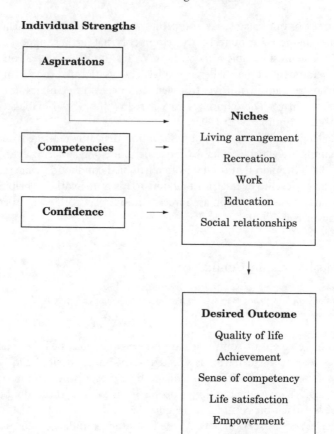

Figure 2.5 Aspirations, competencies, confidence

Interaction of the Elements of Individual Strengths

> Proposition: At any one point in time, people who are successful in living have
> at least one goal, one relevant talent and confidence to take the next step.

The quality of a niche is determined by individual and environmental elements. Individual elements include aspirations, competencies, and confidence. The individual elements interact with each other. For example, a person with confidence is more likely to set ambitious goals. In contrast, it is difficult if not impossible for a person to dream if they live in fear. If you do not think much of yourself, it is hard to have a dream without that dream becoming a source of disappointment and pain rather than inspiration and energy. Similarly, people who are attuned to their competencies are more likely to set goals and have the confidence to pursue them.

Snyder's (1994) exploration of hope demonstrates other interactions. He defined hope as "the sum of the mental willpower and waypower that you have for your goals" (p. 5). Willpower refers to thoughts such as "I can, I'll try, I'm ready to do this, I've got what it takes" (p. 6). This corresponds to confidence in the strengths theory. Waypowers are "the mental plans or roadmaps that guide hopeful thought" (p. 8). In the strengths model, the ability to formulate plans would be one of the competencies. The third part of the definition concerns goals, which corresponds nicely to aspirations.

The research on hope suggests that hopeful people set more goals, set more difficult goals, and attain more goals. They also recover better from physical injury, report less burnout at work, and have superior coping skills. Most important, hopeful people report greater happiness and less distress.

People who are successful in living do not necessarily have large quantities of each element but they do have some of each element. It can be stated mathematically:

$$\text{Aspiration} \times \text{Competency} \times \text{Confidence} = \text{promise and possibilities}$$

If any element is zero then the product will be zero; no possibilities exist.

A case vignette may be illustrative. Sarah is 29 years old and experiences symptoms associated with paranoid schizophrenia. She has been in and out of the state hospital for the last ten years; nine times in the last five. She wanted a full-time clerical job. Sarah had a work history limited to two attempts to work in fast food businesses that lasted less than two weeks, and a one-week clerical job eight years ago. She has limited typing skills (accurate but slow) and no skills using a computer. She requires quiet and few people around because the noise and activity increase her anxiety. Sarah is persistent. If given a task to do that she wants to do, she will stay with it until completion. In fact, her nickname in the program was "Bulldog." The other dilemma is that, despite a myriad creative efforts by Sarah and her case manager, she seems incapable of getting out of bed before 11 A.M. Using the equation:

Aspiration	$\times$	Competency	$\times$	Confidence
Full-time clerical job		accurate typist		willing to apply
		persistence		willing to interview
				willing to start work

With the case manager's assistance, Sarah got a job at the rural public library working from 1:00 P.M. to 9:00 P.M. From 1:00 to 6:00, she worked in the office typing card file entries, filing, doing the mail, and similar tasks. When the library closed at 6:00, Sarah shelved books in the library proper. The only people around at that time were the janitorial crew. For three years, Sarah has been working at the library and there has not been a return to the hospital.

It is probably obvious, that at least on the surface, Sarah did not have an enormous reservoir of relevant competencies but she had something. Combined with her goal and confidence, it was sufficient for her to achieve; to find an enabling niche.

As can be seen by this example, the niche required certain ingredients from Sarah but also required environmental possibilities. It is to this side of the ledger that we now turn.

Environmental Strength: Resources

Proposition: People who are successful in living have access to the resources needed to achieve their goals.

Access to desired niches and the quality of those niches are influenced by the environmental resources available to a person (Figure 2.6). Some resources are needed to make a niche accessible. Public transportation, a car, or carpooling are resources that would allow someone to accept a particular job. Having appropriate clothing would allow others to accept a job. Other environmental resources affect the quality of the niche itself. A television, a cleaning service, or a Monet print could contribute the quality of one's home environment.

Environmental resources are those tangibles and services that the wealthy tend to purchase. Tangibles would include food, clothing, housing, appliances, furniture, a car, or compact disc player. Services are viewed as people who do for you what you cannot or prefer not to do for yourself. Examples would include travel

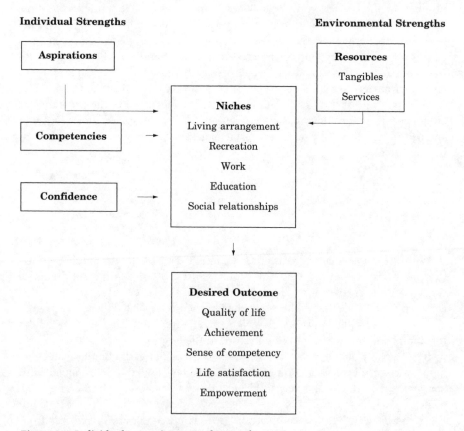

Figure 2.6 Individual vs. environmental strengths

agents, baby-sitters, maids, teachers, team organizers, repair people, public transportation, and typists.

Entrapped niches by definition tend to be resource poor and restrict access to resources outside of the niche. Of the people with psychiatric disabilities who are poor, many are trying to eke out an existence on a modest income from Social Security. The services with which they are most familiar are those specialized mental health services.

Yet, the environment can also be a rich source of resources. A client worked at a chain pizza restaurant in a small community. She loved her job and found satisfaction and confidence from working. Her hours were 3:00 to 10:00 P.M.. The community she lived in had public transportation (bus) that ran throughout the day but ended at 7:00 P.M.. She had a way to get to work but relied on friends and family to pick her up and take her home. After several weeks of this, her friends and family were getting tired of this task. She was in jeopardy of losing her job because of lack of transportation at the end of her shift. The person elicited help from her case manager. The two of them sat down and brainstormed options and resources. The one that was used: the restaurant had an evening delivery service in the community at the end of her shift. The consumer would ride along with the delivery person and then be dropped off near her apartment.

Environmental Strength: Social Relations

Proposition: People who are successful in living have a meaningful relationship
with at least one person.

Access to and the quality of a person's niches is influenced by the social relations that the person enjoys (Figure 2.7). Social relations concerns people and the benefits that accrue from these relationships. "People" would include family, friends, acquaintances, coworkers, church members, a local grocer, or others. "Benefits" would include companionship, emotional support, caring, partnership, sexual relations, recreation, socialization, and opportunities to give or share. In entrapped niches, social relations are constrained. Typically, a stigmatized group's interaction is dominated by intragroup relations. For many people with psychiatric disabilities, their social contact is dominated by interaction with other clients and staff. Although this is obvious in psychiatric hospitals, it is also true for that larger group of "deinstitutionalized" people. For many, the waking hours may be spent in day treatment or a psychosocial clubhouse, and their evenings in a group home or other form of group residence. Those that live in apartments may have another client as a roommate and may spend evenings closeted in their apartments.

The dilemma is that this constricted social network denies opportunities. The interaction is with people who themselves lack resources and who are otherwise similarly situated. For example, it is not unusual for somebody to find a job possibility or a recreation opportunity (e.g., club or team to join), through "word of mouth" by friends. Yet if all your friends are jobless and only recreate at programs sponsored by mental health providers, the chances of such possibilities occurring are slight.

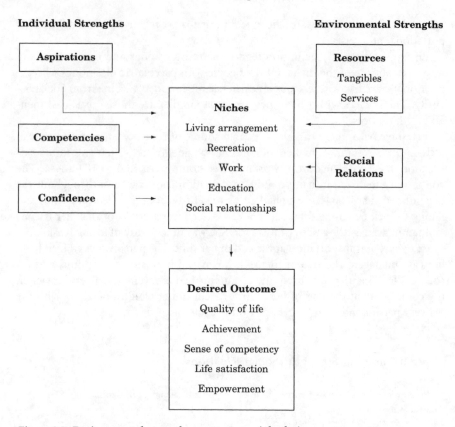

Individual Strengths

Aspirations

Competencies

Confidence

Niches

Living arrangement

Recreation

Work

Education

Social relationships

Environmental Strengths

Resources

Tangibles

Services

Social Relations

Desired Outcome

Quality of life

Achievement

Sense of competency

Life satisfaction

Empowerment

Figure 2.7 Environmental strengths, resources, social relations

Even so, every community is composed of many people; all unique: people who care; people who would enjoy and benefit from relationships with people who happen to have a psychiatric disability. This is not to deny the presence of stigma, discrimination, labeling, or other detriment, but rather to open our eyes to the good, if only we can see it. As Charles Kuralt (former television journalist) said,

> The country I see on my television screens and on my newspaper front pages is not quite the country I see with my eyes and hear with my ears or feel in my bones.

Environmental Strength: Opportunities

Proposition: People who are successful in living have access to opportunities relevant to their goals.

The notion of niche conjures an image of a space waiting to be filled or, in other words, a vacuum. Our society and its communities contain many such vacuums

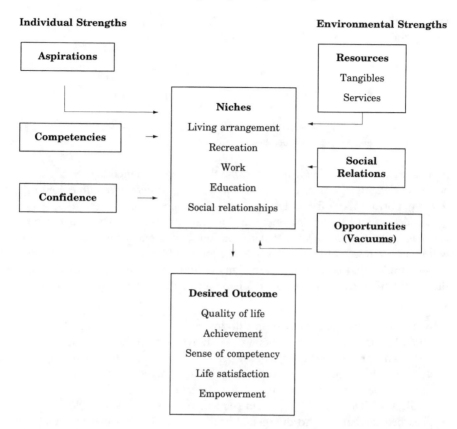

Figure 2.8 Opportunities

that are potential opportunities for people with psychiatric disabilities (Figure 2.8). For example, in the previous vignette of Sarah, the vacuum was the library's need for clerical assistance. Other common examples include a vacant apartment, a team that needs another player, a junior college class that has room for another student, or an older adult person who needs companionship.

Despite the many opportunities available in communities, people with psychiatric disabilities have rarely taken advantage of them. Inculcated with a deficit or problem-oriented viewpoint, mental health professionals rarely are able to perceive a client's strengths and the vacuums that would match those strengths. We tend to see not only the weaknesses in people but also weaknesses in communities and therefore have created a "protective bubble" around people. In fact, we have developed professional sounding explanations, like "setting a client up to fail", to justify decisions not to pursue opportunities.

We need to develop a mind set that recognizes the community as the primary source of opportunities that are not formally constituted mental health programs. Funding for specialized mental health programs has always been, is now, and will always be limited. Instead of bemoaning this situation, we need to see the naturally occurring resources and opportunities in our communities that are expandable, reusable, renewable, and almost infinite in possibilities.

Interaction of the Elements of Environmental Strengths

Proposition: People who are successful in living have access to resources and
opportunities and meaningful relationships.

As was the case with individual factors, the three environmental factors are interactive. For example, different people bring access to different resources and different opportunities. A friendship with an artist is more likely to lead to access to artistic decorations for an apartment than a relationship with an athlete who may allow access to sporting events or participation. Employment may place a person within a certain web of people that another job would not.

A person's behavior is largely a function of setting and resources. People behave differently in church than they do at a pep rally or dance. For example:

A student case manager had been working with a person with a psychiatric disability for three months. They would always meet in the community: at restaurants, parks, coffee shops or the person's apartment. The case manager described the person as talkative, humorous and energetic. At one meeting, the client noted that he had to go to the mental health center to pick up his medication. The case manager said she would drive him. As the client approached the entrance to the mental health center, he slouched his shoulders, shuffled his feet, and pointed his eyes toward the ground. He walked down the hall, received his medication, and shuffled back. Upon entering the car, he asked with great animation whether the case manager had time for a cup of coffee.

Although the student was befuddled, the explanation was clear. The client had learned how to act the as the "client" or "patient" and knew when to do so. Similarly, the wealthy behave differently than others. They spend their time differently; they meet their responsibilities differently; they interact with different people who in turn have access to many resources.

This then places a premium on where life occurs and who is involved. Naturally occurring community resources are more likely to engender "correct behavior" and allow access to more people, more resources and more opportunities. Examples:

- Art classes offered by a recreation department or by a private artist are preferable to those offered by a day-treatment program.
- Daily living skills taught by a junior college home economics department on campus is preferable to a partial hospital program.

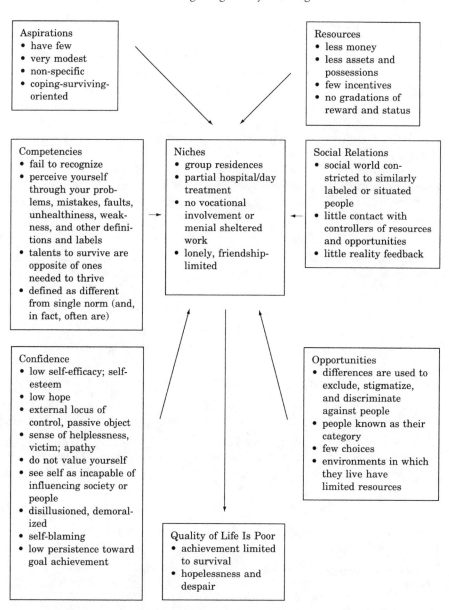

Figure 2.9 The theory of strengths and characteristics of the oppressed

- A residence that is an apartment is preferable to a group home.
- Membership on a bowling team is preferable to the weekly outing of clients in the van with the agency name on the side.

Not only are natural resources preferable and more plentiful but it is possible to make them work on behalf of the people we serve.

Summary of Strengths Theory

The strengths theory posits that a person's quality of life, achievement, and life satisfaction are attributable in large part to the type and quality of niches that a person inhabits. These niches can be understood as paralleling a person's major life domains such as living arrangement, work, education, recreation, and social relationships. The quality of the niches for any individual is a function of that person's aspirations, competencies, confidence. and the environmental resources, opportunities and people available to the person.

This formulation helps explain the poor life circumstance of so many of the five-and-a-half million people with psychiatric disabilities. Figure 2.9 seeks to explain these life circumstances by placing the research (reviewed elsewhere in this

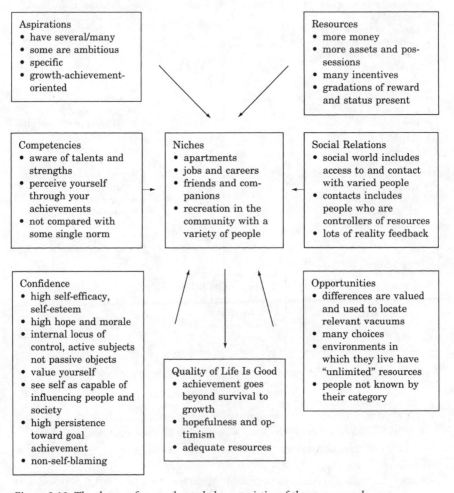

Figure 2.10 The theory of strengths and characteristics of the empowered

TABLE 2.2 Key Propositions of the Strengths Model

1. The quality of the niches people inhabit determines their achievement, quality of life, and success in living.
2. People who are successful in living have goals and dreams.
3. People who are successful in living use their strengths to attain their aspirations.
4. People who are successful in living have the confidence to take the next step toward their goal.
5. At any given time, people who are successful in living have at least one goal, one relevant talent, and confidence to take the next step.
6. People who are successful in living have access to the resources needed to achieve their goals.
7. People who are successful in living have a meaningful relationship with at least one other person.
8. People who are successful in living have access to opportunities relevant to their goals.
9. People who are successful in living have access to resources and opportunities and meaningful relationship.

book) in the context of the elements of the strengths theory. It is these elements that the strengths model seeks to influence. Figure 2.10 provides a contrasting example of the factors that contribute to empowerment, achievement, growth, and good quality of life. A recap of the nine key propositions of the strengths theory can be found in Table 2.2.

CHAPTER THREE

The Purpose, Principles, and Research Results of the Strengths Model

The Purpose

The purpose of case management in the strengths model is to assist people recover, reclaim, and transform their lives by identifying, securing, and sustaining the range of resources both environmental and personal,, those needed to live, play, and work in a normally interdependent way in the community. Furthermore, case management is individually tailored to the unique needs of each person who requests services: "A strengths model of case management helps people achieve the goals they set for themselves" (Rapp, 1993, p. 145).

The purpose is to assist another human being, not to treat a patient. The work and decisions are done with people in partnership, not to someone. As the theory would suggest, a case manager works to "identify, secure, and sustain" resources that are both external (i.e., social relations, opportunities, resources) and internal (i.e., aspirations, competencies, confidence) rather than a focus on just external resources (brokerage model of case management) or internal (psychotherapy or skills development). It is this dual focus that contributes to the creation of healthy and desirable niches, niches that provide impetus for achievement and life satisfaction.

It is common in mental health to express our ultimate goal for people as "independence." In contrast, dependency is abhorred. It is common for professionals to express concerns about a person's dependency and to formulate decisions based on these considerations: "They must do it themselves"; "He is becoming too dependent on his therapist and case manager." This dichotomized thinking of "independence versus dependence" is overly simplistic and harmful to clients.

All people are interdependent. All people rely on resources, opportunities, and social relations, and contribute to these. People use travel agents, baby-sitters, and dry cleaners. Are they dependent? Is this some form of universal pathology? The very wealthy, by this conception, are the most dependent people, yet we not only do not think of their lives as pathological, but many aspire to their circumstances. It is ironic then that for people with psychiatric disabilities a different standard is set, one that often acts as a professional excuse for not helping.

Most of life is interdependent. In the strengths model, the purpose is to help a person establish a mutually satisfying interdependence between important people in their lives (e.g., landlords, employers, friends, family, neighbors, clergy, teachers).

The following six principles are derived from the previously described theory. The principles are the transition between the theory that seeks to explain people succeeding in life and the specific methods for assisting people toward that end. The principles are the governing laws, values, or tenets on which the methods are based.

Principle 1: People With Psychiatric Disabilities Can Recover, Reclaim, and Transform Their Lives

The key word here is "people." The people we work with have the ability to recover their lives. It does not say that "We have the ability to make people recover". Have you ever done any gardening? Would you say that gardeners make plants grow? No, the capacity for growth is already inherent within the seed. So what do gardeners do? We would say they help create the conditions in which growth is most likely to occur (e.g., good light, water, soil).

The strengths model emphasizes that the capacity for growth and recovery are already present within the people we serve. Our job as case managers then is to help create the conditions in which growth and recovery are most likely to occur. It is important that we recognize that we do not possess the power to control or predict how one's recovery journey will unfold.

Lambert (1992), reviewing over forty years of outcome research in psychotherapy, attempted to find out what were the common principles, or core elements, that promoted positive change for people. Although the setting was outpatient therapy, it has several applications to what may promote growth and change within case management services. The authors identified four major factors that seemed to produce positive outcomes in therapy. These factors are:

1. *Client attributes:* Things already present in the person's life that promoted health and wellness (coping strategies, supportive relationships, skills or talents they formerly had). These were things already possessed by the individual before entering into the therapeutic relationship. In the strengths model we would call these things *strengths*.
2. The *relationship* between the therapist and client—this is the amount of trust and connection that the person felt for the therapist. It also included whether the person really believed that the therapist had the right tools to help them—for example, do they understand my cultural traditions, my views, and my perspectives on what would be helpful to me?

3. *Hope and expectancy:* Did the person really believe that change was possible? As stated by Leete (1993), "Hope is critical for recovery for our despair disables us more than our disease ever could." Also important in this is the extent to which the therapist held out hope for the person they were working with.
4. The *model:* There were certain therapy models that seemed to work best for certain types of problems. For example, cognitive behavioral therapy seemed to be most effective when working with people experiencing depression, and systematic desensitization seemed best when working with people experiencing phobias.

The fascinating part of their research was that they used both qualitative and quantitative techniques to see what percentage of each of these things were significant in promoting positive change. Client attributes or strengths accounted for 40%, the relationship was 30%, hope was 15%, and the model was 15%.

About 85% of positive change was attributed to the strengths the person already possessed, the relationship between the person and therapist, and the hope and expectancy that change was possible. The model is not insignificant, but it is only 15%. So, when we talk about the "strengths model" we are talking about a model that has as its primary focus the person's strengths, the relationship, and building hope. In other words, there is no magic in the model, the magic is in people, in the relationship you build, and in the hope that is fostered.

This principle overlays the entire perspective. The central belief of the strengths model is that people are not "schizophrenic" or "chronically mentally ill" but that they are people who may experience particular distressing symptoms. A person's symptoms are only one part of their being. They, like us, have a history of pain as well as accomplishment, of talents and foibles, of dreams and aspirations. Interestingly, a study of effective programs in Kansas found that the most prevalent common denominator was the managerial and direct service staffs' holistic view of clients (Gowdy & Rapp, 1989).

In so many ways, the mental health system has institutionalized low expectations. In contrast, data from the 20-year follow-up study in Vermont more than suggests that most people with psychiatric disabilities can eventually merge into the fabric of a community having jobs, families, friends, and homes (Harding et al., 1987a, 1987b; Harding, Zubin, & Strauss, 1987). What has to be built into any strengths perspective of social work practice is an absolute belief in the individuals' capacity to better their lives. Many people recover their lives, despite our "best efforts." With a recovery-oriented view toward helping people along with concrete actions, many more may do so.

Principle 2: The Focus Is on Individual Strengths Rather than Deficits

The mental health field has traditionally been preoccupied with illness because of the dominance of the "medical model" geared toward assessing, diagnosing, and treating what is wrong with an individual. Although the medical model has been useful in understanding particular physical conditions, it has not always translated well into mental health. When you work with someone by focusing primarily on his or her illness, it shapes the way we view individuals and often has the result of socializing people into disability rather than helping people recover their lives.

The strengths model does not suggest that problems be ignored. People do experience symptoms they find distressing, people often find themselves overwhelmed with life, and people do experience barriers and challenges to reaching their goals in life. At the same time, recovery is not fueled merely by overcoming problems, distress, and challenges. People recover despite the problems, distress, and challenges in their lives.

People tend to develop and grow based on their individual interests, aspirations, and strengths. We tend to spend time doing things that we do well, that we enjoy, and that have meaning. We tend to avoid things we do poorly or that we think we will do poorly. At best, solving problems returns us to equilibrium, but exploiting strengths and opportunities promotes growth.

Our work with people therefore should not be directed at their symptomatology, psychosis, or, for that matter, problems, weaknesses, and deficits. Rather, the work should focus on what the person has achieved so far, what resources have been or are currently available to the person, what the person knows and those talents possessed, and what aspirations and dreams he or she may hold.

Mona Wasow's (2001) account of her son's struggles with psychiatric disability is illustrative:

> My 44-year old son David has had a particularly virulent form of schizophrenia since late childhood, and I do not believe the illness itself has abated over the decades. The newer medications cause fewer side affects,[sic] but in David's case, they do not otherwise seem to be more helpful than the old ones. Nonetheless, there is a dramatic difference between the David of 20 to 30 years ago and the David of today.
>
> In the old days, David's life consisted of sitting and staring into space, chain-smoking, walking a lot, listening to his beloved folk music, and coming home once a week for dinner. Today he still smokes and walks a lot, but he also works at a restaurant an hour a day, gets himself to a clubhouse for lunch every day, and has learned to ride the buses so that he can get to his music and pottery lessons every week. On his weekly visits home, he often helps me prepare dinner, cracks a few jokes, and plays some live music with the rest of us.
>
> I do not believe that these changes came about because of the possible tendency for schizophrenia to improve over the years. Nor do I believe that the newer medications played a role, since he had been taking them for many years before these positive changes occurred.
>
> David's changes came about rather quickly when professionals and family members began to focus on his considerable strengths instead of his illness (p. 1306).

A focus on strengths should also enhance motivation. The typical assessment process, for example, subverts motivation with its obsession with problems, weaknesses, and deficits; it is a process people undergo every time they confront yet another mental health professional. If the person has not entered the encounter depressed, by the time she has completed the process, she is sure to be depressed and unmotivated. As Disraeli stated, "The greatest good you can do for another is not just to share your riches but to reveal to him his own."

The strengths model enhances the individualization of people. The idea that we can help only once we comprehend the person as an individual has been a hallmark of psychology, social work, and mental health practice. It transcends specific methods and applies whether speaking of Freud, behavior modification (i.e., person-specific menu of reinforcers), or cognitive approaches (i.e., the person's specific thoughts and sentences). Despite this, current mental health practice with people with psychiatric disabilities is dominated by a generic imagery of "client."

The last decade has provided us at the University of Kansas the opportunity to witness the professional practice of thousands of mental health personnel in scores of agencies in over three dozen states. The development of treatment plans is central to virtually all efforts at helping and, despite great variations in formats, all treatment plans include as their centerpiece a delineation of goals. In the more typical program, one might conclude that there are only two or three clients being served in all these venues because the treatment plans and goals vary little or are all the same: They are generic. Ninety percent of the goals are included in this listing: (1) improve personal hygiene, (2) improve daily living skills, (3) improve socialization skills, (4) improve prevocational skills or work readiness, (5) take medication as prescribed, and (6) show up for appointments and follow through with treatment plan. Although these plans can often be criticized for lack of specificity and behavioral referents, inadequate specification of the actions to be taken to reach these goals, and the absence of time frames and participation of the person receiving services, the most abhorrent observation is that they reflect a form of practice that sees all clients as the same.

Our first reaction to the generality of treatment plans was that it reflected poor practice, poor supervision, and poor training. In other words, it was technical. The prevalence of these plans, however, suggested that it maybe less technical than conceptual. This explanation gained plausibility when we found that "generic brand" treatment plans were found in some of the best agencies and written by otherwise exceptional professionals. We therefore believe that the problem or pathology model of practice promotes the homogenization of people and prohibits individualization.

The lesson seems to be that human problems are finite and shared by many of us, although how we experience these problems is highly personal. On the other hand, our uniqueness as individuals seems to be more a function of strengths that are highly idiosyncratic, and the configuration of these strengths in a given individual is even more so.

To enhance and reveal people as individuals, then, assessment and treatment-planning methods need to be based on an exploration of a person's strengths. To do otherwise is to direct our minds and our practice toward "standardized" human beings and thereby do injustice to the cardinal value of social work and mental health, which places the individual, in all of his or her elegance and uniqueness, at the center of our concerns, and ultimately to reduce the effectiveness of our efforts.

The domination of the "generic client" idea can be experienced through talking with long-time recipients of services. In the vocational domain, for example, women receiving services will often state their job interests as some form of domestic or secretary work, despite one woman's having a profound interest in art, another who had a long-time gardening hobby, and still another who was devoted to animals. But they have all been socialized to accept that the job for them is a maid at a hotel at minimum wage. The irony is that these women are not necessarily even interested in keeping their apartments or room in a residential care facility orderly and clean. Then we wonder why people do not follow through on job opportunities or fail to keep jobs for more than the briefest time. They do not need more skill development or more medication to control their symptoms, but jobs that they are interested in, if not passionate about. And this kind of job can only be arranged by being fully apprised of a person's unique strengths.

We, as professionals, can sometimes deceive ourselves by thinking that we are using a strengths assessment perspective when we actually are reframing problems positively and thereby operating from a problem (or deficit) assessment perspective. For example, a professional who has assessed a person as being overly dependent on her parents may discuss with the person her enormous capacity for caring about others as exemplified by her relationship with her parents. This would represent a positive reframing of a problem to make it more palatable for the person to hear and therefore grapple with the problem. It is a problem focus leading to a treatment plan aimed at the parent-child relationship. A strengths assessment would identify and develop strengths that may have little to do with parent-child relationships and issues. Treatment plans based on a person's strengths lead in an entirely different direction, and a result of developing strengths is usually greater autonomy. The diminution of the identified problem—reframed or not—occurs spontaneously in the process of human growth. The initial focus of the professional's work, not a reframing of that focus, is the determinant of whether the strengths or problem orientation is being employed.

A shift in paradigms from a pathology orientation to a strengths and resilience focus allows for a different way of thinking about people. It provides a framework for helping that uncovers strengths and the power within people. It is more than "add strengths and stir" to existing pathology paradigms. Instead, a shift in paradigms allows for new and creative ways to work with people that honor their skills, competencies, and talents as opposed to their deficits.

Principle 3: The Community Is Viewed as an Oasis
of Resources

This principle is the corollary of the previous one. The strengths model attends not just to the strengths of the individual but the strengths of the environment. Often the community can feel like a desert of burned bridges, blocked doors, and discrimination. From a strengths perspective, we must be able to find the pockets of

strengths in our communities—the employers, landlords, neighbors, business own-
ers, and community members who want to be part of building a supportive community. While the community can contribute to a person's distress in life, it is also
the community that can be the source of a person's well-being. It is the community that provides the opportunities: the people to care and support and the resources necessary.

Two assumptions underlie this principle. First, a person's behavior and well-
being are in large part determined by the resources available and the expectations
of others toward the person. Second, people have a right to the societal resources
they need (Davidson & Rapp, 1976; Rappaport, 1977). The case manager's task is
to create community collaborators; to become a catalyst for others in the community to be involved with people's recovery. Juxtapose this position with the more
common stance of blaming the community for lack of employment, housing, and
recreation opportunities. The community as scapegoat can be just as inimical to
effective helping as blaming the person receiving service. Both can lead to a sense
of paralysis, frustration, and impotence.

The task of resource acquisition should emphasize normal or natural resources,
not mental health services, because community integration can occur only apart
from mental health and segregated services. The assumption, which has been largely
confirmed in our experience, is that in any given population there are a sufficient
number of caring and potentially helpful people available to assist and support one
another. "Each community boasts a unique combination of assets upon which to
build. A thorough map of those assets would include an inventory of the gifts, skills
and capacities of community residents . . . associations . . . formal institutions like
schools, banks, businesses" (Kretzman & McKnight, 1993, pp. 6–7). The burden
of proof on case managers should be that to use a mental health service, it must
be first demonstrated that, natural helpers, community services (e.g., recreation
department), and social services (in that order) cannot be organized on behalf of
the person. As depicted in Figure 3.1, the size of the ring reflects the size of the
available resource pool. Also, as you move outward from the center, integration
replaces segregation. *The identification and use of community strengths and assets
are as critical as the identification and use of individual strengths.*

The case management research seems to bear this out. Common to the case
management models with demonstrated effectiveness (e.g., assertive community
treatment [ACT], rehabilitation, strengths models) is that service delivery minimizes the use of formally constituted mental health services in favor of direct provision by case managers and use of natural community resources. For example,
both ACT and strengths models target initially the provision of assistance with the
basics of housing, income and entitlements, and medication and health. Except for
medication, these domains involve work with landlords, social security, housing
authorities, social service agencies, food pantries, and other services, not mental
health providers. As people pursue vocational, socialization, and living skills, the
two models encourage the case manager to do this rather than make referrals to
specialized programs. For example, the case manager may work with employers to
find and maintain employment rather than refer the person to vocational rehabilitation, teach the living skills rather than refer the person to a day treatment or

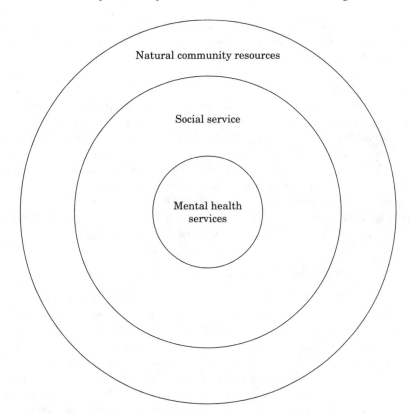

Figure 3.1 Levels of resources

partial hospital program, and locate recreational and social opportunities in the community rather than relying on mental health programs. The strengths model goes even further, in explicitly requiring the exploration and use of non-mental-health and non-professionally driven resources before consideration of these formally organized services. Research has found that:

1. Accelerated participation in in vivo-supported employment is more efficacious than transitioning through clubhouse prevocational activities that are generally viewed as effective (Bond & Dincin, 1986; Test, 1992).
2. Brokerage of services was the only variable negatively associated with client satisfaction (Huxley & Warner, 1992).
3. The treatment condition that fared best was that in which the case manager provided the most services directly and had "minimal contact with community based direct service providers other than for medication review" (Rydman, 1990, p. 233).

Referrals and community or environmental work do occur. Even though not precisely "a referral," the strengths model and one ACT project placed a premium on the use of available or natural community resources (e.g., families, volunteer opportunities, neighbors, junior colleges, sports leagues, YMCAs, art clubs). The results of this approach have included lower rates of hospitalization and a high ratio of goal achievements in most life domains (Santos, et al., 1993; Rapp & Wintersteen, 1989).

The evidence strongly suggests that case managers who deliver the preponderance of service and use naturally occurring resources and avoid traditional mental health services (except medication) produce significantly better outcomes and they do so over a wide range of outcomes (e.g., hospitalization, employment, independent living, satisfaction with services, goal achievement by clients). In contrast, common to each of the brokerage model studies is the reliance on referral, with an emphasis on mental health services (Franklin, Solovitz, Mason, Clemons, & Miller, 1987; Hornstra, Bruce-Wolfe, Sagduyu, & Riffle, 1993; Curtis, Millman, & Struening, 1992). These studies uniformly found poor outcomes.

Principle 4: The Client Is the Director of the Helping Process

A cornerstone of the strengths perspective of case management is the belief that it is the person's right to determine the form, direction, and substance of the case management help he or she is to receive. People with psychiatric disabilities are capable of this determination, and adhering to this principle contributes to the effectiveness of case management. Case managers should do nothing without the person's approval, involving the person in decisions regarding every step of the process. Many people receiving services have a difficulty feeling empowered to make decisions because they have been in a system for many years that has taught them to be compliant, helpless, and dependent. Continued messages of "Follow your treatment plan, attend these groups, take your medications, show up for all your appointments" can become a regular part of a person's life. If a person does resist, then we often attribute this resistance as a symptom of the person's "illness."

Opportunities to move each client closer to being the director of the case management situation should be found, created, and exploited. A benefit of this stance is that it keeps the case manager centered on what is important and meaningful to the person, not what the system deems is "best" for the person. Having the person direct the helping process, allows case mangers to work with the person's natural energy for recovery, rather than wasting energy trying to convince (or at worse coerce) a person to do something the client does not want, which often leads to undue resistance, tension within the helping relationship, or passive acceptance. With the person as the director, we are also more likely to find the "right" resources that have the "right" fit for the person, thereby moving toward empowering niches for people.

People often ask, "What do people with psychiatric disabilities need?" The answer is, "What people need is what they want. What they want is what any of us want: a decent place to live and adequate income, friends and opportunities to have meaningful recreation, an opportunity to contribute (e.g., work, family, helping others), and recognition for that contribution." A study by Ewalt and Honeyfield (1981) found that people with psychiatric disabilities who were hospitalized viewed the following as their needs to "make it" in the community: (1) money, (2) availability of health care, (3) a decent place to live, (4) transportation, (5) opportunities for socialization, and (6) availability of help if needed. Of those interviewed, 33% (N = 253) also stated the importance of the need to "be of help to others." These findings parallel the recent findings of successful programs (Gowdy & Rapp, 1989); that is, the programs that have produced the best results are those that conscientiously address these areas. In contrast, "Efforts at deinstitutionalization that rely primarily on professional judgments, at least in the mental health field, have failed miserably, with an overwhelming proportion of discharged long-term residents unable to maintain ongoing community tenure" (Ewalt & Honeyfeld, 1981, p. 223).

The tension between clients and clinical workers is often obscured by the professional lexicon, including such phrases as "resistance to treatment," "noncompliance," and "setting up the client to fail." The first two phrases have the wonderful effect of camouflaging the conflict by explaining the behavior as a rather natural occurrence in the helping process and as a function of the person's personality. It is therefore neither upsetting nor remediable by the professional attempting to change the person's behavior. The third phrase is heard when a person suggests a goal or aspiration that the professional views as unrealistic and thinks giving permission to pursue it could lead to pain, suffering, exacerbation of symptoms, and regression. Its effect is to deprive the person of one of the most precious elements of humanness: the need for a dream. It further suggests a parent-child relationship of unequal knowledge, power, and protection, guarantees not of a partnership but of an adversarial relationship.

Believing and adhering to a strict code of client self-determination and the skillful assessing of strengths seem to facilitate a partnership between client and worker. The professional works on behalf of the person, and the person's goals and aspirations become the centerpiece of the work. Why do people not follow through with taking prescribed medications? Why does a person refuse to take a bath? Why doesn't this person show up for her group session and when she does, why is she disruptive? Peoples' lack of compliance and lack of progress seem as much a function of their hostility toward a system that is irrelevant to their needs and hopes as it is a function of their personalities and disability. In fact, failing to follow alien prescriptive demands is often the only way we allow people to express their opinion and their sense of power.

Adherence to a strict code of client self-determination should not suggest that the case manager assume a passive posture in the helping relationship by becoming a servant to the person: "If the client wants a doughnut, I will run over and get him a doughnut." This is no more a partnership than when the professional dictates to the person. In almost all cases, however, this exaggerated perspective comes from a sincere acceptance of client self-determination. It also assumes the person knows all rather than the person knows best—two very different ideas.

An alternative perspective is for the case manager to help the person explore new vistas. Guitar lessons can turn into getting paid for working in a music store, or giving lessons, or performing—ideas that the person may never have considered or may have discarded years earlier. This is not talking a person into something, but creating new possibilities by blending different strengths. In some cases it may be nothing more than "planting seeds" that can be regularly watered. It may mean visiting a music store, talking to musicians, attending performances, or scanning classified ads for "gigs." The person has the right to make the choices, but freedom may best be served by knowledge of the choices possible and the confidence that the person could successfully select from among these choices.

Principle 5: The Case Manager–Client Relationship Is Primary and Essential

The relationship is primary and essential because without it a person's strengths, talents, skills, desires, and aspirations often lie dormant and are not able to be mobilized for the person's recovery journey. It takes a strong and trusting relationship to discover a rich and detailed view of someone's life and create an environment where a person is willing to share what is most meaningful and important to her or him, the person's passions for life.

Many case management programs ignore the importance of the case manager–client relationship or prohibit it. The brokerage model of case management is built with an assumption that the work can be done without a close relationship. Nationally, case management caseloads have often exceeded 80 to 1 and have even reached 200 to 1. A close collaborative relationship cannot be established with 80 people. In contrast, Richard Lamb (1980) advocates a therapist–case manager model for the central reason that a therapist is the one professional with a relationship of sufficient intensity and intimacy necessary to carry out case management. As Deitchman (1980) stated:

> Economic survival is not successfully dealt with by referral; neither is psychological survival. For the chronic (*sic*) client to survive psychologically, he needs someone he can have a relationship with, someone he can confide in, someone he can depend on. The chronic (*sic*) client in the community needs a traveling companion, not a travel agent. The travel agent's only function is to make the client's reservation. The client has to get ready, get to the airport, and traverse foreign terrain by himself. The traveling companion, on the other hand, celebrates the fact that his friend was able to get seats on the plane, talks about his fear of flying, and then goes on the trip with him, sharing the joys and sorrows that occur during the venture. (p. 789)

It is the relationship that buffers the demands of challenging and distressing times. It is the relationship that attenuates the stress and prevents or mitigates the exacerbation of distressing symptoms. It is the relationship that supports the person's confidence in tackling the multiple requirements of the environment and other people.

A cooperative relationship often starts with playing basketball or doing the dishes or going shopping together as the person tests the worker's sincere commitment to the person as an individual. As confidence in the relationship replaces skepticism, the person becomes reaffirmed as an individual with assets and valid aspirations, goals become more ambitious, communication more honest, and assistance more accessible.

Principle 6: The Primary Setting for Our Work Is the Community

Given the stated principles of client self-determination and the priority of naturally occurring resources, it should be clear that office-based interventions are contraindicated. A case manager cannot sit in the office and locate, arrange, and support an employer with a job the person desires. The work must occur in apartments, restaurants, businesses, parks, and community agencies. Office contact with people should be limited to the few instances where the person prefers it (usually for psychological safety), and this is rare and usually time limited.

A community outreach mode offers rich opportunities for assessment and intervention. Office-bound assessment limits the sources of data to what the person says, the case manager's observations of the person, and the 10-inch stack of paper referred to as a case file. This is simply not enough for a variety of reasons.

First, a person's behavior in a mental health program is often different from behavior in other settings. The "Thorazine shuffle" disappears in many cases after the individual leaves the mental health center and work on developing strengths begins. The opposite is also true. Many people can and do cook, clean, and socialize while in structured day treatment or partial hospitalization programs, but fail to do so in their own apartments and neighborhoods. Skills learned inside agencies do not appear to generalize easily to more normalized settings (Gutride, Goldstein, & Hunter, 1973; Jaffe & Carlson, 1976; Liberman, Massel, Mosk, & Wong, 1985). Second, the person's perception of resources available is just that, a perception. Most people are unaware of the potential resources available. There have been many examples of this in the 25 years of our program. In one case, a person wanted to earn his GED certificate and attend classes to do so. The case manager helped the person arrange such classes only two blocks from the boardinghouse, but discovered that the person did not go to the first two sessions. The indication was that the person was scared. Because the case manager was doing the work in the community and more specifically in the boarding house, he came to know another resident without a psychiatric disability who was more than willing to walk the person to class. After three sessions, this was no longer needed and the person went on to earn his certificate. It was unlikely that successful resolution of this problem would have occurred if the work had been done in an office.

Finally, part of a case manager's job is to assist people in their decision-making process, provide information on options, and at times to teach new skills for successful community living. Working with a person in the community helps us to avoid generalization of problems and keeps the work centered on what is most relevant to the person. Mental health centers often have groups that teach community living skills, but often what is taught is not easily transferable to the person's specific living situation. As has been already suggested, teaching a client to cook spaghetti for 20 people in a day treatment program on a gas stove can be perceived as very different from cooking spaghetti for one on a hot plate. When people see our services as useful and practical, they are more likely to stay engaged.

The case management research supports this principle. The average retention rate of clients in services for at least a year is 84% across ACT studies, which produces a highly significant ($p = 0.001$) difference with control participants. The more than 80% retention rate for a year greatly exceeds traditional aftercare, where retention rates seldom exceed 50% for even 6 months (Bond, McGrew, & Fekete, 1995; Axelrod & Wetzler, 1989). This is no small achievement given the historical difficulty in engaging and keeping people engaged in service.

Another study found that a number of assertive outreach variables, including out-of-office visits, were correlated with a person's satisfaction with service accessibility (Huxley & Warner, 1992). Bond (1991) commented that "one program using office visits because of a reluctance to make home visits had minimal success until it changed its treatment strategy" (p. 75). McGrew and Bond (1995) found nearly unanimous agreement of ACT experts on the importance of outreach and in vivo service delivery. The failure of the brokerage model of case management, which is largely office bound, and the positive results of the other models (e.g., ACT, strengths, rehabilitation) argue for the criticalness of an outreach mode of operation.

Strengths Orientation Fosters Empowerment

Two of the most oppressed groups in mental health are clients and their case managers. Although the oppression of clients has been well documented (Goffman, 1961; Szasz, 1970), that of case managers has not. Basically, they are the lowest paid, the lowest on the organizational hierarchy, and the least credentialed, yet work most intensely with people and have the most ambitious goals established for their work. They also have to complete the most paperwork, go to the same meetings as others, and are the most supervised members of the organization. They have the least control over their jobs and have the least influence over organizational or service matters.

The strengths orientation cannot address this body of factors. In some small way, however, it may provide some enhanced sense of power for both people receiving services and case managers by: (1) replacing the mutual conflict with a partnership; (2) encouraging the vigilance needed to identify strengths, which forces the individual to look for the good rather than the bad and to enhance the positiveness of worker activities; (3) defining the community as an oasis, allowing individuals to see possibilities where only limitations were seen before; and (4) leading to improved client outcomes, so that both worker and client can see results and experience the satisfaction they can bring. In short, we have seen workers (and clients) with a new sense that they can make a difference.

One indicator of this perspective as an empowerer of people is the consistent phenomenon of client achievements in areas not targeted or attended to by the case manager. Here is an example:

John R. is a 27-year-old man who has a diagnosis of schizophrenia, paranoid type. In the absence of a group-home bed or transitional apartment in the community, John was discharged from a three-month admission at the state hospital to his parents' home. At intake, the following problems were recorded for attention by the treatment team at the Community Support Program where he was referred for aftercare: (1) lacks motivation to engage in social activities; (2) displays poor judgment regarding how he manages his money; (3) needs to improve communication skills with peers; (4) needs to become more compliant with medication regimen and reduce abusing alcohol; and (5) needs to individuate effectively from family of origin. The chart also noted that John enjoyed sports, was in good physical health, and was assertive with staff in expressing his wants and needs. In order to achieve these treatment goals, John was scheduled to attend the partial hospitalization program, attend a medication clinic, and work with a case manager.

During the subsequent weeks, John's behavior began to concern the staff. His parents were reporting that he was staying up very late watching TV, drinking despite their protests, and not attending the partial program on a regular basis. The case manager made a home visit, and reluctantly John agreed to come downstairs to talk with her. At this meeting the case manager focused on identifying John's strengths (aspirations, confidence, and competencies) and learned several things: He did not want to move into his own apartment at this time, and he did not want to go to the partial program and spend all day with "those crazy people." What he did want to do was to get his driver's license and save up enough money to buy a car. This information led to a discussion of cars.

John showed the case manager the many model cars he had put together, and they talked of how much he enjoyed the auto mechanics class he had taken in high school. They agreed to meet the following week at a local gas station, where the case manager knew the manager. The manager agreed to allow John to volunteer for two hours each day, doing odd jobs and going to pick up needed parts at the nearby parts dealership. During the next few weeks, John began to take his medication more regularly, and his attendance and participation at the partial program showed marked improvement. His parents also reported that he was no longer staying up late watching TV and that he was not abusing alcohol at home. After three months of volunteering at the gas station, John began to talk of trying to move to his own apartment with a roommate, a mechanic he had met at the station. The owner of the station was also considering hiring John as a part-time paid employee.

The observed pattern over the last 25 years is so strong as to demand an explanation: Regular trips to the library lead to a person's placing more attention on personal appearance and starting to shower regularly; joining a bowling league leads to taking better care of their apartment so they can entertain friends; participation in the local theater group leads to a person thinking about their own personal health and nutrition; and work on moving to an apartment leads to a person making a decision to be more active in promoting their own recovery through medications and other enjoyable activities. These secondary achievements occur without explicit attention by the case manager. Rather than appealing to some notion of "spontaneous recovery," it may be that success in one area breeds efforts and success in other areas; that success empowers people to try areas where they lacked the confidence or willingness to try before.

Research on the Strengths Model

There have been nine studies testing the effectiveness of the strengths model as delivered to people with psychiatric disabilities. Four of the studies employed experimental or quasi-experimental designs and five used non-experimental methods (Table 3.1 provides a summary of each). This section reviews the client outcomes from this body of research.

Hospitalization

Six of these nine studies include hospitalization as a dependent measure. In the three nonexperimental studies, the incidence of hospitalization was 50% lower than the usual rate for that locale. In the Modrcin, Rapp, and Poertner (1988) experimental study, the 50% reduction in hospitalization was not statistically significant, owing perhaps to the small sample size. Macias, Kenney, Farley, Jackson, and Vos (1994) did find a statistically significant reduction in hospitalization incidences for the group receiving strengths model case management. In addition, they found that the frequency of contacts with the crisis center was dramatically reduced over time while participants in the control group increased the number of crisis center contacts. The study by Ryan, Sherman, and Judd (1994) also suggests that clients receiving strengths model case management had fewer hospitalizations or emergency room visits.

Independence of Daily Living

Rapp and Wintersteen (1989) and Kisthardt (1993) found that the people receiving strengths model case management set more goals in this life domain than any other. Of the 2,624 goals set in this area, 2215 were achieved (84%). Macias et al. (1994) found that people receiving strengths model case management demonstrated statistically significant greater competence in daily living than the control group as rated by both clients and case managers. Modrcin et al. (1988) and Stanard (1999) found participants in the experimental group to score higher on community living skills and community behaviors. Research by Ryan et al. (1994) suggests stability of residence was enhanced by strengths model case management and Stanard (1999) found statistically significant results favoring strengths model group in residential living outcomes.

TABLE 3.1 Strengths-Model Case Management Research

Nonexperimental Strengths-Model Case Management Research

Study (location, study leaders)	Sample size	Character of sample	Design	Outcomes
Lawrence, Kansas Rapp & Chamberlain (1985)	$N = 19$	Seriously mentally ill	Nonexperimental	A = +, H = + I = +
Kansas Rapp & Wintersteen (1989)	$N = 235$	Seriously mentally ill	Nonexperimental	A = +, C = +
Colorado Ryan, Sherman & Judd (1994)	$N = 382$	Multiple hospital diagnosis of psychosis	Three group post hoc Correlational CSS, strengths, traditional	C = +
Kansas Kisthardt (1994)	$N = 66$	Seriously mentally ill	Nonexperimental	C = +, E = +
Barry et al (2003)	STR (81)* ACT (93)†	Seriously mentally ill	longitudinal comparison of strengths and ACT	A = 0, C = 0 G = +

Experimental Strengths Model Studies (N = 4)

Author(s)	Research Design	Sample	Attrition (%)	Follow-up duration	Outcomes
Modrcin et al. (1988)	Experimental	STR (23) S (21)	51	4 months	A = 0, B = 0 C = +, D = + E = +
Macias et al (1994)	Experimental	STR + PR‡ (20) PR (21)	17	18 months	A = +, C = + G = +, H = 0 I = 0, J = +
Macias et al. (1997)	Quasi Experimental	STR (48) S (49)	24	9 months	F = +, G = + H = +
Stanard (1999)	Quasi Experimental	STR (29) S (15)	9	3 months	A = 0, B = + D = +, F = +

A = Hospitalizations, + = fewer, − = greater, 0 = no difference (n.d.); B = Quality of life, + = increase, − = decrease, 0 = n.d.; C = Social functioning , + = increase, − = decrease 0 = n.d.; D = Occupational/Vocational functioning, + = increase, − = decrease, 0 = n.d.; E = Leisure time activities, social isolation, + = increase or less isolation, − = decrease, greater isolation, 0 = n.d.; F = Independence of residential living, + = more time housed, more stable, less structured, improved, − = less time housed, less stable, more structured, 0 = n.d.; G = Behavior symptomatology, + = reduction, − = increase, 0 = n.d.; H = Social support networks, social support, + = improved, increased; − = fewer, lesser, 0 = n.d.; I = Client satisfaction with treatment, + = high satisfaction, − = low, 0 = n.d.; J = Family burden, + = decrease, − = increase, 0 = n.d.

*STR = Strengths

†ACT = Assertive community treatment

‡PR = Psychosocial rehabilitation

Vocational/Education

Three nonexperimental studies all found high rates of client goal setting and goal achievement in the vocational/educational life domain. Combining the Rapp and Wintersteen (1989) and Kisthardt (1993) results, people achieved 1,541 of 1,998 goals set (77%). Modrcin et al. (1988) found a statistically significant different in favor of the strengths model grouping the number of people involved in vocational training.

Leisure Time and Social Support

In keeping with other conclusions, three nonexperimental studies found high rates of goal setting and goal achievement in this life domain. Combining the Rapp and Wintersteen (1989) and Kisthardt (1993) results, people achieved 2,225 of the 2,766 goals set (80%). Modrcin et al. (1998) found significant differences favoring the strengths model in terms of people's use of leisure time. Social support was measured in both Macias studies with one finding statistically significant differences favoring the experimental group.

Financial/Legal

Two of the nonexperimental studies (Rapp & Wintersteen, 1989; Kisthardt, 1993) found that people receiving strengths model case management achieved 701 of 902 goals (78%) set in this life domain. Ryan et al. (1994) also found "a stable and secure income" to be associated with people who received strengths model case management. Macias et al. (1997) found a statistically significant differences in income favoring the strengths group.

Health

Macias et al. (1994) found the people receiving strengths model case management showed statistically significant greater overall physical and mental health. Rapp & Wintersteen (1989) and Kisthardt (1993) found that people achieved 85% of their goals in the health domain (1,834 of 2,157).

Symptomatology

Macias et al. (1994) found that people receiving strengths model case management reported fewer problems with mood, fewer problems with thinking, and greater psychological well-being than the control group. Family members rating of cognitive psychiatric symptomatology was significantly more positive than the control subjects as were ratings of anger and of paranoia. Similarly, professional staff assessed the strengths model group as less depressed in mood and more clear-thinking and rational than the control group. Statistically significant differences in symptomatology favoring the strengths group were also found by Macias et al. (1997). Barry et al. (2003) found a statistically significant difference in symptomotology favoring the strengths group over the ACT group. Modrcin et al. (1988) found people who received strengths model case management showed statistically significant improvement in tolerance of stress over the control group. Ryan et al. (1994) suggest that strengths model case management was associated with better adherence with medication regimes and being judged not to be a danger to self or others.

Family Burden

In the one strengths model study to measure family burden, Macias et al. (1994) found that family members of strengths model clients reported feeling less burdened than family members of the control group. Furthermore,

> family members of case managed consumers reported being less depressed when around their consumer, less in need of help in dealing with consumer, less trapped, less frustrated by an inability to plan ahead, and less strained by tension and conflict caused by the consumer. (p. 333)

Research Summary

The research on the strengths model of case management is suggestive of its effectiveness (see Table 3.1). On the downside, the research is limited to two experimental, two quasi-experimental, and five non-experimental studies. The size of the samples in three of the experimental studies was small. The measure used across studies varied and questions have been raised about many of them (Chamberlain & Rapp, 1991).

On the plus side, in the ten outcome areas, improvements were found for 18 and no difference found for ten. In no study on no measure did strengths case management clients do worse. In the four experimental studies the ratio was 13:5 (positive outcome to no differences). The two outcomes areas where results have been consistently positive is reduction in symptoms and improved social functioning. The strengths model research results have also been remarkably resilient across settings. Even within studies, consistency is shown. Rapp and Wintersteen (1989), Kisthardt (1993), and Ryan et al. (1994) all used multiple sites with different case managers, different supervisors, and affiliations with a total of 15 different agencies. Notwithstanding the potential problems, the research is beginning to accumulate that the strength model can make a positive difference in people's lives in a range of outcome areas.

Functions of Strengths Model Case Management

Strengths model case management includes a practice theory, a set of principles, and a set of methods. These methods can be best organized into five functions:

1. Engagement and relationship: The initial meetings with a person, where the purpose is to begin the development of a collaborative helping partnership.

2. Strengths assessment: The process of gathering information regarding seven "life domains," which appear to be directly related to successful community tenure. Information focuses on the current situation, what the person wants (may indicate a change or desire to sustain), and information regarding resources and activities that have been exploited in the past. The goal is to collect information on personal and environmental strengths as a basis for work together.

3. Personal planning: The creation of a mutual agenda for work between the person and case manager focused on achieving the goals that the person has set. Personal planning requires the person and case manager to discuss, negotiate, and agree on the long-term goal, short-term goals, or tasks; assign responsibility to each task; and target dates for accomplishment. A primary activity is the generation of options used to guide the decision-making process. The strengths assessment is the primary source of information and guidance.

4. Resource acquisition: The purpose is to acquire the environmental resources desired by people to achieve their goals and insure their rights, to increase each person's assets. A primary focus is to break down the walls separating people from the community, to replace segregation with true community integration. To be successful, case managers require new perspectives concerning "community" and a wide variety of interpersonal and strategic skills.

5. Collective continuous collaboration and graduated disengagement: Typically thought of as "monitoring," this concept addresses the multidimensional nature of ongoing modification and adaptation that takes place during the helping process, determining the extent to which people are able to engage in activities noted on the personal plan. In the strengths model, case managers are less concerned with assuring "patient compliance" with a treatment plan, and more concerned with a person's ability to creatively use their own strengths and community resources to cope from day to day in ways that promote self-efficacy, community integration, and recovery. Graduated disengagement refers to the helping behavior that is consciously designed to replace the case manager or program staff in something they are doing with or for a person.

Subsequent chapters are devoted to each of the first four functions. "Collective, Continuous Collaboration and Graduated Disengagement" depicts the ongoing nature of strengths-based case management. The methods used are the same as those in the first four functions.

CHAPTER FOUR

Engagement and Relationship: A New Partnership

Purpose: To create a trusting and reciprocal relationship between case manager and client as a basis for working together.

ENGAGEMENT IS MOST FREQUENTLY thought of as the initial coming together of clients and case manager. Although there are a few considerations and methods unique to this stage, most apply across the helping process. In a sense, with each contact, the relationship becomes reengaged. So, before turning to engagement as a specific function, the importance and nature of the client-case manager relationship need attention.

Nature of the Relationship

The relationship between the client and professional is seen as a keystone in virtually all approaches to casework, psychotherapy, and counseling. Some approaches view the relationship as the crucial therapeutic ingredient (Rogers, 1959), whereas other approaches see it as the context for practice thereby enhancing the effectiveness of techniques (Fischer, 1978). Even more recent empowerment models of practice underscore the importance of the relationship (Gutierrez, Parsons, & Cox, 1998; Lee, 1994; Dodd & Gutierrez, 1990; Simon, 1994).

The relationship between professional and the person with a psychiatric disability has been shaped by its context. Traditionally, mental health workers practiced within the confines of the state hospital, group residence, office, day treatment program, or sheltered work enclave. Contact with others was severely limited; the work was "private." Within these walls, the rules governing the relationship between worker and client were similarly constrained. Each had roles to play and rules, professional and organizational, were established to maintain those roles. The quest was for "professional distance," with its lack of reciprocity, rules against self-disclosure, and power differentials. Although the relationship has always been viewed as critical to helping, it was a very limited relationship that was of concern. The brokerage model of case management places little emphasis on relationship; rather, it focuses on assessment and referral. "It stops short of coaching the client or taking responsibility for making sure the client gets the services" (Robinson & Bergman, 1989). This is the only case management model that has failed to demonstrate its efficacy (Rapp, 1995). The ineffectiveness of these types of services with people with psychiatric disabilities suggests that something else is needed.

Case management, when characterized by out-of-office/in-community work, interaction with a variety of community actors, emphasis on relationship, and other modalities, is a dramatic break from past modes of helping people with psychiatric disabilities. Case management, literally and figuratively, breaches or extends the walls of mental health services. Many old rules become irrelevant within this new context and methods of helping others need adaptation (Curtis & Hodge, 1994). The characteristics of this new partnership are described below.

Purposeful

The relationship is best seen as a medium to achievement. For many clients, the relationship with the case manager becomes a primary mechanism for increasing confidence, identifying goals and risking dreaming, and recognizing talents and strengths. The relationship acts as a rocket booster and a safety net. The stronger the relationship, the more powerful are the rocket booster and the stronger the safety net. Everything that the case manager does in the interpersonal sphere should be done for the person's benefit. We return later to purpose when discussing boundary dilemmas.

There are two levels of purposefulness in case management. The ultimate purpose of our work is to help a person recover, reclaim, or transform his or her life. The relationship should be goal directed and growth oriented; sharing a common agenda that defines the work you do together. This overall vision provides a foundation for the second level, the purpose of each helping encounter.

For many case managers, the work tends to be reactive and passive. The purpose of seeing a client is often described as to "check on," "monitor," "visit," or "see how they are doing." In answer to "how's the client doing?" the answer is often, "Howard's doing fine." This language is reflective of the perception of the role and purpose of the case manager.

In contrast, a case manager who has adopted the vision of recovery tends to use phrases like, "planned next steps in getting a car," "while doing a strengths assessment found the following information helpful to the person recovery," "reviewed his goal achievement for the last week," "I learned the reasons he doesn't like to take his medications," and "we celebrated his first week on the job by going out for coffee together." These words convey a purpose that leads to achievement, growth, and increased confidence on the part of the client.

Reciprocal

The role of the case manager should resemble being more like a traveling companion with the person on their recovery journey rather than a travel agent. Both parties should learn from each other and enjoy the time spent together. The opposite of this would be a relationship that is one sided or hierarchical.

There is an inherent pull in the client-case manager relationship for it to be one sided: The case manager gives and helps, and the client is the recipient. After all, the case manager is being paid for this. As Curtis and Hodge (1994) write:

> However, when staff are always the "givers" and consumers are always the "recipients", we perpetuate the idea that what staff have what is most valuable and that staff hold the power to allocate or give based on their judgment. Very few of us would describe this as a normal adult-adult relationship. Most of us look for a kind of balance in our personal and professional relationships, and often this balance is based on mutuality and reciprocity. Refusing offers of reciprocity—whether it is an offer of a cup of coffee, a small gift, or of knitting lessons—may be as rejecting as outright stating to the person "You have nothing of value to offer this relationship." And it is downright unfriendly. (p. 348)

There is a Chinese proverb, "The greatest gift you can give someone is to allow them to give to you." Among people with psychiatric disabilities, the desire to give and help is prevalent and strong. Too often we have shut off this opportunity.

A powerful frame of reference that helps avoid this temptation of being "one-sided," is viewing the relationship as an experience in mutual learning. In fact, the best case mangers and therapists are also the best learners. Clients are learning about themselves, their environment, and ways to better achieve the goals they set. The worker has the opportunity to learn about that individual's highly personal experience of life. In particular, the case manager has a real-world classroom to teach him or her what it is like to live with a psychiatric disability and the societal oppression that coexists. How does one survive? How does one recover? The case manager is in daily contact with the experts.

Rose and Black (1985), based on the work of Freire (1970), describe the process as one of dialogue. The case manager seeks to enter the reality of the person by learning the objective conditions of their lives and their subjective experience of that reality. "The dialogue cannot be reduced to the act of one person's depositing ideas in another, nor can it become a simple exchange of ideas to be consumed by the discussants" (Freire, 1970, p. 77). Rather, it is a dialogue based on reflection, respect, and mutual learning.

Friendly

One can view relationships on a continuum from the stereotype of detached and limited psychoanalysis to intimate friendships. The case manager-client relationship would generally fall a little to the right of normal friendship on this continuum. In other words, case managers are not paid friends. In fact, case managers should devote considerable effort to clients building "real" friendships with others. On the other hand, the relationship should be friendly. The relationship should be characterized by warmth, acceptance, caring, respect, and even fun. It should be uplifting for both parties. "People do not want to interact with neutral detached helpers, nor do they want to meet a new professional each time they seek help. One cannot establish a secure relatedness with staff who are disrespectful—condescending, not listening, infantilizing, having low expectations, being culturally insensitive, uncaring, untrustworthy, and devaluing. These attitudes hinder people's sense of self, and undermine motivation, self-determination and recovery." (Onken et al, 2002, p. 109)

Trusting

The relationship needs to be based on a high degree of trust. For many people with psychiatric disabilities, their relationships have been limited, and many times a source of frustration and pain. Messages received within past or present relationships have sometimes reinforced their sense of inadequacy.

Sometimes it is a strength for clients to not trust because of past circumstances that have created pain and discomfort. The professional needs to allow for the trust process to evolve naturally as opposed to jumping in and saying "you can trust me." Clients will set the pace when they are able to trust; to be mistrustful is normal considering what most clients have gone through in their lives and with other helping professionals. Trust involves several dimensions. First, trust means honesty. There will be no lies or shading of the truth. Second, trust means that promises will be kept, or if doubt is present, promises will not be made. Rather, the case manager will develop trust through action. When a case manager promises to do something, the person can "take it to the bank". This also means that limits must be set. "I'll be there for you" does not necessarily mean forever or within 10 minutes of a person's call in every situation. Third, trust is the assumption that the person is always doing the best she or can can do given an understanding of the situation and herself or himself.

Trust for clients is the perception that "they can risk sharing thoughts, feelings, mistakes, and failure with the worker" (Schulman, 1992, p. 60). Mistrust is grounded in fear of imagined hurts, exploitation, rejection, criticism, punishment, and control by others. Given the past history of relationships, trust is given reluctantly by most clients. It is therefore built in small steps, with each encounter. Empathy, nonconditional acceptance of the client, and honesty are required (Hepworth & Larsen, 1986). The case manager should demonstrate this through a consistent display using words, actions, and body postures. The case manager strives to create an environment in which the person feels comfortable sharing their hopes, fears, and dreams. The case manager refrains from being judgmental and instead seeks understanding and meaning. The opposite of this would be a relationship that is characterized by mistrust or lack of respect.

Empowering

Client–case manager relationships should be empowering; they should provide strength to the person. "True partnership, having the sense that you are viewed and respected as an equal, and that the other person will be there through thick and thin, conveys secure relatedness and fosters intrinsic motivation" (Onken, 2003, p. 109). An empowering relationship is one in which clients see themselves as the director of the helping process. Case managers make a conscious effort to assist the person exercise his or her own power in such areas as establishing an identity, making personal decisions, exercising a right to fail, and accessing information. Given the discussion of empowerment in chapter 1, an empowering relationship would: (1) increase the person's abilities and perception of his or her abilities; (2) increase options and perception of options; and (3) increase the opportunities and confidence of the person to choose and to act on those choices.

Even allowing the person to choose where to meet begins to reflect a relationship that empowers.

Spirit-Breaking and Hope-Inducing Behaviors

Most mental health professionals want to do whatever is best to help facilitate the recovery journey of the person with whom they are working. Even with this sincere intention, many professionals exhibit behaviors at times that can be deemed spirit-breaking (Deegan, 1990). We refer to spirit-breaking behaviors as those behaviors that diminish or even possibly extinguish the hope held by the person that he or she can move forward in the journey of recovery. Hope-inducing behaviors are those that enhance and strengthen the hope that individuals hold (Russinova, 1999).

Here are some examples of spirit-breaking behaviors (see Appendix I for a more complete list):

- Treating adults as children (e.g., telling the person that they can't drink or that they need to be more quiet in public; "You can't have a dog; you can't even take care of yourself.")
- Taking a parental stance/chastising (e.g., "I told you . . . If you would have listened to me . . .")
- Being rude to people (e.g., using derogatory expressions, forgetting phone calls, breaking appointments, being tactlessly direct (e.g., "You need to work on your hygiene.")
- Attributing everything to the psychiatric disability and making generalizations (e.g., the person is manipulative, noncompliant; a person can't have a bad day or express anger without it being seen as a symptom.)
- Imposing one's own standard of living on other people
- Restricting a person's choices (telling a person they have to do either this or that)
- Making decisions for the other person (e.g., telling a person who wants to go to college that it has been decided that they should go to vocational training instead)
- Telling people they are not yet ready for work
- Insisting that the person be forced to take medications

It should be a goal of all case managers to increase their hope-inducing behaviors while reducing and hopefully eliminating many of their spirit-breaking behaviors. For case managers to do this, they must become critically aware of their words, actions, and behaviors and what impact these have on the people they serve. This is not always easy because many times people do not let us know when something we have said or done has been spirit breaking. Often our words and actions are internalized by the people we serve over time and its impact is subtle yet powerful. Other times we can mistake a spirit-breaking response for a person's symptoms. For example, when a person is already severely depressed, we may not even be able to notice the impact of one of our specific behaviors. We can also get so caught up in the other person's response that we fail to see its connection to our spirit-breaking behaviors. For example, when a person becomes angry, we can become reactive to what we label as inappropriate behavior on the part of the other person and therefore not see that the person's response was directly related to our behavior. In addition, case managers can sometimes view what we call "spirit-breaking" behaviors as good practice. Sometimes case managers might feel that the best way to help a person in their recovery is to provide "tough love" or that "telling the person the way it is" is the most honest and sincere way of helping people. Instead it is further spirit-breaking for the person.

To assess whether a particular behavior is spirit breaking, we must become critically reflective toward our practice. One option is to evaluate our behaviors after each meeting with a person. We can ask ourselves: (1) What were the specific words or actions that I said or did during this meeting that might have been perceived as spirit-breaking? (2) How did the person respond to my specific words or actions? (3) What can I do to acknowledge and make amends for my spirit-breaking behaviors?

Spirit-breaking behaviors are not necessarily intentionally done to inhibit a person's recovery journey, but they can have that power nonetheless. The ultimate goal of a mental health professional should be to assist in facilitating a person's recovery journey; therefore we must always be mindful of the messages we communicate to the person we are serving. It is a hope-inducing behavior to ask a person whether your behaviors are helping or hindering their recovery journey.

Hope-inducing behaviors communicate a message of hope and demonstrate that we are committed to assisting a person in their recovery journey. This would include building hope through caring interactions, focusing on a person's strengths and celebrating accomplishments, promoting choice, helping people achieve goals that are important to them, and promoting a future beyond the mental health system. Here are a few examples of hope-inducing practices (Appendix II contains an inventory of hope-inducing behaviors):

- Demonstrating care and kindness
- Communicating that "I believe in you" and "I am on your side"
- Asking a person's opinion/choice about all aspects of the helping process
- Supporting a person's decisions and desires by accepting them and helping achieve them rather than putting down or minimizing (even subtly) a person's choices and desires

- Normalizing a person's experience by letting him or her know that other people experience similar things
- Pointing out achievements/success
- Going with a person to a doctor's appointment or court hearing for support and to help reduce fear
- Making sure the goals you are working on are actually the client's goals
- Acknowledging and supporting the right for all consumers to make their own life decisions and having control of their course of treatment
- Promoting integration by using community resources and engaging consumers in activities not related to mental health

An important thing to keep in mind is that there can be many gray areas between hope-inducing and spirit-breaking behaviors. For example, focusing on the positive is listed above as a hope-inducing behavior, but when a person is in deep despair about a particular life situation, they may perceive only focusing on the positive as a spirit-breaking behavior. We sometimes call this the "cheerleader approach" to case management. The strengths model is not solely about focusing on the positive, but rather being there in the moment with people during all the ups and downs of their recovery journey. Every encounter with a person has the potential to be hope-inducing (or spirit-breaking). Our goal is to maximize this potential.

Methods

Core Conditions

The foundation for the client-case manager relationship is empathy, genuineness, and unconditional positive regard. Maluccio's study (1979) of client's opinions of social workers included these characteristics among the most frequently mentioned.

Accurate empathy refers to the ability of the worker to perceive and communicate accurately and with sensitivity both the current feelings and perception of experiences of another person and their meaning and significance (Truax & Mitchell, 1971). "It's sometimes described as the ability to step into someone's shoes and see and feel life as that individual does" (Sheafor, Horejsi, & Horejsi, 1991, p. 84). The focus is often on feelings, whether they be frustration, pain, loss, anger, pride, happiness, or satisfaction. As the definition suggests, empathy must be communicated if it is to contribute to the relationship. The case manager shares an understanding of the client's feelings and perceptions with the person. The job of the worker is to be sensitive to exposed and apparent feelings but also to go further and clarify and expand what may only be hinted at by voice, posture, and content cues (Truax & Mitchell, 1971).

Unconditional positive regard "refers to the worker's communication of respect, acceptance, liking, caring and concern for the client in a non-dominating way" (Fischer, 1978, p. 196). These feelings are not conditional on the production of thoughts, feelings, and actions by the client that are acceptable to the worker. This does not imply approval of all behaviors and actions but, rather, even in the face of destructive or harmful behavior, the case manager can convey to the person that they continue to value them as a person and their inherent worth.

Genuineness refers to a worker being themselves in the moment rather than presenting a fascade (Truax & Carkhuff, 1967). As Fischer (1978) states, "it would be difficult to conceive of the meaningful communication of empathy and warmth by someone who was not at least minimally 'real'" (p. 199). He goes on:

> Genuineness is not synonymous with being totally honest. Workers need not disclose their total selves . . . they do not employ [negative responses] in ways that will be destructive to their client. (p. 199)

The case manager should convey a sense of sincere commitment to the helping relationship. The person should feel that the case manager has a genuine investment in his or her recovery journey that goes beyond merely being a paid professional. The opposite of this would be a relationship that seems distant and cold.

Mirroring

People develop their identity and perceptions of the world, in large part, based on the cumulative feedback they receive from others. In a sense, each of us acts as a mirror to other people. All mirrors are distorted to some degree; they mute some things and exaggerate others. As has been discussed in earlier chapters, the lives of people with psychiatric disabilities have been dominated by weakness-oriented mirrors that have muted their strengths and exaggerated their deficits.

A strengths-model case manager consciously uses herself as a countervailing mirror. Where it has been concave, it is now convex. This new mirror is highly sensitive to the abilities and talents of clients. It is highly sensitive to the courage and resilience they have recurringly demonstrated. It is highly sensitive to their achievements, no matter how seemingly insignificant. The purpose is to allow clients to see this other side of themselves that is as real and present as the side of the problems and deficits.

> I knew that Noreen's only way out was to suspend her pain, to see her past not only as a stumbling block but also as a challenge, and to recognize her own resilience. I also knew that she would resist. I remember the first time I suggested the idea to her. She was talking about her mother:
>
> My mother had a label for all the kids. My sister had big breasts, so she was the "tramp." The babies—the twins—were "ugly"; my mother said she wanted to hang veils on their faces. I had something wrong with my eyes, and I had to wear a patch, so I was "defective." A lot of times I would fall or bump into things because I had an eye problem, and she would berate me for being clumsy and out of control. I wouldn't let myself cry. I would stare at her and think of something else . . . like, "I'll know how to be a good mother. I'll do the opposite of everything she does, and my children will love me, and maybe then, I'll finally have a family."

Noreen related the incident for the same reason she had told other similar stories in the past: to let me know about her mother's verbal abuse, the total absence of support and love in her family, and her own suffering. Certainly all of this was present in her story. I knew the pain she was feeling, and I would never want to dismiss or minimize any of it. But from my outside perspective, I also recognized the affirmation that could be salvaged from her story, and I knew that she would benefit from seeing that side of her story too. I forged ahead and reframed the story to reveal its submerged themes.

"I find it remarkable," I ventured, "that under unbearable stress you could exercise terrific self-control, see your siblings' plight, and keep your hopes for yourself alive." (Wolin & Wolin, 1993, p. 57).

Most interactions with clients offer multiple opportunities to mirror the "good." But the effects on confidence, increased goal setting, and improved recognition of the person's competencies may take quite some time. The feelings of "damaged goods" are usually long-standing; very much a part of the person's identity. In some cases, it is likely to take "a lot of positive mirroring" before change can be ascertained.

Contextualizing

People who are oppressed have a high degree of self-blame (Fanon, 1968). Many perceive themselves as the major contributor to their unfortunate circumstances. This self-blame then translates into low self-worth, lack of confidence, and constricted life goals. Persons with a psychiatric disability may not only experience internal distress because of particular psychiatric symptoms but also must deal with the social sequelae surrounding psychiatric disability.

Clients need to have accurate information on mental illnesses, including various causes of psychiatric distress. Efforts should be made to help people see that they are not their disability or diagnosis. It is common that people with psychiatric disabilities will refer to themselves as "I am mentally ill," rather than seeing particular symptoms they may experience as being only one aspect of their life. Efforts should be made to help transform a person's self-perception by helping the person to see that the psychiatric disability is not an internal attribute that defines who one is as a person.

Clients also need information concerning the social sequelae of psychiatric disability. Known variously as consciousness raising or contextualizing, it refers to the process by which a person becomes aware of the societal context for their situation and in this process becomes aware of others in similar predicaments. It allows a person to perceive forces other than themselves as contributing to the current situation. In fact, no one has ever oppressed themselves (Rose & Black, 1985).

Contextualizing, then, seeks to teach people the factors that contribute to their poverty, unemployment and underemployment, social isolation, and lack of achievement including stigma and discrimination based on the illness, racism, sexism, ageism, distribution of resources, governmental and agency policies, the models by which professionals practice, and other considerations. Contextualizing also involves demonstrating that others are similarly situated due to similar processes. In other words, they are not alone.

Care must be exercised in using this method so that self-blame does not transform into environmental blame, which Rappaport, Davidson, Mitchell, & Wilson (1975) argue can be as inimical to achievement and helping as individual blaming. There are people who have involved themselves in consciousness-raising activities that get stuck in the stage of awareness and the anger that often results. Much like viewing psychiatric disability as being only one aspect of a person, no matter how distressing particular symptoms may be, the view here is that, "Yes, these social processes go on, they affect me profoundly, I am not to blame, but they are only one slice of the social world." That social world is also constructed of opportunities, resources, and caring people.

Self-Disclosure

Similar to reciprocity, self-disclosure is a normal component of most relationships. The self-help movement is based on the idea that personal disclosure and reciprocal helping are both appropriate and healing. Conventional wisdom has been that workers should reveal little about their personal values, problems, fears, opinions, etc. (American Psychological Association, 1977; Hackney & Corimer, 1973; Wells & Masch, 1986). This stricture places a constraint on staff to act as if they had no problems, emotions, or experience with life. Such pressure is unrealistic and withholds one of the most powerful aspects of a helping relationship.

Ironically, clients and expatients are often hired by mental health agencies with the expectation that they will disclose personal history and openly draw on their experiences in their role as staff. Self-disclosure by workers can help to establish bonds of trust and understanding, to validate the normalcy of a person's feelings and concerns, to provide examples of how situations can be alternatively handled, and to demonstrate effective ways of expressing both positive and negative emotions.

The fundamental points for discussion in self-disclosure issues are "To what degree?" and "For what purpose?" It is important for staff to be clear that the purpose in self-disclosure is not to meet the needs of the worker, but those of the person receiving services. The relationship does not exist to work out the problems of the paid staff person. Staff disclosure of personal feelings, attitudes, and values happens both deliberately and inadvertently through nonverbal cues. Like most people, persons with a psychiatric disability are sensitive to any lack of congruence between verbal and nonverbal messages. It is far better to convey this information explicitly in a way that is constructive to the relationship than to communicate mixed messages.

Although self-disclosure is an intricate part of most relationships, the type and amount varies widely between individuals and relationships. Individual interests and experience are often the most easily shared. Family configurations and relationships (e.g., "My brother is like that too") are usually next. Feelings are often the most difficult. Each case manager needs to determine the amount and nature of disclosure that is comfortable and use that level purposively with each person they work with. Of particular importance is sharing with the person your positive feelings, the benefits you have enjoyed because of the relationship with the person, and what the person has taught you. Maluccio (1979) found that one of the characteristics of social workers most cherished by people receiving services was their ability "to share of himself or herself with the client" (p. 125).

Accompaniment

Walter Deitchman's (1980) wonderful metaphor of the travel companion (Chapter 3) at times assumes a literal translation. Most people are scared or anxious when confronting a new task or situation. For many people with a psychiatric disability, that fear and lack of confidence can be acute and immobilizing. For some, even obviously simple and mundane tasks, can be a source of great anxiety.

Accompaniment refers to the case manager going with the person, and acting in partnership with the person while he or she does a task. Just the physical presence of a trusted person can often provide the emotional support and courage for the client. Accompaniment in this regard does not necessarily refer to doing part of the task for the person (although at times this can be another justification for accompaniment). Many times, a person's lack of follow-through on tasks they already established as desirable is due not to resistance or lack of skills but, rather, to overwhelming fear.

> Joe was 46 years old and had spent the last 18 years in a Veterans Administration hospital for paranoid schizophrenia. Upon release, Joe needed to apply with Social Security for Supplemental Security Income benefits. Joe readily wrote this goal on his personal plan but while working on defining the steps necessary (e.g., finding the address in the phone book, looking at a map, locating transportation), the case manager began noticing some hesitation. A week later, Joe admitted how fearful he was. The plan was changed. Over the next few days, the case manager drove Joe past the Social Security office several times. They then walked past it several times. They walked into the lobby and then returned to the street several times. Only then was Joe able, again with the case manager accompanying him, to apply for benefits. At no time did the case manager do any of the tasks. Joe got the appointment, completed the forms, talked to the receptionist, and answered the eligibility worker's questions. The case manager was just there.

For many professionals, this type of assistance raises the specter of dependency and is therefore contraindicated. The position here is that simple and unrealistic notions of "dependency" have undermined client achievement and at times have acted as professionally sounding excuses for *not* helping. No person is independent in any pure sense. Human beings are, rather, interdependent. We all exist and survive based on our interactions with others and resources available to us. The most "dependent" people are the wealthy. They need not cook, clean, drive, or even raise their own children. Yet we rarely describe the wealthy as dependent in some pathological sense.

The aim is not to do for a person what they can do for themselves, although at times this is necessary. This could undermine a person's sense of achievement and confidence. Rather, it is to provide the interpersonal support necessary for the person to do; to achieve.

Reinforcement and Achievement

Most satisfying relationships involve the regular if not frequent exchange of reinforcing comments (e.g., "That's great," "I'm proud of you for . . . ," "You really did a nice job on the . . .") Reinforcing comments are usually contingent; they are based on the occurrence of something caused by a person's behavior. In this way, they are different from statements that communicate unconditional positive regard. (e.g., "I really like you," I am in awe of your courage").

Most people respond positively to praise. For maximum effect the praise should: (1) be for a specific behavior, and (2) have immediacy—some temporal proximity between the behavior and the reward.

Praise is often warranted for the smallest achievements. Given the lack of confidence and the fear that dominate the lives of many people with psychiatric disabilities, even the accomplishment of some small and seemingly mundane task is worthy of recognition. In the previous case of Joe, walking past the Social Security office warrants a "pat on the back." It is as important for effort to be recognized as for a tangible achievement. In fact, one can argue that praising effort, possible learning, and the "little" accomplishments within a "failure" is more important than praising successes because successes inherently contain positive feedback where failures rarely do.

The reinforcement need not be limited to verbal communication. Writing notes or giving certificates of achievement can be used. One case manager used little stickers, affixing one next to each task that the person achieved. For some people, this would be demeaning, suggesting an adult-child relationship. This same case manager used this technique only with this one person; discrimination is required.

This leads to another dimension: The nature of the reinforcement, its frequency, and its form need to be individually tailored. What is most meaningful for one person is not necessarily most meaningful for another. For example, telling another person of an accomplishment in front of the client may embarrass one client while for another their face beams with pride. This is especially true of "celebrations." Celebrations are those events involving the case manager and the client, designed to recognize a specific and special achievement. In Joe's case, completing the application process could warrant a celebration. For another person, this would be demeaning. A celebration for one person who got a job may be a celebration for another person who stayed on the job for two weeks. The nature of the celebration needs to be similarly tailored to the individual, the relationship, and the achievement. Going to lunch or a ball game or an art exhibit would have differential meanings for different people.

The relationship between case manager and client should be infused with reinforcement. In this way, case managers help people to feel competent and confident that they can achieve, often achieving what they could not achieve before. The goal is to make every person "feel like a winner." The old adage that "nothing succeeds like success" has some scientific basis:

> Researchers studying motivation find that the prime factor is simply the self-perception among motivated subjects that they are in fact doing well. Whether they are or not by any absolute standard doesn't seem to matter much. In one experiment, adults were given puzzles to solve. All ten were exactly the same for all subjects. They worked on them, turned them in, and were given the results at the end. Now in fact, the results they were given were fictitious. Half of the exam takers were told that they had done well, seven out of ten correct. The other half were told that they had done poorly, seven out of ten wrong. Then all were given another ten puzzles (the same for each person). The half who had been told that they had done well in the first round really did do better in the second, and the other half really did do worse. Mere association with past personal successes apparently leads to more persistence, higher motivation, or something that makes us do better. (Peters & Waterman, 1982, p. 58).

Positively reinforced behavior slowly comes to occupy a larger and larger share of time and attention and less desirable behavior begins to be dropped.

Engagement

Although engagement, in a sense, is a recurring theme throughout the relationship and even with each contact, engagement in the initial stages of helping has some unique properties and methods. In the strengths model, engagement is a separate function unlike most formulations that prescribe assessment as the initial stage (Levine & Fleming, undated; Kisthardt, 1992). Given the importance of the relationship as the bedrock of work, and the often spirit-breaking histories of professional and interpersonal relationships experienced by people with psychiatric disabilities, engagement is viewed as the indispensable and critical first step.

Some people enter a new relationship with a case manager eagerly and easily, but for many the encounter is a reluctant one, characterized by suspicion. So many past relationships, professional or otherwise, have been a source of disappointment, pain, and messages of incompetence, damaged goods, and inadequacy. Many have had professional helpers before, if not case managers. So I am still sick, still poor, still lonely, and similar statements. Given the nature of most professional practice, the professional held most of the power. "They told me what to do and how to do it. They committed me. They would not adjust the medication when I told them of my side effects. They made me work as a janitor and blamed me when I quit. They made me make Halloween masks in their program and criticized me for being disruptive."

The reluctance and sometimes downright rejection of a newly assigned case manager is understood not as a symptom of paranoia but as an understandable and logical response to the person's experience. On the other hand, reluctance is normal for most people as they confront an uncertain and somewhat invasive interpersonal situation. Most people experience some misgivings and doubt when asked to become involved in an endeavor that is new or has not turned out well for them in the past. Most people are somewhat guarded and distrusting when being persuaded to become involved in a relationship of which they are unsure. We need to give that same consideration to clients as we reach out to them, without resorting to familiar labels that place this normal reaction in the context of paranoid ideations or other forms of symptomatology.

Given this situation, specific methods of engagement need to be added to methods identified for relationship. Some of the following methods have been lacking from other helping formulations or have been deemed unprofessional, unnecessary, or even harmful to people. Therefore, these methods can easily be viewed as nontraditional.

Location of Engagement   The first meeting, as well as subsequent ones, should occur where and when the client specifies. Most people will select a community location: their apartment, a coffee shop, a park. Some will assume, based on past experience, that it has to be at the mental health center or other agency. A few will actually prefer an agency office, usually based on familiarity or psychological safety. Whenever possible, the case manager should encourage a community location comfortable to the person (see "Rationale" in Chapter 3 in section on "Outreach"). At times, this may simply be a matter of the case manager asking the person where they would feel most comfortable meeting and if necessary proposing options. As one person stated:

> Sometimes we do it at Pizza Hut, we both like to eat, I don't mind meeting with my therapist here at the center, but it's kind of nice to meet other places, it's just easier to talk about things when I'm out of here.

In many situations, just the offering of this choice of time and place can signal to the person that this relationship may be different. Kisthardt (1993) reports that this is important to people. As one person who, at the time, was not engaged in service reflected:

> When we first got together Kim (CM [case manager]) would say things like "Let's get together and have some coffee and talk and get to know each other." She would let me pick out the places I wanted to go. This made me feel like she was respecting me, she was saying you make the decision and I'll go where you want to go. In other words, Kim was serving me and me not serving Kim [*sic*]. She accepted me for the way I am. I could feel it, she projected warm, caring feelings. (Kisthardt, 1993, p. 176)

A community location also enhances the likelihood of contact. It is less reliant on the client to necessarily get somewhere (and in the face of some suspicion) and more reliant on the case manager following through.

Engagement is often facilitated when an activity is used as a backdrop to conversation. It is often more relaxing. A conversation in a closed office heightens tension and pressure; all you have is conversation. Going for a walk, feeding pigeons, working, cooking, shooting baskets, or washing a car can make that set of initial meetings more comfortable. It also allows the client and case manager to early on "share" an event or experience. If the activity backdrop is unfamiliar to the case manager, shooting baskets for someone who has never picked up a basketball, it places the client in the position of competence, an expert, and perhaps a teacher.

Attempts should be made to contact people you will be working with prior to the first face-to-face meeting. This strategy appears to serve three purposes. First, it represents a non-threatening way to introduce yourself and the case management process to potential clients. In addition, it demonstrates a respect for the individual's right to privacy, as well as the right to be informed regarding decisions made by the treatment team. Usually, case managers attempt to reach people by phone if this is possible. They have also used correspondence and report that this seems to be valued by some people. The following example of such contact attempts to incorporate the philosophy of a strengths approach:

Dear Mr. Johnson,

My name is Brian Smith and I am a case manager at Walnut Valley Recovery Center. As a case manager, my role is to assist people in their journey of recovery by helping them reach goals that are important to them in their life. I understand that you have never received case management services before. I have been a case manager for two years and would love the opportunity to talk with you more about what case management is and see if you would be interested in working with me.

I would enjoy getting to know you better. I am available to meet here at the program, at your home, or at another location where you feel most comfortable. I will be calling you this week to see if there might be a good time for us to meet. Please feel to call me though anytime Monday through Friday between 8:00 A.M. and 5:00 P.M. if you have any questions. My office number is (_____) and my cell phone number is (_____).

I look forward to meeting you.

Sincerely,
Brian Smith
Case Manager
Walnut Valley Recovery Center

Conversational

The focus of the first and early client–case manager encounters should be conversational. The flavor should be similar to that used when any two people are first meeting. As Kisthardt (1992) describes:

During the initial meetings, case manager's attempts to model the belief in mutuality and a helping partnership by engaging in a normative social dia-

logue rather than a more formal question and answer interview. These meetings involve a bilateral information exchange. In contrast to the traditional
mental health intake interview, where the clinician typically asks most of the
questions from which the diagnosis or psychosocial assessment will be
generated, the engagement process encourages mutual sharing and self-
disclosure of the part of the case manager. These relate to efforts to establish
areas of common interest, such as music, sports, television, or other interpersonal common denominators, which serve to establish an emerging helping relationship. (p. 67)

It almost resembles "chatting," an informal process of getting to know another person, not a client. This is in direct contrast with the interrogation style often displayed by mental health professionals during intake and early encounters.

Interviews with people receiving services have tended to support specific helping strategies that may serve to increase the desire to engage in the case management process. When asked about the first meeting with case managers, people stated
such things as "being easy-going and laidback," "having a good sense of humor,"
"asking me about the things I wanted to do," "not asking me a lot of personal questions" (one client said that the case manager "did not impress him as a snooper-
visor"), and "sharing things about themselves," as being important to them
(Kisthardt, 1992, p. 166).

Doing the Concrete Task

In contrast with or, rather, in addition to chatting, engagement can be facilitated
by doing a concrete task with the person. A person who has no food would rather
receive help in getting food than waiting for a relationship to form before tangible tasks get pursued. People who work with individuals who are homeless have
learned that the provision of a cheese sandwich is more welcome than some stranger
who wants to talk. Almost 85 years ago, Mary Richmond (1922) discussed the power
of helping another with a tangible task as a way of promoting a relationship.

Many people are living in circumstances where basic needs are not being met
and these are blatantly obvious. If the person desires, the case manager should seek
to assist with these needs immediately. Care must be exercised, however. For some
people, their definition of basic needs may be different from the case manager's
and their desire for assistance may not be welcomed. Except in the most dire circumstances, where there is an immediate danger to themselves or others, the case
manager needs to receive sanction for action from the person.

At times, the case manager may want to provide information to the person that
sets the tone for the focus of their recovery-oriented work together. The following
is an example of a packet of information an agency could give to a person when
they first begin services:

1. Brochure that provides information about the agency, its mission, and
   the values and services offered.

2. Introduction to the concepts of recovery (possibly articles written by people in recovery).
3. Description of how case managers assist people with recovery.
4. Information on the recovery-oriented tools used by case managers along with blank copies (i.e., strengths assessment and personal plan)
5. Statement of someone's rights as a service participant
6. Information on benefits and entitlements the person may be eligible for
7. Information on employment incentive programs
8. Voter registration packet

Although people receiving services have repeatedly expressed the importance of the relationship and there is some empirical evidence of its contribution to outcomes (Gehrs & Goering, 1994; Neale & Rosenheck, 1995; Solomon, Draine, & Delaney, 1995), some people do not desire a relationship that may be characterized by friendliness and intimacy. Some prefer a rather "business-like" relationship focused on getting tangible help with specific life tasks. Sometimes this will evolve into something more and sometimes it will not. In these situations, the case manager should not force intimacy but, rather, respect the person's desire and proceed to provide the assistance the person wants.

Role Induction

Strengths-model case management is different from other mental health services and other models of case management. It entails a different and unfamiliar way of working for most people receiving services. The expectations of clients and case managers are different. Role induction refers to the beginning efforts to describe and manifest in behavior this new way of being together. The elements would include:

1. The purpose: The case manager will assist a person achieve the goals he or she desires (goals can be to maintain things the way they are).
2. The client is the director of the helping process. He or she decides the content, the pace, the location, the resources, and the goals.
3. The case manager helps the person locate opportunities, options, resources desired.
4. The case manager works with the person to ensure his or her personal rights are made known, respected, and enforced.
5. The case manager gets to know what is working well in a person's life despite the challenges the person may face.

Added to this list are any limitations on the work as directed by agency policy, personal preference, funding source, ethics, or resource constraints. Early in the relationship, discussion of confidentiality and situations where the person is in immediate danger to themselves or others is useful.

TABLE 4.1 Engagement

Purpose: To create a trusting and reciprocal relationship between the case manager and client as a basis for working together.

Behavior

1. Schedules meeting with the person at a time and place (provides community choices) as mutually agreed. (In most situations, minimum contact is once weekly.)
2. Case manager and client are involved in a leisurely activity as a backdrop for getting to know each other (e.g., cup of coffee, shooting baskets, walking).
3. Case manager engages person in a conversational manner, exploring common interests and experiences.
4. Case manager uses empathy and reinforcing comments, both verbally and nonverbally.
5. Case manager discusses purpose of case management and mutual expectations. (Discuss concept of recovery, look toward replacement of self, focus on graduated disengagement.)
6. Case manager uses every opportunity to identify personal and environmental strengths.
7. Case manager reviews in group supervision (by presenting clear, concise consumer situation reviews to generate new ideas) if having difficulty engaging (after three "no's" with person).

The most powerful way of conveying the differences, however, is based on action and consistency of action. Table 4.1 contains those core behaviors required for engagement in the strengths model.

CHAPTER FIVE

Strengths Assessment: Amplifying the Well Part of the Individual

Purpose: To collect information on personal and environmental strengths as a basis for work together.

THE COMPELLING PULL FOR SOCIETY to the negative pole of life (Weick et al., 1989) is reflected in mental health and that of the relevant professional disciplines. The entire field is dominated by assessment protocols and devices that seek to identify all that is wrong, problematic, deficient, or pathological in the client and at times in the environment. "The *Diagnostic and Statistical Manual of Mental Disorders IV (DSM-IV)*, although only 7 years removed, has twice the volume of text on disorders as its forebear" (Saleebey, 1996). Although Axis V in this method evaluates a person's highest level of adaptive functioning, there is little evidence it is being used in practice, and serious questions have been raised about its reliability (Kirk & Kutchins, 1987). With some perplexity, Lois Barclay Murphy (1962) writes:

> It is something of a paradox that a nation which has exulted in its rapid expansion and its scientific-technological achievements, would have developed in its studies of childhood so vast a "problem" literature: a literature often expressing adjustment difficulties, social failures, blocked personalities, and defeat . . . ! There are thousands of studies of maladjustment for each one that deals directly with ways of managing life's problems with personal strength and adequacy. (p. 2)

Taking a behavioral baseline on people's deficits and examining the ability of social workers to correct these deficits have become the standard for evaluating the effectiveness of the profession (Kagle & Cowger, 1984). The same may be said of psychology (Rappaport, 1977) and psychiatry (Wolins & Wolins, 1993). The skills orientation of much of psychiatric rehabilitation (Liberman, 1992; Anthony, 1979) is focused on *identifying* skill deficits and then teaching those skills to people.

A Brief Critique of Current Approaches

Regardless of method or orientation, the purpose of assessment is to collect information needed to establish the direction and means of intervention. In chapter 3, problem or deficit models were criticized as homogenizing people and reducing motivation. Current deficit-oriented assessment protocols do this in part by amplifying the sick or weak part of the individual. The message once again is one of ineptness. It is like "painting by numbers." Ask these questions and explore these areas and the portrait that emerges is of a weak and helpless person:

> In my psychiatric residency that followed medical school, I glibly applied the terminology of physical disease to the "disorders" of behavior and the mind. Eventually, I became so immersed in pathology that I no longer even used the word healthy. Instead, I conceived of health as the absence of illness and referred to people who were well as "asymptomatic," "nonclinical," "unhospitalized," or "having no severe disturbance." In retrospect, the worst offender was the term "unidentified," as if the only way I could know a person was by his or her sickness. (Wolin & Wolin, 1993, p. 13)

The result is that the professional must take charge and lead the way: They obviously know best.

Beyond the images created for the client and worker, assessment dictates-it seems inevitably-the nature of the intervention. Skill deficits lead to skill training. High expressed emotion leads to efforts to reduce it. Seeing current problems as rooted in historical family dysfunction leads to efforts to understand that history. Provoked by the assessment, therefore, the entire helping relationship and process are contoured.

Another ramification of the dominant approaches to assessment is *the* dearth of content related to the environment. At best, some attention will be devoted to family but again it usually reflects problems and conflicts. There are a few exceptions. Good vocational rehabilitation practice ought involve a detailed description of desirable characteristics of the workplace and subsequent efforts to make "reasonable accommodations." Such an approach is suggested here for all life domains and niches.

Although other professions have little in their evolution suggesting a consideration of strengths, social work is different. Since its earliest days, social work has acknowledged the criticalness of people's strengths as a basis for helping. "Actually, social work has been long on philosophy and theory that flaunts a client's strengths, but short on practice directions, guidelines, and know how for incorporating strengths into practice" (Cowger, 1989). As Hepworth and Larsen (1986) state: "Social workers persist in formulating assessments that focus almost exclusively on the pathology and dysfunction of clients, despite the time honored social work platitude that social workers work with strengths, not weaknesses" (p. 167). As Beisser (1990) states:

> If we scrutinize a person selectively to discover his [*sic*] weaknesses, his faults, or the ways in which he is deficient, we can always find some, although in

varying degrees of obviousness. If, on the other hand, we look to ways in which that person is whole or healthy, we will also discover many things. So it will appear that the point of reference determine the characteristics we will find. Seek and ye shall find. (p. 181)

If we are to help throw off the yoke of oppression, enhance a people's sense of empowerment, and help themachieve whatever is important to them, we must remove the pathological imagery that our current assessment methods inculcate. As Rappaport (1990) states:

> To work within an empowering ideology requires us to identify (for ourselves, for others, and for the people with whom we work) the abilities they possess which may not be obvious, even to themselves. . . . It is always easier to see what is wrong, and what people lack. Empowering research [and practice] attempts to identify what is right with people, and what resources are already available, so as to encourage their use and expansion under the control of the people of concern. (p. 12)

Table 5.1 portrays one depiction of contrasts between a strengths assessment and a problems assessment

TABLE 5.1 Assessment Comparison

Strengths Assessment	Problems Assessment
What the person wants, desires, aspires to, dreams of; person's talents, skills, and knowledge. A holistic portrait.	Defines diagnosis as the problem. Questions are pursued related to problems; needs, deficits, symptoms.
Gathers information from the standpoint of the consumer's view of their situation. Ethnographic.	The problem assessment searches for the nature of client's problem from the perspective of a professional. Analytical.
Is conversational and purposeful	Is an interrogative interview
The focus is on the here and now, leading to a discussion on the future and past—asking how they have managed so far.	The focus is on diagnosis assessment procedures to determine the level of functioning.
Persons are viewed as unique human beings who will determine their wants within self and environment.	The client is viewed as lacking insight regarding behavior or in denial regarding scope of problem or illness.
Is ongoing and never complete with the relationship primary to the process.	Clients become passive receptacles for interventions as providers direct decision making.
Encouragement, coaching, and validation is essential to the process.	
Strengths assessment is specific and detailed; individualizes person.	Places the person in diagnostic or problem category using generic, homogenous language.
Explores the rejuvenation and creation of natural helping networks	Emphasizes compliance and management of problems and needs with formal services seen as a solution
Consumer authority and ownership	Is controlled by the professional
The professional asks: "What can I learn from you?"	The professional dictates "What I think you need to learn/work on."

The Strengths Assessment

The strengths assessment is a tool that helps the case manager stay purposeful in helping people recover, reclaim, or transform their lives. It is a tool that, when used well, offers a holistic view of the individual. It does not reduce the complexity of the person to a diagnosis or set of problems, but rather it is used to search for understanding and meaning from the person's viewpoint. The creative practitioner does not see the strengths assessment as paperwork, but rather a canvas on which to create a portrait of the unique person that is before them.

What Are Strengths?

Think of a person whom you hold in high regard. What are that person's strengths? The typical responses are that the person is "hardworking," "kind," "considerate," "funny," "honest," "compassionate," "intelligent," or representative of some other desirable quality. In the strengths model, there are four types of strengths: personal qualities/characteristics, skills/talents, environmental strengths, and interests/aspirations. All of the previously mentioned strengths fit into only one of the four categories: personal qualities or characteristics of the person. Although these are good things to know about the person, in terms of helping people to reach their goals and recover their lives, these are the least useful of the four types of strengths for the strengths-based practitioner. Yet, when we think of strengths, these are the ones that people tend to think of first. We have seen several traditional assessments that have tried to incorporate a "strengths" section. This usually consists of a small box or a few lines with the question, "What are the person's strengths?" Here we usually see language that focuses only on the person's personal attributes.

There are four types of strengths: personal attributes, talents and skills, environment, interests and aspirations.

Personal Attributes   We do not want to completely devalue personal qualities and characteristics; after all, they are one of the four types of strengths we want practitioners to be aware of in the strengths model. Personal qualities are those traits that define who we are, either how we perceive ourselves or how others perceive us. It is possible that a person can lose sight of any positive qualities he might possess, especially when his life is externally portrayed as a history of failures, negative behaviors, and disappointments. People can begin to internalize negative outside messages when they are consistently reinforced by people around them. For example, a woman who has struggled to raise her children the best she can despite being overwhelmed herself with life's challenges may not recognize the heroic journey she has managed to travel. Instead, she may be continuously bombarded with messages from family, friends, and professionals about the things she is doing wrong. In time, she begins to perceive of herself as a "bad mother," and begins to question her own self-worth and her abilities to carry on.

It is important that we help people recognize personal qualities and characteristics that are meaningful to them. To say to the woman just mentioned that she is a "nice person, has a great sense of humor, and is intelligent," may only be perceived as vague comments. But for her to hear that she is a "devoted mother" might hit on something that is important to her. What can make this category of strengths useful for recovery is when something is recognized externally that a person perceives or desires internally. Part of recovery for a person is reclaiming their sense of who they are.

Talents and Skills   Personal qualities and characteristics are not enough in and of themselves. They must be grounded in something concrete that the person has competence in. Some examples of talents and skills could include being a good guitar player, knowing how to put up drywall, making excellent chili, knowing how to fix lawn mowers, being able to take quality photographs, a knack for writing humorous stories or poetry, or being skilled at shopping for groceries efficiently. It is easy to think about people's positive qualities, but it is sometimes more difficult to identify a person's talents and skills, especially our own. We all desire to be competent in something, but even more important to many of us is having others recognize that we hold a competence in a particular area.

For the person in recovery, the identification of a talent and or skills may be instrumental in that person's recovery. This example from Professor Hideki Tanaka of Nagasaki Wesleyan University (Japan) vividly highlights this:

He would not get out of bed on time nor participate in the daily ward program. Even though he had diabetes, he took 3 or 4 cups of coffee a day putting a lot of sugar in it. He hated taking a bath. He was just wandering around all day long in his dirty pajamas that had not been washed for many days. When he had a difficulty in falling into sleep at night, he came to the night-shift staff room again and again until he got sleeping pills. He was very stubborn and found himself quarrelling over trivial things with patients who shared the room. His doctor was concerned about his many hypochondriac complaints. He was offered a job at a sheltered workshop, but rejected the simple work by saying "This cannot be called a profession." All he had was $500 left from an inheritance but he refused to apply for social benefits. He also owned a single lens reflex camera. As such, he was three months behind in contributing to hospital expenses. Since his mother died five years ago, he was left with no relatives.

The professional case conference requested the psychiatric social worker to persuade him to apply for benefits, pay the hospital, and address the problems listed above. I learned from the first interview with Mr. U. that he was sociable, that he still wanted to be a professional photographer, he polished his camera everyday, that he had only a few changes of clothes (to save money), and that he had a strong feeling that he did not want to be on welfare. During the interview he showed me a collection of photographs that he took when he was young. So I made a proposal to him saying, "Is it all right to exhibit your photos in the hospital that I know?" With this proposal he looked pleased and loaned me some photos for the exhibition. A few days later I called him to come to the outpatient waiting room of a public hospital, where I had made an arrangement to put his photos in frames and exhibit them. At the bottom of the frame his name and the date of when the photo was taken were posted. When he saw them, his face brightened.

When we came back to his ward, I borrowed other photos from him. This time I asked a coffee shop that I used to go to put them on the wall of the shop. Then I took him there. After that I asked a bank and a supermarket to put his photos at the exhibition corner. Most of the works featured land-scapes of old streets from the 1950's. They were received well by people there. A few days later Mr. U. came and talked to me. He said, "I have no more photos for exhibition." I said to him, "Why don't you take new photos?" He looked troubled and said, "I have no money to buy a roll of film." I advised him that he could buy some rolls if he applied for the public assistance." He immediately made a decision to do so. Now he was able to pay hospital ex-penses in 12 month-installments that he had let fall into arrears. It meant that the first problem that the hospital had asked me to resolve disappeared.

To my surprise, Mr. U. dramatically changed more that I expected. From the morning, there was no sight of him in the ward. Where had he gone? Hanging his camera from his neck, he was here and there such as an outpa-tient waiting room of the public hospital that I mentioned, the coffee shop, the bank, the supermarket, photo shops, and other parts of the town. He be-came busier day by day. Two months later he was discharged from the hospi-tal. His doctor said that Mr. U. did not have to stay in the hospital. The doc-tor's report said that his insomnia was gone and the he was lively and engaged.

Years later, I happened to meet him in a coffee shop. He wore a beret and a checkered jacket, pulling the collar of his open-neck shirt over the jacket. While smoking a pipe, he was enjoying lecturing about photos to two female students over a cup of coffee. He looked like nothing but a professional pho-tographer. His photos did not sell at all, but he was never admitted to a hos-pital again during the rest of his life. Twenty some years later it came to my attention that he died of pneumonia. All that I still remember is his carefree and bright expression that he had when he saw his works displayed for oth-ers to see (personal communication, March 3, 2005).

In this story, it was the identification of a concrete skill that opened the doors for this person's recovery. By drawing the person's skill in photography to the fore-front, it amplified the well part of this particular individual in the midst of many apparent deficits. It is empowering for the individual, because it is something they possess, not something that needs to be added to them or corrected.

Environmental Strengths   Environmental strengths are those strengths that exist outside the person but are resources that can assist the person in being able to reach their goals. Some examples might include a person's support system (e.g., family, friends, a pet), a car, a supportive faith community, a job, a place where the person feels safe, an educational degree, and a person's personal possessions. It is important to not only know what environmental resources a person has ac-cess to, but more important how they can be used by that person as a strength. For example, a person might have a supportive brother in his/her life, but what makes this person a particular strength is that the brother might be someone he/she can call if they feel stressed or the brother might be able to transport them to places they need to go.

Interests and Aspirations   It may be difficult to see interests and aspirations as a strength, but it actually might be one of the most critical in terms of helping people reach their goals. We are not only more likely to pursue a goal we have an interest in, but we are also more likely to pursue that goal with more passion and derive a higher satisfaction from the process of attaining it (Deci & Ryan, 2000; Sheldon & Kasser, 1998). This intrinsic motivation may be the strength that sustains momentum for a person throughout his or her recovery journey.

Interests and aspirations may be connected to the other types of strengths, but this is not always the case. Sometimes we do not always enjoy things that we are skilled at and sometimes things we are most interested in we do not posses a high skills level. For example, a person might be very good at reupholstering furniture but find the work extremely tedious and tiring. Although the person is skilled in this area, it may not be a strength the person desires to further develop. On the other hand, the same person may be very interested in flowers and plants but not know anything about the subject. This interest and aspiration about flowers and plants is a strength that the person can use as they develop or build other strengths in this area (i.e., knowledge, skills, resources).

Table 5.2 shows the four types of strengths and some examples under each category. As we get to know a person, the list of strengths the person possesses should grow. We will also find that many will begin to overlap and can be grouped together. For example, we may initially find out that a person owns a guitar (environmental strength), and that he is actually quite good at playing it (talent/skill). We may later learn that he enjoys playing folk songs most (interest/aspiration) and at one time earned money for playing it (environmental strength). He no longer

TABLE 5.2 Types of Strengths

Qualities/ Personal Characteristics	Skills/Talents	Environmental Strengths	Interests/ Aspirations
Honest	Good card player	Has a safe home that he/	Wants to be a rock star
Caring	(Spades)	she really likes	Loves to fish
Hopeful	Good at math and	Big brother	Loves to watch old
Hard-working	tracking money	Her dog Max is her best	movies on TV
Kind	Works on cars	friend	Likes to go to coffee
Patient	Can put up drywall	Gets $535 SSI each month	shop and "hang out"
Sensitive	Arranges flowers	Was part of a local faith	Wants to spend more
Talkative	Knows all about	community two years ago	time with niece
Friendly	baseball cards	Sweat lodge—cultural	Hopes to have his own
Willing to help	Computer wizard	healing tradition	car one day soon
Stands up for the	Knows a lot about		
underdog	classic rock music		
	Great memory		

plays for for money, but loves to play at church (environmental strength, interest/ aspiration) and when his grandkids are visiting (environmental strengths, interest/ aspiration).

Through the door of one strength (the guitar), we begin to see more about who this person is and what motivates him in his life. This is where the engagement process begins to overlap with the assessment process and skilled case managers will see that the questions they ask, what they take note of, and how they build on the strengths discovered will lay the foundation for the recovery-oriented work that follows.

Strengths Assessment: Content

The Strengths Assessment is a tool that allows us to organize and make use of the multiple strengths people possess. Few of us have good enough memories to be able to hold all the information we learn about people we work with in our heads. As we mentioned in the previous chapter, case management often tends to be re-active as we respond to the crisis of the day or help people access resources as events arise. We may recall information about a person that relates the specific task at hand, but rarely do we stop to think about more reflectively about what we know about a particular person, what we do not know yet, and how this information could be useful in the person's recovery.

The strengths assessment tool (Figure 5.1) is organized into seven life domains (daily living situation, financial/insurance, vocational/educational, social supports, health, leisure/recreational, and spirituality) and three temporal orderings (past, present, and future).

Life Domains

Daily Living Situation   This would include not only where the person is currently living, but what they like about it or don't like about it. What makes this place a "home" for the person (e.g., furnishings, pictures on the walls, lots of windows, a balcony, an aquarium). What environmental resources are available to the person (i.e., living on a bus route, on-site laundry facilities, etc.)? What daily living skills do they draw on (i.e., keeps daily "to do" list, good cook, makes use of coupons for grocery shopping)? What would their ideal living situation be?

Financial/Insurance   This area focuses more than just on how much money they make and whether they have insurance. What is important to the person regard-ing their finances (i.e., "having money in savings is important to me," "I want enough money to be able to go on vacation someday," "I want control over my fi-nancial decisions,")? How has this person earned money in the past? Are they sat-isfied where they are at financially?

Vocational/Educational   This domain pertains to employment and its features, for-mal and informal education activities, specialized training, credentials, and simi-lar considerations.

FIGURE 5.1 Strengths Assessment Worksheet

Consumer's Name		Case Manager's Name
_____		_____

Current Status:	**Individual's Desires, Aspirations:**	**Resources, Personal Social:**
What's going on today?	What do I want?	What have I used in the past?
What's available now?		

Daily Living Situation

Financial/Insurance

Vocational/Educational

Social Supports

Health

(continued)

FIGURE 5.1 *Continued*

Leisure / Recreational

Spirituality/Culture

What are my priorities?

1.   3.

2.   4.

Consumer's Comments: Case Manager's Comments:

_____   _____
Consumer's Signature   Date   Case Manager's Signature   Date

Social Supports   This includes not only who these supports are (i.e., family, friends, co-workers, neighbors, pets, etc.), but also the nature of the relationships (i.e., "my friend James is always there to listen when I am feeling overwhelmed," "I feel most safe when my dog sleeps on the bed with me," "my mom takes me to and from work each day").

Health   This is to include and emphasize aspects of the person that are mentally and physically well (i.e., has blood pressure under control, stopped smoking three years ago, is able to remember specific details about each person she meets). This area could also include specific health strategies that people use to promote their own wellness (i.e., takes a walk every evening for relaxation, knows yoga, finds the nicotine patch has been helpful for smoking cessation, does crossword puzzles to keep mind sharp).

Leisure/Recreational   This domain includes what the person likes to do for fun (i.e., enjoys reading mystery novels, goes to movies once a week, just joined church softball league).

Spirituality/Culture   This category has been added to the strengths assessment since the first edition of the book. It was added primarily at the insistence of people in recovery who consistently stated the importance of spirituality and cultural factors in relation to their recovery journey. For spirituality, it is important to be able to go beyond just organized religion to make the most extensive use of this domain and to explore what brings meaning and purpose to a person's life. Culture includes those identity-forming and support-sustaining pieces of ourselves so manifest in rites and rituals, language, stories, values, and beliefs

These life domains correspond to those life areas that people are most concerned about. They also reflect the major niches that people occupy. The focus is on actual life activities that reflect the well aspects of the person and those resources, personal and environmental, that are still being, and have been, employed. Tied to the theory of strengths, the case manager is seeking information reflective of the person's talents, aspirations, and confidence, and the opportunities, resources, and social relations from the person's environment.

Each individual's behavior is influenced by the aggregate of their own personal history, their present social context, and their visions of what they would like to achieve (Kisthardt & Rapp, 1992). Each life domain is therefore divided into three temporal categories: (1) current status, (2) desires and aspirations, and (3) history.

Current status includes the personal competencies and environmental resources being used in the person's present life circumstances. Moore-Kirkland (1981) has added that by "identifying what the client persistently and recurrently is engaging in will help the worker understand what motivations are important in the clients life" (p. 46). Desires and aspiration refer to the future. What does the person want? How would the person like to configure her or his lives?

Finally, there is an attempt to learn what kinds of resources the person has used in the past. The importance of this category is twofold. First, it is important for helpers and clients to recall that there are many histories embedded in their lives. Competence is a cumulative history of involvements with the environment. In most cases, there have been periods, sometimes lengthy, of productivity or more successful community living. This helps both the worker and the client avoid the creation of artificial ceilings on expectations. Second, these past involvements may provide clues for additional goals or may represent resources or involvements that the people may wish to reestablish. The following story is an example:

It had been a long time since Bonita had tried to crochet. Only two afghans in her home served as a reminder of something she loved at one point in her life. She smiled as her case manager inquired about who made them and commented on how nice they looked. Bonita's main joy in life now was being able to spend time with her only granddaughter, Cloe, who was in the third grade. Seeing the connection between the two, the case manager asked her if she had ever taught Cloe to crochet. Bonita said no and didn't even think Cloe would be interested. One night when Cloe stayed overnight with her, she asked if she would liked to learn. Cloe ended up loving it and would constantly ask her grandmother to teach her how to make new things.

There are three additional sections at the end of the strengths assessment instrument. First, there is a space for the case manager and/or the client to record positive personal attributes as perceived. This would include comments such as "good sense of humor," "persistent," "resilient," "energetic," or "personable and friendly." Second, there is space for the person to identify their priorities. At this point, what are those desires that are most important to the person? Third, there is a place for the client and case manager to sign the document symbolizing that it was a joint effort and accurately reflects the information that was shared. It does not mean that the identification and recording of strengths has been completed. As will be seen later, the strengths assessment is a continuous process.

Figure 5.2 is an example of a strengths assessment with information filled in. For another example see Figure 5.3 later in this chapter.

Strengths Assessment: Process

The strengths assessment tool does not resemble other assessment instruments. Therefore, the process used in developing it is also unique. The process of doing the strengths assessment itself is a recovery-oriented activity because its focus is on amplifying the well aspects of a person's life. Used purposefully, it should flow directly from the engagement process and ultimately lead to the development of goals that are meaningful and important to the person. The following are five critical components of the strengths assessment process that help keep this tool dynamic and centered upon the person in recovery:

FIGURE 5.2 Strengths assessment worksheet, filled out—Anne P.

Consumer's Name
Ann P.

Case Manager's Name
Rick G.

Current Status:
What's going on today?
What's available now?

Individual's Desires, Aspirations:
What do I want?

Resources, Personal Social:
What have I used in the past?

Daily Living Situation

27 yrs old; lives in 2-bedroom apartment with 2-year-old son.

Nicely decorated with paintings (landscapes) she did.

Ann uses public trans.—likes to cook, maintains apt. well.

SRS involved re: welfare of son.

I want to stay out of the state hospital.

I want to keep my son.

I want to have "some time to myself" away from child care duties.

Has been hospitalized 2 times in past. Longest admission was 6 months.

Has lived in current apt. for 5 months.

Previously lived with family.

Lived with father of child for 2 years in San Francisco.

Financial/Insurance

Has TANF–Food Stamps.

SSI ($202.00 per month).

Section 8 apartment.

Medical card.

Family helps out occasionally.

No child support.

I want to increase my monthly income.

I would consider applying for SSDI.

Used to earn "good money" as a waitress (see vocational).

103

FIGURE 5.2 Continued

Vocational/Educational

Not employed presently.	I would like to attend art classes.	Worked as a waitress for "a couple of years" before getting severely depressed. Did not like "having to put up with customers' complaints."
Days are devoted to child care. This is her primary role now and Ann states that "sometimes I don't know how to handle him."	I want to be a "better parent."	
Has GED.		

Social Supports

Son is very important to Ann.	I want to keep my son.	Used to "have a lot" of friends.
Family (parents, 2 older sisters) live nearby—some support but "they want to take my son," and "they don't believe me when I tell them things."	I want to make more friends.	Used to enjoy dancing, and painting—was a source of support.
	I want my family to "understand" me and "believe" me.	Her last case manager "really helped" and was very supportive.
		Used to go to church.

Health

Ann is in good health—her DX is Bi-Polar, but says it is the depression she finds most disabling; she actually enjoys feeling some mania at times. She smokes cigarettes; says she has a beer "now and then." Some days she feels "very anxious." No major medical concerns.	I want to cut down on my smoking.	Used to be a vegetarian.
	I want to exercise more.	
	I want to stay well and out of the hospital.	

Leisure/Recreational Supports

Ann has little time to do "the things I like to."

She has painting supplies but lately has not been motivated and her time is taken taking care of her 2 year old.

Reads romance novels.

I want to have a few hours during the week when I can do the things I want to do.

Used to love to ride bikes.

Used to play on girls' softball team.

Used to meditate.

Spirituality/Culture

Attends First Christian church on a periodic basis with sister.

Reads Bible on occasion.

I would like to go to church more.

I would like to learn meditation techniques.

Attended Methodist church growing up.

"Has been difficult to believe in God after all I have went through".

What are my priorities?

1. "I want to keep my son."

2. "I want to stay out of the hospital." (psychiatric)

3. "I want to have some fun."

4. "I want to get back into my painting."

FIGURE 5.2 *Continued*

Consumer's Comments:
I'm glad I have a new case manager who wants to understand me better.

Ann P.
7/2/05

_____   _____
Consumer's Signature   Date

Case Manager's Comments:
Ann is a wonderful person; good sense of humor—<u>Devoted mother!</u>

Rick G.
7/2/05

_____   _____
Case Manager's Signature   Date

1. The Strengths Assessment Should Be Thorough,
Detailed, and Specific

Considering that each person's recovery journey is unique, the strengths assessment likewise should highlight the uniqueness of each person you are working with. We sometimes find that case managers put general things like "enjoys music," "has own apartment," or "has worked in the past" on strengths assessments. These statements do little to distinguish between one person you are working with and many others. Most people enjoy music, but not as many can play a musical instrument. Even fewer can play the guitar, and even fewer have performed in front of other people and been paid for it. A little active listening and a few additional questions can take you from "Brian enjoys music" to "Brian used to get paid for playing guitar at weddings."

A good case manager is one who is curious and constantly seeking to find out more about the person they are working with. We want to get a holistic view of the person, so we strive to be thorough and gather information in each domain. As the case manager is getting to know the person, they should listen intently for things that are important (or have been important) to the person and then strive to get more specific details. The goal is to find information that is useful for the person's recovery journey.

2. The Strengths Assessment Should Be Part of an
Ongoing Process In Which Information Is Updated
on a Regular Basis

The gathering of strengths-oriented information begins at the first contact with the person and continues to occur throughout the service. It is not often that a case manager will use the strengths assessment device during the first meeting. A piece of paper for recording information is often awkward during the initial attempt at engagement. It is not unusual for several meetings to go by before introducing the tool. With every meeting, however, the case manager is gathering information about interests, talents, goals, and resources. These are to be recorded on the strengths assessment tool.

There usually comes a time when the client and case manager focus on filling out the strengths assessment. This can take from one to three meetings. After these sessions, the case manager and client will continue to identify the person's strengths. Life is continually evolving. The person will experience new people in different situations. As the person's life story evolves, new achievements and resiliencies will be identified. Each of these pieces of data warrants inclusion on the strengths assessment and, perhaps more important, to be verbally fed back to the person.

The surest way for the strengths assessment to feel like paperwork is to fill it out during one meeting with a person and then have it filed away in the chart never to be seen again. If the strengths assessment is to be a tool for recovery, then it must be an integral part of the ongoing working relationship. The longer we are in a relationship with someone, the more things we will learn about that person. The things we learn about a person during the beginning stages of the relationship usually represent surface knowledge. As we build trust and show our sincere investment in the other person's life, we will slowly begin to find out more about what the person's values and what that person finds important and meaningful in life.

> Nancy had noticed Julie's bear collection around her apartment before but had never asked her much about them. About six months into their working relationship together, Julie was holding one in her arms and the bears became a topic of conversation. "Is this one of your favorite stuffed animals?" Nancy asked her. "Jerry doesn't like to be called a stuffed animal. He's very sensitive about that." Nancy apologized to both Julie and Jerry and proceeded to ask her more about her bears. Nancy found out that there was a story with each bear that signified different points in her life. She referred to her bears as her friends and explained how they had supported her in being able to stay out of the hospital and have hope in life. Over time she also found out that Julie had made all the outfits for the bears and had let other people take home her bears when they were feeling extremely depressed.

Used in an ongoing manner, the strengths assessment can help guide our conversations with people. A quick glance at the strengths assessment periodically tells us what we currently know about the person and which areas are still unexplored. Like Nancy in the example above, we may have noticed things in the person's life that we have not explored. As we learn more and gain more details, we can record this new information on the strengths assessment. This in turn should lead to more questions that warrant further exploration.

We should never set deadlines on when the strengths assessment should be completed. The strengths assessment will never be completed because we will never cease to learn new things about a person. In addition, people's lives change over time and what is important to a person at one point in life may not be important later on. Life is not static, so neither should a person's strengths assessment be static.

Agencies may require that an initial copy of the strengths assessment be put in the chart with a certain time frame (i.e., the first thirty days after meeting with someone). This should only be seen as a starting point. We may work with people who are very reticent to speak or with whom we have not developed a trusting relationship and therefore there could be many empty spaces on the strengths assessment. We take what we get, knowing that over time we will learn more. Even if we meet with someone who is talkative and could help us fill out every box in one setting, we should be careful not to see the strengths assessment as complete. We are only seeing that person at one instance and will only be scratching the surface of the complexities of the person before us.

3. The Strengths Assessment Should Be Conducted in a Conversational Manner

The client should never experience the strengths assessment as an interrogation. The worst thing we can do is start in the upper left-hand corner of the strengths assessment and go from box to box asking people questions. Information obtained from the strengths assessment should flow out of natural conversation with people. With some people, we start talking about what they like to do for fun whereas others might want to talk about their family and their importance in their life. Remember from the strengths principles that it is the relationship with the client that is primary and essential, not any tool that we use. The tool should serve the person's recovery journey, therefore what we want to know from the person is what brings meaning to their life. We get this through conversation with a person, paying particular attention to not only a person's words, but their nonverbal cues.

> Joline had been living in the group home for three weeks and was progressively becoming more depressed. She had met with her new case manager and stated that her goal was to get her own apartment. The case manager wanted to know more about the importance of this goal and what images she had when she thought of having her own apartment. Through natural conversation, Joline talked about wanting to have her own space and not having to share a room with someone, being able to cook meals she liked (e.g., she said she made great Italian and Mexican dishes) rather than the set meals at the group home, getting a bookshelf for all her books, and having lots of windows so the sun could shine in her home. Joline really lit up though when she started talking about her grandkids. She wanted her own place so they could come over and visit whenever they wanted and she could buy games and toys for them to play with. The case manager showed Joline a blank strengths assessment and asked her if he could use this tool to help her reach this goal. He proceeded to record some of the information she talked about and showed her how he would use information to stay focused on her goal.

It was through natural conversation that Joline's passions (i.e., books, home cooking, grandkids) emerged, but the case manager was not just having a conversation with her. He was assessing for strengths that would help Joline in her own recovery journey. The act of writing these valuable pieces of information is important, especially considering that case managers work with several individuals and are continuously bombarded with information throughout each day. Writing down what emerges though conversation helps to keep the work focused and purposeful.

The strengths assessment should not be something done to someone. It is desirable for the process to have the flavor of mutuality, of dialogue. It is also desirable for the person to feel some ownership of the assessment and the process. The strengths assessment can be viewed as a developing "portrait of the well-side of the individual." Like any work of art, it should be a portrait that brings some pleasure and insight to the viewer.

4. The Language Used on the Strengths Assessment Should Be From the Client's Perspective and Be Written in the Person's Own Words

Taking what people reveal to us in conversation and turning into clinical language on a form (e.g., "I want a girlfriend" becomes "increase socialization" or "I want to be able to think more clearly" becomes "stabilize and manage symptoms of mental illness") can be a spirit-breaking practice for someone. We want to record not only what the person says but also the meaning they attach to it. A person may tell us about several jobs they have held over the years but may be very emphatic about what they did and did not like about each one of them (i.e., "I loved working third shift; I'm a night-time person," "Working at the animal shelter was my favorite job, especially when I would see a dog or cat go home with someone who really wanted them," "Working at the restaurant's drive-through window was too fast-paced for me"). Getting people's quotes is a good way to show that we have heard what the person told us. It helps to validate our commitment to the person's recovery. It shows that we are trying to understand what is important to them and that they are the director of the helping process.

Writing things down in the person's own words can also serve as a reference point in future discussions. For example, a person might say they want to go to work or back to school at some point in their life. Periodically, you may be reviewing the strengths assessment and point out a quote pertaining to this goal, "Here is something you said several months ago, where are you now with this?"

5. The Strengths Assessment Process Should Evolve at the Client's Pace

We must always put into perspective why we are doing the work we do, which includes using the strengths assessment. Our goal is to help people recover, reclaim, and transform their lives. Because recovery is viewed as a journey, we must remember that people travel at different paces. We must not rush our conversations with people, just to get information on a form. The strengths assessment is a tool that should at various times come to the forefront or recede into the background depending on what is going on at the time. Some people are reluctant to discuss the details of their lives. For some people, asking them to identify their strengths and recount their achievements is so dissonant with their past experience that it engenders discomfort. There are times when "whipping out" a strengths assessment is inappropriate to the situation (e.g., when a person is in immediate crisis or when the day's activities involve taking concrete action steps). A case manager should always have a copy of the strengths assessment available, because you never know when it can enhance the work you do with the person. For example, a person may be trying to decide whether they want to have a roommate. You might suggest looking at the strengths assessment to see how this decision might have an impact on other important areas of their life. In another example, a person might be considering moving from a group home to their own apartment and the strengths assessment could be used to see what supports and resources the person currently has available to them to make this move successful. Information could be added to the strengths assessment as the discussion proceeds, such as what might have helped to make previous housing experiences successful.

If the person finds the strengths assessment intrusive, then the tool should recede into the background. Remember, the relationship is primary and essential. This does not mean that the case manager ceases to record information on the strengths assessment, but only that things might be written down when the case manager gets back to the office. The case manager might reintroduce the strengths assessment at a later point (e.g., when the person has a goal they want to work on, such information might be helpful in written form on the strengths assessment).

6. The Strengths Assessment Should Occur in the Community

The assessment of strengths should be done in the person's natural environment whether it is in the person's apartment, café, or park. Not only does this facilitate the person's comfort but it also provides rich possibilities for strengths assessment. A person may never mention a love for art and Claude Monet when sitting in an office, but a case manager noticing two Monet posters in a person's living room may lead to information in a previously unmentioned area. The case manager can also meet neighbors, friends, family, and coworkers who are within the person's sphere.

Susan James is 47 years old and has been diagnosed with schizophrenia. She has been married for 14 years. Her husband, Art, also has experienced distressing symptoms that have resulted in hospitalization. Both are unemployed, living on Supplemental Security Income benefits. Susan has been hospitalized nine times in the past year for what she terms anxiety. While she was interested in the services of a case manager, she was reluctant to leave her home. In completing the strengths assessment the case manager learned that Susan enjoyed soap opera. They agreed to spend some time together watching soap operas over the next several weeks. During this time, the case manager learned that Susan and her husband were formerly very interested in playing cards. The case manager came to meet other tenants of the apartment building and through chatting found out that there was a weekly card game among the neighbors. The case manager helped Susan, and eventually her husband, join the group. Ultimately this led to increased activities outside the home and even a vacation in a neighboring state. Susan has not been hospitalized for the past two years.

Without the being case manager having been in the community with the person, it was unlikely these environmental opportunities and resources would have been discovered.

Recording

The strengths assessment tool requires brief narrative statements that are descriptive, not inferential. As such, the recording must be specific. For example, it should be recorded that a person says he likes to play basketball. It should also include information on where (e.g., park, YMCA, backyard), format (e.g., organized team in league play, pick-up games, just shooting baskets), how often, and perhaps with whom. This information would be recorded in the leisure time category in each of the three temporal columns (e.g., currently, desired future, past). The specific information will likely be different in each column, although "playing basketball" would appear in each column.

A second recording guideline is: Do not obsess over the cell in which to place each piece of information. Life domains do not exist apart from other domains; overlap regularly occurs. For example, a person is sharing information about friends with the case manager. John is considered the person's best friend and the client talks about their relationship and the activities they share. It does not matter whether the case manager places those activities under social supports or leisure time activities. The important thing is to get the information somewhere. Because there are no "right" or "wrong" places to record information, the person can be asked where it fits best for them.

After some discussion, if the person is still uneasy, the worker should gather the information and shortly thereafter (preferably in the car) place the information on the device. In some cases, the case manager has left a copy of a blank strengths instrument with the person, briefly described it, and asked whether the person would write their ideas before the next visit. Occasionally, the actual form is dispensed with and the person is asked just to write down some talents or achievements or resources. The case manager may want to do a parallel recording; then at the next contact, the two documents are compared.

In most situations, the strengths assessment is placed between the client and case manager and described, and a choice is given to the person of whether the client or case manager should act as recorder. If the person selects the case manager, whenever possible the form should be easily viewed by the person. Sitting next to each other, rather than across a table, facilitates this. The case manager should also find frequent opportunities to show the person what is being written (and checking its accuracy with the person).

Questioning

The guidelines for questioning during strengths assessments include some that are common to most approaches and a few that are different.

1. Use open-ended questions because they have the potential for facilitating more and enriched information. For example, if you are interested in a person's leisure time activities, do not ask, "Do you like to garden?" Rather, ask, "Do you have any hobbies or activities you like doing?" or "What kind of activities make you happy?"
2. Use questions that are reflective of behavior as well as opinion. In addition to or instead of asking, "Do you have any hobbies or activities you like doing?" ask, "What do you do for fun?" or "What is a typical day for you?" or "Could you describe yesterday for me?" or "What did you do last week that you enjoyed the most?"
3. Probe until you have specifics and an understanding of what is being reported. If the person answers the last question above, "I went to

movies and saw *Mrs. Doubtfire*," the case manager could ask questions about "Who went with you?" "How often do you go to movies?" "What are your favorite movies or types of movies?" "When do you like to go?" "What kind of snacks do you get?" "Which is your favorite theater?" "Which movie roles or actors are your favorite?" "How often would you like to go to the movies?" "Do you ever rent movies?" You get the idea!

4. Go where the person takes you. Because the strengths assessment is to be done conversationally, adhering to a row or column on the forms is contraindicated. For example, mentioning that the person went to the movies with two friends from church suggests a focus on the friendships or social and spiritual domains. Reflective of a conversational style is a strengths assessment with information scattered across cells (i.e., life domains and temporally) and others possibly blank (for now). In contrast, a form with some rows filled in and others blank strongly suggests that it was done in a nonconversational and perhaps even in an interrogatory style.

5. Reflect and self-disclose. As a person shows a piece of themselves, the case manager is encouraged to share a piece of themselves or a reaction: "I loved *Mrs. Doubtfire,* too. In fact, I love almost everything Robin Williams is in!" or "For some reason I have never felt comfortable going to a movie alone as you do. Sometimes I wish I did." These kind of responses help develop a personal bond between people and demonstrates that the case manager is listening.

6. Demonstrate empathy and the hearing of feelings. Most of these guidelines have related most directly to the content of the conversation. The case manager must also be able to hear the emotional content. Do the person's statements suggest sorrow, fear, disappointment, frustration, anger, inadequacy, anxiety, confusion, rejection, loneliness, guilt, or embarrassment? Or do they suggest joy, fulfillment, happiness, caring, love, satisfaction, competence, strength? The case manager must then communicate the feelings heard back to the person. "I sense you are feeling frightened"; "You seem to have received great satisfaction from . . ." (readers are referred to *Direct Social Work Practice* by Hepworth and Larson, 1986, for a fuller discussion of this topic).

7. Help people see the well part of themselves. A person's life and the experience with the mental health and other systems is such that many people have difficulty seeing their lives as one of strengths, talents, and achievements. A person who says, "I only completed one year of college and then I had to drop out," is conveying that self-identity as a failure. On the other hand, the case manager might respond, "So you have a high school diploma and one year of college under your belt." The case manager may also go on to check out the emotional content, "It sounds as if this is of some disappointment in not going further in college. Is that true?" Case managers should exploit every opportunity to feed back to people that while their lives contain pain and disappointment,

like others it also contains a history of achievement (e.g., "This is a strength I've noticed about you"). As one person reflected:

We work on things each week, like goals and stuff. I remember her doing the strengths assessment. I think she saw a lot more in me than I saw in myself. It felt better talking about me as a person rather than as a manic-depressive.

8. In addressing areas that may be awkward or embarrassing, maintain a matter-of-fact composure. It is more likely to be received that way.

Appendix III contains a set of possible questions that a case manager might ask a person to help facilitate getting information within each of the domains on a strengths assessment. These questions are not meant to be used as a one-time interviewing tool, but as questions that can be inserted in the midst of a natural conversation that might get some discussion flowing. A case manager might also want to refer to these questions if they are having difficulties getting information in a particular area.

Contrasting the Strengths Assessment with the Psychosocial Assessment

David was required to attend the day treatment program five days per week as a condition for residing at the program's Transitional Living Facility. Over the past two weeks he was becoming increasingly more aggressive with staff and other clients. He was suspended for one day last week for yelling at clerical staff when they refused to give him bus tickets. David stated that he did not want to be at day treatment and wanted to go to work. Staff were saying that he was not "ready to go to work," but that he could demonstrate his "work readiness" by his behaviors at the day treatment program. A staff meeting was called to decide what to do with David. The prevailing thought was that he would probably need to be rehospitalized and have his medications adjusted.

This is the situation that a newly assigned case manager walked into. The case manager has recently been to a training on the Strengths Model of Case Management and felt conflicted about what he learned in training regarding starting where the person was at, allowing the person to be the director of the helping process, building on a person's strengths and the prevailing consensus of program staff that David was "decompensating" and needed an immediate involuntary intervention.

The following contains partial information from an actual person's psychosocial assessment on admission to a community support service program.

Client's Name: David
Age: 42
Axis I: 295.10 Schizophrenia: Disorganized Type

Axis II: 301.7 Antisocial Personality Disorder
Axis III: high blood pressure
Axis IV: illiteracy, unemployment
Axis V: GAF score: 20

Living Situation
Client has been living in Wichita for two years. Spent first five months living
either in either homeless shelters or on the streets. Now resides in the
Sedgwick County Transitional Living Apartments with three other
roommates. Does not interact much with roommates. Has been accused of
taking food belonging to roommates. Becomes hostile when confronted.
Client came to Wichita via bus from Little Rock, Arkansas. Had been living
in group home there for eight years. Ran away from group home to find an
uncle who he thought lived here in Wichita. No record of uncle living in
Wichita. Transported to shelter by police after trying to spend the night at
bus station.

Psychiatric History
First psychiatric hospitalization at age 17. Mother committed him after he
became threatening to her. Spent 14 years in Arkansas State Hospital.
Discharged in 1978 to group home. Re-hosptialized 12 times between 1978
and 1986.

Vocational/ Educational History
Client attended public schools until 3rd grade. Was withdrawn by parents to
be home schooled. Client has limited reading and writing skills. Has never
held paid employment. Only vocational activity has been work crew units
(janitorial) at Arkansas State Hospital.

Social History
Client's father died when he was 12. Mother died when client was 33. Client
has no social support network here in Kansas. Has difficulty making friends.
Client has never been married.

Financial
Client receives $376 in Supplemental Security Income. Sedgwick County
Department of Mental Health is client's payee. Is not able to manage money
well.

Prior to the staff meeting, the new case manager decided to begin a strengths
assessment with David. The case manager got permission from the program to take
David out of day treatment for part of the day and hang out at the mall where they
also shopped for shoes together. The strengths assessment was not filled out by sitting down in an interview, but through casual conversation as they went about the
mornings activities at the mall. Figure 5.3 is the actual initial strengths assessment
(later versions continued over time) that the case manager took to the staffing.

Over the next few weeks, the case manager and David went around looking
for jobs instead of going to day treatment. David eventually got a job taking tickets at a local movie theater. What he liked most about this job is that one of the

FIGURE 5.3 Strengths assessment worksheet, filled out—David

Consumer's Name: David

Case Manager's Name: Rick

Current Status: What's going on today? What's available now?	**Individual's Desires, Aspirations:** What do I want?	**Resources, Personal Social:** What have I used in the past?
	Daily Living Situation	
Living in Transitional Living Apts. (I don't want to stay there, but its better than the shelter).	I want a place of my own	Lived in Bellview group home (hated it!—could only watch TV until 9:00pm, they decided what you could watch and they told you when to go to bed).
Likes to cook hot dogs, corn dogs, mac & cheese, burritos, etc.	I want to learn how to cook more Mexican food.	
Has bus card.	I need new shoes!	
	Financial/Insurance	
$376 SSI ($120 goes for rent) $78 food stamps	I want to be my own payee (They are messing with my money and it's not right).	Mom used to be payee until she got real sick. Transferred payeeship to Bellview. Mom used to give me extra money.
Sedgwick County is my payee I get $50 per week for spending money.	I want to have more money to do the things I want.	
They make me put the rest in savings (I don't need savings, I need food).		

Vocational/Educational

I go to classes at day treatment: symptom management, money management, etc. (Those things don't help me at all.)

I want a job

I want out of day program

I used to sweep floors and clean bathrooms at ASH. I did a good job. Would sometimes wash dishes in the kitchen.

Social Supports

Tony—roommate (He pays for cable, sometimes we put our money together and rent movies).

I don't like my other roommates. They're weirdos, something's really wrong with them.

I wouldn't mind getting married. There is a girl at day program I like. She likes me too. Staff don't like it. They say you can't date in day program or TL. I'm going to ask her out when I get out of here.

Mom—she was always there for me. Never got along with my dad.

Uncle (Bud)—we used to go fishing. He moved here to Wichita when I was a kid, but I don't know where he is now.

Cousins.

Health

I'm in good health, but my teeth hurt.

Medications (Prolixin, Cogentin) make me drowsy and sometimes like I'm coming out of my head. I do better at night.

I need to get my teeth looked at. I think they might have to pull a couple.

I want to stop taking medications. I don't like the side effects.

I used to have asthma when I was a kid, but I do better now, as long as I don't try to run when it's cold outside.

Leisure/Recreational

I like to watch TV—old westerns, Vincent Price movies. I watch any movie that is on TV.

Tony and I rent movies. He likes comedies, but I like action (It doesn't matter though).

I know a lot about movies.

I want my own TV for my room. I have enough in savings to get one, but they say I can't use it for that.

I want a VCR.

Used to go fishing a lot.

Used to have my own pole and tackle box.

Used to go to the movie house when I was a kid, sometimes with mom, sometimes with friends.

FIGURE 5.3 *Continued*

Spirituality/Culture

My family attended First Baptist when I was young. I didn't like going to church, but I liked Sunday school.

What are my priorities?

1. I want a job

2. I want to be my own payee

3. I want out of day program

4. I want my own place

Case Manager's Comments:

David is a very funny guy. He tells great stories. I have also never met a person who knew so much about movies (knows who starred in just about every movie).

Consumer's Comments:

_____   _____
Consumer's Signature   Date

_____   _____
Case Manager's Signature   Date

benefits was getting to go to movies free when he wasn't working and all the pop-corn and soda he wanted. As of the writing of this book, David has now been em-ployed continuously for seventeen years, although he had a few job changes in be-tween (e.g., better pay, nicer theater).

Contrasting the information contained in the psychosocial assessment and the strengths assessment, you might not think they were referring to the same person. What is written comes from the perceptual framework being used. In one, all of David's deficits and shortcomings are made the focus and interventions by staff are centered around "fixing" David. In the other instance, David's strengths are brought to the forefront, even in the midst of a challenging situation. What David wants in life is what drives the helping process and his natual energy and intrinsic motivation are drawn on.

The Experience of Strengths Assessment

There are several conclusions that have been drawn based on 20 years of experi-mentation and implementation of the strengths assessment process. For profes-sionals, there is great difficulty in moving from an interrogation mode to a con-versational mode. The tendency is to fire questions at the person. Despite the less rigid format of the instrument and the attendant protocols, new case managers tend to rigidly pursue their questions by sticking to one life domain until "com-pleted." A second difficulty is to develop the skills needed to be specific, to get the details of a strength.

For clients, there is considerable difficulty at times in their willingness and abil-ity to engage in the strengths assessment process. For some, it remains just another instance of some professional "nosing around" in my life. Their easily understood skepticism can be exacerbated when insufficient time has been devoted to engage-ment. For other clients, reflecting on strengths is a totally unique experience and, as with most new experiences, it can be difficult. Some have never been asked for their talents and dreams before. Others have used their diagnosis and deficit iden-tity as a shield to more pain and disappointment.

Despite the difficulties, the benefits of strengths assessment are clear. Clients tend to experience the assessment process as comfortable and energizing in and of itself (Kisthardt, 1993). As one person stated:

> The strengths assessment helped me to integrate the different parts of my life. There's so much to keep straight, so many areas to think about, it really helped to make sense of it. It kind of helped me to see that where I am to-day is O.K. (p. 177)

Many other clients found the process motivating: "I have done things"; "I'm not such a bad person"; "This is a side of me I forgot." Kaplan and Girard (1994) write:

> People are more motivated to change when their strengths are supported. Instead of asking family members what their problems are, a worker can ask

TABLE 5.3 Strengths Assessment

Purpose: To collect information on personal and environmental strengths as a basis for work together.

Behavior

1. Information is gathered conversationally (not by interview or interrogation).
2. Assessment process occurs over time in a variety of community settings to look for a person's strengths in the natural environment.
3. Information is specific, detailed, individualized (can tell who it is by reading it), and in the person's voice.
4. Case manager points out, brings up, and records person's skills, talents, accomplishments, abilities, what they know about, care about, and have a passion for in each life domain.
5. A person's interests, wants, desires, and aspirations are recorded in each life domain (including desires to sustain the current circumstance).
6. Past and present attempts to use community resources are identified in each life domain in a manner that suggests successful coping rather than lack of success or failure.
7. Various ways are used to increase a person's ownership of the strengths assessment process (e.g., person writes their own, person gets a copy, person asked which cell to record information in).
8. Reflects cultural, ethnic, racial information that holds meaning for person.
9. Case manager uses strengths assessment in group supervision to develop stronger plans.

what strengths they bring to the family and what they think are the strengths of other family members. Through this process the worker helps the family discover its capabilities and formulate a new way to think about themselves. . . . The worker creates a language of strength, hope and movement. . . . (p. 49)

This suggests that motivation is a transactional phenomenon that results from the interaction of the person and the environment rather than the usual perspective that motivation is a quality processed or not processed by people subject to assessment (Moore-Kirkland, 1981). The strengths assessment process is one instance of a motivating transaction. The process itself is often enjoyable. It is rather common for laughter to accompany the discussion. (How often does laughter occur during intake interviews or other assessments?)

The strengths assessment process often begins the process of building a more complete picture of a person. Experience with the strengths assessment suggests that in recounting and remembering past involvements, interests have been re-stimulated, past successes long forgotten are relived, and ultimately the self-perception of the life history has shifted.

The strengths assessment process does produce the information needed to develop effective interventions. Cowger (1989) opines, "Basically, client strengths are all we have to work with" (p. 4). If this is correct, the process detailed here gathers this information better than any other process we know of. Table 5.3 is a listing of key behaviors required to do a strengths assessment with fidelity.

CHAPTER SIX

Personal Planning: Creating the Achievement Agenda

Purpose: To create a mutual agenda for work between the person receiving services and their case manager, which should be focused on achieving the goals that the person has set.

PERSONAL PLANNING IS ANALOGOUS to case planning and treatment planning, but it is different in many ways. In the strengths model, personal planning is viewed as establishing the mutual agenda of work between the person receiving services and the case manager at any one point. Personal planning reinforces the client as the director of the helping process because it focuses on the person's unique journey of recovery. Goals are highly individualized and the paths toward goal achievement are limited only by the creativity generated through the helping process. The personal planning process flows from and is tightly intertwined with the strengths assessment. Similar to the strengths assessment process, the personal planning process develops within a conversational style, is consumer paced, strives for detail and specificity, uses a specific tool that is updated regularly, and employs the language used by the person. The personal planning tool is shown in Figure 6.1.

The Importance of Goals

Humans are purposeful organisms; we do things for a reason. Goals are inherent to hope and indispensable precursors to achievement. First-person accounts of recovery place having a purpose squarely in the center of that process. In the strengths theory, aspirations and goals occupy a cell to themselves underscoring their importance. As Locke, Shaw, Saari, and Latham (1981) state: "The beneficial effect of goal setting on task performance is one of the most robust and replicable findings in the psychological literature" (p. 145).

FIGURE 6.1 Personal Plan

For: _____   Case Manager: _____   Date: _____

Long-Term Goal (The Passion Statement):

Measurable Short-Term Goals Toward Achievement (Tasks or Action Steps)	Responsibility	Date To Be Accomplished	Date Accomplished	Comments:

_____   ____   _____   ____
Consumer's Signature   Date   Case Manager's Signature   Date

                                     _____   ____
                                     Other   Date

Goals are cognitive representations of a future event and, as such, influence motivation through five processes (Locke & Latham, 1990). Goals:

- direct attention and action toward an intended target. This helps individuals focus on the task at hand and marshal their resources toward the accomplishment of the goal.
- mobilize effort in proportion to the difficulty of the task to be accomplished.
- promote persistence and effort over time. This provides a reason to continue to work hard even if the task is not going well.
- promote the development of creative plans and strategies to reach them.
- provide a reference point that provides information about one's performance.

Of particular interest is which goals do you think are most effective, easy, or difficult goals? Surprising, more difficult goals lead to a higher level of performance than do easy goals if the task is voluntary and the person has the ability to achieve the goal (Locke & Latham, 1990). People tend to expend more effort to attain a goal they perceive as difficult. However, the goal must not be difficult that it seems to be unachievable because most people will avoid a task they perceive as impossible.

Why Goals Are Not Achieved

The protocols for personal planning in the strengths model have been designed to facilitate the achievement of a person's goals. It is instructive to first understand why sometimes goals are not achieved. Based on the assumption of human purposefulness, the strengths model does not accept that people, including those diagnosed with mental illnesses, have no goals. Our experience suggests that the reasons goals are not achieved by clients are rarely due to mental illnesses. Rather, goals set by people with psychiatric disabilities fail for the same reasons that all people may fail to achieve.

Think of a goal that you set for yourself at some point in your life that you did not achieve. Write down the specific reason(s) that this goal was not achieved. Some people may point to a specific defining event (i.e., "I blew out my knee and that ended my football career," "When I got pregnant I decided that going to college overseas was no longer a viable option."). Others may express a change in perspective toward a goal (e.g. "I decided that the goal wasn't something I really wanted.," "Something else came along that took a higher priority.," "When I first started, the goal sounded fun, but then it became more work than it was worth."). Sometimes people even give reasons that are self-defeating (e.g. lack of motivation, laziness).

When we hold workshops, we always like to press people for a little more information on their reasons a goal was not achieved especially if they give answers such as, "I wasn't motivated" or "I got lazy." When we get responses such as these, we might ask them whether they are unmotivated or lazy in all aspects of their life.

Of course, they will tell us they are not. We then ask them what was it about that specific goal that they lacked the motivation to complete it. When pressed further, people realize that why the goal was not achieved was more about the nature of that specific goal than it was about their personal attributes. They may conclude that the goal was really never theirs in the first place or that the cost of working toward that particular goal was not worth the benefits they imagined they would receive.

Even though, in most cases, the reasons goals fail for clients are the same reasons that goals fail for all people, traditional or typical mental health practice often places the blame for goal failure on clients by using generic and spirit-breaking language such as the person's being "unmotivated" or "noncompliant." In the strengths model, we do not think there is ever any such thing as an "unmotivated" or "noncompliant" client. We are all constantly "up to something" as human beings. It is the nature of being human. The question is not so much about being unmotivated but rather what is it about the goals we put on client's treatment plans that are not worth the person's energy. The question is not so much about non-compliance but rather why is the goal not one that holds any value for the client to pursue.

At the end of this paragraph is a list that you could pull out any time that a goal is not achieved by a client. Rather than moving us toward labels that attack the person's character, it help open us to the various possibilities that might influence the person's motivations for pursuing any particular goal.

1. The goal as written is not the person's goal.
2. Resources that are needed to complete the goal are not available.
3. Access to needed resources are blocked.
4. Resource people do not accommodate particular needs of person.
5. Skills needed to complete goal are lacking.
6. Client lacks or has inaccurate information needed to complete goal.
7. Fear of failure/ fear of success felt by client.
8. Client has too many goals going at one time.
9. Not enough time is available to client.
10. Goal is set too high/ goal is set too low.
11. Client has no fun in attempting goal.
12. No positive reinforcement/ reward is evident to client.
13. Circumstances have changed, so that goal no longer desirable or feasible.
14. Influence of significant other who does not support the goal is evident.
15. Person changes their mind.
16. Too tired/ becomes ill and so goal is dropped.
17. Client forgot about goal.
18. Goal has not been broken down into manageable steps; too abstract.
19. Goal is not in the person's power to achieve alone (relational goal).

This list could be expanded further because there are limitless reasons why any particular goal is not achieved and multiple factors could also be at work. Using the strengths theory as a framework, the following is a more in-depth discussion of some of the common factors that affect goal attainment.

Aspirations

The nature of the goal itself has much to do with its probability of attainment. Goals that are not the person's or not owned by the person are rarely achieved. We have all experienced goals being set for us by parents, teachers, friends, and bosses. How many of your parents set for you the goal of working at a mental health center when you were a teenager? Has your supervisor ever set an improvement goal for you that you did not share? There is often a natural resistance to goals that are set for us by other people.

Mental health professionals often think of goals that they think a client "should be doing." (e.g., stay out of the hospital, take medications, improve daily living skills) but that may not hold any meaning or value for the person. Goals such as these lack any contextual reference that would point to something the person actually aspires toward. Why would a person want to stay out of the hospital, or take medications, or increase particular skills? We may be able to think of several reasons, but for some clients, these types of goals may lack meaning in the context of their personal aspirations. For example, a person may have a desire (aspiration) to be around other people or to feel safe. The person may view the hospital as the only place that people actually express care and concern for them or a place where they feel safe. A person may desire more energy in their life to do things that they enjoy, but the medications they take actually make them feel more sluggish. The person may want to live on their own but detest cooking or feel that they have sufficient enough skills to survive (the authors survived our undergrad degrees on hot dogs and macaroni and cheese); therefore learning how to cook may hold no appeal. When we choose goals for clients that hold no aspiration or value, no matter how much we see their benefit, this is a recipe for "noncompliance."

Sometimes people establish too many goals at the same time, leading to diffusion of effort and thereby rendering some or all of the goals unattainable. From Ann's strengths assessment in the previous chapter (see Figure 5.2), we see from the middle column that she has many things that she wants for her life, yet not each of these wants and desires hold the same level of value. If we were to try to work with Ann on all of these goals simultaneously, there is a good chance that little would get done. If you read further down to the priority section, we see that keeping her son and having some fun are the top priorities for her. Goals set for Ann that she does not see as being directed toward these ends have little chance of being achieved. It is also important to note that people's aspirations are not necessarily static. While "going to church more" (from spirituality domain) did not make the top priority list at this particular setting, it may at some point rise to the top, whereas "get back into my paintings" might diminish.

A goal may be too ambitious to be met given time or resources. Conversely, if goals are set too low, feelings of personal excitement and interest may be insufficient to fuel efforts designed to achieve the goal.

Goals may be too vague and lack a clear and concrete set of behavioral referents. For example, goals related to "feeling better about myself," "having meaning in my life," "feeling more connected," or "getting a job that makes me happy" may exist in an amorphous manner with little feeling of progress toward achievement.

Failure to achieve goals can result from goals that conflict or produce fear. Conflicting goals are experienced by anyone who seeks simultaneously to achieve high levels of achievement as parents, spouses, and professionals. At times, visions of goal achievements can produce fear. The person who wants a job can easily become fearful that mental health–related benefits will be reduced or eliminated: "What if I cannot do it?"

Mental Health Practices

Many times, the identified goal was never really the client's but someone else's. The situation typically occurs in programs that have a predetermined list of treatment goals that apply generally to all clients. Case managers report that clients frequently agree with the goals as stated by the program only to "sabotage" them by acting out in some way or by not following through on designated short-term goals or tasks. This situation may reflect more about the client's lack of a sense of ownership of the goal than on identified pathology such as resistance to treatment or denial of what it is they need to do.

Because expectations of people with severe psychiatric disabilities have been typically low, goals are often mundane or irrelevant. A person with an engineering degree does not necessarily want to be on a "janitorial crew." A person who wants their own apartment will not be motivated to "earn" the privilege by first staying in a group home. Professionals sometimes justify their setting of a less ambitious goal in terms of "not setting them up to fail."

For many professionals, there is a logical progression of goals that are far too global in scope, thereby requiring clients to do too much. It is important to recognize that although many clients have led successful lives before experiencing debilitating symptoms, the process of integrating and reintegrating into the community involves learning and relearning skills. Thus, many of the kinds of activities that others take for granted represent significant steps or obstacles for clients.

Consider, for a moment, the number of steps and skills it takes to take a bus from one place to another. First of all, one must become aware of the bus schedule in some fashion. This may require calling the bus station (if one has access to a telephone) or securing a schedule from the station. Then, one must learn where the bus stops and where one would be best advised to depart. If a transfer is involved, there are special behaviors involved in this procedure such as securing a transfer pass. Not insignificant is the need to learn the fare for the ride and to determine whether exact change is necessary. Once on the bus, there are a variety of spoken and unspoken rules and norms to bus travel that one must learn such as how to signal for the bus to stop and general rules for bus behavior.

When considered in this fashion, it becomes quickly apparent that riding the bus, a seemingly uncomplicated procedure, is very complex. The list of tasks presented could have been extended and decomposed to a greater degree. Such a breakdown does not even account for the potential for fear and anxiety associated with bus transportation that many clients face. Added up, it becomes increasingly clear that there are many potential avenues for a person to fail in an attempt to navigate the bus system successfully.

What is most problematic about this example is that few case plans even go so far as to suggest learning the bus system as a goal. Instead, riding the bus is embedded in an even larger goal such as applying for a job, keeping a medical appointment, or attending therapy. The transportation is considered only a means to another, more important, end. Thus, the inability to understand the person's most basic struggles is lost. Inevitably, of course, the job application is never delivered and the two appointments are missed. In the end, the client is viewed as disorganized, unmotivated, and/or resistive and is continually viewed as unable to attack the larger and more ambitious goals.

Often goals are written in professional language. For example, "increase socialization skills" is a commonly recorded goal. No client has ever asked for "improved socialization skills," but many have said they would like more friends or do more with their sibs. Sometimes workers take responsibility for task accomplishment, and at other times, clients are expected to do it all with little help.

The mental health system can powerfully constrain achievement-oriented goal setting. In some systems there is a tendency to focus only on the ongoing problems facing clients in their lives. This problem is particularly salient when case management caseloads have climbed to unreasonable numbers (here defined as more than 20). Crisis is a predominant feature of many client's lives. These crises may come in the form of interpersonal trauma, strained family relationships, financial problems, and so on. There is always a pressing crisis for the practitioner to turn to. This often clouds the attempt to establish client goals which are, by nature, future oriented.

When attention is focused exclusively on a client in crisis, little developmental work that is necessary to enhance community capacity is possible. The consistent crisis focus also represents poor modeling on the part of the practitioner. Although there are clearly times in the lives of all people where personal trauma makes it nearly impossible to function, case managers must convey to clients the importance of continuing to function in a variety of life domains regardless of difficulty in one aspect of life. This is not to suggest that legitimate crises should be ignored. It is suggested, however, that neglecting to address future-oriented goals is ultimately a great disservice to clients. It is important to always remember that a case manager is not likely to spend ten years or longer working with one client and therefore should always strive to project how today's activities will benefit the client throughout the client's lifetime.

Competencies

At times goals fail because there is a mismatch between the goal and needed information or skills. For example, a person whose goal is to acquire financial aid for college may resort to a loan in lieu of information on available scholarships and grants-in-aid. An example of goal-skill mismatch could be the desire to fix a leaking faucet but not knowing how to organize goal-directed activities.

Goals fail when practitioners do not have a complete picture of a person's talents or underestimate these abilities. This leads to not pursuing some goals because they seem "unrealistic" or placing numerous steps in the way of the client. A client who wants to be a hairdresser, for example, is asked to complete a prevocational program, vocational testing, vocational school, and apprenticeship. The first two steps, at least, are often undesirable to clients and unnecessary.

Sometimes practitioners overprescribe the necessity to acquire a certain level of skills before actually pursuing a goal a client desires. For example, often clients are required to demonstrate that they have learned a sufficient amount of "daily living skills" before a goal of actually living independently is pursued. Like many people, my daily living skills repertoire was fairly sparse on getting my first apartment. Many of those skills (i.e., paying bills, cooking), I eventually learned through the trial and error of life in the real-life setting of my own apartment. Some skills (i.e., cleaning up my bedroom, ironing), I never quite learned adequately and found that no one else really cared anyway. Other skills (i.e., doing laundry), I found that I could use the time-honored tradition of getting a roommate who either possessed these skills or could be talked into taking on these chores as part of the living arrangement.

Confidence

Many times goals fail because people lack the confidence to take the first step. How many dates have not occurred simply because one person did not have the confidence to ask the other person out? Asking a person out requires venturing a certain amount of risk. The fear of rejection might be enough to deter a person from taking a chance. The same is true when considering embarking on an ambitious goal. When people lose confidence in themselves due to a multitude of reasons (e.g., recollections of past failure, others telling you you cannot do something), they may not even be willing to try.

Another aspect concerns goal-setting situations in which people experience feelings of powerlessness and fatigue. Powerlessness refers to feelings of anger, frustration, and dependency as efforts to make decisions and engage in behaviors to change circumstances fail to yield desired results. The constant emotional energy that is expended in this process may serve to decrease the level of energy needed to sustain goal-oriented efforts.

Practices in mental health systems can deflate one's confidence or at least not support it. The focus on what people cannot do versus what they can do places a *pall* on helping. Goals established without the identification of small incremental steps to accomplishment deny people opportunities for a sense of achievement and movement. Undermining client self-determination sends a message of incompetence.

Environment

Successful goal attainment is frequently the product of a complimentary match between the goal and the environment. Goal attainment may fail if the necessary resources are not available, accessible, or accommodating. If the goal is to go to the movies on Saturday night, the failure of the babysitter to show up means one stays home unless some emergency child care resources (e.g. parent, grandparents) are available. In our society, lack of money is the single most prevalent resource deficit affecting goal attainment.

Sometimes goals fail because of the lack of social relations or lack of social feedback. Sustained efforts toward goal achievement often requires the support and affirmation of others they trust who are "right there with them." As was seen earlier, our social networks help determine access to resources, other social relations, and opportunities. Entrapped niches constrain these.

Goal achievement is affected by feedback from the environment, especially from people. Locke et al. (1981) in their review of the literature stated that "both goals and feedback are necessary to improve performance" (p.136). People's opinions of us are important. Goal achievement is enhanced when there is encouragement, reinforcement for accomplishments and efforts, and information suggesting progress.

Goal achievement is also affected by the opportunities available in the environment. A goal of making the basketball team or being cast in a play is limited to a few slots or opportunities. Economic opportunities within inner cities are severely constricted.

Mental health practice often reflects a limited view of the environment and its role in goal achievement. Resources, social relations, and opportunities are often perceived as those present in the formal mental health service system. Learning daily living skills means a partial hospital or day treatment program. Leisure time pursuits mean groups of clients going bowling or making ceramics. Friendship means pairing a person with another person with a psychiatric disability. Work means jobs at the mental health center. Completion of tasks on case plans are dominated by the case manager and the client. Rarely do responsibilities suggest roles for other people in the client's social network.

Too often environmental factors are taken as given or fixed and therefore the options offered to clients are narrow. The lack of options represents de facto disempowerment. In contrast, the assumption that the social environment is susceptible to change leads to creativity and increased environmental support for goal attainment. For example, one program director negotiated effectively with the local transportation authority to include in the bus route the street where a number of people were residing in transitional living apartments. Another created a network of retired school teachers in her rural community who served as mentors for people engaged in getting their general equivalency degree (GED). Another case manager, who was working with a person on the goal of getting her hair done, talked with beauty shop operators in the community until she found one who was willing to accommodate the special need of a highly anxious client. The client, who was scheduled as the last appointment, was allowed to smoke; she was reassured that if she needed to get up and go outside it would be acceptable and that if she left before the hairdresser was finished with her, she would not be charged.

Long-Term Goals: "The Passion Statement"

In the strengths model, we make a distinction between long-term and short-term goals. A *good* long-term goal is one that the person has some "passion" about. It is a statement that is reflective of their true desires, hopes and dreams in life. Not all people will share with us these "passion statements" during our first few meetings together. It is only through sincere, persistent engagement where trust and mutual respect are built that the person may allow us to share in their journey toward recovery.

The following are examples of good long-term goals (passion statements) that you might see on a person's personal plan:

- I want to keep my son.
- I want my own place to live.
- I want a job where I can work with animals.
- I want my own car.
- I want to have more friends.

Compare these with the following poor examples of long-term goals that are frequently found on treatment plans. These are hardly goals for a person to get "passionate" about!

- Increase socialization.
- Improve personal hygiene.
- Increase community tenure.
- Increase vocational activity.
- Improve daily living skills.

Goals written in this type of language, although often convenient for staff, do not inspire the hope and passion that is needed for anyone to commit their time, energy, and resources to attain that goal. On the contrary, these statements are spirit breaking in that the fail to recognize the true aspirations of the person and instead reduce their dreams to mere general statements that reflect the interests of the service delivery system.

So where do we get the "passion statement"? The long-term goal "passion statement" is: (1) derived from the aspirations section of the strengths assessment; (2) written in the person's own words; (3) specified precisely as the person understands it; and (4) is not debated but rather accepted and further explored.

Use of the Strengths Assessment

The strengths assessment is a tool that can help us uncover a person's passion statement. Because a good strengths assessment is conducted in conversational mode, the passion statement should also arise naturally through conversation. If we are attentive to people, we will see a shift in their body posture, tone of voice, or facial expressions when we hit on a subject that they are interested in. One person may light up when they talk about their grandchildren, others during a discussion of their favorite sports team, others when talking about their faith.

Person's Own Words   When you write down a person's passion statement, it is important that you keep it their language. This is not the time to think about how you can reword this into professional sounding or funder-friendly language. Things like "take meds as prescribed" or "improve hygiene" are statements that hold little passion for people. No one lives to take their meds as prescribed. Yet, a person may take medications if they see it has a connection to something they do value. For example, what is Ann's passion statement from the previous section? "I want to keep my son!" Now *this* is a statement that holds some passion. By writing down this passion statement, Ann sees that the case manager has understood what is important to her.

This is the time to make sure you understand what it is that the person values in life. In essence, you trying to understand what is this person's internal motivators for beginning or continuing on their journey of recovery.

Specified as Precisely as the Person Understands It   A person may say that they would like to go back to work. From looking at their strengths assessment, you see that they have had multiple jobs at fast food places. From their perspective, they may have disliked each of these jobs and instead be thinking that they would like to work with animals. The passion statement would be "I would like to have a job working with animals," rather than merely, "I would like a job." This distinction is important because it gets more specifically at the particular meaning a goal holds for a person. Sometimes, it is good to ask a person why a particular goal is important to them or why is it that they wish to attain that particular goal. When one person expressed an interest in going back to work, I asked them why they wanted to go back to work. He told me that he had always wanted to own a motorcycle and had seen one that he really liked. He wanted to go back to work to earn enough money to purchase the motorcycle. Here the passion statement is to "get a motorcycle" more than it is to "go back to work." Understanding this places the person's quest to go back to work in context and can inform the process of exploring strategies toward achieving this goal. In this case, *where* the person worked wasn't as important to him as was earning the most amount of money in the shortest amount of time. After exploring multiple options, he decided to take a job loading trucks at $6 per hour. He was able to achieve his goal in three months. Once he had purchased the motorcycle, our attention turned to maintaining the motorcycle (e.g., insurance, gas, repairs along the way). Now that he had made his purchase and now that he had transportation, he decided to look at other types of jobs that seemed more interesting to him and that could provide enough income for him to keep his motorcycle running.

Not Debated but Rather Accepted and Further Explored   In the strengths model, rarely is a goal to be the subject of negotiation, but rather accepted as something about which the person is passionate. Most goals then can be written exactly as the person states it on the personal plan. The only exceptions to this are goals that are illegal or unethical. If a person states that they would like to be the biggest drug dealer in California, it would hardly be good practice to write this down so as to break it down into smaller steps. It does not mean that goals like this cannot be further explored. Why would a person want to be the biggest drug dealer in California? Possibly, the perception is that they could make a lot of money? Or have nice cars? Or hold power? Knowing the reason why a person wants to explore a particular goal serves the purpose of trying to find a way to relate it to the case management process. Although we may not be able to help a person start a drug-dealing business, there are ways we can help a person increase their income through case management.

What if the person wants to pursue a goal that does not fit into our moral values? An example of this was a case manager who worked with a person who said she wanted to go work in a strip club. Even though this is not an illegal activity, the case manager felt uncomfortable with the woman's goal and didn't know how she could help her move forward without violating her own values. Before rushing to judgment, she asked the woman some more questions about her goal. She asked her why she wanted to work at a strip club. The woman responded that working at a strip club was the best money she had ever earned and she wanted money to get a car so she wasn't dependent on others to take her places. She also didn't think anyone else would hire her because she dropped out of school when she was 17 and had very limited work experience. The case manager asked her if she had any reservations about going to work at the strip club. The woman responded that when she worked previously at a strip club she did not always feel safe and was often harassed by not only customers but her employer. She also stated that she often felt embarrassed telling people she worked at a strip club and this had an impact on being able to meet new people. Rather than the case manager refusing to work on this particular goal with the client, she acknowledged that this was something the client wanted to do. She also pointed out the person's own reservations of pursuing this goal and asked if she wanted to have her team help generate a larger list of job options that might help her meet her goal of getting a car and minimizing the negative aspects that the woman stated herself about working at a strip club.

The ultimate decision belongs to the client. In the above situation, the case manager did not refuse to accept a goal that she felt uncomfortable with, but rather attempted to help the person understand her own reasons for wanting to pursue a particular goal along with any reservations. The case manager only assisted in generating a more comprehensive list of possible options for the person after exploring the goal further with the client. The case manager kept the client as the director of the helping process.

If a client *does* choose a goal that a practitioner is uncomfortable with, the agency should find a staff person who would be able to help the person pursue that particular goal.

Common Challenges

Goals That Seem Unrealistic, Delusional, or Grandiose   Some of the most difficult goals to accept as stated are those that *seem* unrealistic, delusional, or grandiose. I emphasize the word "seem" because we must be careful how we label what a person says before truly understanding the meaning that a particular goal holds for a person.

Mrs. J. was due to be discharged into the community after several years of hospital residence. When faced with her compulsory discharge, she was considerably panicked. She stated her wants in terms of residence in a nursing home with no responsibility plus daily care activities. Everyone agreed that her likely self-care skills and anxiety levels seemed to indicate that this would be the best plan. Once a trusting relationship had been established, Mrs. J. divulged that she hated the idea of living in a home and going to day centers, and that she really wanted to be the Queen. She challenged the Practitioner to work toward that aim. Without promising too much, the Practitioner began to work out with Mrs. J. what she felt the Queen did that was worth aiming for. It emerged that Mrs. J. believed that the Queen did not have financial or administrative worries, she always knew where she was going to live, people respected her because she helped them, and most importantly, she has "companions" and "ladies in waiting" who helped her and kept her company. The subsequent assessment stated that Mrs. J. needed a strong sense of financial security and the guarantee of help with day-to-day organization, she needed to move to one location and be promised that she need never move again, she needed to feel she was helping people and feel respected for it, and she needed some "old-fashioned" companionship. Mrs. J. eventually began considering a house with another person being discharged who was already a firm friend and an effective organizer both of good works and administration (Bleach & Ryan, 1995, p.175)

By understanding the meaning that imbedded within Mrs. J.'s goal of being Queen, the creative process was opened up that allowed for the case manager to enter into Mrs. J.'s journey of recovery.

Hanging in there with someone when a goal seems delusional or grandiose can be very difficult for many case managers. We often feel more comfortable confronting delusions because we think that a person needs to get past them to recover. It is also sometimes uncomfortable to discuss things that we perceive to have no basis in reality. For people to invite us to join them in their journey of recovery, we sometimes have to "step into the tension." The following is a story that highlights a case manager entering into unfamiliar territory in order to find a foundation onto which to help a person begin their recovery journey.

The case manager first met Susan at the agency's Crisis Intervention Services program. Susan had been picked up by police and taken there to assess her need for hospitalization. After determining that Susan was not a danger to herself or others, the case manager was called over from the agency's homeless program to see whether shelter could be acquired for her and to see if she met the criteria for that program's services. The case manager helped Susan get into a local shelter and then went back to visit her to see how he could help her. She told the case manager she was in the Central Intelligence Agency and was wanted to "set up operations here in Kansas" and she wanted his assistance in keeping her identity concealed.

The case manager "stepped into the tension" by finding a common ground between the goal as stated by Susan and one that he felt he could invest in as well. While Susan perceived the goal to be "setting up operations," the case manager viewed it as getting an apartment. For the next few weeks, they went around looking for places to live that Susan deemed acceptable for her to "set up operations." After moving into one she liked, she began to go to Wal-Mart and purchase "rabbit-ear" TV antennas that she would place all over the apartment. She would tell the case manager what each antenna did and what county it was picking up signals from. The case manager just listened and would always notice when Susan would purchase a new antenna.

Over time he got to know Susan better and found out that Susan had actually completed two years of a political science degree from the University of Wisconsin-Green Bay and had two family members who had high ranking political positions in the state. Underneath what seemed to be a delusion, there were small kernels of truth that were embedded in what Susan was saying. Susan was very articulate and extremely intelligent and after working on the strengths assessment he saw incredible potential. Because of her identified passion in politics, the case manager asked Susan if there was something of a political nature that she would like to do locally, in addition to all the "other" things that she was doing nationally that she couldn't talk about. Susan agreed to let him brainstorm with his team some possible things Susan could get involved in.

During this particular year, Joan Finney was running for governor in Kansas. One of the other case managers on the team had a friend who was volunteering to help out with this campaign on a local level. She said that maybe Susan could help out as well. Although the case manager had some reservations about including this idea on the list, he left it on and this is what Susan chose. Two weeks later Susan started a volunteer job going door to door hanging flyers on people's doorknobs.

Over the next few months, Susan started talking less about the CIA and more about the Joan Finney campaign. Yes, she did embellish a few facts about how her family and Joan Finney's family grew up together, but she was taking some pride in her new job. Several years later Susan took a paid clerical position in a state-level political organization.

Goals That Are Too Vague   Sometimes clients may give us goals that are too vague. For example, "I just want to be happy" or "I wish I could feel normal." If this is all we can get from a person, then this is a passion statement worth writing down. We should still strive for further understanding of the meaning that underlies statements such as these to help the person create a clearer passion statement. If a person were to say that they just "wanted to be happy in life," here are some possible follow-up questions that a case manager could ask to gain further understanding.

1. What does being happy mean to you?
2. Was there a time in your life that you felt you were happy? What was going on in your life at that time?

3. Who is someone that you consider to be happy? What makes you think that person is happy?
4. If you were to reach a point in your life where you considered yourself "happy," what do you think would be going on in your life?
5. What are some things that make you unhappy in life?

By asking further questions, we might gain further clarity on what it is that the person is passionate about. For example, a person might equate happiness with having people who care about them in their life.

Person Has No Goals   In response to goals, some people might say that they do not have any or that they "don't know." As was stated earlier, the strengths model holds that all people have goals. Just because people do not readily communicate to us their goals does not mean they do not have any. We should ask a question of ourselves as practitioners: "Why should the people we serve entrust us with their innermost dreams, desires, and aspirations? For many people with psychiatric disabilities, they have had dreams discounted, ridiculed, or even ignored by people within the mental health system. These spirit-breaking practices often lead to future mistrust when interacting with professionals. We are often too quick to jump to the question of "What are your goals?" or "What would you like to work on?" before we have even developed a relationship with the person. Without a relationship, people often give us surface goals that are more practical (e.g., "I need to get a ride to the grocery store" or "I need someone to help me fill out this form for Social Security") than passionate in nature.

Often passionate goals emerge in time through the engagement process. A good case manager is constantly on the lookout for information that might be used to help the person develop goals. Careful observations of the person's residence, listening attentively to what a person talks about, and clues from the person's past can all be potential areas that goals can emerge from.

We must remember that most people don't talk in terms of "my goals." If one were to ask us right now what our goals are, we might have to stop and think for a while. But as we get to know people, we can often pick up on things that are important to them or things that they find interesting. People may not always equate an interest with a "goal." For example, a person may be interested in meeting more people they could do things with, but not necessarily see this as a goal of theirs. A case manager can help a person to formulate interests into goals by asking if this is something the case manager might be able to help them with.

Case managers should also be cautious about too readily moving toward a goal just because someone expresses an interest in something. For example, a person may say they are interested in fishing and the case manager may ask the person if they would like this to be one of their goals. A person might respond "yes," even though it is not a top priority for them out of courtesy to the case manager or because they might be able to think of anything else they want to work on. Case managers should be patient with people in setting goals if they truly want to find things that hold "passion" for the person.

Client Involvement

It is required that if the client is to be the director of the helping experience and client self-determination is to be taken seriously, the personal plan should be created with the full involvement of the client. This would include the setting of goals, steps to the goals, strategies to be used, designating responsibility for carrying out each step, and timelines. Increased goal attainment occurs when the person is committed to that goal (Naylor & Ilgen, 1984). People who have been in a dependent social position for some time, where their preferences have not mattered, have often lost sight of their own preferences, are seemingly unmotivated, and are reluctant to make decisions (Carling, 1995). This is not sufficient reason for case managers to jump in and start prescribing goals. It is rather the case manager's task to be "continually encouraging choices, no matter how small and then supporting successively more important life choices" (Carling, 1995, p. 288).

It is important that we do not mistake passive acceptance for client involvement. There are many reasons a person might agree with a goal that is written on their treatment plan without it being their goal: (1) They are worried that if they do not agree to a goal then they might lose their services; (2) they have lost hope in their life and thereby become apathetic to the entire goal setting process; and (3) they wish to be liked by their case manager and therefore accept what goals they have written.

Locke et al. (1981) suggested that participation leads to more ambitious goals, increased commitment, and acceptance of goals. Goals set by others reduce motivation (Naylor & Ilgen, 1984). The importance in using client-directed goals lies not only with the improved performance that results but also in potential long-term benefits. Moore-Kirkland (1981), for example, views collaborative goal-setting as an important aspect of promoting confidence in people:

> By being involved in the setting of goals, the client sees them as coming largely from him/her and more easily incorporates them. As a result chances for success are enhanced since the problem is one he (or she) has helped define rather than one that has been thrust upon him. Equally important is the feeling of competence resulting from satisfaction demonstrates to the client that change is possible and rewarding, and it lays the groundwork for subsequent success instilling hope. (p. 46)

The core of empowerment is returning to consumers the responsibility for choices about their lives and their lifestyles. (Carling, 1995, p. 287)

Based on the work of Berg and Miller (1992), DeJong and Miller state that the first characteristic of well-formed goals is:

> Goals are important to the client. Goals are well formed when they belong to the client and are expressed in the client's language; they are not well formed when, first of all, they are thought appropriate by the worker and are expressed in the worker's categories. This characteristic constitutes a practice principle that rests on the belief that clients whose goals are respected are more motivated than those whose goals are over-looked. The principle

is not compromised except in cases where the worker, after exploring for clients strengths and coping capacities, is convinced that the client is over-whelmed or a danger to self or others. (DeJong & Miller, 1995, p. 730)

When we set one goal, others may be activated (Ford, 1992). For example, one may start out with a goal to get their bachelors degree. This goal may activate oth-ers at the same time (e.g., wanting to have more friends, wanting to get involved in more campus activities such as going to sporting events or joining an organiza-tion on campus, wanting to have a boyfriend or girlfriend, wanting to get a car).

Goal Setting and the Stages of Change

The Transtheoretical Model or the "Stages of Change" (DiClemente & Velasquez, 2002; Prochaska, Norcross & DiClemente, 1994) offers a helpful way to conceptu-alize people's decision-making about goals. The Stages of Change suggest that be-havioral change for a person is not a static event, but rather people progress through different stages as part of a change process. This is important for case managers to be aware of because not all people are "ready for change" or desire to take imme-diate action on a particular goal that they have expressed or implied a passion about. Rather than assuming that all clients are ready for action when they express interest in a goal, the strengths model recognizes that many people may initially be ambivalent about pursuing some life goals. The Stages of Change are:

1. Precontemplation: In this stage, a person is not thinking seriously about changing. In regards to a particular goal (e.g., to be sober, to get a job, to take medications), the person does not see how pursuing action toward this goal would benefit them, while seeing many reasons against pursuing it.
2. Contemplation: In this stage, the person is more aware of the benefits of pursuing a particular goal, but there is some ambivalence about taking any action. If the person were weighing the benefits versus the costs of pursuing a goal, the person would have reasons on both sides of the scale.
3. Preparation/Determination: In this stage, the benefits of pursuing a particular goal has clearly outweighed any costs for a person to the point that they are committed to taking some type of action.
4. Action: In this stage, the person has taken the first steps toward reaching a goal.
5. Maintenance/Retention: In this phase, the person has progressed to the point that reaching the goal or maintaining the benefits of the goal is a routine part of the person's daily life.
6. Re-evaluation: Because the transtheoretical model was written with addictions in mind, relapse is listed as the sixth stage in the change process. Although the word "relapse" doesn't fit well within a psychiatric disability context, the concepts behind this stage of change still has relevance for any goal directed behavior, because people often

turn away from goals they once pursued for a multitude of reasons (see the section on Why Goals Fail). For the purposes of goal related decision making in the strengths model, this step might be better reworded as the "reevaluation" phase, where a person may reevaluate whether this particular goal now has any relevance or importance for the person.

When working with people on goal setting, it might be important to keep the stages of change in mind to avoid working at a pace that is not set by the client. We hear many stories about how people tell their case managers they want to pursue some goal, only to sabotage steps toward reaching that goal along the way. An example would be a person who says they want to work, so the case manager sets them up with an appointment with a supported employment worker. As the appointment date approaches, the client either wants to cancel, reschedule, or just fails to show. It is tempting for the case manager to become frustrated and label the person as noncompliant or unmotivated or manipulative. Case managers are geared primarily toward the action phase and this is reinforced by funding sources who want to see goals written down for each person for whom a case manager is working. In our desire to help people recover and reach personal goals, we can often find ourselves at a mismatch with the stage of change that the person is currently in. Although a person states they are interested in a particular goal, they may be actually in the contemplation stage with a lot of ambivalence about actually pursuing the goal.

It is important for case managers to spend some time talking with people in more depth about goals they seem interested in. Some ideas might be to:

1. Ask them what it is about this goal that is important to them.
2. On a scale of 1 to 10, how important is this goal to them? (1 being not important at all and 10 being of highest importance.)
3. What do they see as benefits of reaching a particular goal?
4. Do they have any reservations about pursuing a goal?
5. On a scale of 1 to 10, how confident do they feel they would be able to reach this goal? (1 being no confidence and 10 being extremely confident.)
6. List the pros and cons of this goal.
7. Where does this goal rank in relation to other goals the person might have set?

The more we seek to understand how the person perceives a particular goal, the better we are able to help them begin to take steps toward attaining that goal.

The Methods of Personal Planning

How many people do you know who keep "to do" lists? When you count things like grocery lists, weekend project lists, and daily planners, the majority of Americans keep some type of "to do" list. If you ask people why they do this, you will hear varied reasons including: "it keeps me organized," "it helps me prioritize what I need to get done," "it brings me a lot of satisfaction when I am able to check something off," "it keeps me from forgetting to do something," "it allows me to set aside tomorrow's tasks so I can concentrate on today's tasks," or "it gives me energy about my ultimate goal because I see that I am continuously making progress toward it." What about clients of community support service programs? How many clients with whom you work keep "to do" lists? Although some of course do, my experience is that most do not. You would think that a person who had difficulty concentrating, felt overwhelmed with life's circumstances, had disorganized thoughts, or felt frustrated about not making progress toward their life goals would that much more need a "to do" list for many of the exact reasons as already listed. Well, the personal plan is the "to do" list of the helping relationship.

Personal planning and goal setting are considered normal and routine aspects of case management practice in the strengths model (Table 6.1). This suggests that goal setting is not something one does apart from normal activities but should be woven into the daily routine with clients. The case manager should always have goal sheets available, referring to them, writing new goals, and discussing them with clients. Like the assessment process, goals can often be deciphered and

TABLE 6.1 "Miracle Question"

The "miracle" question is often a good way to stimulate thinking about aspirations: Suppose, while you are sleeping tonight, a miracle happens. The miracle is that the problem that has you here talking to me is somehow solved. Only you don't know that because you are asleep. What will you notice different tomorrow morning that will tell you that a miracle has happened?

This question is the starting point for a whole series of satellite questions designed to take the client's attention away from difficulties and to focus it on imagining a future when the problem is solved. The following satellite questions might be used:

- What is the very first thing you will notice after the miracle happens?
- What might your husband (child, friend) notice about you that would give him the idea that things are better for you?
- When he notices that, what might he do differently?
- When he does that, what would you do?
- And when you do that, what will be different around your house?

The intent of these questions is to help the client formulate, in detail, what will be "different" in his or her life when the miracle happens. As the client struggles to describe these differences, the client also often develops both an expectation of change and a growing sense of the goals toward which to direct effort. The satellite questions mirror the characteristics of well-formed goals. Thus, when a client responds to the miracle question, "I'd have a sense of peace," the worker might ask, "What might your husband notice different about you that would tell him that you are beginning to 'have a sense of peace'?" With this question, the worker is attempting to help the client develop more concrete goals that are more the beginning of something rather than the end and that respect the client's language. Or, to give another example, when a client responds to the miracle question with, "I'd cry less," the worker would ask, "What would be there instead of the crying?" recognizing that well-formed goals are the presence of something rather than the absence. (DeJong & Miller, 1995, p. 731).

created in conversational style. For neophyte case managers, the goal-writing procedures often seems unnatural and mechanical. It is important, however, to learn to incorporate this into the normal flow of activities.

Standards for Short-Term Goal Statements

1. Goals should be concrete, specific, and behavioral. It should be unambiguous as to whether a goal was accomplished. For example, "Ralph will do more things with friends" would be replaced with "Ralph will go to the movies with Terry next week." Two guidelines are helpful. First, avoid adjectives and adverbs (e.g., "Tom will wear a shirt to his support group meeting" rather than "Tom will dress appropriately"). Most adjectives and adverbs seek to capture qualitative differences that are usually open to wide interpretation (e.g., "appropriately," "successfully," "diligently," "regularly"). Second, each goal should set a single behavioral standard. The desired outcome should be explicit. For example, "Fred will work ten hours this week," rather than Fred will increase his hours of work." In the later situation, is one hour enough? Is five hours enough?

2. Goals should be stated positively. The goal should identify what a person is expected to do, rather than what a person is expected to stop doing. For example, if the person's goal was to stop smoking, a poor short-term goal to write on the personal plan would be "Jim will not smoke this week" or even "Jim will decrease the number of cigarette's he smokes this week." A better short-term goal statement would be a list of concrete task the person could do to occupy their time instead of smoking. For example, "Jim will take a 30-minute walk every evening after dinner." This of course would assume that walking is something that Jim enjoyed and that targeting the time after dinner was important for Jim in his quest to stop smoking. For example, "Harriet will work until 5:30 P.M." rather than "Harriet will not leave work early." Goals seek presence rather than absence (Berg & Miller, 1992). "Practice outcomes are improved when clients are helped to express their goals as the presence of something—for example, 'taking walks,' rather than the absence of something" (DeJong & Miller, 1995, p.730) like "not being bored." Another example, "Sara will exercise at the YMCA on Monday and Wednesday" rather than "Sara will decrease stress," although the latter may be sufficient as a long-term goal.

3. Goals are broken down into discrete tasks with a high probability of success: "Mere associations with past personal success apparently leads to more persistence, higher motivation, or something that makes it better" (Peters & Waterman, 1982). Successful achievement of goals for people, not just people with psychiatric disabilities, is dependent on being able to identify specific behaviors or steps toward its achievement. When helping people work toward a desired goal, especially one that might be challenging for the person, one that requires many steps, or

one that require a lengthy passage of time, it is important that a person see that progress is being made. It is also important that people experience some success in striving toward a goal, because there will be times that set-backs can occur. For example, "Martha will lease an apartment" can be broken down into myriad steps that might begin with "select areas of the city that would be desirable" or "buy a newspaper." Any goal or task can be further subdivided. The author has seen the task of folding a piece of paper in half divided into 23 separate steps.

4. Breaking down a goal is a principal mechanism for building realism into the process. A person's goal of being an airline pilot could start with enrolling in junior college. Finding a girlfriend could start with thinking about enjoyable activities you might take a person to or practicing asking someone on a date with a case manager.

How far to break down a goal is a judgment made based on the client, the goal, and the current situation. The standard is achievability. For some clients, "doing wash on Wednesday" is adequate. For others, this would be asking too much. Perhaps it could be divided into the following tasks:

1. Sort clothes into a pile of darks and a pile of lights.
2. Place one pile in laundry basket.
3. Place detergent and apartment keys in basket.
4. Carry basket down to laundry room.
5. Place clothes in washer with one cup of detergent.
6. Set dial to "REG" and push button.

Breaking down a task like doing laundry this finely is not only not needed for some clients but may also be considered insulting. But for others, each of these tasks can be seen as a challenging goal in and of itself and worthy of recognition.

Helping People Set Goals

Whenever a client begins a discussion about possible activities, the goal-planning process can concretize these activities. Case managers have found it useful to make copies of the goal-planning forms for people to refer to. The personal plan helps them to recall the plans that have been agreed on.

Many clients have goals and can articulate them quite well. Other clients have great difficulty in doing so. Goals can be vague. Clients often state goals that they have been socialized to believe that the mental health professional wants to hear them choose. Others state that they have no goals and do not want anything. Sometimes a client does not want what previous mental health professionals have offered and assumes that the strengths-based case manager will "follow suit." Others believe that the goals they do have will be discounted and ignored. Still others are fearful of embarrassment over their goals as being too mundane, too childish, or too ambitious. Refusal to express goals is a protective devise. If one assumes that human beings are purposeful organisms, then it is impossible to not have goals although they may be quite different from those commonly thought of as typical.

A well-done strengths assessment with proper attention paid to how the person spends the day and the cues provided by the possessions or other environmental factors can often suggest goals that have gone unstated. For example:

A case manager was assigned to work with a client who agreed to meet with the case manager in the client's home. When the case manager was invited into the home, he noticed right away a large bookcase in the living room that had hunks of dried mud and rocks on every shelf. As the engagement process unfolded, the case manager asked the consumer, Jim, to tell him about the items on the bookcase. Jim explained he enjoyed going to the river and finding rocks and fossils. The case manager listened and learned about Jim's interest while observing that Jim became more animated as he talked about the rocks and fossils. This was noted on the strengths assessment. The case manager asked Jim how he knew so much about the subject. Jim replied he'd picked it up by spending time at the river and remembering what he had learned in a high school science class. The case manager asked Jim if he would be interested in finding out more about this interest. Jim replied, "Yes." The community Jim lived in had a university. The case manager assisted Jim in securing a scholarship to take a geology class. Jim enjoyed the class immensely and signed up for more classes on geology. Eventually Jim was hired by the university to classify rocks and minerals.

This would have been less likely to happen if the case manager had not employed assertive outreach and looked for clues in the consumer's environment based on the interest, abilities, and strengths of the consumer. Success in this case also stems from the case manager's belief in the person ability to recover their life. The case manager is not merely seeking to help the person "stabilize and maintain" in his apartment, but creatively seeking areas of importance, meaning, and passion that might be developed into personal goals.

Some clients only want to discuss "what's wrong" with their lives, relating a history of problems and obstacles. It is important for the worker to listen, to respond empathically, to use these opportunities to convey that the client is not alone, and to reflect back the resiliencies embedded in the story. The case manager should be attentive to opportunities to reframe problems into statements of aspirations or goals. One technique, the miracle question, has been proposed by DeJong and Miller (1995; Table 6.2).

With some clients who have difficulty becoming comfortable with the personal planning process, case managers have left forms with them to fill out on their own. In addition, case managers and clients have sometimes found it helpful to fill out personal plans retroactively in those cases where clients have taken significant strides in a manner not previously discussed.

Marshall had talked of locating some old friends ever since he had left the hospital. While he talked about how good it would be to see these acquaintances, he did not actively seek them out. During the early phase of the case

TABLE 6.2 Personal Planning

Purpose: To create a mutual agenda for work between the client and case manager focused on achieving the goals that the client has set.

Behavior

1. The long-term goal reflects something that the person wants, desires, dreams about, and hopes for, as reflected in the wants column on the strengths assessment.
2. Goals and tasks are specific, measurable, observable, and reflect as much as possible the consumer's own language.
3. Goals are broken into small meaningful steps that have a high probability of success.
4. Target dates set for each task (no "ongoing" tasks); in most situations, target dates are set within one week.
5. Goals and tasks are written positively: something the person will do, not what they will not do.
6. Strengths that are recorded on assessment show up in goals, action steps, and resources.
7. Case manager uses natural resources, (e.g., community recreation league, postsecondary educational classes), in addition mental health center resources to increase options for consumer goal achievement.
8. Case manager involves family, community members (not mental-health professionals), friends, partners, and others (as wanted by consumer) to assist in achievement of action steps and goal plans.
9. The personal plan short-term goals are revised, updated, and changed, and accomplishments are celebrated in every contact between the consumer and case manager.
10. Various ways are used to increase the person's ownership of the personal plan (e.g., person writes their own, person has a current copy, person signs or initials plan and changes, case manager teaches person how to use strengths to attain goals).

Definitions: goal = person's long-term goal tasks, short-term goals, objectives; steps = the steps established to reach long-term goal

management process, Marshall found a volunteer job that he liked a great deal. Later, he decided to buy a used car with some savings he had accumulated. Soon afterward, the case manager was surprised to learn that Marshall had recontacted two old friends, one of whom lived in the same neighborhood. Now, Marshall had an alternative to spending his leisure time watching TV.

Even though retroactively recording client accomplishments can be overdone and not reflect the true impact of case management, the opposite is also true. It is important to measure as precisely as we can the range of activities that clients embark on after becoming involved in case management.

Resource Options

A centerpiece of strengths model practice is the generation of alternative paths to goal attainment.

More often than not people rise to the occasion when they are given positive options. People typically strive to set their lives straight, and given time, usually succeed (Peele & Brodsky, 1991).

An inherent element in empowerment is the presence and perception of options among which to choose. It is the case manager's job to help the client generate the various resources and pathways available. By doing so, the case manager will inevitably emphasize naturally occurring community resources, because in most cases it is the community, not the mental health system that contains the most options.

Long-Term Goal: I Want to Be Healthier

Alternatives:
1. Aerobics class offered through the psychosocial program
2. Classes offered by the town's park and recreation department
3. Classes held by the local YMCA
4. Classes offered by Body Boutique (a private fitness center)
5. Start a consumer-run aerobics class at the drop-in center.
6. Start an aerobics class at the church after Bible study.
7. Buy a video tape or DVD and use it alone in your living room.
8. Buy a video tape or DVD and use it with a friend or family member.
9. Do aerobics as a volunteer.
10. Lead an aerobics class for senior citizens.
11. Be an aide to an aerobics teacher.
12. Get a job teaching aerobics.

To maximize options, the case manager requires a broad knowledge of the community and knowledge of the client's strengths and interests. For example, a strengths assessment that has church or religious involvement as a prominent area of importance in the client's life would stimulate option 6 whereas for others the idea of a church-sponsored aerobics class might not be appealing. Similarly, a client who has talent and experience in aerobics, even in the past, suggests considerations of options 10 and 11, but for a novice, this would be premature and probably frightening. The presence of a sib could make option 8 viable. There is simply no shortcut to effective case plans without being apprised of the client's unique configuration of strengths.

Knowledge of the community is as much about perspective as about detailed information on all possibilities. Our experience is that a case manager who asks the question, "Where do adults in Springfield, U.S.A., do aerobics?" will find a way of finding an answer. Be clear! The question is neither "where do adults with psychiatric disabilities do aerobics?" nor "where do most adults do aerobics?" although the latter question is a good starting place. Rather, the case manager is asking the millions of people in the United States who do aerobics and the hundreds who do it in Springfield, what is the range of options available?

The first short-term goal or task is often finding information about options through the telephone book, asking around, talking about it with the case manager's supervisor or the team, and making phone calls. As in other situations, the client should do as much of the work as possible.

With options generated, the case manager assists the client in choosing which are most desirable and worth pursuing. Each option is unique and its features need to be discussed. Relevant features in the previous example could be location, cost, schedule, type of people enrolled in the class, among other factors. Clients often rule out some options immediately. Selection from the shortened list often takes more discussion. Sometimes more information is needed or the client would like to visit and preview different options. Sometimes the desired option, aerobics class offered by Body Boutique, for example, requires money, so the initial short-term goals might focus on getting sufficient money or acquiring a "scholarship" from the fitness center.

Fear of losing supports can affect a client's selection among options. As Carling (1995) writes:

> Often consumers will choose from a very narrow range of options (e.g., a group home or a boarding home) because of their past experiences of only being offered support in a very narrow range of settings. A powerful strategy for increasing choice is to offer consumers support wherever they choose to live, work or learn, and to assume that working out the complexities of offering services in this way is the service provider's responsibility, not an obstacle that should be used to force consumers to choose only from among those places where services are traditionally available. At times, this offer of support may be met with skepticism by family members or even by consumers themselves, given past experiences. In this case, it is the task of the service provider to build trust that the supports will be there, and to be diligent about providing them. (pp. 288–289)

Assigning Responsibility

There is a hierarchy of desirableness in assigning responsibility. It is most desirable for the client to be responsible for goal/task completion. The next level of desirableness is that the client with assistance from the natural support network (e.g., family, friends, and neighbors) completes it. The third level is when the client and case manager do the task together. The least desirable level is when the case manager does it for the client. The more a client can achieve independently or in a normally interdependent way, the greater will be the sense of achievement and empowerment, and the greater the likelihood of subsequent goal-directed efforts being exerted. It also frees the case manager from these tasks.

The client should be the primary decision maker. If the case manager did a good job of role induction to define mutual expectations, the client will know that tasks whenever possible should be done by the client and that the case manager's aid has limits; the case manager is a helper, not a slave. Beyond this, the case manager helps the client configure the tasks so that the client has the ability and confidence to accomplish it. If the task is set by the client, therefore it is important to them, and they have the ability (competency) and confidence to do it, the task will have a high probability of achievement.

The case manager facilitates this process of assigning responsibility by not only helping the client to break down goals but also by providing options. A well-done strengths assessment will have identified a client's social network. Each of the members could be considered for accompanying the client in performing tasks. The case manager helps the client evaluate the possibilities for each person. Often the selection of a person leads to new tasks like "Jenny will call sister," "Jenny will ask sister if she would go grocery shopping with her on Tuesday," "Jenny will set a time with her sister," "If Jenny's sister cannot go, Jenny will call the case manager." Even if Jenny's sister could not, Jenny had completed four tasks that she would not have done in the past and this deserves some celebration. Perhaps Jenny is too scared to call her sister; it is too big a step. In this case, the case manager can offer to be with Jenny when she calls (accompaniment), and Jenny could decide if she desires this.

There are situations when the case manager's involvement and responsibility are warranted. The most frequent reason for case managers to do something for a client is time. Picking up an application for a loan, for example, takes less time for the case manager to do it on the way home than to pick up the client, take him to the office and bring him back home. Sometimes, the client's level of anxiety is so troublesome that it is just easier for the case manager to do it. On other occasions, the task is so complex (e.g., understanding low-income housing loans) that the case manager again may choose to do it alone rather than have the client do it alone or with the case manager. In real-life agency practice, time is precious and it does affect decisions. The case manager needs to be acutely aware, however, that a fuller opportunity for empowerment and learning by the client has been sacrificed.

Establishing Target Dates

For each goal/task, a target date for achievement should be set. A target date further structures and directs the goal achievement process and enhances the likelihood of its completion. Most frequently, target dates are set for tasks that are to be accomplished between client-case manager visits so that the next visit can be used to review these tasks and set new ones.

A common practice in mental health is to write "ongoing" as the target date for some tasks such as "take medications as prescribed," or "shower daily," or "attend groups each day." This form of practice is contraindicated for several reasons. First, for many clients, if it was this simple to do they are probably already doing it. If they are not doing it, a simple statement to do it with "ongoing" probably will not work. Second, it deprives the client (and case manager) of a tangible benchmark for success and feelings success engenders. Therefore, in most cases, the task of "showering daily" would have seven target dates for the week. With each one, the client would mark its completion. Each shower taken would therefore be seen as the achievement it is for this particular client.

A Note on Pacing

For some clients, time is measured in days, if not hours and minutes. One source of goal failure is the presence of too many goals (both long-term and short-term) during any one point in time. For clients, this can lead to confusion, diffusion of effort, and feelings of anxiety and being overwhelmed. Clients and case managers both can be the instigator of too many goals. When this derives primarily from the client, the case manager may suggest directly that the focus be on a few areas for this week. The case manager could also share information on the deleterious effects of too many goals. Another response could be:

> This seems like a lot. It feels a little overwhelming. I know when this happens to me, I am less likely to accomplish things. Have you ever felt like this? What about just focusing on your number one priority?

The client has the final say, but the client would be best served by having the information needed to make the best decision.

In other situations, the case manager is the major force in setting too many goals. As Kisthardt (1992) describes:

> Do not attempt to generate a comprehensive plan that includes a wide range of goals during the first planning meetings. Sometimes, in their enthusiasm to implement the personal planning function, case managers generate a lengthy list of goals, but soon discover that they have proceeded too quickly. Consumers may become overwhelmed if they feel they have agreed to a plan where they are over-extended. The following example illustrates this point: During a goal planning meeting, a case manager recorded thirteen short-terms goals with a consumer after having been working with her for only three weeks. (This session was videotaped for evaluation purposes.) During the meeting it was evident that the case manager was strongly directing the development of the plans by making suggestions regarding what the consumer could do. The consumer was agreeing, but her facial expression and body language indicated that she was becoming increasingly anxious as the case manager recorded each goal. The case manager, enthusiastically writing the goals on the form, missed these very important cues. That evening the consumer, feeling overwhelmed and fearful that she would "let the case manager down," called the crisis line. She received the reassurance she needed, and the plans were scaled down at the next meeting with the case manager. (p. 76)

The following excerpts of a letter to the author best captures the subtlety of pacing:

> I know my work with Stuart began with assertive outreach. He was historically withdrawn and isolative. His parents frequently expressed their concern about his inability to initiate and to connect with others. It was their fear that he would be forgotten about because he rarely expressed any needs. When Stuart and I began working together, we would go to lunch. Stuart enjoyed eating out and from his viewpoint, this was an exciting part of his day.

As case manager, I felt pressure to address his parents concerns—especially around Stuart's need for dental care. During our weekly lunches Stuart and I would talk about a number of things—he appeared most energized when talking about his past life in Arizona and going to college; he appeared most apprehensive when I brought up the dentist. So I would back off.

Stuart expressed interest in going back to Arizona to complete his degree in geology. His dream was to be a copper miner. We talked over lunch—week after week—about pros and cons and started looking at options. Stuart was aware he had been out of school for many years and that having his parent's support was important. We went to an area community college to explore the possibility of his volunteering in the geology department. And to make a long story short, Stuart became increasingly excited about his life and possibilities—he had me taking him to the library so he could get the address of the University of Arizona and send for his transcript. We went to Johnson County Community College and he wanted to take a chemistry class for audit to see how he would do in school again. He had also agreed to go to a Dental Fears Clinic just to talk about his anxiety about going to the dentist (we had just driven by the clinic weeks prior to help him feel more at ease). In the end, Stuart chose to see a dentist and got new dentures (I really praised his wonderful smile!). He also decided to go to Kansas University after successfully completing his chemistry class and moved to Lawrence!

The work with Stuart was paced by him and I remember wondering what was so productive about eating lunch once a week. Looking back, I can see how instrumental our lunches were because it sustained contact. Stuart was not being forgotten. It was a part of being assertive and reaching out. By doing so, I was able to tap into those window opportunities and support Stuart in reaching his goals. It was fascinating to see a man who had seemingly little going for him come alive when he realized he could, in fact, do what he has always loved the most—be a student . . . It was impossible for me to know when Stuart's time for change was—I did know that I was going to be there when it happened.

Related to pacing is that sometimes no plan is the best plan. Sometimes a need is so important (e.g., food, clothes) and the client desires it that there is no need to pull out the personal plan and strengths assessment before acting. Just do it! With some clients, doing something immediate and concrete can be the best way to establish trust and caring early in a relationship. Recording the set of goal-directed activities on the personal plan later may be useful to meet documentation requirements, to show the client how the personal plan works, and to provide an initial sense of accomplishment.

Reviewing Personal Plans

A centerpiece of client and case manager interactions is the personal plan. After all, it is the basic agenda for work together. Review of personal plans occurs at each contact. This entails a review of short-term goals to be achieved since the last meeting. Dates of accomplishment would be filled in if not already filled in by client or case manager. Achievements warrant compliments if not celebration.

Short-term goals that were not achieved usually require some discussion to locate the obstacles that were confronted. Listening carefully to the client's story in a nonjudgmental accepting fashion is necessary. A case manager is well served by being familiar with why goals fail. This can allow the case manager to "diagnose" what may have gone wrong and thereby better assist the client in setting achievable goals.

The comments section allows for the case manager or client to make any further remarks about the status of a goal. It is a place where the case manager might wish to reinforce the client further by noting exemplary performance. It is also a place to note any obstacles or change that might have occurred or to note the help of a friend or resource. The important aspect of this column is that it continues to direct attention to goals that have been set rather than allowing them simply to fade away unattended.

From Strengths Assessment to Personal Planning

The purpose of assessment is to gather information necessary for development of a plan and its implementation to occur. We have found the strengths assessment as described in chapter 5 to be the best method of gathering helpful information. We have all reviewed assessments that seem to have no or only superficial relevance to the case plan. The same phenomenon can occur in strengths-based practice as well. But in the hands of a skillful practitioner, the link is unambiguous. The strengths assessment seeks information on the individual and involvements with environmental resources in the past and the present and desired in the future across all life domains or niches.

Goal Setting

The strengths assessment views the presence of aspirations as a strength. The column labeled "Individual's Desire/Aspiration: What Do I Want?" is the first place where possible goals are located. The client's list of priorities is usually a direct source of goal statements although often the priorities need to be made more congruent with the standards for goals (e.g., specific).

The strengths assessment often contains other information suggestive of goals. Past activities or involvements may be long-buried in the client's mind or relegated to "well, that was then." Sometimes, these can be rekindled by gaining confidence or being presented with new options. For example, in the fossil anecdote, the client had no desire to work until he reinvolved himself in this area of interest and became aware that you could get paid for it. The strengths assessment provides a variety of clues for activities and interests that can be combined to generate goals. Thus, an interest in swimming can lead to volunteer employment at the city pool or simply an activity worth pursuing in leisure time.

Options

The aerobics example highlighted the use of a strengths assessment to generate alternative resources and pathways. To recap:

1. Considerable skill in aerobics suggests the option of leading a class, not just participating.
2. Past successful involvement in aerobics classes suggest group options. In contrast, if group options were associated with pain and failure, more individual options need to be generated.
3. The possession of a VCR or DVD player suggests the possibility of in-home aerobics. Similarly, owning a car makes other options available.
4. Involvement with a consumer organization or the consumer-run drop-in center suggests a consumer-run class.
5. The presence of a friend, a sib or other relative, or a neighbor suggests an in-home pairing arrangement.
6. Knowing that Jane Fonda is one of the person's favorite movie stars provides leads to which DVD or video to select.
7. Knowing that the person is gregarious or desires friends suggests a group option.

It was mentioned in the assessment chapter that interests that appear inconsequential may be the key to a success. Consider the following example:

Martha claimed that the only thing she liked to do was to drink coffee and smoke cigarettes. Rather than ignoring this, the case manager listed it a personal interest on the strengths assessment. Eventually the case manager, working with the strength, talked to Martha about meeting at a nearby restaurant for coffee. This constituted Martha's first trip into the public for over a year. After several trips to the restaurant, Martha asked the case manager if they could go shopping together someday.

A strengths assessment that contains detailed information on the social relations and supports used by the client can provoke a variety of creative options. A situation from England is illustrative:

Mrs. C was being considered for discharge into residential care at the reluctant application of her husband who was concerned for her safety because of bouts of disorientation particularly when he had to work on nightshifts. The Practitioner established that Mr. C had considerable support from neighbors and family but felt that he would be overloading them and was at risk of losing his job if he was absent from too many nightshifts as a result of his wife's "bad days." With their permission, the Practitioner negotiated with the potential carer network that Mrs. C would be "looked in on" or could stay elsewhere when required, providing that this was convenient to all concerned. The Practitioner also arranged to be responsible for ensuring access to local respite care if the support network could not provide it. Both Mrs. and Mr. C were pleased to be able to avoid the breakup of the household and the other carers felt much happier about not always being obliged to put Mrs. C's needs before their own. (Bleach & Ryan, 1995, p. 187)

Short-Term Goals/Tasks

One of the most difficult skills for practitioners to develop is using strengths to configure strategies toward goal achievement. Many personal plans, even otherwise good ones, lack the presence of a person's strengths in the short-term goals. Perhaps an extended example can help demonstrate the methods. This is a person whose "passion statement" was to be able to "keep his apartment and be able to care for Muffy (his cat)." He considered his medications to be important to his own well-being, because they helped lessen the distressing voices he experienced and helped him to think more clearly so he could do the things he needed to do to care for his cat. He had difficulty remembering to take his medication which he found frustrating. Because he found his medications to be helpful in meetings his goals, he wanted help in this area. The following was the initial plan that was developed for him:

Goal: To stay out of the hospital and continue living in my apartment. To take medications as prescribed and see Dr. Holly.

Short-Term Goal:
1. John will take his meds as prescribed for two weeks.
2. John will buy a five-day pill box for his medications by 7/26.
3. John's case manager will call him twice a day for a week to remind him to take his medication.
4. John will see Dr. Holly one time this month for scheduled appointment on 8/6.

This is a typical goal plan for many people with psychiatric disabilities in many agencies. After using this goal plan, John still was not able to remember to take his medications. What is missing in this goal plan? Now look at John's strengths assessment (Figure 6.2). By using the strengths and resources from the strengths assessment, these other options were generated:

1. John's neighbors (Roger and Amy) will check on John twice a day to help remind him to take his medication for one week.
2. John's mother will call him two times a day to remind John to take his medication for one week.
3. Get a Bible that is organized with daily readings and put markers in it to remind him to take his medications.
4. Tape daily medications/reflections from Alcoholics Anonymous on his mirror along with a reminder to take medications and the reasons he thinks he his medications are helpful.

FIGURE 6.2 Personal plan, filled out

Current Status:
What's going on today?
What's available now?

Lives alone in 1 bdrm Apt (2 years)

Has Cat—Muffy

Apt. is on bus route

friend April cleans his Apt 1x per week

Goes out to eat a lot

Apt. has pool & laundry facility

Has sec. 8 apt.

Has a fish aquarium

SS $442/month

Has Medicaid

Has Medicare

$200 per month spenddown

Individual's Desires, Aspirations:
What do I want?

Daily Living Situation

Keep my apartment

Get a car

Own my own home someday

Financial/Insurance

Wants to earn money working and get off social security

Resources, Personal Social:
What have I used in the past?

Lived in a group home for 3 yrs.—liked Fred who also lived there

Enjoyed sharing meals

Lived with his parents for 5 years and enjoyed helping with yardwork

Had a dog "Jake" growing up

Was on parents' insurance until 1988

"I used to live off $3 a week when I lived at the group home."

152

Sec. 8 Apt

Foodstamps $20/month

Parents give him extra $ occasionally

Vocational/Educational

Wants to work full time at Radio Shack

Helps father in his job as Real Estate Appraiser (volunteer)—goes out with him 2–3×/month

McDonalds (3 months in 1986)

Dishwasher (2 months in 1988)

MHC prevocational library unit in 1990

Loves electronics

High School graduate 1985

Types

Beginning to learn to use a computer at dad's

Has looked into electronics program at DeVry Institute

Social Supports

Mom and Dan—June and Brett

Wants more friends to do things with

Best friend in high school—Pete—who is an electronics graduate

Friends—Scott and April

Wants a girlfriend

Past girlfriend—Kerry

Neighbors—Roger and Amy

Friends from state hospital—Jeff, Eldon, Ray, Sue

Case Manager—Mary

Church Youth Group (Lutheran Church)

AA sponsor—Bob

(continued)

153

FIGURE 6.2 *Continued*

Health

Stay out of the hospital and keep and keep apartment

Wants to pump iron at a gym

Wants to quit smoking

Used to do a lot of active sports for exercise—basketball and tennis in high school

Hospitalized 3× at Os. State Hospital—usually for 3 months to 1 year

Leisure/Recreational

Wants to do more fun things

Played basketball in high school

Used to read a lot of science fiction

Was on the debate team in high school

Used to go to rock concerts—loved them!!

Meds—Haldol, Cogentin

Psychiatrist—Dr. Holly

Physician—Dr. Rayton

Walks a lot

Substance free for 3 years

AA meetings—2× per week

Loves music—listening to rock

Likes electronics—"messing with machines"

Board games (chess)

Attends movie and bowling 1× per week with day program

Smoking and drinking coffee with friends

Watches sports on TV

Plays with cat—Muffy

154

Spirituality/Culture

I would like to find a church that has lots of activities for people to do

was raised Lutheran, but didn't always like going to church

enjoyed being a part of the youth group at church

I still read my Bible on occasion. It helps me keep hope when I am really down.

What are my priorities?

1. Keep my apartment

2. Be able to care for Muffy

3. Get out and do more things

4. Get a girlfriend

Consumer's Comments:
Muffy likes Linda, so I guess she's okay.

Case Manager's Comments:
John is funny and likes to tell jokes

He is friendly and outgoing once he gets to know someone

His favorite foods are hamburgers and ice cream (Chocolate!!)

_____   Date

Consumer's Signature

_____   Date

Case Manager's Signature

155

5. John will call his old friend Pete to ask him if he would work with him to make a buzzing medication box that will remind him when to take his medication.
6. John will take his medication when he feeds Muffy for one week.
7. Tape a reminder to take medications around the fish-food dispenser.

The case manager took the above list to John as some possible options that might help him. If John didn't like any of these options, the case manager was willing to brainstorm more options with John go back to her team and generate more ideas based on his strengths assessment. John liked option 5 involving his old friend Pete and wanted to try that first. Figure 6.3 contains the personal plan that they developed together.

This example highlights three points:

1. People have a multitude of strengths and resources they can use to get what they want.
2. Options increase as you explore and use the strengths and resources people already have.
3. The strengths assessment and goal plan are connected in such a way that you must use them in combination for highest effectiveness.

In terms of John, this personal plan allows him to reconnect with a friend and to engage in an activity he enjoys and because of this investment it has a heightened chance of working. By using the strengths assessment, John's personal plan will be unique, that is tailored to him.

Because spirituality is an often neglected aspect of assessments, another case anecdote may be helpful in demonstrating the critical connection between the strengths assessment and personal plan:

A case manager was working with a woman who recently displayed multiple symptoms of a mental illness. She was off her medications and was on the verge of losing her apartment and her job in the community, which she did not want to do. The consumer, despite distressing symptoms, never missed a day in church and this was recorded in the strengths assessment. When the case manager asked why she wasn't taking her medications, the woman stated that she was worried that they were "evil and could be poisoned." What the case manager did was simple . . . yet showed creativity and innovation. The case manager asked the woman, "Would you be willing to take your medication if a priest blessed it first?" The woman agreed and the case manager went to the priest with the request. The priest was happy to help. The woman has taken her medicine ever since. The case manager learning about her interest in spirituality made a significant difference.

Responsibility

The client should do as many of the short-term goals and tasks as he or she is willing to do. By breaking goals down to manageable pieces, expressions of confidence

FIGURE 6.3 Personal plan, filled out—John

For: _____ John _____   Case Manager: _____ Linda _____   Date: _8/5/96_

Long-Term Goal (The Passion Statement): "I want to keep my apartment and be able to care for Muffy"; "I want help being able to remember to take my medications, which help me"

John will call his old friend Pete to ask him if he would work with him to make a buzzing medication box that will remind him to take his medication.

Measurable Short-Term Goals Toward Achievement (Tasks or Action Steps)	Responsibility	Date to Be Accomplished	Date Accomplished	Comments:
1. Call Pete and ask if he would help	John	Tues. (8/6)	Tues.	Pete was Excited!
2. Visit Pete to discuss plan for building the device	John & Linda (CM)	Thur. (8/8) 3 p.m.	Thurs.	Diagram drawn.
3. List materials needed	John & Pete	Thurs.	Thurs.	List created (about $15 needed)
4. Withdraw $20 from bank for materials	John	Fri. (8/9)		
5. Pete will pick John up at 1 P.M. on Sat.	Pete	Sat. (8/10)		
6. Go to Ace Hardware and buy materials	John & Pete	Sat.		
7. Work on device in Pete's basement	John & Pete	Sat.		

Consumer's Signature   Date   Case Manager's Signature   Date

Other   Date

by the case manager and client ownership of the goal as meaningful to them enhance the likelihood of achievement. When the client is uncomfortable in performing, other alternatives need to be considered.

The strengths assessment provides possibilities beyond the case manager. In particular, people currently or formerly involved in the client's life can be considered in the personal plan. These social relations are a strengths on which to build. The sister who attends church with the client can be the sister who goes to the movies with the person. The friend with whom the client plays cards can be the friend who goes grocery shopping with the person. The coworker can be the person who takes the client to work and back. A landlord or apartment superintendent could be a source of companionship or reminders. A coach from many years ago may use influence to get a client on a basketball team.

Most times a client has the competency and skill to perform a task. The distress a person experiences, overwhelming living conditions, and the lack of resources may interfere with its accomplishment. For others, it is fear and lack of confidence. Mobilizing social supports for prompting (i.e., reminding the client) and accompaniment are critical. Just the presence of another person can make a task doable and enjoyable.

The Client Experience with Personal (Goal) Planning

The personal planning methods described in this chapter are believed to mightily contribute to the positive outcomes found in the strengths model research. Clients themselves attribute part of their success to the personal planning process. This section captures the client experience in their words.

Client-Determined

- "She asked me if I wanted to write my own. That blew me away. I was afraid at first but I did it, and it felt really great, like I was in charge."
- "She told me I was in charge. Like this was my own to-do list, and I was not locked in and could change my mind whenever I wanted."
- "I was working on things that were important to me, not what somebody else said was important to me."
- "When I told her I wanted to go back to school she did not try to talk me out of it like some other people did, saying I was not ready and needed to do a whole bunch of other things before I could try this big step. She wrote it down and then we talked about all of the things that needed to get done for this to happen."

Organizing Lives

- "Before I met my case manager all my goals were up here (points to his head). Now they're more real, like I can see that I'm making progress, and it makes me feel like I can do it, and I want to do more, like when I write them down, where I can see them, it helps me to remember. I have trouble blowing things off."

- "The personal planning usually keeps it in writing, and kind of more up front for both of us [the worker and the client]. It becomes a major concern, and we try to maintain contact with people in the community, and we try to accomplish it in a certain time, we review these at least once a week, sometimes twice a week."
- "Personal planning is a process anybody could benefit from. Sometimes your life is like a rerun, it keeps going over and over, and sometimes you got to change the channel. Don't let the future be twenty years down the road, you want something a little bit sooner. Writing it down is important because sometimes my memory gets bogged down, writing it down where you don't just talk about it, where you visually see it, there's that visual contact, my personal appointments or other things I got to do, anything that helps your mind stay improved, I'm all for it."
- "I'm gonna try now to not have case management for awhile, I think I can do it. I told my case manager I'm going to keep using the personal plan as my stress management strategy."

Breaking Goals Down

- "The personal planning is pretty helpful for me. I had a hard time getting things done like the housework. We would break it up (the goal, not the house). When we do it that way I can do better. Fran [the case manager] has taught me to do that."
- "I get, really overwhelmed real easy, and my case manager (using the personal planning tool) helped me to break them up into real small, comfortable steps that I could manage no sweat."

Collaboration

- "We set a lot of goals. We have these goal sheets, when I do my laundry, take my medication. We set goals and then we talk about it, and I usually complete all my goals, and we usually go out. Sometimes she helps me pay my bills and get them all arranged. The goal planning is, well, I'm a real restless person, and sometimes I don't want to do the things that are on my goal sheets, and she tells me, 'you don't have to do them,' but that 'they are important,' and I trust her so much that I want to do them. It's not that I do it because she wants it but because I want to do it. Those goal sheets have been really helpful."
- "I never worked this closely with anyone down here before, I've never confided my deepest thoughts, I never made out goals before or had somebody to help me make out my goals. When she [case manager] came here it was kind of a miracle for me."

Sense of Achievement/Feedback

- "Completing the goals made me proud of myself, because I accomplished so much. She would say, look here, look at how much you have done, and it made me feel good because I had something to look at and something to be proud of, and I didn't feel that my life was going to waste. I felt like I can't do this, and I can't do that . . . but I can do this, and it was a great feeling. She gave me the ability to renew my mind, she taught me how to use my mind to go out and get the things I want on my level."

- "Personal planning helped me to see what I was doing in all parts of my life, and I could see the progress. It was all me. I could see how much I was doing and how much I advanced. It helped me to keep track of where I was going and to see the changes I've made. It made me feel a lot better about myself, I wasn't just existing . . . I was going someplace."
- "It felt great to actually accomplish things, I could see that I was making progress in my life."
- "I didn't want to do the plans at first, but she said she would write down what we were doing anyway and I could see what she was writing anytime I wanted. When I decided to see them, it was neat to see how far I had come."
- "I get copies of my plan, and I keep them and look back on all the things I've done when I'm feeling depressed, and it lifts me up."
- "We get together and we review the sheets and I check off all of the things that I've done, and my CM puts a sticker on the page and I love that. One time she forgot to put my sticker on and I let her have it!"
- "Normally I wouldn't have liked the goal sheets. I was afraid to have goals, but there was a sense of accomplishment. Just reminding me that there were different areas of my life. Maybe I didn't want to be that positive, maybe that day I didn't feel like I had any strengths, but I do now."

CHAPTER SEVEN

Resource Acquisition: Putting Community Back into Community Mental Health

Purpose: To acquire the environmental resources desired by clients to achieve their goals and ensure their rights, to increase each person's assets.

Mental health is a sense of achievement, a sense of belonging, a sense of self-worth, a sense of choices, and the power to choose. Individual mental health, in this sense, is inseparable from the community. Belonging, achievement, and self-worth can only occur in context and in transaction with others. The quality of the niches a person inhabits is dependent on the match between individual characteristics and the resources, opportunities, and social relations of the environment.

The mental health of people with psychiatric disabilities will continue to suffer as long as mental health is seen as separate from community, is only seen as a group of professionals with specialized talents, or is only seen as formally constituted services largely segregated from the rest of life. Although the community is not the source of mental illness, it is the community that is the source of mental health. It is the community that is rich with opportunities, resources, and people. Therefore, a primary task of the strengths model case manager is to break down the walls separating clients from the community, to replace segregation with true community integration.

The Mental Health System as Barrier

Our current system of mental health care acts as a primary barrier to integration, achievement, and decent quality of life by fostering and enforcing segregation. In many locales, a specialized program has been established for virtually all life domains:

Housing: group homes, residential treatment, nursing homes, staff supervised apartments

Employment: sheltered workshops, prevocational skills classes, work crews at the mental health center

Recreation: partial hospital and day treatment programs

Education: GED classes at mental health center, daily living skill classes or groups

Spiritual: clergy visit congregate program (e.g., day treatment, group home)

Friendship: linkage with other clients, socialization groups run by the mental health center

These programs are usually delivered to groups. These programs mean that much of a person's life will be limited to interaction with other clients and paid staff. Their world becomes segregated and severely constricted or as Charlene Syx (1995) describes "an entire pretend world inside that transparent bubble" (p. 84).

Mental health workers come to believe that these programs are the service of choice for the person with psychiatric disabilities. The range of options offered to the person is limited to these mental-health-sponsored programs. The uniformity of treatment plans found in many programs is derived directly from this limited view of resources. The community support program initiative was focused on creating a "caring community," but too often "community" became limited to mental health staff, other professionals (e.g., vocational rehabilitation staff), and clients. As Carling (1995) writes:

> By labeling all of the needs of individuals as originating with their "mental illness," and then by offering only treatment-oriented responses to such common human needs as housing, work, education, and social connections, these programs continued to reinforce the notion that their clients should be centrally defined by their impairment rather than their citizenship. (p. 110)

Stigma within the mental health system created the current system and continues to maintain it. Two stigmatizing myths are particularly important: (1) people with psychiatric disabilities cannot make reasonable choices; and (2) people with psychiatric disabilities are too disabled for regular housing, work, and social relationships.

These myths are used to explain failures and "difficult" clients. For example, failure to maintain a community job is presumed to be confirming evidence of their incompetence rather than due to inadequate support or to features of the job setting.

A major effect of disregarding people's choices is the widespread pattern of "treatment resistance" reported in the literature (e.g., Bachrach, 1982). The real problem, as Estroff (1987) has suggested, may actually lie in what people are offered. Carling (1995) states that "the problem appears to be one of unappealing programs rather than of unmotivated or resistant consumers" (p. 112).

The stigma leads to "blaming the victim" and the perceived need for protective segregated program responses.

This view is further reinforced by "blaming the environment" beliefs. The view is that the community is uncaring if not hostile to people with psychiatric disabilities. The community is unaccommodating and therefore options available to other citizens are unavailable to people with psychiatric disabilities. Blaming the victim combined with blaming the environment is the epoxy that adheres people with psychiatric disabilities to segregated environments and entrapped niches where recovery is unlikely.

Mental health financing has reinforced the use and overuse of formally constituted services. Medicaid is the major source of funding for the care of people with psychiatric disabilities. Clients in this "fee-for-service" system are viewed as income-generating. The more service that is provided, the more income can be received up to the limit set by the state for their contribution (about 50% of the cost). Group services often bring in the most reimbursement relative to expenditures. Often, work with collaterals (e.g., landlords, employers, ministers) and transporting clients do not get included as reimbursable activities. Sometimes, entire life domains are not reimbursable (e.g., vocationally oriented activities). Thus, there are often powerful financial disincentives for delivering individually tailored services using existing community resources.

Another obstacle is that the identification, orchestration, and ongoing support of existing community resources is more complex and more time consuming than reliance on formally constituted services. Referral processes for formal service (e.g., vocational rehabilitation, partial hospital) are usually well-specified and comfortable for the case manager. In contrast, work with highly idiosyncratic community settings and people places a premium on flexibility, creativity, and skills in relationship building. Some case managers, especially newer ones, find this prospect uncomfortable, if not scary.

The presence of specialized mental health programs, stigma within the mental health system, blaming the environment, financing structures, and task difficulty powerfully conspire to reduce dramatically the true integration of clients in communities.

Redefining the Possible

At the root of the current system is a narrow definition of what is possible. Therefore, we need to develop a new vision of the possible. A few anecdotes may help. The first three reflect the success three programs have had in putting the community back in community mental health. The fourth story is a specific situation from a client in England.

Sumner County Mental Health Center is located in rural south central Kansas. In 1991, the CSS program under the leadership of Mike Lawson had 1-1/2 staff and access to a psychiatrist and responsibility for 55 clients. They obviously did not have the client base or resources to develop specialized programs. They did not have a partial hospital or day treatment program, specialized employment program, group homes, or other offerings. Despite this, in 1991 Sumner County had not one person enter a state psychiatric hospital, had no one in nursing home or other residential placement, had 82% of their people living in apartments, and had 42% of their people in paid, competitive employment.

In 1991, the Horizons Mental Health Center's CSS program produced these results for the 65 clients enrolled: (1) 90% were living independently; (2) 62% were receiving wages for work; (3) only 10% were not involved in some form of vocational or educational activity; and (4) only two people were hospitalized.

These results were produced by two staff members. How did they do it? They had no psychiatrist so they worked with general practitioners. They had no group homes, so they worked with landlords. They had no "group room" so they used a local fast food restaurant. They had no vocational program so they worked with employers. They had no drop-in center so they worked with churches and ministers. They had limited crisis services so they worked with the police. They had no special GED program, so they organized a group of retired school teachers. They had no special social and daily living skills program, so they used the home economics department of the community college.

The staff created a CSS without walls. They turned the communities into a community support program. They worked with police, ministers, general practitioners, the Chamber of Commerce, community colleges, landlords, employers, and even the owner of the all-night convenience store where some people receiving services tended to hang out. They educated them about psychiatric disability, told them the role and behaviors they needed to do to help, nurtured the relationship (e.g., going out in police cars, going to the convenience store to shop), and always left them a card with a number to call if they needed anything. The program coordinator for Horizon's Mental Health Center, Cheryl Runyun, termed this the Tom Sawyer Principle: Get everyone to help you paint the fence.

Dean was adamant that the mental health center, who was his payee, was stealing his money. All attempts to show him the center's record of his finances were unconvincing to him. Dean told the center that he wanted to be his own payee. Several barriers stood in the way of Dean's becoming his own payee, including the fact that he could neither read or write. Dean refused to go to any literacy classes. The case manager, wanting to be supportive of Dean's goal, assessed what other supports might be available for him to do this. One person who Dean trusted most in his life was his landlord, who was also a retired school teacher. She did not want to be Dean's payee but was willing to help him pay his bills and budget his money. A letter was written to Social Security requesting that Dean be his own payee, detailing the supports that would available for him to do this. Whenever Dean received one of his utility bills he would take it to his landlord, who would keep them all in a file for him. When he received his Social Security check, he would cash it and get money orders for the amounts his landlord had written down for him. She was patient with Dean and would show him everything she did and how she arrived at certain amounts. She even taught him how to read and used the mail he received as practice material. Before she died eight years later, Dean was able to handle his own finances by himself.

A local community center became worried about Mr. L.'s behavior when he used to wander around the reception area begging for cigarettes and being abusive, including shouting at his "voices." The Practitioner was able to provide them with information, resources, and strategies for dealing with the situation, and at the same time negotiate a role for Mr. L. in helping out with the cleaning and tidying up. The cleaner, a keen Union member, was resistant to the idea because of the risk of being made redundant by a volunteer. An agreement was negotiated whereby the cleaner was given permission to achieve their job targets in whatever way seemed best, and as long as the job was done it did not matter how. The cleaner, a heavy smoker, made friends with Mr. L., and they shared the work, their cigarettes, and the leisure time they created by working together. The center was no longer troubled by Mr. L.'s presence in the foyer, Mr. L. had what he regarded as a meaningful way of passing the time, and the Practitioner negotiated a mutual monitoring agreement. Mr. L. required fewer visits, because if there were any problems they would be picked up quickly by the center staff. (Bleach & Ryan, 1995, p. 101)

Lessons

1. People want to help. These examples indicate that in any community there are people who want to help, to share their time and resources with people with psychiatric disabilities. Not everyone wants to help, nor are people equally eager to be involved. In some cases, helping is in their self-interest. For example, the mission of community colleges is to provide flexible post-secondary education to citizens. Their funding is often based on enrollment. Helping people with psychiatric disabilities participate in their colleges helps them meet their needs as well. Other people give because of social or religious reasons. Some have talents that they want to share with others. Others give just because giving is a part of who they are.

2. People need information and support. In each of these examples, the case managers devoted considerable time to providing information on psychiatric disability and recovery, the goals people have, and ways of being helpful. In Hutchinson, Cheryl Runyun was part of the training program for serving police officers and for the orientation for new officers. The case managers also made themselves available to these community people to answer questions, check on how things are going, and to help in case of disruption or crises. The community people knew how to contact the case managers at any time. Parenthetically, these people rarely abused this privilege.

3. Client desires drive the work. In each of these examples, precise goal statements set by the clients directed the search for community

involvement. When asked how to achieve such consistently high levels of client outcomes, Kathi Gale of the Family Life Center stated, "We ask the clients what they want and then we help them get it." Case managers will use natural community resources more if the desires of people receiving services are taken seriously. All client preference studies, whether in housing, employment, socialization, or other areas, overwhelmingly find that people desire those niches that are apart from the mental health system. (Tanzman, 1993)

Further evidence to support the use of natural community resources is found in the research. People with psychiatric disabilities who work, live, and play in integrated settings spend less time in psychiatric hospitals, are more satisfied with their lives, and achieve more than others whose lives are dominated by the mental health system (Chamberlain, Topp, & Lee, 1995; Levstek & Bond, 1993).

Dimensions of Resources: The Four As

The use of naturally occurring resources entails attention to four dimensions of the resources: availability, accessibility, accommodation, and adequacy.

Consider the person who enjoys working on cars and would like to become a mechanic. As an advocate, the case manager begins with the availability issue. Are there continuing education courses at local high schools or junior colleges that provide such training? Are there mechanics in the community who would be willing to have the person help out at the service station in return for some hands-on training? Are there junk-car businesses that would provide an opportunity for the person to become familiar with car engines by stripping parts for resale? Identifying the availability of opportunities constitutes the first step in the advocacy process.

Accessibility becomes the next important area for consideration. Identifying obstacles such as lack of transportation, or expectations of the service system such as attending prevocational group at the center five days a week, may functionally render this resource inaccessible for the person. In such cases, efforts of the case manager may involve initially transporting the person to the resource site, or arranging for a family member, friend, or other collateral to meet this need. Additionally, efforts may need to be made to alter normal rules of access to be more responsive and supportive of the client's plan.

After issues of availability and accessibility have been addressed, the case manager must consider how accommodating the resource will be. This refers to the nature of the relationship, that is, interaction and communication, that the client will experience in any given resource context, whether a garage or the Social Security office. Case managers who have worked with people with psychiatric disabilities know that clients who have been treated in an abusive or less than compassionate manner in a given context in the past will be reluctant to involve themselves in a similar situation. Consequently, addressing this area of accommodation frequently involves initial work in educating and supporting the potential resource person (e.g., employer, landlord). Explaining any special needs the person may have may help set the stage for a more successful advocacy effort.

A focal point of work is creating a demand-competency match. *Demand* refers to the normal requirements of the setting or niche. *Competency* refers to that individual's unique configuration of desires, talents, and confidence.

> A case manager was working with a particular person who wanted to have her hair permed but was extremely fearful about going in the beauty shop to have it done. With her approval, the case manager went in to talk with the woman who ran the shop to explain the person's wishes and her particular situation. As it turned out, the beautician had experienced psychiatric disability in her family and was very receptive to accommodating the needs of the person. She scheduled a time at the end of the day when there would be no one else in the shop, she gave the person permission to smoke if she needed to, and was reassuring and friendly in her approach to the person. The client received the perm which made her feel wonderful, and the beautician gained a regular customer.

In this situation, the normal conditions of the beauty shop had from three to seven people present and did not permit smoking. Competency in this case refers to the person's ability to get her hair done if there were fewer people and she could smoke. The case manager found a setting and helped the owner to accommodate. More traditional approaches would have been: (1) engaging a hairdresser to do the woman's hair at the partial hospital program; (2) using a desensitization approach with client and gradually increasing the number of people in a room with the client and the length of time without a cigarette; and (3) having the case manager or other professional give the perm.

For a particular client in a particular situation, these approaches could be desirable. For this person, however, the case manager made a "normal" arrangement possible. The side benefits include increasing confidence in normal community activity, providing an opportunity for the salon owner to "give," and creating an ongoing relationship between the owner and client that in the words of Sullivan (1992) was "reusable and expandable" without cost to the service system.

A final dimension in the resource acquisition effort is that of adequacy. This issue relates to the extent that the resource meets the needs of each particular person. Is the connection giving the person a sense of personal fulfillment and satisfaction? Does their living situation meet minimal standards for decency and safety such as adequate heat, cooling, freedom from infestation, and other considerations? Does the person's vocational or volunteer involvement allow them to use their own unique talents and abilities, or are they involved exclusively in what the program has to offer?

The Perfect Niche

Much of this chapter will be devoted to strategies for making naturally occurring community resources more accessible, accommodating, and adequate for clients. In many situations, the case manager is called on to help the setting adjust in some way. There are times, however, when adjustments are not needed, by the setting or the client, or are very minor. This occurs when the case manager can find the "perfect niche" where the requirements and needs of the setting are perfectly matched with the desires, talents, and idiosyncracies of the person. In the previous example, perhaps the case manager could have found a beauty salon that is rarely crowded, operated by one hairdresser, and already permits smoking. If such a setting had been found, there would have been no need for the case manager to help the salon operator to make any accommodations. The following situation vividly depicts the "perfect niche":

Harry, a 30-year-old man, grew up in rural Kansas. Within a nine-month period, three years ago, both his parents died. Harry, with the help of his aunt and uncle who owned the contiguous ranch, continued to operate a large farming operation. After a while, his relatives began noticing that Harry was "forgetting" to fulfill responsibilities or doing them wrong, and was increasingly not eating, not bathing, and ignoring other personal necessities. They reported that he was increasingly "talking strange." A visit to the mental health center led to a diagnosis of schizophrenia and entrance into the state psychiatric hospital. After discharge, Harry was placed in a group home with services provided by the local mental health center. Although not disruptive, Harry failed to meet the group home's hygiene and cleaning requirements, did not attend mental health center services, and resisted taking his medication. It was reported that Harry would pack his bags every night, stand on the porch, and announce his leaving although he never left. Over the next two years, Harry's stay at the group home was punctuated with three readmissions to the state hospital.

Harry was referred to a social worker trained in the strengths model. Although Harry was largely uncommunicative, the case manager slowly began to appreciate Harry's knowledge and skill in farming. The social worker took seriously his expression of interest in farming and began working with Harry to find a place where he could use his skills.

They located a ranch on the edge of town where the owner was happy to accept Harry as a volunteer. Harry and the owner became friends and Harry soon established himself as a dependable and reliable worker. After a few months Harry recovered his truck, which was being held by his conservator, renewed his driver's license, and began to drive to the farm daily. To the delight of the community support staff, Harry began to communicate and there was a marked improvement in his personal hygiene. At the time of case termination, the owner of the ranch and Harry were discussing the possibility of paid employment.

Why Is This the "Perfect Niche?"

1. The case manager did not ask Harry or the rancher to change anything. Harry's desires and skills were a perfect match for the setting's demands and needs.

2. Harry's so-called deficits (e.g., noncommunication, poor hygiene) were irrelevant to the setting. In fact, the rancher did not talk any more than Harry.
3. Both parties, the client and the key actor, benefited.
4. The "natural" resource only cost a little case management time.

That his communication and hygiene improved was never targeted by the case manager. Yet, this "radiating impact" is a consistent finding of strengths model practice where success in one area seemingly leads to sometimes dramatic successes in other areas.

Locating "perfect niches" should be a primary goal of all strengths-model case managers. When successful, these niches tend to be stable produce high levels of client satisfaction and achievement, contribute to the community, and contribute to gains in other areas. Because case managers do not have to change or "fix" the person and the resource, it is also inexpensive in terms of case manager time and auxiliary mental health services.

Wanda was in her late 30s and had spent much of the last 10 years in and out of state hospitals. She wanted a job as a maid at a motel/hotel, which she had done for two brief periods during the last decade. She had all the necessary skills. Wanda, due to tardive dyskinesia, had a rather rigid style of walking with her head always tilted to one side. She also said "Hi, how are you?" indiscriminately whenever she confronted or passed someone. If she passed you, turned around, and passed you again, she would say it twice. The hotel of choice has always been a lower scale establishment. The strengths case manager, in contrast, recognized that it was up-scale hotels that devoted considerable resources to having all employees be friendly and greet their guests. The case manager helped Wanda get a job at a more expensive hotel where her goal, her skills, and even her "inappropriate" behavior were valued.

Strategies

Choose-Get-Keep

In chapter 1, the transition or continuum model of services was critiqued. The contrasting approach has been termed "choose-get-keep" by Anthony, Cohen, and Farkas (1990). In this model, the client and case manager: (1) set a goal and choose among the alternative settings and resources, (2) get access to the desired resource, and (3) make the adjustments and providing supports to keep the desired resource (Sullivan, Nicolellis, Danley, & MacDonald-Wilson, 1994). In the transition model, clients are asked to complete certain prerequisites before receiving (earning) the opportunity. For example, a person who wants to live in his or her own apartment may have to first demonstrate "success" in a group home, half-way house, or supervised apartment. The choose-get-keep approach avoids these hurdles and focuses on the client's goal directly and immediately.

The choosing phase includes specification of a long-term goal, the generating of options, and client selection. A long-term goal of enrolling in college or earning a bachelor's degree is the most frequent kind of beginning. With case manager assistance, the goal becomes more precise: to enroll and complete a creative writing course. The next step is the generation of options. The question is: Through what means and settings do people take a creative writing course? A list might look like the following:

1. Community college
2. University
3. Correspondence course
4. Interactive video
5. Independent study (perhaps with a local person who receives adjunct status to a community college)

Because the person's long-term goal is a degree, all alternatives should be credit bearing. If this was not the desire, other alternatives could have been generated (e.g., pair up with retired teacher or local author). Within each of these setting options, there are other alternatives, such as which creative writing course is most desirable. This step often involves the gathering of information (e.g., class schedules, course outlines). The last step within the choosing phase is the actual selection. Given the fear and anxiety that accompany new ventures, the person may want to visit campuses or classes, talk to current students, or do other forms of personal research.

The getting phase is focused on gaining access to the desired resource(s). In the previous example, this could include locating enrollment procedures and schedules, finding scholarships or financial support, and formulating transportation plans. As always, the client should do as many of the tasks as possible with help, if necessary, from people within the person's social network. Often, however, the case manager is the principal companion in "getting" activities. (Specific getting strategies are later.)

The getting phase may lead to a "rehabilitation crisis" (McCrory et al., 1980). This is described as:

> The experience of the disabled person who has accepted the challenge to grow, has achieved significant movement toward his goals, and is feeling overwhelmed by his changing/changed state. The client has advanced far enough in the process to begin to experience a transition in his activities, his relationships, his sense of himself. He is proud of his progress, yet sad for what he must give up and frightened of the uncertainties he must face. (p. 136)

The case manager needs to understand that the reaction is a rational response to fear, rather than some pathological resistance. Emotional support, reinforcement for steps already taken, slowing the pace of the "getting," and further breaking the goal down may be indicated.

The keeping phase is devoted to helping the client and the setting to sustain the arrangement in a satisfying and successful way for both parties. Frequently used strategies include:

1. Constructing reasonable accommodations (e.g., test-taking procedures, hours of work)
2. Pairing the person with a "travel" companion (e.g., another student, coworker, neighbor)
3. Celebrations for achievements
4. Easy access to the case manager by the client and setting (e.g., give them a card)
5. Arranging for supplements (e.g., tutor, job coach, cleaning service)
6. Brokering the use of supportive services (e.g., community college disability service office, academic counselors, transportation services, clubs)
7. Ongoing education and consultation to the key actors in the setting

The case manager needs constantly to assess the satisfaction with the arrangement and be prepared to help make adjustments.

In the keeping phase, the rehabilitation crisis as described above in the getting phase may also be a factor. As McCrory (1991) discusses, intense conflict can occur when the student is face-to-face with his or her own growth in connection with going to school and leaving the previous illness-related role. This may result in a recurrence of symptoms, or even possible rehospitalization. "The stronger the alliance, the easier client and practitioner will face this challenge . . . together, to acknowledge the struggle and support the [student] as decision maker in his or her own life to move ahead, to step backward, or to take a time out if it is too hard" (pp. 61–62).

Supported Living and Wrap-Around Services

Supported living refers to the collection of service approaches consistent with choose-get-keep that are called supported employment, supported housing, supported education, supported recreation, among other services. A central tenet of this approach is to separate the setting of activity from the receipt of services. For example, traditionally, people with psychiatric disabilities were required to live in certain residences (e.g., group homes, nursing homes, superrvised apartments) to receive medical care, meal preparation, case management, counseling, household maintenance and laundry services, and transportation services. This can be seen most vividly in total institutions like nursing homes and psychiatric hospitals. These settings provide for most needs: housing, food, socialization, medical care, and the like. One of the rationales for the judgment that people with psychiatirc disabilities cannot live in their own apartments has been doubts about their ability to cook, clean, socialize, structure their lives, and at times be supervised. These services were only available in professionally operated living arrangements.

The supported living perspective separates setting from services and asserts that it is the professional's job to arrange the needed supports to make the desired setting work. In other words, services and supports are "wrapped around" the person in the settings or niches of their choice. Johnson County Mental Health Center's Community Support Program (Merriam, Kansas) used the wraparound perspective when they closed their nursing home for people with psychiatric disabilities. Most of these people had spent much of their adult lives in psychiatric hospitals or nursing homes. Their symptomatology were severe and many showed signs of having been institutionalized. After nine months, 78% were still living in apartments and three people were living with families. A full 50% were involved in some kind of vocational activity. Thirty percent were working for wages and one person was attending college. Johnson County achieved these results in part through individually tailored personal plans using the wraparound perspective. A few examples:

1. People who were erratic in taking medication: A program called Med Drops was started in which a nurse went to the apartment and administered medication one to three times a day
2. Self-maintenance, apartment maintenance, and supervision-attendant care up to 24 hours a day
3. People fearful of the community environment: Case managers, attendant care workers, and significant others accompany people out of their apartments
4. People without transportation: Client-operated van service to get people to community locations and the mental health center
5. People without meaningful social roles: Heavy emphasis on vocational activity and work

These clients were among the most disabled. For most people with psychiatric disabilities, this level of professional service is not desired or needed but the concept still has currency.

Joan is a 52-year-old woman who had been a resident of the RCF [Residential Care Facility] for about two years after being referred from a state hospital. She was diagnosed with schizophrenia in her mid-20s, after she had completed college and begun a career in civil engineering in New York City. When she began experiencing distressing symptoms, her family brought her back to Kansas so they could assist with her care. However, Joan's symptoms were so severe that her family could not manage her at home and she began a series of state psychiatric hospital admissions and nursing home placements that would continue for more than 20 years. Joan bounced from state hospitals to nursing homes to community hospitals back to state hospitals frequently. Typically, she would be started on medication at the hospital and seem to do very well for a time. She would then be discharged to a nursing facility where she began to refuse medications; her delusions and paranoia would increase. She would become angry and sometimes threatening and she would often begin to steal clothing from other residents. At that point she would usually be sent back to the hospital and the cycle would begin again. She was in five different nursing homes in Kansas, every state hospital in Kansas, and numerous community hospitals.

Joan had her typical ups and downs at the RCF, but the difference was they didn't send her to the hospital unless she insisted on going; then they would take her back after a short stay. They capitalized on her love of people—she developed a number of friendships with CSS clients and with staff. When they first talked about closing the RCF, Joan was pretty scared. (In fact, she had a couple of hospital stays around that time because she was so stressed out.) She really wanted to have her own place, but she was fearful that she wouldn't make it. Probably the key was assuring her that she would have attendant care from someone whom she already knew on the RCF staff—for as long as she needed it. And, telling her over and over that they believed in her ability to do it. Also, they had the flexible funds to buy furniture and stuff and she really liked picking out stuff for her own place.

Joan has now lived in her own apartment for over 18 months! She still has attendant care, but only a few hours, two or three times a week. She has daily medication drops, which are critical. She is working with a vocational staff person trying to get a job and she was interviewed on a Kansas City TV station—they did a story about people diagnosed with schizophrenia who were doing well in the community. Joan says she was able to do it because the staff were the first people who believed in her.

A Strengths-Based Approach to Employment

Work is a critical element in many people's recovery (Onken, Dumont, et al, 2002; Steele & Berman, 2001). Studies suggest that 60% of people with psychiatric disabilities desire paid employment (McQuilken et al., 2003; Muesser, Salyers et al., 2001; Rogers, Welsh, Masotte, & Danley, 1991). Despite the desire, fewer than 20% are employed (Dion & Anthony, 1987). In fact, employment assistance is a major unmet need based on consumer surveys (Crane-Ross, Roth & Lauber, 2000; Noble et al, 1997).

The individual placement and support model of supported employment is a well-specified practice with over 13 studies (nine of which are randomized controlled trials) attesting to its effectiveness (see Becker and Drake, 2003 for a review of the research and details on the practice). In some studies, competitive employment rates exceeded 70%. The principles of this strengths based approach are the following (Becker & Bond, 2002; Bond, 1998):

1. Services focused on competitive employment: The agency providing supported employment services is committed to competitive employment as an attainable goal for its consumers, devoting its resources for rehabilitation services to this endeavor, rather than to intermediate activities (e.g., day treatment, sheltered work). Supported employment programs focus on helping consumers obtain their own permanent competitive jobs.

2. Eligibility based on consumer choice: No one is excluded who wants to participate. The only requirement for admission to a supported employment program is a desire to work in a competitive job. Consumers are not excluded on the basis of "work readiness," diagnoses, symptoms, substance use history, psychiatric hospitalizations, or level of disability.

3. Rapid job search: Supported employment programs use a rapid job search approach to help consumers obtain jobs directly, rather than providing lengthy preemployment assessment, training, and counseling.

4. Integration of rehabilitation and mental health: The supported employment program is closely integrated with the mental health treatment team. This principle means that supported employment staff participate regularly in treatment team meetings and interact with treatment team members outside of these meetings.

5. Attention to consumer preferences: Services are based on consumers' preferences and choices, rather than providers' judgments. Staff and consumers find individualized job placements, based on consumer preferences, strengths, and work experiences.

6. Time-unlimited and individualized support: Follow-along supports are individualized and continued indefinitely. Supported employment programs remain committed to the support of consumers long after they have achieved employment, thus avoiding artificial deadlines for program terminations that may be dictated by funding sources.

Supported Housing

People with prolonged psychiatric disabilities often encounter difficulty in achieving a stable living situation in the community. The complex reasons for this difficulty include personal, social, and environmental factors. The disability can impair functioning, whereas recurrent acute symptoms and repeated short hospitalizations often result in loss of benefits and housing. The extreme poverty of the target population, due to low levels of employment and low entitlement income provided by government programs for people with disabilities, make it difficult to afford a place to live. The lack of low income housing, both within the private market and through government-assisted programs, makes decent affordable housing a very scarce commodity in almost all areas of the country. Stigma and discrimination, fragmentation of services and supports, and the general lack of integration of housing, social welfare and mental health programs add to this problem.

The lack of attention to housing and support needs of this population has been linked to unnecessary transfer to other institutional settings (Lamb & Goetzel, 1971); incarceration; residential instability, and homelessness (Bassuk, 1986); unnecessary and costly inpatient stays and emergency services episodes (Chafetz & Goldfinger, 1984); social segregation in substandard housing (Aviram & Segal, 1973; Lamb & Goetzel, 1971); and excessive burden on families who often serve as primary caregivers (Doll, 1976; Wasow, 1982).

In the late 1980s, supported housing emerged as programmatic response to this situation. These programs seek to reduce common negative outcomes and improve the quality of life for people with prolonged psychiatric disabilities. At its core, supported housing combines scattered site, socially integrated housing with individually tailored support services in which clients control their personal space and have typical tenant roles and responsibilities (e.g., the lease in their name, control over keys) (Blanch, Carling, & Ridgway, 1988; Carling & Ridgway, 1988; Ridgway & Zipple, 1990; Hogan & Carling, 1992). In many states and local mental health systems, such programs quickly became viewed as an indispensable element of community support services. Approaches using normal housing and individualized supports to meeting residential services needs were endorsed in national policy by the National Institute of Mental Health (NIMH, 1987) and the National Association of State Mental Health Program Directors (NASMHPD, 1987).

The research indicates that people receiving supported housing are more likely to be stably housed and less likely to be hospitalized or homeless (Rog, 2004). Some studies have found positive difference in symptoms (Lehman et al, 1994; Hough et al., 1994), functioning in daily life (Goldinger, et al., 1994; Shern, et al., 1994; Lehman, et al., 1994); and quality of life (Goldfinger, et al., 1994).

Effective supported housing services combine housing assistance with high quality case management. The housing assistance includes rental subsidies and help in obtaining and establishing a home. A recent qualitative study in Kansas (Eichler, Gowdy & Etzel-Wise, 2004) found the following elements as critical:

1. Consumers considered by CMHC [Community Mental Health Center] staff as "difficult to serve" can succeed with supported housing. All consumers were living in homes of their own, averaging over two years subsequent to their last significant period spent in an institutional setting.
2. Intensive case management is the most essential service in supported housing. Case managers spent a considerable amount of time in the life space of these consumers. Frequency and intensity of contact clearly contributed to improved outcomes with consumers. The eight main activities are:
   • Advocating for the consumer: supporting his or her goals
   • Honoring consumer decisions and goals
   • Obtaining resources
   • Teaching skills
   • Providing emotional support/reassurance
   • Meeting the challenges of transportation
3. Living independently increases consumers' opportunities to pursue interests, relationships, goals, and future plans of their own design. Having a home of their own increased their ability to act on their choices and preferences.
4. Vehicle ownership appears to contribute to consumers' success in staying out of institutions and in their own homes. Fifty percent had

their own vehicle, much higher than expected. Vehicle ownership expanded personal choice and freedom in practical and meaningful ways.

5. Feeling a sense of "home" does not happen immediately. Consumers take some time to develop personal "ownership" of their living space and experience the freedoms associated with having private, stable housing.

6. Family members play a significant role in helping consumers get and keep housing. The main areas in which they help include advocating for proper treatment; providing temporary or permanent housing; helping furnish an apartment; providing transportation; and offering emotional or financial support.

7. Case managers and medical staff listen to and act on consumer's concerns about the efficacy of their medications. They take seriously consumers' opinions and experiences with their medications. Consumers stress the need to advocate for the right doctor, the right medicine, the right medical treatment.

Supported Education

Many consumers value education as a means to better jobs and more income,as a way to allow personal growth, and as a mechanism to feel better about themselves. Yet, enrollment in postsecondary education is appalling low. Kansas is the only state that has established educational achievement as one of the five state mental health goals. But even here, in March 2005, Kansas had less than 3% of consumers enrolled in postsecondary education. If recovery is, in part, helping people build lives apart from the mental health system by helping them attain the goals they set for themselves, we are failing in the area of education.

Supported education is defined as:

The provision of post secondary education in integrated educational settings; the target population is individuals with severe psychiatric disabilities for whom post secondary education has been interrupted, intermittent or has not yet occurred because of a severe psychiatric disability, and who, because of this psychiatric impairment need ongoing support services in order to be successful in the education environment. (Unger, 1990, p 10)

Three supported education prototypes have been identified: self-contained class-rooms, on-site support, and mobile support (Anthony and Unger, 1991).

1. Self-contained classrooms: In this model, the young adults with psychiatric disabilities attend separate classes at a postsecondary setting. Students may participate in the activities and use the resources of the educational institution but they are not integrated into regular classes. Regular academic credit may or may not be given. Support is available at the postsecondary site and is provided by special program staff and/or members of the academic institution. Typically, students eventually move out of the self-contained classes into integrated classes, often with on-site support or mobile support.

2. On-site support: In this model, young adults with psychiatric disabilities attend regular classes for which they are matriculated and receive credit. Support is provided by staff from the post secondary site-usually the Disabled Student Service or the College Counseling Service.
3. Mobile support: In this model, young adults with psychiatric disabilities attend regular classes for which they are matriculated and receive credit. In contrast to the on-site support model, the support is provided by community based mental health services. In this model, support can be provided on- and off-site to young adults enrolled at a variety of postsecondary institutions.

There have been 14 studies of supported education with only one employing an experimental design (see Carlson, Eichler, Huff & Rapp, 2003 for complete review). It is noteworthy, however, that each study found positive findings. For the self-contained classrooms, at least 21% and as high as 96% go on to enroll in integrated classes, with employment rates varying from 35 to 100%. Despite the length of preparatory self-contained classrooms (two to four semesters), well over half of the participants complete them. For mobile and on-site studies, between 59 and 100% of students enrolling in regular integrated classes complete the courses and achieve grades at a B average.

Due to the generally weak research designs, conclusions must remain tentative. Concerning self-contained classrooms, the suggestion could be made that in a recovery oriented system, such arrangements may serve as an alternative to day treatment. The content covered in these classes is often similar to content included in day treatment programs and results seem to indicate more movement into "normal" adult roles (e.g., work, integrated classroom enrollment) than day treatment. Changing the location of service to a non-mental health setting could contribute to escape from entrapping niches (Taylor, 1997; Sullivan & Rapp, 2002) and facilitate recovery. Just the location may help reduce consumer fear and rekindle dreams.

While the descriptions of the interventions is cursory in each of the mobile and on-site support studies, a few common features seem to emerge:

- Active recruitment of participants; providing information and encouragement in a variety of ways
- Entrance to the program is based only on consumer desire and meeting any requirements of the college.
- Supports are individually tailored and provided.
- Preenrollment supports include help with financial aid, transportation, purchasing books and supplies, class selection and enrollment, college resources, and how to secure them. The availability of personal accompaniment seems necessary.
- On-going supports include easy access to tutors, work with faculty around accommodations, structuring homework completion, personal support and encouragement, celebrations (e.g., biweekly dinner), access to peer support.

Multiple Strategy Method of Resource Acquisition

A basic premise of the strengths model is that community integration and adjustment can only occur after the client has been removed from the mental health system. For example, who is better integrated: the client doing ceramics in a partial hospitalization program or the client doing ceramics in a class sponored by the town's recreation department? Our current use of segregated services as a first choice often leads to people never reaching the other level and to a waste of resources for those who with some help could make it in a class for "normals." Workers must begin with "normal" resources and naturally occurring supports (e.g., family, friends, neighbors), using segregated services as a last, not a first, resort. The task for the worker is to build the mechanisms necessary for the person to be able to meet the social demands such "normal" settings establish so that a person's sense of adequacy and competence can be respected. This often means engaging in environmental engineering to adapt settings to our client's needs and to providing support to both the person and environmental actors as they seek to make the adaptation work.

The general process through which a strategy is to be selected might be construed as rational problem solving. In other words, there is a goal or a set of goals that are sought and a number of avenues through which those goals can be attained. The selection of a strategy must be based on the information collected in each step of the proposed model.

The model itself contains eight steps and is portrayed in Figure 7.1. The steps themselves are grouped into three phases: (1) assessment, (2) strategy selection, and (3) implementation. Although the steps are described sequentially, in operation there is considerable interaction between steps.

Resource Assessment

Too often this step is ignored because several resources may be immediately obvious. However, the obvious ones may not include all possibilities, nor are they automatically the best. It is important for the case manager and client to generate as many alternatives as possible and to assess the subjective probability that each will fulfill the goals of the person. This phase of assessment will include such tactics as interviewing, brainstorming, and researching.

Who Is in Control?

This step includes two phases determining which of the desired resources are available and identifying who is in control of them. For the available resources, the organization or person in control must be identified specifically. For those resources that are not available or not accessible, the individuals or organizations involved in the general resource area or those that are known to have an interest in the general area may provide a starting point. As in the previous step, it is necessary to push the traditional limits. Frequently, various organizations, groups, or individ-

Resource Acquisition

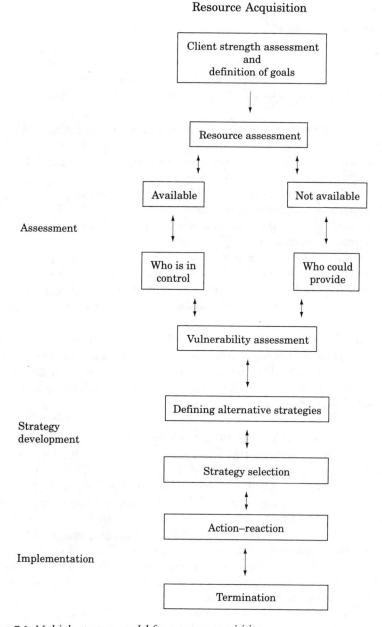

Figure 7.1 *Multiple strategy model for resource acquisition*

uals provide similar resources. Again, the process calls for selecting the resource that will satisfy the desire and is most likely to be available. This step culminates in the identification and selection of an individual, group, or organization that can provide the resource in question.

Assessment of Vulnerability

The fourth step involves an assessment of those factors to which the target individual or institution would be most responsive and would lead to the provision of the desired resources. The case manager will need to assess the target's vulnerability to positive appeals and negative contingencies. Targets may consist of individuals, groups, or organizations. Sample questions that need to be answered include:

1. Does the target have an ideology that would resist or encourage the provision of the resource for the client?
2. Is there any relationship between the case manager or client and the target?
3. Does the target view the relationship as positive or negative?
4. What are the target's self-interests?
5. To whom is the target most responsive: supervisors, taxpayers, consumers, legislators, or pressure groups?
6. How accessible is the adequate time target?
7. Does the target have direct control over the provision of the desired resource or is the target only one part of the decision-making process?
8. Does the target have many potential allies and how influential are they?

This step has many implications for the effectiveness of the strategy. Therefore, and effort should be devoted to developing an accurate and complete picture of alternative targets. It should be noted that an initial positive approach strategy may be needed to attain the necessary information about the target's vulnerability. Consider the following case example.

Bill Riley has been in and out of the VA hospital for 20 years for treatment of bipolar disorder precipitated by a car accident in which he sustained severe brain damage. Bill has been unable to hold a job, maintain friendships, or function in the community. The longest time spent out of the hospital during this period was 18 months. Bill was assigned to a case manager who together with Bill completed the client assessment, identified life domains in which to work, and selected getting a job as the number one priority. Bill was anxious about starting a job and the idea of a full-time job was scary. It was agreed that a part-time volunteer job in food service would be a good first step. The case manager and Bill selected the congregate meal program for senior citizens as "fitting the bill."

The case manager went off to see the person who was responsible for volunteers in this program. During the conversation, the case manager described Bill's situation in some detail including the information in the first paragraph, at which time the target became worried about having "such a mentally ill person" working in their program and denied the request.

Postscript: Through further negotiation, Bill was finally accepted and worked there for 10 months to everyone's satisfaction.

Selected Strategies

The multiple-strategy model suggests two dimensions of strategies. The first dimension consists of a continuum ranging from positive "salesmanship" approaches to aversive or negative approaches. In order to generate or stimulate a particular resource, the advocate must select a strategy that could be positive, negative, or somewhere in between. The points on the continuum include the following:

1. At the positive end, the case manager can attempt to gain the good favor of the person or agency in control of the desired resource.
2. At midpoint, the case manager could select a neutral strategy, often referred to as consultation, in which information would be provided to the critical individual or agency.
3. At the negative end, the case manager could decide to take direct aversive action against the critical individual or agency. If the desired resource is not provided, threats to take such action are also a major component of negative strategies.

The second dimension consists of a continuum of approaches to bring about change that ranges from the individual level to the societal level. The points on the continuum include the following: (1) At the individual level, the case manager could identify the critical person in control of the desired resource;. (2) at the administrative level, the case manager could identify a critical agency in control of the desired resource; and (3) at the policy level, strategies might include situations in which the case manager could identify some political or social system that was responsible for the resource that was lacking.

Interaction of Strategies

As can be seen, the two dimensions will necessarily interact. In other words, the case manager will need to select strategies that are positive or negative and identify individuals or systems that must be changed. The examples showing the interaction of the two sets of strategies cannot be viewed as prescriptive because strategies or combinations of strategies must be executed on the basis of each situation.

The next sections offer a few examples of the interplay of dimensions.

Sample Interventions from Case Management Projects

Advocacy Efforts

Positive Strategy at the Individual Level
- One client wanted leisure time activities and liked to garden but the apartment complex had no provision for gardening. The case manager worked out an agreement with the landlord so that the person could plant a small garden. As an activity, gardening demands ongoing

attention. Once the tulips are planted, they have to be watered, weeded, and cared for.

Neutral Strategy at the Individual Level
- A client had cockroaches in the apartment but was afraid to contact the landlord. The case manager contacted the landlord, explained the situation, and an exterminator was provided.

Positive Strategy at the Administrative Level
- A client who had been institutionalized for many years was interested in getting a job but had little experience. His family had, years ago, been in the food service business. The case manager approached the head of the city volunteer agency and arranged for the person to help serve meals to senior citizens.
- A client in tough financial straits bounced a check at a local grocery store. The person was asked to pay the store a "bounced check fee." The case manager contacted the store manager and got the fee rescinded.

Neutral Strategy at the Policy Level
- The case manager defined the lack of jobs as a prevalent concern of people receiving services. They began thinking about an advocacy effort focused on eliciting job commitments from Lawrence businesses. They contacted some business organizations, presented information, and sought other information that would be needed to develop a plan of action.
- Case managers became increasingly aware of the support needed by clients at the time of discharge from a psychiatric inpatient setting. A peer support program modeled after the compeer program was developed to meet this need. A grant was written and submitted for funding to implement and pay clients for participating in the program.

Table 7.1 is a completed strategy matrix for a client, John, whose goal was "to swim three times a week." The resource desired by John was swimming at the YMCA.

Strategy Selection

A critical element of the model is the selection of a strategy that will produce the resource needed. By necessity, this will have to be accomplished in each individual situation. In the first place, at the heart of the approach is a belief in the rights of clients and the self-control of environmental resources. It is critical, then, that clients be involved in the selection of the necessary resource as well as the selection of a strategy for intervention. It is not yet possible to provide an a priori prescription as to what resources are needed, which strategies are indicated, and who should carry out the actual effort. The action-reaction sequence will provide considerable information for selecting the next strategy.

TABLE 7.1 Strategy Matrix Advocacy Focus

	Individual Level	Administrative Level	Policy Level
Positive approach	Approach the swimming supervisor to allow John to act as his assistant swimming instructor in return for free access	Request an exception to policy in John's case in return for the case manager applying for United Way funds for recreation scholarships to be given out by the YMCA.	Make a formal proposal to the YMCA's board to waive or reduce cost for John and those similarly situated.
Neutral approach	Engage swimming supervisor in a problem-solving session on alternative avenues for John	Present information on the need for recreation of a group of community members like John.	Do a study for the board highlighting groups of citizens who do not have access to the YMCA and identify the barriers.
Negative approach	Send letters to the administration, board, and national organization complaining about the supervisor's lack of cooperation.	Have the media cover the story of one individual being denied access to YMCA facilities because of administrative rules inconsistent with the Y's constitution	Approach the United Way to reduce funds for the YMCA unless special scholarships are provided for those who cannot afford membership fees.

Consequences

The consequences of a strategy are multiple. Fundamentally, a strategy has consequences for three parties: the client, the case manager, and the target. Systems theory has proposed that it is not possible to affect one part of the system without affecting the whole. Therefore, depending on the nature of the resource needed and the strategy used, varying numbers of people would be affected.

A few generalizations about the relationship between the strategy and its possible consequences can be proposed. At any level, positive and neutral strategies have little chance of causing short-term negative consequences. The converse is that negative strategies have a high probability of incurring backlash or short-range negative consequences. Many strategies include combinations of positive, neutral, and negative approaches. The crucial consideration that supersedes all others is how to obtain the resource that the person needs. The client and the advocate must decide which strategy offers the highest probability of attaining the necessary resource at the same time that it minimizes any potential negative consequences. Obviously, in some instances, backlash must be risked to ensure that the position of the client is not compromised.

Implementation

After a strategy is selected, the decision of "who will do what?" becomes critical. In particular, should the case manager act for the person, act with the person, or have the person initiate the effort? Because the goal of our program is to engender empowerment, the model suggests that clients should be given as much responsibility as possible. Therefore, the client should be the primary acquirer of resources if possible. Role playing and instruction may allow people to assume more responsibilities than would otherwise be possible. A few rules can be suggested: (1) Any case manager activity is to be discussed before and after the activity with the client; (2) the case manager should review with the client any activities the person performed on their own; and (3) positive feedback should be profusely given for any activity by the person, even those that may have failed. Look for the smallest increments of improvement in a person's competence.

A strategy that fails to produce the needed resource means either that new sources of resources need to be considered or that new strategies need to be developed. The learning that occurred during the unsuccessful effort often can be used to formulate a revised plan. If successful, the client and the case manager are ready to move to a new task related to the same goal or to a new goal. The multiple-strategy model must be construed as a set of intricately related and interacting components. However, the model does not imply that orderly execution of the phases of assessment, decision, and implementation will lead automatically to a successful disposition. The continual goal of maximizing gains while minimizing losses dictates an ongoing interplay of components. For example, the process of assessment including assessment of strengths and aspirations, potential resources, identified individuals and institutions, and the vulnerability of these groups continues to take place throughout the advocacy effort. In many instances, the best assessment can be carried out by initiating a particular strategy and carefully monitoring the reaction of the group providing the resources.

Developing Agreement: Principles Underlying Effective Persuasion

Resource acquisition requires a set of perspectives and discrete skills. The premium placed on naturally occurring community resources means that case managers are interacting with a wide variety of citizens in a wide variety of settings. In their efforts to make resources available, accessible, and accommodating, case managers seek to influence these key actors.

In trying to influence others, a person may use persuasion, inducement, or constraint (Gamson, 1968). "In contrast to inducement or constraint which requires the manipulation of consequences contingent upon the target's response, persuasion involves changing the way an individual or group perceives a set of alternatives through the provision of new information" (Simons, 1987, p. 244), or as Larsen (1983) puts it, "the process of persuasion involves your presenting good reasons for a specific choice among probable alternatives" (p. 281). The following material on the principles of persuasion is based on Ronald Simons, "The Skill of Persuasion: An Essential Component of Human Service Administration," *Administration in Social Work, Vol. 1,* 3/4, 1987.

The Technique of Persuasion

Theory and research on persuasion are concerned with identifying the characteristics of messages that persons find appealing and with discovering the nature of communications that are perceived to contain "good reasons" for adopting the position being advocated. Based on the findings of several decades of research, the following principles appear effective persuasive appeals.

Cognitive Principle 1: Emphasize Advantages or Rewards

People are constantly processing the information available to them and making decisions as to how they might best satisfy their needs and achieve their goals. Hence, the probability that individuals will change their behavior in response to a communication is increased when the message provides information indicating that the change will enable them to satisfy more effectively their needs and desires.

Several studies show that a target audience is more apt to adopt a favorable attitude toward a behavior or procedure when they perceive it to have a relative advantage over existing or alternative practices (Coleman, Katz, & Menzel, 1966; Leventhal, 1970; Rogers, 1983). Rogers (1968) notes that the advantages or reward associated with an action may not be economic or material. The benefits of adopting the line of action being advocated may be largely psychological, leading to an increase in prestige, status, or satisfaction. People must have sufficient reason for modifying their behavior or for adopting a new procedure. One good reason for doing so is because the new approach yields rewards at a level unavailable through existing practices or alternative action.

Cognitive Principle 2: Be Comprehensible

The action being advocated must be presented in a language that is readily understood by the target audience. Technical jargon should be avoided if possible. People will not adopt a line of action that they do not fully comprehend. Simple, easily understood ideas are more likely to be accepted than arguments that are complex and hard to follow (Glaser, Abelson, & Garrison, 1983; Rogers, 1983; Zaltman, 1973). Comprehension can sometimes be enhanced by augmenting verbal discussion with graphs, charts, or through site visits where the target can view the innovation in action. Clarity and comprehension are important to addressing a person's fear of the unknown.

Cognitive Principle 3: Show Compatibility of Values

There is substantial evidence that people are more apt to accept an idea if it is perceived as consistent with their present beliefs, values, and ways of doing things (Rogers, 1983; Zaltman, 1973). For instance, Woolfolk, Woolfolk, and Wilson (1977) found that students who were shown identical videotapes of a teacher using reinforcement procedures evaluated the teacher and the technique more favorably when the videotape was described as an illustration of "humanistic education" than when it was labeled behavior modification. Sanders and Reppucci (1977) reported that the reaction of school principals and superintendents to a program proposal varied according to whether the program was identified as employing a behavior modification approach. Such studies are a clear demonstration of the way that one can destroy an audience's receptivity to an idea by using words or phrases that the group perceives as representing beliefs or practices that are contrary to their value commitments.

Various groups—whether human service agencies, funding bodies, or civic organizations—are often committed to a particular sociopolitical ideology. An idea is more apt to be accepted or assimilated by a group if it is perceived to be compatible with the assumption, principles, and procedures that make up the group's ideological orientation (Glaser et al., 1983). Compatibility promises greater security and less risk to the receiver while making the new idea appear more meaningful (Rogers, 1983). Enhancing organizational performance, client-centeredness and client outcomes comprises an attractive ideology and set of values that can be difficult, but far from impossible, to disagree with.

Cognitive Principle 4: Cite Proven Results

An audience is more apt to accept an idea if its consequences have already been observed. When people can see the positive results of an action or procedure they are more likely to adopt it (Glaser et al., 1983; Rogers, 1983). Given this finding, a stepping stone approach is often the most effective way of selling an idea. First, a small group is persuaded to test the procedure. The positive results obtained in this demonstration project or pilot program are then cited in persuasive communications designed to promote the idea across a broader population.

Cognitive Principle 5: Allow for Trialability

The target group will perceive less risk if the new ideal can be tried on a piecemeal basis prior to wholesale adoption of the procedure (Rogers, 1983; Rogers & Svenning, 1969). As Glaser et al. observe:

> The extent to which a proposed change is known to be reversible if it does not prove desirable may affect its adoption. Not all innovations can be discarded later with impunity; the bridges back to the status quo may have been burned. Situations in which the user need not "play for keeps" provide more opportunity for innovation. (1983, p. 61)

People are reluctant to commit themselves to a line of action that does not allow for a later change of mind. An idea is more apt to be adopted if it can be broken into parts that can be tried one step at a time, with the group having the option of discontinuing the new procedure at any time in the process should they decide that it is not producing the anticipated results (Rogers, 1983).

Cognitive Principle 6: Link Message to Influential Others

Consistent with the predictions of Balance Theory (Heider, 1958), several studies indicate that people tend to adopt the same attitude toward an object or idea as that held by someone they like and that they tend to adopt the opposite attitude toward an object or idea as that held by someone they dislike (Tedeschi & Lindskold, 1976). In this way, individuals maintain cognitive balance.

These findings suggest that an idea is more likely to be accepted if it is linked to persons whom the target likes. The most direct method for doing this is to have someone the target likes or respects deliver the persuasive appeal. When this is not feasible, reference might be made to influential others as part of the communicated message. For instance, if a city council member is known to be a firm supporter of the state governor and the governor is known to have the same views on an issue as the case manager who is trying to influence the council member, this information could be presented to the council member. This general tactic can be used whether the favored person is the president, a movie star, a well-known expert on some topic, or the target's colleague, friend, or spouse.

The case manager might cite individuals similar to the target when information about whom the target likes or respects is lacking. This strategy is based on the extensive body of research indicating that people tend to be attracted to people they perceive as similar to themselves. Thus, when attempting to persuade a landlord to make repairs, the worker might name other landlords who have made such repairs.

Cognitive Principle 7: Avoid High-Pressure Tactics

Research based on Reactance Theory shows that when individuals feel pressured to select a particular course of action, whether through the promise of rewards, the threat of punishment, or intense appeals, they tend to increase their valuation of alternatives to the position being advocated (Brehm, 1966; Wicklund, 1974). High-pressure tactics create a boomerang effect. The use of pressure to persuade people to adopt an idea frequently creates resistance and a determination to act in a manner that is contrary to the proposed action. Human beings value their freedom and will resist attempts to circumscribe their choice or self-determination. Therefore, messages should be presented in a manner that minimizes any threat to the target's feeling of freedom. Phrases such as "It's your decision," "But, of course, it's up to you," and "Think about it and see what you want to do" serve this function, whereas words such as "must," "should," and "have to" are likely to arouse resistance (Brehm, 1966).

Cognitive Principle 8: Minimize Threats to Security, Status, and Esteem

Case managers often commit the "rationalistic bias" of assuming that people are reasonable beings who when presented with the logic of a new and better approach will recognize its merits and embrace it without hesitation (Zaltman & Duncan, 1977). However, events frequently fail to unfold in this fashion. People's logic and reason are often distorted by less rational processes. Sound judgment may be clouded by a defensive emotional response. Emotional defensiveness may be produced because a group fears the new procedure will signal a diminution in their prestige or power (Bright, 1964; Berlin, 1968). Those persons who have benefited the most from existing practices are likely to be threatened by a change in procedures. Other individuals may fear that the new approach will devalue their knowledge and skills and that they will have a difficult time learning the new procedures (Bright, 1964; Glaser et al., 1983). In still other instances, persons may be reluctant to adopt a course of action because they feel they will lose face with their friends or some constituency.

The wise case manager will construct his or her communications in a manner that alleviates such threats. Whenever an idea might be interpreted as threatening to the target group's security, esteem, or sense of competence, these fears should be discussed and objectively examined as part of the communication process. By acknowledging and evaluating these concerns through the two-sided approach discussed next, defensiveness may be reduced and reason allowed to prevail.

Developing Agreement: Cognitive Strategies for Persuasion

The previous section describes principles of persuasion, those dynamics that seem to work. This section transforms these principles into specific interpersonal strategies of documented effectiveness.

Ronald Simons (1982, 1985, 1987) has conducted an extensive review of the social psychology literature on cognitive strategies for persuasion and influence. Although it is natural to think of cognitive strategies to be the exclusive realm of oral interchanges, they are also useful with written communication channels, such as letters, memos, and reports. These strategies will be reviewed by describing the strategy and providing an example within the context of strengths model case management practice. This is no substitute for learning and practicing these experientially. Case managers are encouraged to practice each of these with another person (e.g., supervisor) who can observe the use of the strategy and the effect on the audience and provide feedback.

Cognitive Strategy 1: The Two-Sided Argument

This strategy recognizes that there may be several points of view on any point of discussion. To use this strategy, you present the other position or positions first and then present the position you would like supported. The presentation of the other positions is more effective when it is accompanied with clear appreciation for each position. The advantage of this strategy is that it demonstrates understanding and appreciation of the other positions. It tends to reduce defensiveness and preempt counterarguments.

We have devoted several hours of discussion over the last several days to deciding if Marge should be returned to the Welcome Group Home or placed in an apartment upon discharge from the hospital. The task today is to decide. There seems to be two positions on this issue. The first position is that Marge would be better served by placement in the Welcome Group Home. The reasons include:

1. Marge has not been responsible about taking her medications for at least two years.
2. Marge has not demonstrated an ability to care for herself in terms of food.
3. Marge tends to isolate herself and resists attending the partial hospital program; she does not know how to structure her day.

Furthermore, under these conditions, we all know Marge is likely to decompensate and be rehospitalized, probably sooner rather than later. This scenario is quite possible and the reasons given are very much based on Marge's behavior over the last year and a half. If we do not address these needs, an apartment surely will not work.

Discharge to an apartment, on the other hand, has some promise for the following reasons:

1. Marge wants to live in an apartment and has wanted to do so for over a year. As a program, we have increasingly respected client choice and, in fact, it is part of our mission statement.
2. Besides eating, Marge does possess and uses self-care skills in other areas. Her living quarters and clothing are always immaculate.
3. What we have been doing has not really worked. Marge had been in the Welcome Group Home for almost a year and was in another group home before that. During that 18-month period, Marge has been rehospitalized four times.

My own position is that we try the apartment and arrange for the supports needed to address the medications and food. If it does not work, we still have the group home. Remember Robbie and Gus? We had similar trepidation in their situation but for the last six months it seems to be holding. I would like to use today to brainstorm alternative ways for meeting these needs. I have brought copies of Marge's strengths assessment. As you can see, Marge is not without strengths and has a fair amount of supportive people in her life. Let's take the medication issue first.

Woven into this monologue are several ideas. First, the task before the group is made clear. Second, the contrary position is detailed first and its credibility established. Third, the group's wisdom is acknowledged and the opinion that they are the best people to work on it implied. Fourth, the desired position is described and a specific person recognized. Fifth, threats to security and control are attenuated by suggesting that a decision to go ahead is not a done deal *i* and everyone will continue to be involved in designing it correctly. The reader may also notice how the monologue also introduced compatibility of values, cited proven results, and allowed for trialability.

Cognitive Strategy 2: Cognitive Dissonance

In this strategy, when people sense a contradiction between a behavior and an attitude, they tend to want to change to resolve the dissonance. That is, if they are aware of a contradiction between a behavior and an attitude, they are likely to change the attitude or the behavior to bring the two in line with each other. There is a danger in using this strategy. Some people who see there is a contradiction point it out, and with an attitude of "I got you." Some people think about this strategy as confrontation with a negative emotional component. Our experience is that by including a negative emotional component in the delivery, that resistance results or increases. One definition of confrontation is to bring face to face, or to compare two things by placing them side by side. The challenge is to place the two contradictory items side by side within a relationship that engenders change rather than resistance. This strategy may also be used in a more active way by inducing or rewarding a person or group to perform an action that is in the direction of the desired position without examining attitudes that would contradict this behavior. When the audience sees that there were rewards from the behavior despite contradicting their original attitude, they are more likely to bring the attitude in line with the behavior. In the previous example, the case manager noted the values of the group (i.e., client choice) and used it as one of the reasons for selecting the apartment alternative.

Cognitive Strategy 3: Specify the Consequences of a Stance

With this strategy, the audience is involved in exploring the consequences of a position through logical reasoning. When the consequences of the desired position are seen as more beneficial or more likely to satisfy a need, then the audience is more likely to move toward the desired position. This strategy is essentially thinking through positions and their consequences. It is more common than unusual to adopt a position without systematically thinking through the consequences. After all, we are all busy people with workloads that seldom allow time for reflection. This strategy works best when the audience or target describes their position and the anticipated consequences of this position. The case manager's job in this situation is to help clarify the position and the consequences. The case manager also has to ensure that negative or possible undesired consequences are identified. In other words, the case manager must have done her homework and be a skilled interviewer. When the position and consequences are clear, the leader points out how these consequences are not as desirable as those emanating from the desired position.

In the previous example, the case manager did say that the group home "solution" has not been working. The case manager could have listed other consequences such as:

1. Working with the Welcome Group Home staff is time-consuming and often not pleasant.
2. If Marge returns there, there would not be a bed available for Joe or Sam when they are discharged.
3. Because the group home is a 40-minute drive from the program, many of the transportation problems for Marge would continue.

Cognitive Strategy 4: Weight of the Evidence

While specifying the consequences of a stance relies on logic, weight of the evidence relies on documentation. You present all of the evidence for your position and this suggests to people that they might adopt a new position based on the evidence. It can also be used by comparing the evidence for one position with the evidence for another position. Similar to a courtroom analogy, the position with more evidence tends to be sustained. Just as in court, you need to consider the nature of evidence. In court, there are specific rules of evidence. In the area of the social programs, evidence tends to come from empirical literature, theoretical literature, and the experiences of others.

In the previous example, the case manager pointed to Robbie and Gus as two clients in similar situations where the apartment choice worked. The case manager could also have included: (1) the research on the favorable results of supported housing; and (2) the success another program (familiar to the participants perhaps) has had with similar clients or a successful program that does not have access to a group home.

Developing Agreement: Behavioral Strategies

Behavioral Strategy 1: Do Work (Tasks) with Them

One of the most powerful techniques for developing a consensus with a group of people is to get them involved in doing a *task*. All too often meetings are a waste of time. The agenda is unstructured or absent and the desired outcomes are not specified. Few participants take responsibility for helping structure or lead the meeting. The meeting operates at such a level of abstraction and verbal interchange that few results could be expected. As case managers, a common strength is verbal ability. Much of case management is conducted with verbal skills. We probably selected case management in part because we had well-developed verbal skills. It is this very strength that can become a problem in the meeting. Discussion of "issues" at a conceptual level passes for doing work in the context of many meetings. We attempt to talk a participant into taking our position. We try to change minds.

The variety of cognitive strategies that, in fact, may exercise influence do have a role. However, we have found that these strategies and social workers' heightened verbal abilities are even more effective within the context of doing a *task* together.

For example, you are trying to get acceptance to start a new "Med Drop" program that will deliver medications up to three times a day to people who would desire this service. There are many concerns among the staff including potential to foster dependency, the expense of the program, and therefore the number of clients has to be limited—so how will the service be rationed—and suggestions that the funds could be better used elsewhere. Your research has convinced you that such a service would dramatically reduce hospitalizations by helping people have access to medications they find helpful. One approach would be to use a variety of persuasion strategies (e.g., two-sided argument, cognitive decisions) to convince people. It may, however, just continue the discussion of whether it should be done.

The task-centered approach in this situation would change the focus by getting the group to do work together rather than engage in verbal argument. In this case, the case manager, as the instigator, would note the difficulty in defining who will receive this service and get the group engaged in developing the criteria that will, as unambiguously as possible, determine which people will be served and not served.

If you are successful in getting the group engaged in this *task,* you are accomplishing several things at the same time. You are building on the groups strength in terms of analytic and verbal ability by directing this into a critically important *task.* You are developing ownership for the product, which enhances the implementation of the product as intended. You are drawing on the collective practice wisdom of the group, which is bound to be larger than yours alone. As items are put forth as suggestions for the in-take checklist, you are provided opportunities to reward individuals as well as the group for their specific suggestions. Consequently, the group is going to experience increased feelings of competence and probably cohesion. As the group struggles with the difficulty of the *task,* you are provided with a natural opportunity to provide the group with information you acquired in your research. But most important, you have begun to change the central question from "whether to do it" to "how are we going to do it."

No single example can demonstrate the richness and variety of this strategy. However, the list of benefits is quite impressive. Of course, the group or individual members must have the specific skills required to complete the *task.* The group may simply not have any history in doing work together, which may make it difficult to engage them in *a task. You* may also select *a task* that they just do not have the ability to complete. In either case, it is likely that the original *tasks* can be broken down into a small *task* or set of *tasks* at which the group can be successful.

It is also frequently the case that part of the *task* cannot be finished because someone needs to do some other work outside of the group meeting, such as checking case files or state policy. In this situation, the work is delegated to group members. The more responsibility each member can take for a part of the *task,* the more the benefits of this approach will accrue. Volunteering to do a part of the *task* shows commitment on your part as well. One advantage to the delegation of *tasks* to be done outside of the group is the natural establishment of the agenda for the next meeting as well as prior commitment to work at the next meeting.

In short, case managers who are skilled at translating issues into concrete tasks and involving others in their completion are often quite successful in change efforts.

Behavioral Strategy 2: Modeling

Modeling as a strategy for building consensus is simply doing. Much of what we want people to do is a set of behaviors that are much too complex to explain or attempt to talk people into doing. When a person does the set of behaviors (models), the components of the behavior are demonstrated. This also allows the audience to compare their behavior in similar situations to the demonstrated behavior. Not only are the behaviors demonstrated, but the rewards possible or accruing from the behavior are also demonstrated. This includes both extrinsic and intrinsic rewards. That is, modeling not only demonstrates the rewards available from others but also demonstrates the ways in which the behavior is intrinsically energizing or exciting.

This strategy is often useful in working with employers, ministers, or other people who are predisposed to helping but are uncertain how to respond to a person who is experiencing severe psychiatric symptoms, such as hearing distressing voices. The case manager can demonstrate how to interact with the person during times when the voices are most apparent and how assistance can be most helpful. The case manager can model recovery-oriented behaviors such as talking about the person with the highest respect, valuing what they have to say, and being accommodating to any specific needs they have. Viewing the case manager interacting in a way that is effective and comfortable can reduce discomfort and fear and vividly portray the necessary behavior.

This description has several implications for use by case managers. The audience has to be able to see the behavioral components, the extrinsic rewards, and the intrinsic rewards. The audience has to believe that the rewards would also be available to them. The audience has to believe that they could perform the behavior. These conditions mean that the case manager using modeling must establish the conditions for modeling to be effective. That is, the case manager must remove any real or perceived barriers to performing the behavior. The case manager must make certain that the rewards are available to others who perform the same behavior. The case manager must explicitly demonstrate the implicit rewards through demonstrating the excitement or joy felt by performing the behavior.

Behavioral Strategy 3: Inducements and Rewards

This strategy comes directly from the various behavioral schools of thought. People exhibit behavior they believe to be rewarding. Either the conditions are established to assure the person that rewards are forthcoming or the behavior is exhibited and rewards accrue, which increases the frequency of the behavior. Of course, the link between the behavior and the inducement or reward must be explicit. In addition, for inducements and rewards to work they must be valued by the person and must be perceived as fair and not patronizing.

This strategy is yet another instance where the case manager must know what is valued by people in the environment and what specific individuals find rewarding. Possible rewards for an employer could include:

1. Having a reliable worker for a job that has high turnover;
2. Receiving a tax credit for hiring a person with a disability;
3. Suggesting program staff try to shop at businesses that employ clients;
4. Arranging that the participating business gets free advertisement through the vocational newsletter that is distributed to over 500 people in town;
5. Having on-call access to the case manager or other program staff.

The case manager must explicitly link the inducement or reward to the desired behavior. In many behavioral models, this is emphasized through temporal placement of rewards and behavior. Given the environment in which case managers operate, "being there" when the behavior occurs is unlikely. Consequently, the case manager needs to be explicit in the link between the inducement, reward, and the desired behavior. Linking rewards from the case manager to rewards that occur more normally within the environment also enhances their effect. Again, being explicit about intrinsic rewards in creating a reward-based environment is a large part of this strategy.

Innovative Community Strategies

The separation of community mental health from "community" has stifled the integration and quality of life of people with psychiatric disabilities. The community support program initiative grew from a profound recognition that to enhance successful community living for people required attention not only to their medical (psychiatric) needs but also to housing, employment, income, food and clothing, socialization, and other factors. The reluctance of communities to provide adequately, in part, led to mental health centers assuming major responsibility for these needs. The last 20 years have witnessed the growth of mental-health-sponsored housing, employment, education, daily living skills, socialization, transportation, and recreation programs. Mental health has assumed responsibility for functions that our society has delegated to other institutions and entities. With mental health resources being limited, such an undertaking is always limited and frustrating.

The strengths model, in its call to return "community" to our work, requires new strategies besides replacement. Although much of this chapter has been devoted to case managers working on behalf of individual clients, often targeting an individual key actor, there are times when more programmatic approaches are indicated. This section details four strategies for involving community stakeholders.

Data-Based Approaches

Many problems facing our clients can only or best be addressed by mobilizing a diverse group of community people. The data-based approach has several components: (1) gathering the needed data and information; (2) identifying people and organizations who have a stake in the topic reflected by the data; and (3) urging the group to take responsibility for acting on the data.

An example from Sedgwick County, Kansas (Wichita), is illustrative.

Community Support Program (CSP) staff became aware that only 12 out of 874 clients were enrolled in postsecondary education. They knew that a sizable increase could not be accomplished by the program alone. The staff invited representatives from affiliate mental health agencies, the Kansas Alliance for the Mentally Ill, consumers from the program's advisory board, consumer drop-in center, representatives from universities and junior colleges, and a few employers.

At the meeting, the CSP Director, Kevin Bomhoff, distributed the data and expressed his shock and dismay. He went on to say, "We need to do something about this and the people in this group are the ones who could make it happen. The purpose of this meeting is to figure out how."

One result was the hiring of a person whose only responsibility was supported education. A liaison with each postsecondary institution was designated, and responsibility for collecting information on scholarships and financial aid and various courses of study was delegated. Methods for educating consumers, parents, and case managers were formulated. Within six months, there was a 58% increase in the number of clients enrolled in college.

This example demonstrates the three elements of a data-based strategy. One key to this strategy is that the data must be viewed as valid, accurate, and objective. If they are not, doubts will be raised and the time will be devoted to discussing whether this is a problem and where we can get better or additional data rather than strategies for correcting the situation. The results of this scenario show how community resources and energy can be mobilized with the case manager acting as but one partner.

The Caboolture Approach

An interesting experiment occurred in the 1990s in Caboolture, Australia, on the outskirts of Brisbane. Under the leadership of Dr. Kalyanasundaram, community integration of people with psychiatric disabilities became the principal mission of the program. Their vision statement stated:

The rights, options and opportunities of the citizens of the Caboolture and Kilcoy Shires who have a mental illness shall be the same as those of all other members of the community. All citizens have the rights to be accepted, supported and respected in their choice of lifestyle as contributing members of the community. (Caboolture Adult Mental Health Services, 1995, p. 2)

Acutely aware of its limited resources, the program had since its inception made a major effort to reach out to community people and involve them in the lives of the clients.

While individual case managers were viewed as "community resource workers" and devoted much of their energy to supporting community people's efforts on behalf of individual clients, programmatically Caboolture created the Mental Health Network of Caboolture involving community actors (Figure 7.2). The network in turn helped create the Access Arts Program, which matches artists with clients. One of their projects was to decorate a neighborhood park. Loneliness was a problem for many people so they created the Open Door Volunteer Program that matches community people with clients. They found families for crisis services and laypeople to help in respite care; this became the basis for the Host Family Program. As they describe:

> . . . the emphasis is on the informal system. It is the informal system which provides the restorative experiences of friendship, understanding, and a sense of belonging. (Caboolture Adult Mental Health Services, 1995, p. 12)

Another major initiative was supporting the development and operation of a consumer organization. Under the leadership of Helen Glover and Melanie Scott, this organization now offers the following:

1. Chat Line providing peer counseling
2. Community Movement Project, which befriends people who are lonely
3. Building Blocks—a lunchtime socialization opportunity with a library of videos on mental health
4. Quiet Support—room in a house that people can use for respite
5. Publication of an anthology of consumer poetry
6. An education program for community groups
7. Lunchtime series involving consumers and staff to discuss topics such as recovery and partnerships

The group also does consumer advocacy, provides consultation to the professional staff, and assists consumers in finding employment and other opportunities.

One of the strategies is to funnel funds to community groups rather than using those funds to expand the mental health center services. For example, rather than applying for a grant to establish a day treatment center, Dr. Kalyanasundaram helped the Neighborhood Centers to apply for the funds. The Neighborhood Centers already served other populations and this step allowed them to provide skill instruction, socialization activities, and some additional linking to other community resources.

The benefits of this approach include fostering integration and avoiding segregation, increasing access to people and resources beyond the mental health system, exploiting the talents of existing organizations, and developing new partnerships. (For more information on this exciting experiment, contact the author or Dr. Vaidyanathan Kalyanasundaram, Caboolture Adult Mental Health Services, Locked Mail Bag No. 4, Caboolture, Queensland, Australia.)

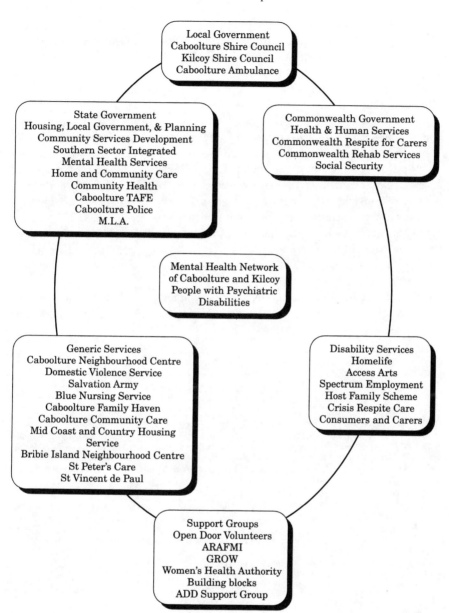

Figure 7.2 Mental health network

Communiversity

People desire enjoyable activities to fill their lives and opportunities to learn and be in the company of people who share common interests. These are mechanisms for growth. Day treatment centers and partial hospital programs have been established by the mental health system to contribute to this life domain. Even when done well, these programs foster segregation and oppression. Clients' interactions are with other clients and staff, the program activities are defined and supervised by staff, options and therefore choice is limited, and this is done at considerable expense to the mental health system. The increase in clubhouses and other consumer-operated programs are a desirable trend but even these are segregated and run on limited funding.

An alternative framework is to create a "program without walls" open to the public. One such effort by the University of Missouri at Kansas City is called "Communiversity." This program recruits community people to offer "classes" on hundreds of subjects including arts and crafts, cooking ethnic foods, meditation and massage, taxes, gardening, language, music, dance, computers, healing, and travel. As you can imagine, the offerings are too varied and extensive to capture here. Classes vary in schedule from six sessions of two hours each to a single six-hour day. Classroom sites have been donated by libraries, churches, community centers, and universities but many of the classes occur in people's homes. The cost of each course averages about $9. If you take as many classes as you want for a semester, the cost is $40.

While mental-health-sponsored programs will always be limited, the Communiversity offers an inexpensive and almost infinite array of possibilities. It taps the

---

Samantha Travis
1424 Windswept Ave., Apt. #2
Carson, CA. 95032
(304) 354-6654

Benefit:

With a fleet of 30 cars, your business is currently paying the rate of $35–$40 per hour to have an outside auto mechanic maintain and perform simple repairs on your automobiles. I propose that you hire a full-time auto mechanic to perform the same work for one third the present hourly rate. An added benefit of having an auto mechanic on duty will be appreciated by your outside salespeople who will not have to wait for repairs from "the shop" or call a towing company to have a battery recharged, tires changed, or minor repairs.

Qualifications:

Samantha Travis is an ambitious and hard working auto mechanic who finished in the top third of her class this fall from the Carson College Auto Mechanics Training Course. She has worked on and off for several years in a family-owned gas station, and enjoys working with cars and contact with the public. Samantha looks forward to becoming part of a team where she can utilize her fine-tuned mechanical abilities.

Employment Conditions: 40 hours a week, $12 per hour

References

Deborah Callohan, Manager
Union 76 Station, Carson
(304) 654-3324

Gerald Smith, Instructor
Carson College
(304) 656-7435

Robert Wright, Counselor
Carson College Employment Project
(304) 654-7654

Figure 7.3 Letter

endless talents and strengths of citizens and provides them an opportunity to teach, to share, to give. It is integrated and provides a wide range of choices. Rather than replace community responsibility, the mental health system could join with the community to help the community meet its proper responsibility.

Creating Opportunities

Most resource acquisition activities involve identifying a community resource and then, through a variety of strategies, acquiring it for the client. Its a process of getting what is already there. Another approach has been to create opportunities. The best articulation of this community strategy is from Denise Bissonnette (1994) as applied to employment. The approach is to create jobs that people will fill as solutions to the problems a particular business may be having. In many ways, it is a systematic attempt to create "perfect niches" which were described earlier in this chapter. Figure 7.3 contains one example. Table 7.2 summarizes the differences between "traditional job development" and the creating opportunity model. The approach is a sophisticated application of the strengths model. It places a premium on identifying a person's strengths and aspirations as a basis for locating vacuums in the environment.

TABLE 7.2 Beyond Traditional Job Development Training Workbook: Summary of Paradigm Differences

Traditional Job Development	Entrepreneurial Job Development
Sees a limited job market	Sees a world of possibility
Views the corporate world as impenetrable, inhuman	Views the corporate world as a framework for approachable human system
Sees organizations as static institutions	Sees organizations as ever-changing processes
Expects organizations to make sense	Expects the unexpected from the people who make up the organization
Focuses on the decision to hire; wants to talk to the decision maker	Focuses on the need to hire, the screening and recruitment process, and the decision to hire; will talk to anybody
Recognizes employers as experts in hiring	Recognizes employers as experts in the business they are running but possible amateurs at hiring
Defines a job by the duties and minimum qualifications	Defines a job by the results produced or needs met
Works to give applicants the best edge against competing job seekers	Works to remove applications from competition with other job seekers
Seeks openings in the open job market	Seeks opportunities in the hidden job market
Responds to job orders for existing positions	Proposes to create new employment
Uses resumes	Uses employment proposals and resumes
Sees scarcity of identified employment opportunities	Sees abundance of as of yet unidentified employment opportunities
Hears, "We're not hiring"	Hears, "We're not hiring yet"
Reacts to the whims of employers	Proacts to the needs of the business community
Asking	Offering

TABLE 7.3 Resource Acquisition

Purpose: To acquire the environmental resources desired by consumers to achieve their goals and ensure their rights; to increase each person's assets.

Behavior

1. Case manager educates consumer of rights and responsibilities of citizenship.
2. Case manager identifies and seeks to remove policies of exclusion, stigma, and discrimination.
3. Case manager is persistent in using a variety of influence strategies to gain resources in a positive collaborative manner.
4. Case manager assists consumer to take responsibility to accumulate resources for themselves.
5. Involves consumer and significant others in advocacy efforts.
6. Case manager supports and recognizes community resource people through rewards (e.g., letters, certificates).
7. Case manager shares knowledge of and seeks ideas and approaches to potential resources in group supervision.

Summary

Resource acquisition (Table 7.3) is an intrinsic part of all case management models. The strengths model, however, pushes the boundaries of traditional approaches. It requires a dramatic new set of perspectives of community, integration, and resources. It also recognizes the sophistication needed to do it. The strategies, skills, and judgment needed to successfully accomplish true community integration with clients are as complex and demanding as those required for clinical work. Despite the challenge, case managers in the United States, England, and Australia whose practice reflects the strengths model are demonstrating daily that it can be done.

CHAPTER EIGHT

Supportive Case Management Context: Creating the Conditions for Effectiveness

THIS BOOK HAS DEVOTED ITSELF to exploring the contours and textures of the client, the community, and the case manager. Case management is also powerfully influenced by the organizational context in which it is embedded. *Simply, if strengths model case management practice is to occur and flourish, producing the benefits and outcomes for consumers, the organization and its management must adopt certain perspectives and practices.* (Note: The term management as used in this chapter refers to the people other than case managers or other direct service staff. This would include people with titles such as supervisor, team leader, coordinator, director, and administrator.) This chapter seeks to describe these critical features. Of particular importance is the skillful use of group supervision.

This chapter has value at at least two levels. First, managers need to be well-grounded in the intervention methods being used by their workers (in this instance, strengths model case management) and also need to know and practice those management methods supportive of the model. This chapter speaks directly to those management methods. Second, case managers have many opportunities to influence the operation of their organizations and this chapter provides the elements that they should seek to establish. Case managers, in most organizations, are not totally passive recipients of "management." They attend meetings, sit on task forces or committees, and in a myriad of ways make suggestions or are in a position to do so.

Traditional Management Practice

Current mental health management practice is characterized by separation of management from clients. Buttressed by management theory and methods, management education programs, and public tolerance, mental health management has been systematically separated from the people it is charged to serve. As Miringoff (1980) states:

> As social welfare has grown, there has been an increasing recognition that management is needed, but such management has often been perceived, even by its own practitioners, as an activity almost divorced from the quality of service itself. In this view management is concerned almost exclusively with an organization's maintenance and political functioning; the quality and substance of service provided is seen to be outside the purview of management. Hence managerial measures of efficiency and budgetary concerns have often been viewed by service practitioners as being counterproductive to service delivery. (p. 10)

This separation between mental health managers and the person with severe psychiatric disabilities has had severe consequences. It has produced both short- and long-term goal displacement, whereby the organization's means become its end. "Thus the activities that the organization engages in (interviewing clients, supervising staff, managerial tasks such as budgeting and personnel selection, etc.) are used as criteria to judge the success of the organization" (Neugeboren, 1985, p. 28). This process is characterized by concern for survival or program expansion and the loss of purpose.

Another result of the separation has been that managers frequently engage in reactive management practice; in premature embracing of snazzy new management practices, which consume large amounts of resources before they atrophy and are discarded; and in employing problem-solving modes that seem to solve problems but that never seem to lead to improved performance. The separation between management and clients also is a primary reason why management is seen either as being irrelevant or as posing an obstacle to better service delivery in so many agencies. Management continues to be seen as a major contributor to low morale and job satisfaction and as a major source of burnout (Karger, 1981).

The most profound consequence is felt by clients. Clients bring their problems, needs, pain, and suffering to the mental health agency, seeking help, direction, relief, and an increased sense of control and power. Too often, their feelings of impotence are exacerbated in the face of rules, policies, and protocols that seem unresponsive to their concerns. At times, the process of receiving service is dehumanizing, whether through the physical setting of service or through the behavior of personnel. Also, too often, our services are ineffective, do not help, and fail to produce benefits for clients.

This chapter presents a framework for management practice in mental health that promises to reduce the chasm between managers and consumers and between managers and direct service staff. It does so by: (1) describing the assumptions and principles of client-centered performance management and (2) proposing a new metaphor and resultant strategies for implementing client-centered management.

Client-Centered Management

Assumptions of Client-Centered Management

One of the defining characteristics of management is that it does not directly produce or deliver goods or services. Instead, direct delivery or production of goods or services is accomplished by the teacher, the salesperson, the assembly line worker, or the direct service worker. A person receiving mental health services receives help through the efforts of and interaction with the therapist, the case manager, or the nurse and psychiatrist in the medication clinic. A manager's contribution to the well-being of clients is indirect, mediated through the efforts of direct service workers. By this definition, management would include positions such as administrators, supervisors, program directors, coordinators, and so forth. The ideas in this chapter apply to all of these positions.

The first assumption of client-centered performance management is that management's reason for existing is the well-being of clients and the principal task is to facilitate that well-being. The mental health manager is confronted with a myriad constituencies (e.g., funders, licensing and regulatory organizations, advocacy groups, unions, media, staff, other agencies) that make demands on the organization. Clients are but one of these groups and often have the least power and influence. Also, these varied constituent demands are often incompatible with client goal attainment and well-being. Client-centered managers, rather than succumb to external pressures and become diverted, never lose sight of their purpose and continue to make well-being of the client the centerpiece of their activity with other constituents.

The second assumption is that a manager's performance is virtually identical and inseparable from the performance of the organization or organizational unit to which the manager is assigned. This perspective assumes that managers are placed in those positions to be responsible for the performance of the domain under them, whether it is a team, an office, an area, a program, a division, or an entire agency. It assumes that this is why the organization is paying the manager. It is therefore rare to have a superior manager overseeing an inadequate program or a superior team being run by an inferior manager. They are interchangeable for 80 to 90% of managers and units. This notion is more prevalent in business, where excellence in top-level management is equated with organizational performance: profit, market share, and so forth. The process followed in *In Search of Excellence* (Peters & Waterman, 1982) was to identify first the high-performing companies and then find the managers who made it happen.

The notion that management equates with performance is much more alien in the human services. The most typical initial response is to identify factors that seem to be beyond the influence and control of managers, which affect organizational performance. Common examples of such excuses include civil service or patronage appointments; less than adequate community services; unsympathetic judges, physicians, and other gatekeepers and decision makers; and insufficient staff in terms of amount or quality. The most frequent response is, "We don't have enough resources. "For each manager, the obstacles to performance are numerous and vary in terms of type of obstacle and degree of influence. Mental health managers, however, are responsible for either mitigating the obstacles their units confront or taking such obstacles as unchangeable and seeking performance despite them.

If management equates with performance, then a clear definition of mental health service performance is necessary. The client-centered performance model posits five performance areas: client outcomes, productivity, resource acquisition, efficiency, and employees' job satisfaction. The client-centered manager is responsible for performance in each of these areas.

The centerpiece of agency and managerial performance is the benefits accrued by clients as a result of our efforts. The performance related to client outcomes focuses on the improvement in the *client's* situation or at least the curbing of a deteriorating *client* situation. Client outcomes act as the bottom line of mental health services in much the same way that profit serves business. The business executive needs to closely monitor production, acquisition of component parts, and employee morale but that functionary would never assume that happy employees who seem to be diligently working guarantee an adequate profit. In much the same way, human service managers need to perform in a variety of areas, but adequate performance in these areas is neither sufficient nor a proxy for client outcomes. It is this notion that leads Patti (1985) to argue that effectiveness (client outcomes) should be the "philosophical linchpin" of human service organizations.

Principles of Client-Centered Management

Four principles act as the foundation for *client-centered performance management* (Gowdy & Rapp, 1989; Rapp & Poertner, 1992):

1. Venerate the people called "clients."
2. Create and maintain the focus.
3. Possess a healthy disrespect for the impossible.
4. Learn for a living.

Principle 1: Venerate the People Called Clients   Managers play a key role in communicating the values of the program to those who use it, to those who work for it, and to the community in which it operates. Whether consciously or unconsciously, managers communicate, in their daily words and actions, how people will be viewed and treated by the program. Managers whose programs show effective results for those it serves are managers who create helping environments wherein consumers are seen and treated as human-as people who are more than mere patients or clients (Gowdy & Rapp, 1989). They are seen as whole people; each individual has a life beyond the program, comprising a variety of interests, relationships, and histories. Although a person might receive a diagnosis of schizophrenia, for example, on entering the mental health system, that person is much more than "a schizophrenic." She or he is a person who happens to experience psychiatric symptoms, along with many other life events and processes. Central to seeing people as individuals is the view that people have strengths and can recover, reclaim, and transform their lives.

Among the ways in which managers manifest this principle are: (1) knowing the people receiving services, their stories, their history, their families, interests, and so forth; (2) having frequent contact with clients, characterized by courtesy, friendliness, and respect; (3) promoting clients as heroes; and (4) assuming a client advocacy perspective toward their own jobs.

Principle 2: Create and Maintain the Focus   The organization that performs is the one that has clearly defined its mission, purpose, and performance, and commits all its knowledge, resources, and talents to achieving those aims. The performing agency is conscientiously myopic and single-minded. It systematically excludes the irrelevant and limits the domain of organizational concern. Basically, *the perform-ers* set out to do one or two things and to do them well. For the client-centered performance manager, that focus is defined in terms of clients and client outcomes.

Organizational focus requires the following:

1. The management's job is to select and establish an organizational focus.
2. The management should define the focus in terms of client outcomes.
3. The management's definition of a focus dictates *the elimination* of other potentially worthwhile goals and activities.
4. Management embodies a commitment, a preoccupation, an obsession with achieving that focus.

Principle 3: Possess a Healthy Disrespect for the Impossible   Mental health services suffer from a chronic lack of funds, staff, community interest, and public support. This lack of resources is simultaneously coupled with incessant demands from the program's multiple constituencies (Martin, 1980). Thus, a manager's daily work life is often typified by a continual stream of needs and demands from consumers, staff, funders, providers, courts, regulatory agents, and advocates. There are dead-lines to meet, reports and grants to be written, meetings to attend, phone calls to take, questions to be answered, and crises to be resolved.

In the face of such a chaotic milieu, managers seem to evidence one of two re-sponses: (1) surrender to such constraints and be satisfied maintaining the status quo, or (2) persist in finding opportunities to improve the program in the midst of chaos. *Both responses* mean that managers *work equally hard,* it seems, but they *work differently.* The effective managers are those who take the second course of action. Rather than remain inactive behind excuses of "not enough money," "not enough time," or "not enough staff," exceptional managers are those who say, "This is needed. Let's make it happen." They are people who instill a "make do" attitude in the workplace, in which program participants and staff members become ac-tively involved in making good things transpire in the face of seemingly over-whelming odds. As such, the manager removes barriers to action: needless proce-dures, policies, meetings, and processes. The manager is willing to go with a promising idea and willing to drop one that has not worked, though the manager may have been pleased with the attempt. As Franklin D. Roosevelt stated, "But above all, try *something*." The result of this perspective is that such programs are flexible and changing, sprouting innovations based on emerging needs of clients.

Five characteristics seem to be at the root of these action-oriented managers:

1. A perception of self as powerful and responsible in the situation at hand
2. Flexibility and invention, based on a clear focus on people's needs
3. Highly developed problem-solving skills, with a premium on partializing
4. Ability to blend agendas of seemingly disparate interests
5. Persistence (Gowdy & Rapp, 1989, p. 57)

Principle 4: Learn for a Living   Managers whose programs show effective results are those who seem to "learn for a living" rather than "work for a living" (Gowdy & Rapp, 1989). They actively seek out input and feedback on program performance from sources ranging from program participants and staff, to publications, performance reports, funders, and consultants. Their programs are open to visitors and observers; their offices are open to continual streams of clients and staff; their conversations are laced with stories about what they have learned from reflecting on their own practice. These managers evidence the critical skills of learning, including a total lack of defensiveness about evaluating their work; a drive to critically examine minute helping interventions and decisions to glean their impact; and the ability to brainstorm with others so that truly creative ideas can be identified and pursued.

Rather than deifying existing interventions or program models, these managers are people who approach life with the question, "What can I learn today?" They are open to experimentation. They create learning environments for their staff by paying attention to client outcome data, by constantly putting the work of the program under a critical (but nonblaming) microscope, by encouraging contact with a diversity of people, and by providing support for risk takers.

The Traditional Organization

The most resilient symbol of management is the organizational chart. Originally devised for the military and borrowed by manufacturing companies during the Industrial Revolution, the hierarchical and pyramidal organization chart (sometimes referred to as a table of organization) is ubiquitous in human service organizations. The basic configuration is portrayed in Figure 8.1. The chart typically includes three types of personnel. The first is the *line staff*, the people who actually make the product or deliver the service. The second type is *supervisory and management*, who are responsible for controlling and coordinating the work to be done. The third type of personnel is *support staff*, who perform specialized roles for the organization, such as budgeting and accounting, legal services, information systems, housekeeping, among other functions. In the pure sense, these support personnel have no direct authority over the line and managerial personnel.

This traditional organizational configuration was designed to enhance the manufacture and distribution of products. Efficiency was the ultimate criterion, and control was the principal function of management. The organizational chart por-

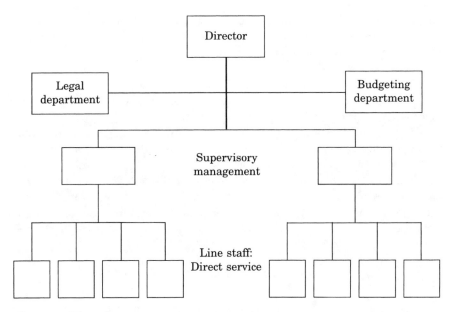

Figure 8.1 Hierarchy

trayed the positions that exist in the organization, how these are grouped into units, and how formal authority and communication flows among them (Mintzberg, 1979). This vertical hierarchy depicts the division of labor and establishes that power is centered at the top.

The criticisms of this organizational configuration are legion. For the client-centered performance manager, the most pertinent consequence is the inherent separation of managers from front-line workers and clients. Furthermore, the larger the organization, the greater the distance grows between day-to-day client contact and the policy decisions affecting these clients. "The vertical, one-way hierarchy tends to separate and give precedence to goals of organizational maintenance over client-oriented goals" (Altshuler & Forward, 1978, p. 58). While this seems to occur in business, with profound consequences (Peters & Waterman, 1982), mental health services—with their plethora of constituencies—make it that much easier to forget about the clients. The typical organizational structure reinforces the tendency to maximal nonresponsiveness to clients and their well-being.

A second implicit consequence of this configuration is that control remains the major managerial function, with its assumption that employees in the trenches will engage in actions that are wrong or bad or inadequate unless their behavior conforms to the letter of the management-established policies and procedures, and that close monitoring is required. Unfortunately, many organizational rules (i.e., policies and procedures) were developed not based on the needs of clients but, rather, on the needs of the organization. For example, most paperwork was not designed to help front-line workers provide better service but, to control who is to receive what form of help for how long, to please other constituencies. Another problem with rules in mental health organizations is that they assume that clients are the same, or at least similar enough that a rule can be implemented uniformly, with rather uniform results. The worker trying to help a particular client knows how farcical this assumption is. The agendas for managers, workers, and clients are, therefore, widely discrepant. Managers seek to control and maintain adherence to the rule book, whereas workers seek to help individuals, who are unique. It is no wonder that management in so many mental health organizations is seen as irrelevant or as the major obstacle to quality service.

A third consequence of the typical organizational configuration is symbolic. Clients are rarely included in the chart. The power is at the top, and all others are subordinate. Subordinate means "inferior to or placed below another in rank, power, importance, etc.; subservient or submissive" *(Webster's New World Dictionary,* 1972). These concepts are abhorrent to the client-centered performance manager. The need for a new symbol, a new metaphor for the human service manager, is needed.

The Inverted Hierarchy: A New Management Metaphor

Mental health organizations that are producing superior rates of client outcomes seem to turn the typical organizational configuration upside-down in everyday practice (Rapp & Poertner, 1992). It is from this observation that the inverted hierarchy was created (Figure 8.2). This organizational configuration is a more ac-

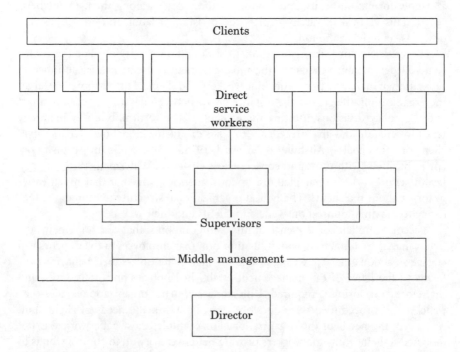

Figure 8.2 Inverted hierarchy

curate portrayal of a client-centered organization and has more fidelity with concepts underlying the client-centered performance model of management. First, at the pinnacle of the chart are the clients, and all organizational personnel are subservient to them. In fact, supervisors are subservient to front-line workers and the person who may be called the "boss" is subservient to supervisors and front-line workers.

The assumption central to the inverted hierarchy is that the principal function of management at any level is *not to control,* but *to help the next higher rung do their jobs more effectively. Subservient* then relates not only to power and authority but also to service. The service provided by management is to help others who want to do the best job possible to do their job better. How do managers help? There seem to be four major categories of organizational helping:

1. Clearly laying out the job to be done and the expectations of how it should be done (providing direction)
2. Providing the tools to get the job done
3. Removing obstacles and constraints to the desired performance
4. Creating a reward-based environment

Providing Direction

One way in which managers can help those who provide direct services is to lay out clearly the job to be done and the expectations of how it should be done. This guidance also includes providing clarity about how a particular employee's job fits into a larger context of program, agency, and society. The cluster of managerial strategies would include the development and use of an inspiring vision, a mission statement, and a well-crafted program design that provides a variety of direction-setting elements such as goals and objectives, target population, and a service plan.

The *service plan* itself describes where the help will be provided, what will be the natural flow of helping phases, what are the existing expectations of clients and workers, and how the emotional elements will be accommodated. It also prescribes the minimum behaviors required of key actors for the program to meet its goals.

If done with precision and tied to client outcomes, *job descriptions* are the most direct source of job prescription for the individual employee. Although direct service worker positions come to mind first, it is equally important to write supervisory and managerial job descriptions that are precise.

If "what gets measured gets done," the data that are collected by personnel and are reported also send a powerful message concerning what is important to the organization. The *selection and reporting of client outcomes* defines the priority domains of the work. The selection and reporting of those worker behaviors most influential in producing these outcomes establishes the most important behaviors. In this respect, the data help guide and direct behavior. Performance appraisal and interpersonal feedback similarly direct behavior and provide a set of tools for improving performance.

A powerful technique for directing behavior is the *modeling* of supervisors and managers. Does their behavior consistently embody the values of the organization?

Are they models of client-centeredness? This modeling helps guide others in how to make decisions and how to behave. There is no more destructive element in an organization's culture than supervisors and managers who pronounce one set of values or prescriptions and then behave in incompatible, inconsistent, or opposite ways.

The modeling of client-centeredness is particularly important. The following are but nine examples that are often within the control of managers:

1. Interact with clients in the hallway or waiting rooms; find opportunities to do so—have an open-door policy concerning clients.
2. Institutionalize a variety of client feedback mechanisms (e.g., client satisfaction surveys, focus groups, suggestion boxes) and respond to them.
3. Ensure client representation on the board of directors or advisory board.
4. Provide membership dues for staff and consumers so that they can join consumer organizations and advocacy groups.
5. Arrange for advocacy group representatives to regularly address staff meetings.
6. Donate honoraria to consumer organizations.
7. Talk about clients in every interaction; make them heroes.
8. Ensure that the manager's personal staff acts as an extension of that manager, in treating clients with the highest degree of courtesy, respect, and dignity.
9. Hire former clients.

Another opportunity for providing direction occurs in many of the myriad day-to-day interactions. The most obvious are those in which staff come to you for advice and suggestions. Others are more subtle. A worker frustrated by a client who has not followed through on a series of agreements will have a natural tendency to be angry with or to blame the client. While acknowledging the frustration, the manager can help the case manager stand back from the situation and think through it more creatively. For example, the case manager and client may be at different stages of change (action versus contemplation), the goal as written may not be the clients, or the person may be fearful or lacking confidence in taking steps toward the goal, etc.

Providing the Tools

With expectations clarified and a variety of mechanisms established to reinforce them, the tools required to meet the expectations must be provided. It is often the discrepancy between expectations and tools that causes job dissatisfaction and low levels of effectiveness-for example, setting ambitious goals for clients and workers and then requiring services on 50 clients at one time.

For the client-centered manager, there are two general strategies for facilitating employees in their meeting of expectations. First, the client centered performance manager seeks to place as many resources as possible in the trenches, where the help occurs. Overhead costs should be kept to the minimum, which usually means reducing the levels of managerial and staff positions. In many agencies, especially public bureaucracies, there are simply too many employees who do not provide service as their primary responsibility. Second, the client-centered performance manager should constantly be asking employees, "How can I help you with your job?" Furthermore, the employees responses should be written down, and the manager should find a way to implement their requests. An eminently worthwhile question that the manager could ask every day while driving home is, "What did I do today that made the jobs of my workers more effective or easier?" Tools can be categorized into three groups: (1) information, (2) structural supports, and (3) tangible resources.

Am I asking the staff to do something they do not know how to do? The answer is too often yes. Information as tools includes training, technical assistance and consultation, interpersonal feedback, and information system feedback, especially that concerning client outcomes.

Structural supports include reasonable case loads (i.e., 20 to 1 or fewer), and interagency agreements that detail the reciprocal responsibilities in behavioral language between agencies and organizations. Structural supports include the design of assessment and case-planning forms that help case managers do their jobs rather than to just meet documentation requirements. The forms included in this book were developed from this perspective. Volunteers, emergency transportation services, case manager assistants, and adequate clerical support can help case managers focus on the job they have to do.

Structural supports also include supportive policies and procedures. Organizations often develop policies and procedures in response to a perceived problem that no longer exists, or these policies and procedures are contradictory to expectations the same organization has for its workers. For example, the agency may expect workers to be available for crisis situations after hours but then places limits on the use of compensatory time. If the expectation is for an outreach mode of service delivery yet billable service hours do not include transportation time, major disincentives are created. The best source of identifying organizational anomalies is the workers themselves. If we *listen* to them, we will be able to identify the areas of change.

Tangible resources for the worker and client are important tools. Tangible resources for the worker can vary widely, depending on the agency and the particular job, so a few examples will have to do. A classic situation concerns the case manager who is expected to do work outside the agency. Resource supports would include cars, adequate travel reimbursement, liability insurance, a beverage holder and trash bag for the car, clipboards or laptop computers for recording in cars or parks, and either cellular phones or pagers. For many workers, easy-to-use resource guides, Rolodex files, adequate office supplies, and so on, would help them to do their jobs more effectively or efficiently.

Tangible resources for the client can vary widely also, but in many agencies, access to flexible funds for emergencies would be critical. These are monies not tied to bureaucratic controls (e.g., forms, permissions, meetings, and several layers of review) but almost immediately available for such things as rent deposits, food, clothing, registration fees for community activities, and so forth. It could mean *a lending closet,* where people who could not afford to buy could borrow items, such as vacuum cleaners, kitchen supplies, furniture, or even fishing poles.

Removing Obstacles and Constraints

The third category of managerial behaviors required by the inverted hierarchy is the constant and conscientious removal of barriers to performance. In a sense, the lack of any of the previously mentioned tools acts as an obstacle. For example, inadequate job descriptions detailing work expectations are an obstacle. Large caseloads are an obstacle. The major theme is "less is more": less paperwork, fewer meetings, fewer priorities, fewer permissions, fewer organizational levels, fewer excuses, less noise.

Reward-Based Environment

The fourth cluster of management behaviors composing the inverted hierarchy concerns creating a reward-based environment in which to work. Mental health practice provides an opportunity to touch others—to make a difference in people's lives. It provides rich opportunities for learning and collegiality. Work should be a source of satisfaction, esteem, achievement, and pride. Work should be enjoyable. Yet, for too many human service personnel, work is frustrating, depressing, punishing, and joyless. The agency environments are often oppressive, and management is often perceived to be part of the problem. Clients and employees *require* a reward-based environment, which contributes to each person feeling that he or she is important and valued.

Positively reinforced behavior slowly comes to occupy a larger and larger share of time and attention, and less desirable behavior begins to be dropped. Yet, most managers appear not to understand the power of this concept; the reward structure is inadequate in terms of the amount and the way in which it is implemented. The first rule of reinforcement is that the rewards need to be valued by the person being rewarded. Even though it is true that all persons have their own sets of job values and unique reinforcement menus, there are probably more similarities among people than differences. For example, most of us respond positively to written and verbal praise, and to formal recognition through awards. Based on the work of B. F. Skinner, Peters and Waterman (1982) observed that high-performing managers follow five additional rules in using positive reinforcement:

1. The reinforcement should be specific as to the behavior being rewarded.
2. The reinforcement should have immediacy-close time proximity between the behavior and the reward.
3. Small achievements (e.g., one client got a part-time job) warrant rewards (try to make everyone a winner).

4. The reinforcement should be unpredictable or intermittent (this happens naturally in large organizations because no manager can be aware of all behavior that warrants reward).
5. A fair amount of the reinforcement comes from top management (not just from your immediate supervisor).

What this portrays is an environment where people are receiving many rewards for many different behaviors at a variety of times from many different sources. This also suggests that those reward systems that are at set times (annual reviews or employee of the month) and are based on general criteria (made the greatest contribution to the agency) are less potent for meeting personal or organizational needs. The most prevalent obstacle to the creation of reward-based environments is the manager's belief that money, promotions, and other tangible rewards are the only or the most powerful rewards. The problem is that these rewards are limited, delayed, and often not under the manager's control. The evidence, however, is that the aforementioned rewards are as powerful as tangible rewards and are controlled by the manager. William Manchester, in describing his World War II experiences as a foot soldier, said, "A man wouldn't sell his life to you, but he will give it to you for a piece of colored ribbon. "Not only are they powerful, but they have a nice effect on the giver as well.

[The reader might find valuable Charles A. Rapp and John Poertner (1992), *Social Administration: A Client-Centered Approach* (New York: Longman), which offers a detailed description of the strategies and methods summarized in the previous section.]

The Case of Estelle Richman: Providing Tools and Removing Obstacles

Case management had been a lower level priority in this Ohio community mental health center for several years. Case managers were given little support and recognition. In early 1986, the executive director, Estelle Richman, identified case management as a number one priority and became committed to providing case management effectively.

Various stakeholders were first identified: the county mental health board, the agency's board of trustees, agency administrators, and case managers. Each group of stakeholders was seen as a team that needed to interact with another group of stakeholders or team. Ms. Richman acted as a facilitator between the county board of mental health and the agency board of trustees and between the agency board of trustees and the agency administrators. The case manager supervisor acted as a facilitator between the agency administrators and the case managers. Once stakeholders had been identified, the process of education began.

Educating the board of trustees was effective due to its simplicity and honesty. First, case management was added as an agenda item every month, as part of the director's report. Topics included: meaning of Community Support Program (CSP), importance of case management, the need for case management, evaluation based on outcome rather than productivity standards, and empowerment versus enablement. The result of this education process was the board's approval of a new organizational structure that created a case management unit separate from the outpatient department. The unit was staffed with a supervisor and 16 case managers.

Second, both the executive director and the case management supervisor took advantage of every opportunity to attend county and state conferences, workshops, or seminars on case management. Articles, books, and other materials on case management were collected, read, and discussed. Policies and procedures began to develop. Simultaneously with their self-education program, Ms. Richman and her program director began an energetic education program for the case managers. This training included teaching a model for effective case management and making workers feel like stakeholders with a voice in determining how the program would function. After a couple of months, these workers were able to contribute invaluable feedback.

The following items were presented by the case managers and, with Ms. Richman's influence, policies were successful adopted or changed to make the program more effective:

1. *The case managers expressed a need for an agency-owned vehicle for them to use if their own car was not available.* Ms. Richman requested that the finance committee of the board of trustees approve leasing a car. The committee learned that assertive outreach was the preferred mode of treatment and availability of an agency-owned vehicle would facilitate this. Further, statistics showed that case managers spent 50% of their direct service time in the field. The committee was impressed by the data and the commitment of "meeting the client on the client's turf" and recommended approval to the board. The leased car arrived two months after the request. The finance committee has continued its support by approving the leasing of additional vehicles.

2. *Punching a time clock acted as a barrier to case-management work.* The time clock had been placed in the agency by the board of trustees, and all staff were required to punch in except the highest level administrators. Data were presented to the personnel committee by the director, showing that case managers were frequently needed by clients prior to 9:00 A.M. and after 5:30 P.M. Each time they came in early or left late, special recordings needed to be done. Large accumulations of compensatory time developed. The paperwork flow through the personnel department tripled. The personnel director and Ms. Richman requested that case managers be permitted to work flexible hours. The personnel committee of the board enthusiastically endorsed flexible time and removal of the time clock for case managers. This was achieved in three months. The removal of the time clock for case

managers not only removed an obstacle to their work but also became a symbol of the organizational importance assigned to case management services, case managers, and their clients.

3. *Visual display pagers became a necessity, as case managers spent an increasing percentage of time out of the agency.* Pagers cost the agency $200 per pager plus air time. The fiscal director had not planned for them in his budget and was apprehensive as to their value. Ms. Richman's program director spent time explaining case management, aggressive outreach, and community resources. The budget director began to understand that case managers working with clients and collaterals in the community were more productive than when in the agency. All 16 case managers received their own pagers.

4. *Case managers frequently complained about required paperwork.* They noted that some forms were redundant and others appeared useless. All paperwork not relevant to the client was reviewed by the county mental health board and the agency quality assurance coordinator. All paperwork that could not be documented as necessary by a primary funding body was eliminated. If the only funding body requesting the document was the county mental health board, negotiations were held to eliminate the document. Required paperwork frequently is reviewed. An agency goal to maintain documentation time at less than 20% remains strong. Clerical workers have been retrained to help with non-clinical documentation and routine paperwork.

5. *Caseload size was an immediate problem as the agency sought to do effective case management.* It was apparent that caseload size had to be reduced. The board of trustees made the commitment to shift resources and to hire additional case managers to effect an overall caseload ratio of 43:1 from the original 75:1. With the identification of priority clients, 3 case managers have 10 to 12 clients, 10 have 35 clients, 2 have 60 to 80 clients, and 1 has 150 clients. (Clients on the 150-person caseload require only medication monitoring. Clients on the 60 to 80 caseloads are currently stabilized and working but have periodic needs for support. These caseloads are the next priority to be reduced to 35:1.)

6. *Many clients have a payee for their disability checks, which is frequently an outside agency with minimal understanding of the mental health system.* The program director and billing coordinator approached Ms. Richman and the fiscal director about the feasibility of the agency becoming representative payee for clients requesting this service. Case managers felt strongly that they would be better able to advocate for clients in the community if the agency was the payee. While very new territory, Ms. Richman and the fiscal director determined that clinically it would be worth the risk. Financially, the agency loses money on this project, but case management successes have far outweighed any fiscal negatives. Currently, the agency is the representative payee for 100 clients.

In conclusion, the agency has been successful in implementing a comprehensive case management system, and this is due to an executive director who was single-minded in her pursuit, who set the direction (e.g., specify client outcomes, job descriptions, designed a model of intervention), provided the tools to do the job (e.g., training, leased cars, pagers, quality supervision), and assertively removed obstacles to performance (e.g., paperwork, time clock, caseload size).

Group Supervision

The once-a-week, 60- to 90-minute meeting between a front-line practitioner (e.g., case manager) and supervisor continues to be the centerpiece of supervisory practice in mental health and the human services more broadly. Since the late 1930s, the principal focus of supervision has shifted from the case to the worker (Burns, 1958). The notion is that by supporting and educating the worker, clients will be better assisted. Unfortunately, the evidence suggests that worker perceptions of supervisory helpfulness are not associated with planning cases or developing practice skills (Shulman, Robinson, & Lucky, 1981), that worker satisfaction with supervision is uncorrelated with worker performance (Olmstead & Christensen, 1974), and that case discussions may be the smaller part of supervision (Kadushin, 1974; Munson, 1979). In fact, Shulman et al., (1981) found case consultation representing only 43% of supervision, and Kadushin (1974) found that case discussion-dominated supervision was practiced by less than 20% of the supervisors.

Teams Versus Individuals

There continues to be considerable controversy in the field between proponents of team versus individual models of case management service delivery. The use of interdisciplinary or otherwise configured teams has been a hallmark of Assertive Community Treatment (ACT) and has often been used as a point of demarcation with other models. The arguments for a team approach include: reduced burnout (Boyer, 1991), enhanced continuity of care (Bond, Witheridge, Dincin, & Wasner, 1991; Test, 1979), increased availability of someone who knows the client (Bachrach, 1992), more creative service planning (Test, 1979). The advantages of individual case managers that have been proffered include: a single point of accountability (Degen et al., 1990; Bond et al., 1991), more efficiency of case management time through less meetings (Degen, Cole, Tamayo, & Dzerovych, 1990; Bond et al., 1991), increased clarity of task assignment (Degen et al., 1990), and one person to develop a professionally intimate relationship (Bachrach, 1992).

The team versus individual dichotomy tends to camouflage the similarities between these two models. For example, since its inception, the strengths model has stipulated a group supervision/team approach for the purpose of creative case planning, problem solving, sharing knowledge of resources, and support to team members (Modrcin, Rapp, & Chamberlain, 1985; Rapp & Chamberlain, 1985; Rapp & Wintersteen, 1988; Modrcin et al., 1988). Responsibility for actual service delivery is lodged with an individual case manager although the supervisor, or even other team members, often act as backup. The distinction between models is further blurred when one considers that several of the reported sites for ACT research were dominated by single-case-manager service provision (Bond, McDonel, & Miller, 1991; Santos et al., 1993; Borland, McRae, & Lycan, 1989).

Both ACT and Strengths prescribe that an experienced mental health professional without preference for discipline act as team leader. PACT (the Wisconsin variant of ACT) recommends that a psychiatrist act as team leader.

The evidence of effectiveness is equivocal. McGrew, Bond, Dietzen, & Salyers, (1994) found that "shared caseloads" were significantly correlated with a reduction in days hospitalized. In the one study that sought to examine this variable, Bond et al., (1991) found less burnout and staff turnover for teams than individuals and reduced hospitalization as time went on although overall no differences were found on program dropouts and hospital admissions. Bond et al. (1995) hypothesized that lack of overall differences may be attributable to the control group also receiving intensive case management, although not using a team approach. In another study, Sands and Cnaan (1994) studied two team approaches where a difference was "corporate responsibility for cases" versus "individual caseloads with team backup. "There were no outcome differences although the authors commented that both groups of subjects were "faring relatively well." The criticalness of a team approach in service delivery also gets tempered by the favorable outcomes found in the strengths model research that uses individual case managers.

One report (Degen et al., 1990) from a project that used the team approach reflected:

> The team method of case management is time consuming and manpower intensive. Staff over-saturation with frequently changing information often results in long or incessant meetings, or communication attempts that are sometimes spurious. Staff have a tendency to "tune out" because of over-arousal or overflow. Additionally, another problem with team case management is accountability in a system where there is no primary case manager except for charting, with resultant ambiguity about who will do the follow-up after treatment planning. (p. 268)

In contrast, one study found that team case managers provided more hours of service than did single case managers (Bond, personal communication, 1995). Teams also may be impractical for rural areas (McGrew & Bond, 1995; Santos et al., 1993).

The conclusion is that both models prescribe a team approach under the leadership of a seasoned professional for the purposes of planning and support. They differ, however, in that service delivery is the responsibility of a single case manager in the Strengths model with supervisory backup but shared responsibility in ACT. The evidence suggests that team delivered services are no more successful in producing client outcomes than individually delivered services. But the consensus is that the team is needed for backup, support, and service-planning ideas. In fact, ACT experts surveyed by McGrew and Bond (1995) "rated shared caseloads for treatment planning as more important than shared caseloads for treatment provision" (p. 117).

Purpose of Group Supervision

Group supervision began for us 25 years ago with the very first strengths model case management demonstration project (Rapp & Chamberlain, 1985). The reason we chose this approach was for efficiency. We did not have the resources to adequately supervise four case managers using the traditional approach of supervision with its once-a-week 90-minute meeting with each manager. Within four months, it was clear that it was not only efficient but more effective. All the case managers delighted in the approach and could point to specific advantages. We have come to believe that group supervision is indispensable to effective case management practice. Group supervision is designed to accomplish three purposes: (1) support and affirmation; (2) ideas; and (3) learning.

Strengths model case management is a demanding job that requires high levels of skills and energy in the face of heretofore intractable situations to achieve ambitious ends. Furthermore, this work is often done alone. Group supervision is a mechanism for case managers to feel connected to a group sharing the same mission and challenges. Its aim is to affirm case managers: their efforts, their ingenuity, and their accomplishments. Group supervision is a good mechanism for exchanging feedback.

The central task of group supervision is the generation of promising ideas to more effectively work with clients. Even the most skilled strengths model case manager will run into a situation where "nothing seems to be working." It is one order of business to know the perspectives and methods of the strengths model, and another to apply these to the myriad idiosyncratic client situations. Brainstorming is central to group supervision. Groups are more likely to generate the "right" answer or richer alternatives than people acting alone or in dyads. This is a major advantage of group supervision over individual supervision.

The third purpose of group supervision is to facilitate learning. By placing individual client situations "under the microscope," case managers have an opportunity to learn things that would apply to similar situations. In fact, an important task of the supervisor is to help the team generalize from idiosyncratic client situations to other client situations. Group supervision provides information on community resource alternatives that could be useful for other clients.

What Is Group Supervision?

The inverted hierarchy framework avers that the central purpose of supervision is to help case managers do their jobs on behalf of clients in an effective, efficient, and satisfying way. Group supervision has been found to be a principle mechanism for achieving these supervisory purposes.

In its most frequent form, group supervision involves a unit or team of case managers (usually four) and their supervisor. At times, specialists (e.g., medical personnel, vocational staff, substance abuse experts) participate. Occasionally, family members or key actors (e.g., friend, minister, employer) may be invited. The group meetings vary in length and frequency. The recommended and most frequent scheduling is once a week for two hours.

During this two-hour period, two to four difficult consumer situations are intensely discussed. The selection of situations is usually delegated to case managers with perhaps consultation by the supervisor. The selection is based on consumer situations on which the case manager desires new ideas. Typically, these are clients who have been unable to achieve their goals. Other situations particularly amenable to group supervision are:

1. Lack of progress in engaging with a person or developing a relationship
2. Situations where case managers are having difficulty identifying client strengths or developing personal plans
3. Difficulties with particular key actors in gaining access or accommodation
4. Client goals where identification of community resources has been lacking or where the "perfect niche" has not been found

Crisis situations are rarely appropriate for group supervision; instead, the case manager should consult directly with the supervisor or specialist at the time of the crisis.

Each discussion of a client situation begins with the distribution of the client's strengths assessment and most recent personal plan(s) and a presentation of the particular situation by the case manager. This presentation should include:

1. A statement of the difficulty or problem
2. A statement of what the case manager would like to see instead (desired state) and how the group can help
3. A complete list of strategies and efforts already tried to achieve the desired state

This presentation is then followed by questions from the group and brainstorming solutions or alternative. Statements of empathy and support are often exchanged. Minimum standards for brainstorming usually include that at least three potential alternatives be generated. Each discussion of a client situation closes with the case manager repeating the alternatives and perhaps indicating the one believed to be most promising. The case manager should also tell the group what the next discrete step is (e.g., consult with client on Thursday; phone Ms. Harris at the Garden of Eden nursery; write on paper the information needed to employ a two-sided argument with the landlord). Each client situation discussion usually lasts between 25 and 40 minutes.

Group supervision also includes each case manager sharing one or more achievements from the past week, some of which could be derived from past group supervision brainstorming. This kind of "celebration" is found to be uplifting and energizing for case managers. Figure 8.3 shows the eight-step group supervision process.

FIGURE 8.3 Group Supervision Process

Step One: Facilitator starts the meeting by asking for 2–3 ideas that came out of the previous group supervision that have been useful. May also invite other client achievements.

Step Two: Presenting staff must bring a copy of the strengths assessment for EVERYONE in the meeting.

Step Three: Presenting staff clearly says what type of feedback they are looking for from the team (e.g., how can I better engage with this person/family; how can I help the person reach a particular goal; what community resources might be available for this particular goal, etc.)

Step Four: Presenting staff gives a brief overview of why they are presenting this particular situation and what has been tried that did _not_ work.

Step Five: Teams ask questions of the presenting staff person that further clarifies what is on the strengths assessment. (1) Let your questions start from material on the strengths assessment, not in your head. (2) Keep your questions focused on the type of feedback the staff person is requesting. (3) NO ADVICE or suggestions can be given at this stage, only curiosity. (4) Everyone should be writing on their copy of the strengths assessment.

Step Six: Team brainstorms a list of ideas to help the presenting staff—the more creative the ideas the better. Facilitator should keep the process moving quickly but help staff get as specific as possible (e.g., if "garden club" is a suggestion, ask quickly if anyone on the team knows of one). The presenting staff must write down EVERY IDEA on paper that is generated from the team, and the presenting staff CANNOT SPEAK during this part of the session.

Step Seven: Presenting staff asks any clarifying questions on the ideas generated from the team (i.e., "you mentioned this resource, do you know of a good contact there?" or "Can you tell me more about _____?")

Step Eight: Staff identifies the top 3 ideas that they think are the most helpful. Ideally, the case manager will be sharing the entire list with the client and together deciding which ideas to follow-up on.

The Methods of Group Supervision

Logistics group supervision is essential to competent strengths model case management. As such, the time set aside for it needs to be protected.

The session should start on time. Interruptions and distractions should be avoided whether from other staff entering the room, telephone calls, or client demands. If interruptions cannot be totally eliminated, the *specific* situations warranting interruptions need to be written and all staff and perhaps clients notified.

The setting for the group supervision should be large enough for the members to arrange themselves comfortably in a circle. Some teams benefit from having a chalk board or flip chart present. Even though the location is most often a room within the case-management agency, some group supervisions have occurred in a church or other community facilities or in the supervisor's home. One case-management team had their weekly group supervision in a gazebo located in a cemetery across from the mental health center. The supervisor said that it was quiet, there were no interruptions, it was convenient, and it modeled an outreach mode of service delivery.

The selection of the situations to be presented and the order should be established before the group supervision or within the first few minutes of beginning.

The case manager should have copies of the client's strengths assessment and recent personal plan(s) sufficient for each person in the group. Group supervision is about clients and the work with them. Discussion of policies, new procedures, or other agency topics should be rigorously avoided unless they directly pertain to the consumer situation under discussion. These topics need to be transmitted and often discussed but this should occur at some other opportunity.

Affirmation and Support   Group supervision is to be an uplifting experience, enjoyable if not fun. Supervisors and case managers should laugh. Energy that case managers expend on behalf of clients (whether they succeed or not), creative or particularly skillful methods that were employed (whether they succeeded or not), and specific achievements (including small ones) should be recognized if not celebrated. When group supervision is really working, the exchange of "pats on the back" come from all team members, not just the supervisor.

The ambiance of group supervision should be characterized as positive and optimistic. This does not mean that frustrations are not permitted or acknowledged. They surely must be. But group supervision needs to help a particular case manager get beyond that by reminding the person of how far the client has come, by recognizing the efforts made to date, by helping the case manager "see the forest through the trees" and regaining a focus on client achievement, and by generating alternative ideas and strategies.

Ideas   There are certain conditions that facilitate creativity and idea generation, and obstacles. One facilitating condition is for everyone to be clear on the desired outcome. This is why the case manager is required to tell the group what the desired state would be and how the group can be helpful. At times, this requires the case manager to do some thinking ahead of time. Its often easier to say "Joe needs to stop swearing in the cafe" than specifying what Joe should be doing. Like work with clients, setting goals as the presence of something rather than absence is more conducive to achievement. At times, a case manager may have difficulty doing this. In these situations, the case manager should state this and instruct the group that this is what he or she wants help with.

Another facilitating condition is for members to have the necessary information. Over the last 25 years, we have found three pieces of information to be critical. First, a clear statement of the dilemma or problem and why it is a problem for the client and others. Second, information on the client's strengths and the client goals, efforts, and achievements reflected in the personal plans. What the client wants in the particular situation is often forgotten and is critical to generating ideas and selecting the ones to try. This is not always obvious. For example, the person who loudly swears in the cafe and therefore will not be permitted to return may want to continue eating lunch at the cafe or wants to talk to someone while eating. Third, all the strategies already tried by the case manager with some level of detail. This last set of information is important to reduce or eliminate some of the "yeah-but I already tried that." "Yeah-buts" waste time and place a pall over brainstorming. Other information, specific to the situation being examined, can be gathered through questioning.

One particularly productive source of questions is the strengths-model behaviors included at the end of chapters 4 through 7 or the fidelity guide presented later in this chapter. Often even the most skilled strengths-model case manager has not followed all the methods specified in the model (e.g., goals are not broken down enough; strategies of interpersonal influence have not been used or have been done inadequately; goals and steps are established that do not employ client strengths). Reviewing the fidelity items may prompt a series of questions that may later produce promising ideas.

Once the desired state has been precisely described and relevant information shared, only then does idea generation commence. The two stages of information gathering and idea generation should be kept separate when possible, otherwise time will be wasted prematurely generating ideas just to have them discounted because all the information was not taken into account.

The brainstorming phase of client situation discussions should be characterized by the free flow of ideas. Evaluation of the ideas should be left to the next phase. The aim is to generate as many different ideas by as many people as possible, not to evaluate or select the best. Often the most "crazy" idea, if allowed to be shared, can provoke a similar but perhaps more feasible idea. Some teams even have an award as in the following example:

> A case manager was having difficulty helping a person keep an apartment because they always said their apartment was covered in roaches. Even after several moves to apartments that seemed to be "roach-free," the person would continue to complain of seeing roaches everywhere and would leave their apartment. The case manager brought this situation looking for ideas, since she had no idea of where to go next and was frustrated. After several minutes of brainstorming, one person on the team offered a very nontraditional idea. She stated that she heard that geckos kept roaches away. The case manager took this idea to the person she was working with and she wanted to try this in her next apartment. In fact, she wanted to get two geckos. We're still not sure if there is any truth to geckos keeping roaches away, but in this woman's mind it was working and never complained of roaches again. We started giving out "The Gecko Award" (a rubber gecko mounted on a piece of wood) to any team member who came up with a "wild and extremely nontraditional" idea that actually ended up working.

If brainstorming is to flourish, evaluation and selection of ideas need to be kept separate from idea generation.

The case manager is responsible for recording all the ideas generated. The use of a flip chart is often helpful because it allows everyone to keep track of ideas already generated. Brainstorming continues until the group has exhausted its ideas and the case manager has at least three promising or "reasonable" ideas to try. The evaluation and selection of ideas are the case manager's and clients' responsibility although the group surely can comment and suggest. Options that require the least change by the client and resource, *if they are attractive to the client,* should be given extra consideration because they often have the most probability of both short- and long-term success (see the section on the perfect niche).

The discussion of a particular client situation concludes by the case manager identifying the "best" ideas and specifying the first (next) discrete step they will take.

Learning   The group supervision format, with its difficult client-situation focus and group involvement, enhances professional learning beyond that allowed by in- dividual form of supervision. Learning can be further enhanced by the supervisor (or others) helping the group to generalize from the discussion of specific clients. The supervisor would point out similarities with other client situations or strate- gies used successfully by other case managers.

Learning also occurs in terms of community resources. Except in the smallest of communities, will any case manager be fully apprised of all the resources avail- able? Often, a resource is identified in group supervision that is eventually rejected for that particular client situation but gets used for another client.

The Role of the Group Supervision Facilitator   The person who facilitates group su- pervision must be focused and able to stay on task. For many teams, the supervi- sor has the role of facilitating group supervision, but some teams decide to rotate responsibilities for facilitating group supervision discussions. It takes some disci- pline to facilitate quality group supervision, because for most people the group su- pervision process presented here is a departure from traditional formats. One su- pervisor stated that a facilitator has to be "a little obnoxious" to keep the various parts of the group supervision process separated and maximized to their fullest po- tential. While overseeing implementation of a high fidelity strengths model case management team in Kansas, it took almost two months of weekly group super- vision, with copies of the process (see Figure 8.3) in front of each person before it finally became part of their regular routine. Without a facilitator helping maintain the discipline required, it will be easy for the team to revert to old ways of doing things.

The Power of Group Supervision   Group supervision is clients, clients, clients. Nothing else should be allowed to intrude. Rather than "talk about" cases, the team works together generating specific alternatives to be implemented. The overall ef- fect is one of empowerment, not continued frustration. The alternatives may not work, but the team will learn from it and other alternatives will be produced.

The advantages of group supervision include the following twelve benefits:

1. More ideas regarding creative alternatives in working with challenging circumstances will be generated.
2. Ethnic and cultural diversity present in the group may help in understanding consumer behavior from a cultural perspective.
3. Support and affirmation from colleagues who understand how challenging, frustrating, and disappointing the work can be put forth.

4. Having others with whom you can share successful helping efforts and consumer success stories will add value.
5. This method of supervision can help with the "can't see the forest for the trees" phenomenon. One may get a different perspective from a colleague who is not as intimately involved with the consumer.
6. When circumstances suggest difficult treatment decisions (e.g., petitioning for involuntary commitment), case managers may feel a sense of sharing and consensus; in effect, the decision becomes a team decision rather than an individual one.
7. The method may be more efficient in terms of time allotted to supervision and communicating information and ideas to each case manager.
8. The entire team becomes familiar with consumers, and on-call crisis coverage may be shared and individualized response delivered.
9. Case managers may gain support in the face of opposition from other providers or family regarding treatment decisions.
10. Team may enjoy sessions and have fun while helping each other.
11. There may be generalized learning-ideas or resources discussed for one consumer may have relevance for others.
12. Case managers may feel a sense of respite—a time away from the telephone calls, consumer requests, other demands on their time.

At the end of this chapter are two tools that have been developed to help guide and evaluate group supervision. The first one, "Case Managers Group Supervision Feedback," was designed for case managers to evaluate the sessions and provide feedback to the supervisors and other case managers. The second, "Supervisor's Group Supervision Monitor" allows the supervisor to evaluate the session and his or her performance. Teams are urged to use these as a basis for exchanging feedback and for fulfilling group supervision's promise of increased efficiency, satisfaction, and effectiveness.

Field Mentoring and Supervision   Another indispensable component of helpful supervision is that which occurs while case managers are actually doing their work in the field. The supervisor accompanies the case manager on visits with people or meeting with particular community resources. The supervisor can observe the case manager and provide feedback on their skills in assessing strengths, formulating goals, and building relationships. The supervisor could model strengths-based methods in real life situations or provide job-coaching. Too often, supervisors are unaware of exactly how case managers present themselves to others. This is a great opportunity for the supervisor to see the strengths of the case managers in action (use this information for rewarding and celebrating) as well as areas where a person struggles.

This kind of field mentoring is very powerful. In the national Evidence-Based Practice Implementation Project (Drake, Goldman, Leff, Lehman, et al. 2001), several sites had dramatic increases in fidelity after such efforts were made. There is nothing more difficult than taking skills taught in formal training and applying them in real practice. It is one of the reasons why the results of formal training on actual practice is so limited (Grimshaw et al., 2001). The supervisor acts as the helpful translator for such skills.

Many supervisors initially feel uncomfortable doing field mentoring because they think their staff will perceive it as micromanaging. It is often threatening to have your skills be on display. If approached properly, we have found that most staff find field mentoring to be helpful and instructive.

Employment staff at a mental health center involved in the implementation of supported employment had been struggling with developing their skills in the area of job development. In fact, many of the staff had avoided going out to contact employers because of their fears and lack of skills. The staff involved in the project had been through training in job development and had some time to practice and role play skills in training and team meetings. The employment staff's supervisor began to go out with her staff to observe how they were doing job development. The supervisor soon realized that her staff did not have the skills or the confidence to adequately engage and work with employers in order to help people obtain employment. The supervisor aggressively set a goal to spend 40% of her time for three months going out with her staff with the purpose to model skills, give feedback on skills, and build confidence. Six months later, one of the employment staff talked about the experience.

> After our training in job development, our supervisor set the expectation that we should be doing job development and set a certain number of contacts that we should be having with employers each month. I didn't really do it. I didn't like to do job development and did not feel comfortable doing it. I wasn't even sure about how to do it so I wasn't doing much. Later, my supervisor said she wanted to help us be more effective with our job development and would be going out regularly with us to talk with employers. At first, I was really upset and did not want to do it. After a while, thought, I realized that I was feeling more comfortable with talking with employers and that my supervisor was really helping me do it better. I really liked it when I started getting clients jobs through my contact with employers. I realize now how helpful it was and how much better I am at job development.

Prior to a field mentoring session, the supervisor and case manager should define the purpose of the session. Is it for the supervisor to model certain skills? Is it to receive feedback on the case manager's skills? For example, "I'm really having difficulty staying purposeful with Joe. Could you give me some feedback on what I could do differently . . ." or "I would like for you to get a better picture of what is going on with Nancy so I can get more ideas during group supervision.. The purpose could be what the supervisor would like to assess (i.e., During our last training we talked about use of motivational interviewing techniques when discussing employment with people, I'd like to see how you are able to use some of these techniques in your practice).

It is important that the goals of field mentoring are clear to keep it purposeful rather than being just a monitoring session. Being clear on the purpose of a particular field mentoring session sets the stage for feedback following the session. The following is a suggested format for doing feedback following field mentoring:

1. Restate the purpose of the particular field mentoring session (i.e., to give you feedback on how you could be more purposeful with Joe).
2. Point out specific strengths of the case manager observed during field mentoring.
3. Point out specific words, behaviors, or actions that might have been obstacles to the case manager reaching his or her desired outcomes.
4. Make a plan for follow-up.

In order to give a case manager good feedback following the session, it is important that the supervisor be an active observer during field mentoring and restrain from trying to do case manager themselves (unless the purpose of the field mentoring session was for the supervisor to demonstrate a particular skill). This does not mean that the supervisor does not interact in the session (i.e., distant observer), but rather is consciously allowing the case manager to do their work so as to give them the feedback requested. Remember, the purpose of field mentoring is to help the case manager improve their skills not to demonstrate how great the supervisor is. Too often supervisors are unaware of exactly how case managers present themselves to others. This is a great opportunity for the supervisor to see the strengths of the case managers in action (use this information for rewarding and celebrating) as well as areas where a person struggles.

Other Conditions for Effectiveness   Adapting the perspectives and methods of the inverted hierarchy and using group supervision as an integrating centerpiece of the framework will increase consumer outcomes and the job satisfaction of case managers. The research on case management with people with psychiatric disabilities suggests several other necessary features to create the conditions for effectiveness. The following material is based on the outcome research on the Assertive Community Treatment (ACT) and strengths model of case management, the two models with evidence of effectiveness.

Staffing

Both ACT and Strengths use teams of "generalists" with consultation by medical professionals and other experts as needed. The strengths model sees B.A.-level case managers as adequate. In fact, in three strengths model studies, the case managers were undergraduate or graduate students in social work. The PACT model (Wisconsin variant of ACT) prescribes interdisciplinary teams including psychiatrists (recommended team leader), nurses, and social workers and could include vocational counselors, substance abuse counselors, and other professionals and paraprofessionals.

ACT research has found that only the degree of nurse participation on the team was correlated with client outcomes (McGrew et al., 1994). The study of ACT experts found "relatively low interjudge agreement for the team subscale with wide variance in size, make-up, and operation" (McGrew & Bond, 1995).

Reports of consumers as case managers or as case manager extenders seem promising (Solomon & Draine, 1994, 1995, 2001; Porter & Sherman, 1988). Both Solomon and Draine (1994) and Kisthardt (1993) found consumers to value the interpersonal characteristics (e.g., emotional engagement, personal support) as more important than credentials or consumer/nonconsumer status.

The evidence is that case managers can be selected from a wide pool of people (e.g., professionals, B.A.-level generalists, students, consumers) but need high-quality supervision (see previous section) from a seasoned professional, and easy access to medical personnel and other experts. The research in supported employment (Bond, 1998) and dual diagnosis treatment (Drake, Mercer-McFadden, Muesser, McHugo, & Bond, 1998) strongly suggests that a specialist of each should be assigned to each case management team or at least be available. Considerable preservice and in-service training and technical assistance has been recommended (Bond, 1991; Sullivan & Rapp, 1991; Modrcin et al., 1988). A benefit of this staffing configuration is that it would be less expensive than requiring case managers to be fully credentialed.

Caseload Size and Frequency of Contact

The expectations of case managers concerning the direct provision of services, the outreach mode of service delivery, involvement with client crises, highly individualized service, the breadth of life domains to be attended to, and the work with naturally occurring community resources inevitably requires a rather high staff-to-client ratio. High staff-to-client ratios received virtually unanimous agreement of ACT experts (McGrew & Bond, 1995). The ACT programs recommended 1:10 ratio (Test, 1992; Witheridge, 1991). The strengths model suggests caseload sizes between 1 to 12 (Rapp & Wintersteen, 1988) and 1 to 20 (Macias et al., 1994). Both approaches suggest tailoring caseload size to the "needs presented by clients and the outcomes or benefits sought by the intervention" (Witheridge, 1991, pp. 52-53). For example, a ratio of 20:1 seems effective when it is composed of people normally distributed in terms of severity (Macias et al., 1994) and 30:1 if composed of people who are stable and more independent (Salyers et al., 1998). the comparison site had high caseloads (typically between 40:1 and 100:1). In two studies where the comparison group to the ACT team had lower caseloads (Bond, Pensec, et al., 1991; Sands & Cnaan, 1994), there were no significant differences in hospitalization outcomes.

Although not the only reason, small caseload sizes are prescribed to allow increased intensity of case manager contact with the client. King, Le Bas, and Spooner (2000) found that caseload size was inversely associated with personal efficacy. With higher caseloads, a case manager's efficacy in areas of knowledge of people's home environment, acute response, linkage to community resources, and advocacy was greatly reduced. Rife, Greenlee, Miller, and Feichter (1991) found that "the strongest predictor of client [homeless mentally ill] engagement in case management was frequency of case management contacts. Clients who received more frequent monitoring were more likely to remain engaged in case management services and not to return to a homeless condition" (p 65). Similarly, Quinlivan et al. (1995) found a strong inverse association between frequency of contact and inpatient use of health care resources. Another study (Dietzen & Bond, 1993) found that "the four [ACT] programs with moderate or substantial impact in reducing hospital days also had moderate to high levels of service intensity, together averaging 11 contacts per client per month. The three programs that had minimal impact on hospital use had moderate to low service intensities, together averaging 6.3 contacts per client per month" (p. 841). Others (McGrew et al., 1994) found that number of contacts, not number of hours of contact, were significantly related to hospital outcomes. This study also found a significant relationship between frequency of telephone contacts and contacts with collaterals and hospital outcomes.

Three conclusions seem warranted:

1. Frequency of case manager-client contact rather than hours of contact makes a difference; the use of telephone may be a helpful supplement, not a replacement.
2. Frequency of contact and hospital outcomes will never be truly linear because those who are most ill will often receive the most contact but may also have higher rates of hospitalization (even if reduced compared with similar control subjects).
3. The quality of the contact, not just frequency, may be a mitigating factor. For example, small caseloads employing ineffective methods or skill deficit case managers would probably be ineffective. The study by Hornstra et al. (1993) is illustrative. A brokerage model intervention with small caseloads and significantly more caseworker contact produced no client-outcomes differences compared with the control group.

Length of Service

Each of the models prescribes time-unlimited case management services. Mental illness are often lifelong with cyclical exacerbation of symptoms. Because of their serious and ongoing difficulties, the members of this group are likely to need lifelong or very long-term access to a broad range of services, delivered in a highly personalized fashion, to maintain their previous gains and make further progress (Ridgeway & Zipple, 1990; Talbott, 1988). In the study of ACT experts (McGrew & Bond, 1995), "time-limited services for some clients, was rated very low (3.7), reflecting the experts' opinions that short-term services were contrary to the ACT model" (p. 118).

The evidence suggests that short-term case management can produce short-term client outcomes in hospitalization prevention, acquiring stable housing, and adequate money management (Bond, 1991). Impressive results have been attained in the strengths model for as little as six months' worth of case management. However, other research strongly suggests that although immediate gains can be made, without long-term services client gains can evaporate and others do not have time to occur (Goering, Wasylenki, Farkas, Lancee, & Ballantyne, 1988; McGrew et al., 1994; Strauss, Hafey, Lieberman, & Harding, 1985). The seminal work by Stein and Test (1980) showed that when services were removed, many clients relapsed or showed loss of gain.

With each of these studies, case management was withdrawn abruptly with little attention given to the transfer process and only brief follow-up periods after transfer. In contrast, Salyers et al. (1998) studied the Harbinger Step-Down program for recipients of ACT services. This effort was designed to preserve continuity of care through a selective and orderly transfer process:

1. Individualized transfer of persons
2. Single agency responsible
3. Continuity of staffing
4. Continuity of basic service model
5. Gradual transfer
6. Communication between teams

Persons with psychiatric disabilities moved to a three-person team with a consumer-staff ratio of 30:1 where previously the ACT team had seven members each with an 8:1 ratio. The new team did not have daily meetings and were not available on an around-the-clock basis like the ACT team. Intensity of service was reduced by one third. The results found that more stable persons actually continued to improve.

The conclusion is that case-management services should be of indefinite duration. Given the importance of continuity of relationship and service, the case manager or team should be constant, not requiring clients to switch to different case managers as needs change.

The preference of these models is to have the ultimate *service* responsibility for the clients assigned to the case managers and their team rather than sharing responsibility with other programs or agencies. The PACT and Strengths programs were started as semiautonomous alternatives to the then current service systems. As Turner and Shifren (1979) argued: Case management is the "integrative mechanism at the client level" (p. 9). Fragmented responsibility is generally the rule and the polar opposite of integration. This does not mean that referrals to other programs do not occur (although the strengths model prioritizes nonprogrammatic resources), but that authority is not delegated. As Bond (1991) concluded: "Outreach teams are likely to have less impact if they are viewed as components of a mental health system than if they have functional autonomy" (p. 77).

24-Hour Availability

Each model argues that case managers should be accessible 24 hours a day, 7 days a week. One of the reasons for team approaches is to spread this responsibility across team members. The ACT experts, however, reached relatively low levels of agreement on this element whereas the early Wisconsin efforts and some subsequent ACT programs adhere to this rigidly. Some ACT programs run only from nine to five. Even with great variation in the dimension across studies, positive outcomes have been reported regardless of the structure employed; therefore this specific components of service seems optional.

What is not optional is that clients need access to crisis and emergency services 24 hours a day, 7 days a week. The effectiveness of crisis services is enhanced by access to staff who have familiarity and a relationship with the client (Carlson, Gowdy, and Rapp, 1998). This would necessarily include the case manager, the team leader or supervisor, the team members, or in some (probably rural areas) the crisis staff themselves.

Fidelity of Strengths Model Implementation

Fidelity is the degree to which implementation of the strengths model reflects the actual ideas and methods of the model. Like with a stereo system where fidelity means how "true" is the sound to the actual recording. In both instances, *high* fidelity means the least amount of distortion.

The last decade has witnessed considerable progress in the measurement of fidelity. Fidelity measures are tools to assess the adequacy of implementation of specific program models (Bond, Evans, Salyer, et al, 2000). Fidelity measures have been developed for supported employment, assertive community treatment, integrated dual diagnosis treatment, illness management and recovery, and family psychoeducation (Drake, Merrens, & Lynde, 2005). In each case, the fidelity items were based on well-defined models with practice manuals. Each requires the use of multiple sources of information: chart reviews, observation of practice and team meetings, and interviews with consumers, family members, practitioners, and supervisors.

The Strengths Case Management Fidelity Scale, (SCMFS) has 12 items with seven pertaining to structural characteristics (e.g. caseload size, use of group supervision) and five items relating to practitioner behavior (e.g. use of strengths assessment, hope-inducing interactions). Each item is rated on a 1 to 5 scale after gathering information from multiple sources. The scale can be found in Appendix V. As was reported in chapter 3, there is beginning evidence that higher fidelity to the model scores are associated with higher rates of client outcomes.

The SCMFS can be used in several ways. First and foremost is as a quality assurance tool whereby areas of implementation strength and weakness can be identified and corrective action plans developed. Periodic administrations (i.e., 6 months to a year) would help prevent "slippage" between the strengths model and actual implementation. Second, the SCMFS can inform program leaders of the core set of structures and practices required by the model and thereby decide whether they are in the position to embark on implementation. Third, state mental health authorities can use the SCMFS for state-level monitoring.

The skillful use of strengths assessment and personal plans are cornerstones of the strengths model. The skills used by a case managers in working with consumers around these documents can best be assessed through field supervision (see earlier section). Some of the skills, however, are obvious by reviewing the documents themselves. Appendix IV contains two supervisory tools to guide these reviews. We recommended that supervisors devote an hour a week to reviewing strengths assessments and personal plans, and whatever time is necessary to provide feedback and instruction to their staff.

There is initial evidence that as fidelity of strengths model implementation improves, so do client outcomes. Between 1996 and 2000, Rick Goscha was director of program serving people with psychiatric disabilities who experienced prolonged homelessness. After he took over as director, the program increasingly moved toward full fidelity of strengths-model practice. During this time frame, there was an 86% increase in the number of individuals living independently (73% of whom were able to retain their housing for at least one year), a 433% increase in the numbers of individuals who were competitively employed, and an 87% decrease in the numbers of individuals who experienced psychiatric hospitalization.

Jeff Krolick, clinical director of Options for Southern Oregon in Grants Pass, Oregon began converting his program to a high fidelity strengths model program in 2002. Within six months, they had a 70% reduction in psychiatric hospitalization bed days. Prior to that they had never had anyone at their program involved in postsecondary education and within six months had six people attending college.

In 2004, the University of Kansas School of Social Welfare began a project at one of the mental health centers in Kansas that sought to measure the impact of high strengths-model case-management implementation with client outcomes. The following table (Table 8.1) shows the change in fidelity scores at Pawnee Mental Health Center in Manhattan, Kansas and the accompanying change in client outcomes.

In the above example, there was a 76% increase in fidelity over a 12-month period. More importantly, there was a 125% increase in the numbers of individuals who were competitively employed and hospitalizations decreased by 67%.

Summary of Structural Features

1. Team structure should be implemented for the purpose of creative case planning, problem solving, sharing knowledge of resources and support to team members.
2. Team leaders/supervisors should be experienced mental health professionals.

TABLE 8.1 Fidelity and Outcomes: Pawnee Mental Health Center

Outcome Area	Baseline	6-Months	12-Months
Fidelity score	25	38	44
Employment	8%	15%	18%
Hospitalizations	24%	10%	8%
Education	1%	1%	1%
Independent living	95%	96%	96%

3. Case managers can be B.A.-level workers but need access to specialists; involvement of nurses seems particularly important.
4. Caseload sizes can vary based on client severity, geography, and other factors but should not exceed 20:1 unless the entire caseload is composed of clients highly positioned in their recovery. The average across-program clients should probably be 12 to 1 to 15 to 1.
5. Efforts should be made to enhance the continuity of relationship between the client and case manager.
6. Clients need 24-hour, 7-days-a-week access to crisis and emergency services. That service should require access to staff who have familiarity and a relationship with the client (can be and perhaps should be the case manager).
7. Preservice, inservice, and technical assistance should be available.
8. Length of case management service should be indeterminate and expected to be ongoing (although intensity at any point in time would vary).
9. Case managers should have ultimate responsibility for client services (with the exception of medication). They retain authority even in referral situations.

Case Managers
Group Supervision Feedback

Your group supervision has been specifically designed as a major source of help in your work with clients and as a means of providing mutual support. The items below represent the kinds of help and support you can and should expect from your supervisor and each other. After it is completed, it provides a snapshot for you and your supervisor as to how well these purposes are being met. Please complete this at the end of the supervisory session and return it to your supervisor.

1. Did you receive help in the following areas:
   a. Using the strengths assessment to identify goals, tasks or strategies.

      YES   NO
   b. Identifying nonmental health resources for my client(s).

      YES   NO
   c. Identifying the activities I am doing for or with my client(s) that could/should be done by someone in the community or by themselves.   YES   NO
   d. Breaking client goals into smaller tasks.   YES   NO
   e. Translating "problems" into "goals"   YES   NO
   f. Identifying patterns and similarities between cases to enhance learning.   YES   NO
   g. Identifying what the client wants   YES   NO
   h. Engaging clients and developing a relationship   YES   NO
   i. Identifying client strengths   YES   NO

2. Did the discussion on your case close with at least three options in which you identified for the group your next tasks?
3. Was the supervision atmosphere optimistic and positive (i.e., focused on what can be done rather than what cannot be done)?
4. What did you receive positive feedback for?
5. What successes were identified in your work?
6. Were any of your conscientious efforts which failed acknowledged?
7. Did you laugh during the session?

Any Other Comments or Feedback

Supervisor's Group Supervision Monitor

Group supervision is a critical element in supervisory practice and indispensable to a high-performing case-management program. The following items warrant careful monitoring. It is divided into two sections: I. Group Interaction; II. Client Situation Discussion. Supervisors can use this instrument a prompt to themselves before and during group supervision and as a self-evaluation tool after the section.

I. Group Interaction
1. Did the session start on time?   YES   NO
2. Is the seating arrangement circular (everyone can see everyone else) and comfortable?   YES   NO
3. Was the discussion among all the participants or was it predominantly directed toward the supervisor?   YES   NO
4. Did the supervisor laugh during the session?   YES   NO
5. During the session, did the case managers laugh?   YES   NO
6. Was the supervision atmosphere optimistic and positive (i.e., focused on what can be done rather than what cannot be done)?   YES   NO
7. What interruptions occurred during the supervisory session?
8. Which client situations were reviewed?
9. Which case manager dominated (if any)?
10. Who is generating alternatives?
11. Who made excuses to shoot down a potential resource or idea?
12. What conscientious efforts which failed were celebrated?
13. Who left group supervision feeling energized?

II. Client Work
1. For each client situation, were at least three alternative solutions or strategies generated?   YES   NO
2. Did each client situation discussion end with a specific plan for case manager action or strategy?   YES   NO

3. Did each client situation discussion close with the case manager identifying the specific tasks to be done?   YES   NO

4. If any case manager was frustrated with a client or others, did the supervisor help him/her make more realistic expectations and/or break tasks into smaller steps?   YES   NO

5. Who used the strengths assessment to identify goals, tasks or strategies?

6. For each client situation discussed, what natural resources and helpers in the community were identified?

7. For each client situation discussed, what strategies for involving natural helpers were generated?

8. If words like "problems" and "deficits"were used rather than "interests," "strengths," and "goals," how did the supervisor reframe them?

9. What patterns and similarities between client situations were identified to enhance learning?

10. What successes did group members celebrate?

11. Who received positive feedback for
Use of client strengths?
Use of natural helpers?
Specific client achievements and goal attainment?

12. Did the group identifying policies within the agency or within other agencies or programs which indicate supervisory advocacy?

13. Any other observations?

CHAPTER NINE

Strengths Model Epilogue: Commonly Asked Questions (Objections) and Managed Care

D URING THE LAST 25 YEARS, the mental health team at the University of Kansas School of Social Welfare has presented the strengths model before tens of thousands of people in over 40 states, England, Ireland, New Zealand, Japan, Sweden, and Australia. The challenging questions we have received helped initiate and direct our efforts to better understand the strengths perspective and refine its methods. In this section, the six most frequently asked questions are addressed. Because managed care is a source of increasingly frequent questions, a separate section on this topic follows.

Questions and Objections

What About Real Problems and Crises?

Because all the helping professions and our society as a whole continue to be preoccupied with problems, deficits, and pathology, it is no wonder that this is the most frequently asked question about the strengths model. The incessant focus on problems prevents attention to achievement and usually creates more problems or crises. The following anecdote (Weick & Chamberlain, 1997) is illustrative:

> Loretta, age 34, is diagnosed as having a borderline personality disorder. She had multiple hospitalizations yearly following suicidal threats, gestures such as cutting of wrists, other forms of self-injury, overdosing on medications, and two more serious suicide attempts. In recent years, she had also begun to threaten to hurt other people. Loretta had been in treatment for many years. Creative social workers and psychiatrists had worked diligently with her to help her get jobs and move from her family home into her own apart-

ment. Despite years of treatment focused on understanding and coping with her depression and suicidal impulses, exploring different ways of managing her feelings, each job or new living arrangement ended abruptly with a dramatic crisis involving threats and/or self-destructive behaviors and subsequent hospitalizations.

A newly assigned social worker decided that Loretta's destructive behaviors dominated not only her life but also the years of case planning. In an attempt to rid both she and the client of the emphasis on "the problem," they worked together to arrive at a detailed crisis plan involving a crisis team to respond to Loretta's calls and threats, and arrange immediate hospitalization during crises. After the crisis plan was put into effect, the worker's only job became assisting Loretta in defining her considerable talents and helping her to find ways to express them in work, her home life, and social activities. In the four years that this plan has been in place, Loretta has had two brief hospitalizations. Fortunately, they were not accompanied by the usual spectacle of mental health professionals and emergency vehicles so she has been able to return to her job and apartment following discharge. With the social worker's refusal to be involved in the problem, Loretta has slowly learned to shift her attention to building more satisfying activities in her daily life. For Loretta, putting the problem in its place may, in fact, have saved her life.

The strengths model, as reflected in Loretta's case, did not ignore the problems but "instead of being the star performer in a play, they became minor characters with small roles." (Weick & Chamberlain, 1997). There are three ways for putting problems in their proper place: (1) we recognize problems only in their proper context, (2) we adopt simpler ways of talking about problems, and (3) we pay less attention to the problem (Weick & Chamberlain, 1997).

On the other hand, when called on to intervene in crises or with severe situations, the case manager is probably not implementing the strengths model. For example, when a person is dangerous to themselves and others, the case manager and the entire mental health team are often forced to make decisions, such as commitment of the person. Even during these episodes, the case manager should explore less extrusive options with the person, but in large part the strengths model does not apply. Lack of food, clothing, shelter—the basics of life—requires different approaches. If really dangerous to themselves or others (e.g., children, parents, spouse), the above discussion applies. In most cases, however, the client desires these basics, and as has been already noted, the case manager should help in their acquisition. Doing this is not necessarily the strengths model. Although maximizing options is desirable, any form of decent practice or even basic human kindness would ask no less. You do not need an assessment of strengths or a personal plan.

The point here is that while discrete elements of the strengths model are often applicable, not every situation is amenable to or can benefit from the full application of the strengths model nor should proponents claim it is. The core of case management practice is not these episodic crises but helping people create lives that they desire, to minimize these episodes, to mitigate losses due to these situations (e.g., lost apartment, job) and allow them to rebound more quickly from them.

What About the Illness?

People who pose this question are often reacting to the relative deemphasis of "mental illness" in most treatises and presentations on the strengths model as applied to people with psychiatric disabilities. Given the dominance of medically oriented professional education and training, the strengths model is perceived as virtually "ignoring" the illness. The strengths model in no way "ignores" that people experience intense psychiatric distress that can be disabling, but we refuse to relegate these symptoms solely to the term "illness." There are several reasons for this.

First, strengths-model case management is about habilitation and rehabilitation; its focus is on achievement, empowerment, and the quality of one's life, not on curing an "illness." It is more important for us to understand what is distressing or disabling for a person in being able to achieve what they want in life. Second, since we believe that people receiving services are the directors of the helping process, we also believe that they also have the right to define their own life experiences. Some people find it helpful to talk about the psychiatric distress they experience as a biological brain disorder, others consider their symptoms to be a response to trauma and abuse, others see it as a physiological reaction to stressors in a person's environment, which they find overwhelming. People recover, reclaim, and transform their lives using all these various definitions of "mental illness," therefore we do not feel there is reason to impose one standard view of "illness" to which people should subscribe. Third, our experience and that of others suggest that the "failure" to achieve is due less to what we may label as "illness" than to social and personal processes that are common to the human experience, albeit sometimes a person's symptoms may pose a greater challenge to achievement than for others (see chapter 6).

Having said this, the strengths model does take seriously any psychiatric distress a person may experience and the impact it may have on their life. Recovery is about helping a person achieve a full and meaningful life, and whatever interferes with that, including psychiatric symptoms should be addressed. Strengths model case managers are encouraged to work with clients and medical personnel to explore if medications are helpful in alleviating any psychiatric distress, but at the same time finding things apart from psychiatric medications that promote a person's well-being. It should be noted that recovery stories occur for people without the use of psychiatric medications or limited use of medications. Of critical importance is the work done with clients to identify the earliest possible precursors and indications of symptom interference and to develop plans for early efforts to prevent further interference.

Isn't the Strengths Model Just Positive Reframing?

Absolutely not, although many people who claim to be strengths-based practitioners are doing merely this. Positive reframing refers to the technique of redefining distressing or challenging situations into a positive light. This is devaluing a person's experience of life. The Strengths Model is a unique way of viewing a person, but it is a more holistic way of viewing the people we serve than mere problem-based assessments and interventions. We start from the belief that people can recover, reclaim and transform their lives. We acknowledge that all people have unique strengths, talents, and skills, and that community provides a key to helping people achieve well-being. This philosophical mindset drives our curiosity and creativity toward helping a person achieve a life that is meaningful, purposeful, and most importantly, their own. Any distress, problems, or challenges a person perceives to be interfering with their well-being are acknowledged. These things are put into the context of the person's recovery journey though rather than reframed.

What About Stigma and Discrimination?

This is the environmental corollary to "What about the illness?" People with psychiatric disabilities do experience stigma and discrimination in employment, housing, recreation, religion, and other areas. This is real although progress continues to be made. While education can contribute to a reduction in stigma, the most powerful method is integration. Barriers, whether religious, racial, or economic, are most effectively destroyed when diverse people are asked to work together, play together, learn together, or live together. Nowhere has the hatred, separation, stigma, and discrimination been greater for a longer period of time than that between Israelis (Jews) and Palestinians (Arabs):

> Nablus, West Bank (AP) —The two officers, one Israeli and the other Palestinian, fought each other in the 1982 war in Lebanon. Now, they command joint security patrols to protect the shaky peace.
> Despite the many upheavals of recent months-suicide bombings by Islamic militants, a protracted Israeli blockade of the West Bank and Gaza Strip, a new Israeli government-the two commanders and their men have become friends. They ride in convoys by day and drink coffee by night.
> "Now, some of the teams are really friends and talk about going into future businesses together," said Buganim, a 22-year-old from the Israeli coastal town of Nahariya. "Day by day, our respect grows," he said. "They are like family now." (July 14, 1996, *Lawrence Journal World*)

It is equally true that every community contains numerous people and organizations that want to help or will readily do so if approached. Just as in the case of individuals where achievement is enhanced by exploiting real strengths, the same is true in communities. Although case managers should be aggressive in attacking discrimination and inuring clients' rights, more frequently, better lives are fostered by using the community resources that are there for the asking.

What Is New Here? (We Already Do This)

This can be answered on two levels. First, we admit that the strengths-model legacy is long-standing. Each element or idea or method has its roots in the experience, research, and ideas of many others. The uniqueness, if it exists, is in the borrowing, synthesis, and packaging of these ideas. At a second level, that of actual mental health and case management practice, the strengths model is a dramatic break. Many case managers and mental health organizations "argue that they already abide by the stricture of a strengths orientation. A review of the actual practice reveal that they fall short of full endorsement and application of a strengths-based practice" (Saleebey, 1996, p. 303). As Saleebey continues:

> For example, in many mental health agencies around the country, Individual Service Plans are devised to "incorporate" the strengths of client and family in the assessment and planning. But most ISPs are rife with diagnostic assessments and elaborations, narratives about decompensation, and explorations of continuing symptomatic struggles and manifestations. Axes I and II of the D.S.M. are usually prominently featured. Often, the strengths assessment is consigned to a few lines at the end of the evaluation and planning form. The accountings rendered on these forms are, for the most part, in the language of the worker and employ the mental health system lexicon. (p. 303)

After 25 years of teaching the strengths model to people across the United States, we continuously have people come up to us saying that they currently practice from a "strengths perspective". The following is a list of some common expressions that we have heard from people over the years:

We do strengths . . .

. . . we have a box on our intake assessment that asks people what their strengths are.

. . . we let our people choose between money management and cooking skills in the morning and art and music group in the afternoon.

. . . we bought new comfortable chairs for our day program.

. . . we have a pull-down menu on our computers for clients to pick which goals they want to work on.

. . . but not for our really ill clients. You know we work with the most difficult clients.

. . . we consider work for people once they stabilize and get their symptoms under control.

. . . we help people move along a continuum (residential care facility, transitional living) until they are ready to live on their own.

. . . we make sure people are med compliant so they can recover.

. . . we had a guy who wants to be an airline pilot. We first want to make sure he's serious about work, so we started him in a transitional employment job doing janitorial work.

. . . we had a woman who wanted to learn macramé so we started a macramé group in our psychosocial program.

. . . our staff always make sure to say "hi" to people when they see them in the waiting room.

. . . our staff had training several years ago.

. . . we give clients little jobs around the center so they have something to do.

. . . every year we take all the clients to the State Fair. They have so much fun!

When we hear statements such as these, we see how shallow people's interpretations of what strengths practice can be. Usually after a person hears the entire model laid out before them, most people will say, "Well, we really don't do strengths practice at our agency."

A recent study of supported housing where "client choice" was a linchpin, found that few clients were provided few if any options (Srebnik, Livingston, Gordon, & King, 1995). This is not the strengths model. If a mental health agency has more than a few people working in sheltered workshops or living in residential care, the strengths model is not being practiced. If most clients spend most of their time interacting with other clients or staff, the strengths model is not being practiced. If no consumers are involved in higher education or have never heard of a strengths assessment and personal plan, the strengths model is not being implemented. If descriptions of people received services at team meetings, during hallway discussions, recorded in progress notes, and other places, start, end, and are dominated by their problems, weaknesses, deficits, and inadequacies rather than their talents, dreams, passions, and achievements, then the strengths model is not being practiced.

Client Goals Are Fine but What About Needs?

The answer depends on one's definition of "need." In the strengths model, needs are defined as human needs necessary to sustain life such as food, shelter, absence of self-harm, or danger to others. Addressing these may contain elements of the strengths model, but a full application is unwarranted. "Needs" beyond this should be at the discretion of the client who is helped to convert the need to a statement of what he or she desires.

This approach is different than that generally practiced. Need is often defined more broadly to include not only the basics of life but "needs" for structure, or less isolation, or in terms of services, "she needs partial hospital," "he needs a group home." The position here is that no human or person with psychiatric disability "needs" these. Some may desire them and the task becomes to generate options and formulate a plan to be implemented.

Managed Care and Strengths-Based Case Management

We have been urged by reviewers and colleagues to include material on managed care and its fit with the strengths model of case management. We were reluctant to do so for several reasons, the main one being that this is a practice text not a policy book. We finally were convinced, however, when we concluded that the conditions that augured managed care will only be exacerbated in the future and those conditions may effectively bury not only the strengths model but other reasonable approaches to case management.

Background

Managed care continues to be seen as the most prevalent solution to the problem of rapidly escalating health care costs and of entitlement programs in general. Managed care is, at its core, a financing strategy that caps expenditures for a given period (most often a year). While each managed care approach is unique, the one common denominator is a fixed amount of money to provide a set of services to a predetermined target population. The state determines the specifications, accepts bids and proposals, and selects the contractor responsible for the funds, the services, and the clients. Under most plans, the contractor assumes "the risk" of spending above the contracted amount. Contractors therefore establish risk pools to protect themselves from such circumstances. Any money not spent is kept by the contractor as "profit."

The results of managed care in public mental health has led to these conclusions:

1. The state authority controls the nature and quality of the mental health system through the design of the managed care contract.
2. Managed care will control expenditures no matter how it is done.
3. Money is the primary motivator; financial incentives dictate client service.
4. There will be competition for the contract no matter how rigorous the contract requirements.

Beyond this, generalization is fraught with danger because each managed care plan is unique and those in mental health are only a few years old. It is fair to say, however, that there is no evidence that suggests people with psychiatric disabilities are receiving better service nor are they achieving better outcomes. In fact, most analysis seem to emphasize less service, less timely service, less personal service, less access to appropriate services, less client choice, and huge profits for the contractors (especially for-profit entities).

Incentives

A critical facet of all social policy, financing or otherwise, is the incentive structure it contains. The still dominant fee-for-service mode provides incentives for more service (especially the most profitable) and therefore increased spending. It leads to overuse of services that accrue the most reimbursement compared with cost. For example, partial hospital/day treatment in many venues has been a major source of income for providers despite the lack of evidence demonstrating its efficacy. Because fee-for-service systems by necessity specify "fundable" services, other services or approaches are excluded. Most Medicaid plans do not reimburse supported work, supported education, or consumer-run services despite the evidence of such activities' effectiveness. Flexibility to tailor service packages to individuals is constrained by detailed specifications of who can be served with what approaches.

The fee-for-service financing mechanism tends to result in costs continuing to increase; some outcomes (e.g., employment, education) remain stagnant; some people not receiving the most effective services in the intensity needed; and some people receiving services that are not effective or needed including hospitalization.

In contrast, the financial incentives in the typical mental health managed care system include:

1. Reduced use of expensive institutional care (e.g., state hospitalization, nursing facilities) for those facilities included in the managed care contract
2. Increased use of inexpensive natural resources and a reduction in formal services because services are an expense rather than income generating
3. Increased use of services provided and paid for by others not included in the managed care contract (e.g., nursing homes, jails, shelters) known as cost-shifting
4. Flexibility in the array of services and options due to reduction in program-specific rules—unfortunately this incentive is attenuated by item 5
5. Increased administrative costs for controlling client utilization of services
6. Disincentives to serve the most disabled because they cost more
7. Disincentive to client choice to curtail short-term costs
8. Incentives for crisis response and client maintenance and disincentives for rehabilitation

The negative results of the typical managed care financing structure can be predicted: (1) a dramatic increase in the amount of money diverted from services to administrative costs and profits; (2) people with the most serious disabilities not getting served; (3) many clients underserved; (4) some cost shifting to other entities (e.g., nursing facilities, jails, police); (5) individualized care reduced; and (6) when no financial incentives exist, desired client outcomes decrease.

On the positive side, managed care provides powerful incentives to reduce the use of hospitalization and other forms of expensive and segregated institutional programs. In a related manner, managed care encourages the use of natural community resources because they are either free or of little cost. Although rare, managed care systems could be based on achieving client outcomes rather than units of service with their attendant onerous recording requirements. In this case, dramatically increased flexibility would occur to create client tailored service packages.

Managed Care and Strengths Model Case Management

First-generation managed care operations in mental health suggest strongly that neither strengths-model case management nor other approaches with indicated effectiveness, like assertive community treatment teams or the rehabilitation model,

TABLE 9.1 Case Management Differences Between Community Support Systems (CSS) and Utilization Review (UR)

CSS	UR
Working alliance with consumer	Working alliance with professional
Ongoing interactions with consumer	No interactions with consumer
Decision making usually on-site	Decision making usually off-site
Consumer involved in decision making	Consumer not involved in decision making
Decision makers are case managers and consumers	Decision makers are case manager and professionals
Decision making with same group of consumers	Decision making with different consumers
Case manager may perform other therapeutic functions with consumer	Case manager performs no other therapeutic functions with consumer
Case manager trained in case-management knowledge and skills	Case manager trained in UR knowledge and skills
Tends to have experience working with people with psychiatric disabilities	May not have experience working with people with psychiatric disabilities
Has helping orientation	Has benefit-management orientation
Accesses services directly	Grants permission to access services
Cuts through red tape	Adds to red tape
Recovery vision	Medical necessity vision
Wellness model	Illness model
CSS values	Managed care values
Research shows improved consumer outcomes	No research support for improved consumer outcomes
Consistent with current trends in business reengineering	Inconsistent with current trends in business reengineering
History of using case management team approach	No history of using case management team approach
Underlying comprehensive service system design articulated	No underlying comprehensive service system design articulated

will be used. Rather, practice guidelines for case management in managed care are assuming a utilization review function focused on limiting expenditures in the short term. As the GAO (1996) notes: "By using practice guidelines, plans are making a conscious decision about the care they intend to provide, reflecting the trade-off between costs and benefits" (p. 13).

Bill Anthony (1996) has contrasted this utilization review approach with the community support services (CSS) approach that includes strengths model case management (Table 9.1). The irony is that of the four major approaches to case management in mental health, the only one with a compelling track record of failure in terms of client outcomes, is the broker model that has many parallels with the utilization review depiction.

Can Managed Care Support Strengths Model Case Management?

CSS case management (including strengths) is not being implemented by first-generation managed care programs. Given the early experiences with mental health managed care, it can be anticipated that costs will be controlled, hospitalization will be reduced, clients will be underserved, and client outcomes will decrease. Are managed care and strengths model case management mutually exclusive or can they be mutually supportive? I think the latter is possible.

First, CSS case management and utilization review (UR) case management are two distinct services (with very little but the superficial in common) yet have the same label (see Table 9.1). This must change. One alternative is to rename UR case management to just utilization review or benefits manager, which are more descriptive of function. Another alternative is to rename CSS case management. While none of the present candidates seems comfortable (e.g., community consultant, integration specialist, recovery coordinator, care worker), there are two good reasons to do so. First, "case management" is an awful term that almost everybody, professionals and clients, dislikes or even resents. We seek to *help people* not "manage cases." Unfortunately, for historical and reimbursement reasons combined with lack of consensus on an alternative, "case management" continues to be used.

A second reason to change the label is that it is not accurate and misleads. Case management formally entered mental health in 1978 with the onset of the community support program. Under this program, case management was to ensure that needed services were provided to people with severe psychiatirc disabilities. The early formulation of case management and early implementation of the service were of the broker model type (Levine & Fleming, undated). It was not long, however, before this arid "linkage to a service" model was being replaced by enriched approaches (e.g., ACT, strengths, rehabilitation) that included direct service elements such as skill training, detailed rehabilitation plans, and work with naturally occurring community resources with all approaches requiring a close relationship with the person and increased authority for case manager decision making within the mental health agency.

The point here is that CSS case management is a multifaceted service that seeks to help clients achieve the goals they set for themselves. They are responsible across life domains. It is the one service not limited in focus. It is not limited to formal services but is encouraged to look beyond these. In many locales, especially rural areas, CSS case management acts as a replacement or substitute for specialized programs. Therefore, CSS case management under managed care could be renamed and purchased as a separate service by UR case managers.

There are strengths and dangers in this approach. First, although compared with hospitalization and usual service approaches, CSS case management is significantly less expensive. Given that controlling costs predominates in managed care, CSS case management seems to be a perfect match. In Solomon's (1992) review of the case management research, she identified ten studies that attended to "cost effectiveness/savings." Of these ten, eight found the experimental case management group to be less expensive than the control condition, and one reported no differences. The one reporting no difference (Borland et al., 1989) had most of their clients living in residential treatment where costs paralleled state hospital costs. The only study finding increased costs for the case management group was the study employing a broker model (Franklin et al., 1987).

Second, most people in mental health believe that CSS case management, like medication services and crisis services, should be universally available for individuals with psychiatric disabilities for an undetermined length of time. Under this recommendation, the UR case manager would not have discretion over the rationing of this service. Perhaps states could make universal accessibility to CSS case management a mandated element of their contracts.

The strengths of this approach, beyond "calling a spade a spade," include moving CSS case management to a new level of prominence. Given its efficacy, CSS case management should be able to compete well with other service approaches. The strengths model, in particular, with its focus on community strengths offers the promise of a highly cost-effective service. Initial evidence from the application of the strengths model to older adults requiring long-term care has indicated reduced costs due to "increased levels of informal support, a more sustainable balance of formal and informal services, and fewer transitions between home and health care facilities" (Fast, Chapin, & Rapp, 1994; Fast & Chapin, 1996).

A second step needed for managed care and strengths model case management to be mutually supportive is for managed care contracts to be outcome based rather than service-based. In other words, managed care contracts could place a premium on achieving the core outcomes of CSS: reducing hospitalization and increasing community tenure; improving vocational, educational, and living arrangement status; and increasing community activity and participation. Achievement standards could be set for each. Although some service reporting and standards would necessarily be included, the emphasis could change from carefully counting units of service to "here's your money, here are people who need your services, and here are the outcomes you need to produce." How it is done is less important. Since no form of mental health service has a better record of efficacy, CSS case management would likely be at a premium.

Afterword

JAMES BOSWELL REFERRED to his famous subject, Dr. Samuel Johnson, as his "guide, philosopher, and friend." Charlie Rapp has been no less a figure for me. The first edition of this book crystallized my experiences over 25 years in the mental health field, and this edition reinforces all of my current thinking about evidence-based health care, shared decision-making, and recovery.

Focusing on psychopathology often reinforces the feelings, behaviors, and experiences from which people desire to escape; on the other hand, emphasizing abilities, aspirations, and accomplishments often inspires people to new hopes, new successes, and new senses of themselves.

On reading the first edition, I immediately wrote to Charlie Rapp and congratulated him on writing the finest book about working with people who have mental illness that I had ever read. Nothing else in the published literature so clearly defines and illustrates what it means to be on the person's side, to attend to his or her goals, and to restore and reinforce strengths rather than weaknesses. Since then, I have made many trips to Kansas and worked with Charlie on several projects. His warmth, insight, and practical experience continue to inspire me each time we get together. This man lives his life as he writes his philosophy; he is truly a guide, philosopher, and friend.

Rapp and Goscha have enhanced us all by producing a new edition. Although the "strengths" term has crept into mental health jargon, mental health professionals continue to have difficulty understanding what it means to align oneself with the person's strengths and to find strengths in the natural environment. The second edition of the book is even richer than the first edition in bringing these concepts to life, and it should be standard fare for all who do this work. Strengths case management is a practical and caring approach that we can all use.

Much like the "strengths" concept, "recovery," "empowerment," and other concepts are often perceived as pieces of mental health jargon and presented as shrill ideologies, political battering rams, or wishful thinking. Consequently, professionals sometimes react negatively to these terms, as though they represent non-scientific and potentially damaging approaches to health care. Yet the strengths approach instantiates the true meaning of these concepts.

One of the most unfortunate and destructive trends in the mental health dialogue today is the attempt to separate the very constructive movements toward evidence-based health care and recovery. Some argue that scientific approaches to health care, embodied in the techniques of evidence-based medicine, are somehow incompatible with humanistic and hopeful approaches to health care, represented by recovery. To my total amazement, I hear conference speakers make patently absurd claims: "There is no evidence for any biological basis of what are called mental illnesses." "Evidence-based practices are funded by the drug companies." "Recovery is for some people and evidence-based practices are for others." "Evidence-based practices leave out choice and individualization" "The relationship helping relationship is all that matters." "Evidence-based practices do not apply to people in the real world." And so forth. Without speculating on the reasons for such misunderstandings, let me just lament their negative ramifications. They fragment the mental health community, erode political support and funding for mental health programs, inhibit access to care, slow advances in the field, and undermine people's ability to trust one another. Policy makers at the local, state, and national levels are dismayed by the self-destructive disharmonies within the mental health community.

I mention these unfortunate trends because one of the great strengths of Rapp and Goscha's book is its ability to weave science and humanism together. These authors truly understand that strengths-based case management is an evidence-based practice precisely because it offers choice, individualization, and a focus on the person's goals. I hope that all community mental health stakeholders will recognize the centrality of these concepts and the value of this book.

Robert E. Drake, MD, PhD
Andrew Thomson Professor of Psychiatry
Dartmouth Medical School

Spirit-Breaking Behaviors

1. Restrictive practices or resources
   - Being put on a court order or getting extensions of a court order
   - Having a payee
   - Being "placed" in a residential setting (e.g., group home, nursing home)
   - Telling a person who wants to go to college that it has been decided that they have to go to vocational technical training instead
   - Telling people they aren't ready to work
   - Telling people they can't have relationships with other people receiving services
   - Making people have medications monitored when they are capable of doing it on their own
   - Having the client handcuffed when the person is picked up on petition
2. Negative staff attitudes/perceptions about people with psychiatric disabilities
   - Telling a person that they can't get better unless they take their medications
   - Saying (or thinking) "you'll always be on medications"
   - Attributing things to the illness and making generalizations (e.g., the person is manipulative, noncompliant)
   - Focusing on "labels" or the illness rather than the person as a unique individual
   - Devaluing the person
   - Imposing our own standard of living on people
3. Invasive interventions
   - Medication injections
   - Random urine analysis

4. Disrespectful/belittling interactions of staff
   - ❏ Talking down to people (e.g., talking to the person as if they aren't intelligent enough to understand)
   - ❏ Treating adults as children (e.g., telling the person they can't/shouldn't drink—then they see case manager at a bar)
   - ❏ Giving compliments that are conditional (e.g., "You did this great, but . . .")
   - ❏ Ignoring the person (e.g., talking about someone in front of them, not acknowledging the person and continuing to do paperwork)
   - ❏ Not valuing or respecting a person's time by having him/her wait for long periods of time (e.g., to see someone, to get flexible support funds)
   - ❏ Taking a parental stance/chastising (e.g. "I told you . . . If you would have listened to me . . .")
   - ❏ Under normal circumstances (excluding assertive outreach), going to people's homes unannounced/without calling first
   - ❏ Being rude to people (e.g., using derogatory expressions, not following through on what you said you would do, forgetting phone calls, breaking appointments, being tactlessly direct, "you smell, go home and bathe!")
   - ❏ Not listening to what a person is saying (e.g., A person says they want to earn more money and you refer them to a prevocational program)
   - ❏ Making promises or saying that you will do something that you do not do.
5. Poverty
   - ❏ The person always having to worry about "how am I going to pay for this?"
   - ❏ Accepting charity (e.g., going to food banks, second-hand stores)
6. Services
   - ❏ Focusing services on maintaining people at their current level rather than helping people achieve goals (e.g., helping clients obtain employment, educational pursuits)
   - ❏ Building people up to accomplish something ("You can do this!") and then having it take months to get them the resource
   - ❏ Refusing to do something because "it's not my job"
   - ❏ Having infrequent contact with the person
   - ❏ Changing case managers or psychiatrists once the person has established a relationship with the them
   - ❏ Providing too many services (e.g., the person is referred to every program in the agency)
   - ❏ Changing peoples' medications, which leads to relapse of symptoms or severe adverse or side effects
   - ❏ Setting too many traditional boundaries on the working relationship (e.g., can't recognize person out in the community, "professional distance")
   - ❏ Putting contingencies on resources (e.g., you can only have assistance with housing if you go to groups)

7. Goals
   - Imposing our ideas of what a person "should" be doing or what their goals "should" be on the consumer
   - Ignoring the person's dreams/goals by not pursuing them, not writing them down
   - Family members controlling decisions for the client
   - Reframing the person's goal into the professional's goal (e.g., "I want more friends" becomes "Improve socialization skills")

8. Discrimination
   - Not being able to find decent housing because landlords have had bad experiences in the past with the person or other people receiving services, or not being able to get a desired apartment because the landlord will not take section 8 vouchers
   - Employers/employees treating the person poorly (e.g., making fun, not hiring, and the like . . .)
   - The side effects of medication (e.g., impotence, weight gain) that contribute to the person feeling "different" than others
   - Person being embarrassed about having a mental illness
   - Being looked at as sexual predator

9. Family
   - Lack of support by family (e.g., family does not want much contact, treats the person like a child)

Hope-Inducing Behaviors

1. Building hope through Caring Instruction
   - Listening actively (e.g., good eye contact, feeding back what they are saying)
   - Being available when the person needs to talk
   - Demonstrating caring and kindness
   - Doing things with the person that are fun
   - Communicating that "I believe in you" and "I am on your side"
   - Giving positive, encouraging comments
   - Accepting a person whether they succeed or fail and celebrating the effort if they do not succeed
   - Asking a person's opinion/choice about all aspects of the helping process
   - Showing genuine enthusiasm for what the person is saying or doing
   - Sharing something in common with the person
   - Sharing personal experience when appropriate
   - Letting them know you're "human" (e.g., "yes, I have bad times too," "I make mistakes")
2. Treating people with respect
   - Supporting a person's decisions and desires by accepting them and helping achieve them rather than putting down or minimizing (even subtly) a person's choices and desires
   - Following through on appointments
   - Returning calls and doing it promptly
   - Keeping all promises
   - Being on time
   - Treating people as you want to be treated

3. Focusing on the positive
   - Talking about the future as being positive rather than dwelling on past occurrences that may not have gone well
   - Focusing on what a person has been doing well and their strengths
   - Praising things that are going well
   - When things are not going well, reminding the person of past successes
   - Normalizing a person's experience by letting him/her know that other people experience similar things
   - Communicating a "can do" attitude
   - Pointing out achievements/success
   - Letting a person know he/she can try again if something doesn't work out
4. Celebrating accomplishments and success
   - Giving specific praise about things a person does well
   - Celebrating accomplishments/successes—big and (particularly) small ones
5. Being there for the person/sticking with them
   - Going with a person to a doctor appointment or court hearing for support and to help reduce fear
   - Advocating for a person when he/she is unable to obtain a resource by educating others, convincing the keeper of the resource to assist the person, and in other cases of need
   - Visiting the person if they are in the hospital
   - Helping the person negotiate with the psychiatrist around medications if he/she is having difficulty (support what they need and want)
   - Continuing attempts to engage with a person who may be isolating or leery of the mental health system or becoming more difficult to work with. Do not give up.
6. Helping people work toward the goals that are important to them
   - Helping a person establish goals
   - Helping a person achieve their goals by breaking them down into achievable steps, helping to get resources, recognizing small steps
   - Making sure the goals you are working on are actually the person's goals
   - Letting the consumer know that his/her goals are possible to achieve
   - Showing enthusiasm and excitement towards the person's goals
   - Working on goals that move people to self-sufficiency and independence (e.g., being own payee, jobs/education)
7. Promoting choice
   - Acknowledging and supporting the right for all people to make their own life decisions and having control of their course of treatment
   - Generating many options for what the person wants
   - Linking the person to information and resources to make informed decisions

- ❏ Having choice of services and ability to change providers
- ❏ Including people receiving services in all treatment decisions and discussions

8. Promoting education
   - ❏ Providing education to people about their recovery, methods for dealing with symptoms and medications
   - ❏ Educating family members to help build relationships and understanding

9. Promoting a future beyond the mental health system
   - ❏ Communicating to people that they may not need services forever (e.g., payee, case management)
   - ❏ Spending time with people outside the mental health center in natural community settings
   - ❏ Promoting integration by using community resources and engaging people in non-mental-health-related activities

Areas to Explore through the Strengths Assessment

Daily Living

Current Status
☑ Where do you live (address)? How long have you lived there?
☑ Do you live with anyone else?
☑ What is good about where you live? What do you like about where you live? (e.g., quiet neighborhood, close to grocery store, near bus route)
☑ How do you get around (e.g., car, bike, bus, walk)?
☑ Do you have pets or animals?
☑ What personal assets related to daily living does the person have? (e.g., Do you have a phone, cable, TV, dishwasher, washer/dryer?) Note: This can help identify wants—does the person wish he/she had a vacuum cleaner?
☑ Are there details, special attributes about the home that the consumer is proud of or enjoys? (e.g., collects things, paintings, is particularly tidy, embroiders, has aquarium)
☑ What does the person enjoy doing or is good at doing in terms of daily living tasks, if anything? (e.g., cooking, cleaning, doing errands, grocery shopping)

Desires/Aspirations
☑ Do you like where you live? Where else would you like to live?
☑ Do you like living alone? With other people?
☑ If you could change one thing about your living situation, what would it be?
☑ What would your ideal living situation be? (e.g., living on a farm, buying a home, etc.)
☑ Is there anything you would want to make your living situation easier? (e.g., a vacuum, day care for kids, a care, a way to get to the shopping center more)

☑ What is most important to you in your living situation? (e.g., feeling safe, near friends, near certain businesses, having a pet)

Resources
☑ Where have you lived in the past (list each)? With whom? For how long? What was the type (apartment, group home, house, nursing facility) and location?
☑ Are there things you really liked about any of the past living situations?
☑ What was your favorite living situation? Why?
☑ Are there things you had in a past living situation that you do not have now but you would like to have again?

Financial/Insurance

Current Status

Income (type and amount)	Program Assistance
☑ SSI/SSDI	☑ Food stamps
☑ Income from work	☑ Section 8/HUD
☑ Family/friends loans/assistance	☑ PASS Plan
	☑ Homestead
	☑ TANF
Insurance	Money management
☑ Medicare/Medicaid	☑ Do you have a bank account? What kind?
☑ Insurance Company	☑ Payee? Name & address
☑ Spend-down information (amount)	☑ How do you budget & manage your money?
	☑ How do you pay your bills?
	☑ Do you have extra spending money each week? How much?

Desires/Aspirations
☑ What would you like to be different with regard to finances? How?
☑ What is important to you regarding your finances? (e.g., I want extra money each week to go out to eat; I want to be able to rent movies; I wish I had a savings account).
☑ Are there benefits the person is entitled to, but is not getting?

Resources
☑ What was the person's income in the past? From what sources? (e.g., Has the person worked in the past? Did they get benefits they do not receive now?)
☑ Did the person use/have any resources in the past that they are not using now? (e.g., payee, taking a financial management class, was an accounting major in college, used to have a savings/checking account)

Vocational/Educational

Current Status

☑ What is the person doing with regard to productive activity? Include type, where, and amount of time. (e.g., Junior College classes in art one class per semester).

☑ Activities that could be included in this category: competitive employment, volunteer work, school, odd jobs, helping others, work in the CSS program, job search, involvement in vocational services and/or vocational program, parenting, taking care of sick or elderly friend or relative

☑ Highest level of education (e.g., GED, high school, 22 hours of undergraduate work, B.A.)

☑ What do you like about your current job, activities?

☑ What is important to the person about what they are doing? (e.g. "I like the extra money," "helping people," "being around people," "being in charge of something")

☑ Particularly if the person is not doing anything in this area, what are their interests, skills, abilities related to productive activity? (e.g., "I'm very mechanical," "I enjoy playing with kids," "Art is my passion")

Desires/Aspirations

☑ Do you have any desire to work? Go to school? Volunteer? Earn extra money?

☑ If so, what would that be doing? What do you enjoy doing? What do you have experience doing? (e.g., "I'd like to get a nursing degree," "I like to work outside and with my hands," "I like helping people")

☑ If you could be or do anything you wanted (i.e., career), what would that be? What is it about that that interests you?

☑ If the person is doing some type of activity currently, is the person satisfied with what they are doing? Is there anything about what they are doing they would like to change? Is there other activity they would like to do in addition?

Resources

☑ What type of activity (work, school, volunteer work, training) have you done in the past? For how long? When? Where? What did you like or not like about it?

☑ What kind of vocational services have you received in the past?

☑ Have you been/are you on any work incentive programs?

☑ What work situations have you found most enjoyable and why?

Social Supports

Current Status

☑ Who do you spend time with? Who are your friends? Who do you feel close to? Who makes you feel good when you're around them?

☑ What organizations, clubs, groups do you participate in? (e.g., church, AA/NA, CSS, softball league, neighborhood groups)

☑ Do you have anybody that comes to visit you or that you spend time with? What kinds of things do you do together?

☑ Do you have a pet? Would you like one?

☑ Do you visit with any members of your family? Are the visits pleasant or stressful? Do you rely on any members of your family for support?

☑ What is it you like and dislike about being with other people?

☑ What is it about being alone that you like? What kinds of things do you do when you are alone? What do you do when you feel alone?

☑ Where, outside of your home, do you feel most at ease?

Examples of Social Supports

• Family	• Friends	• Mental health
• School	• Compeer	workers
• Pets	• Spiritual (church,	• People at work
• Acquaintances	minister)	• Support groups
• Social service	• Significant Other	• Self-help/Consumer-
workers		run organizations

Aspirations/Desires

☑ Is there anything that you would like to be different in your social life?

☑ Are there any areas of you life you would like to have more support in? (e.g., spirituality, better relationship with family, more friends, someone to go camping with)

☑ Are there organizations, groups, clubs that you do not currently belong to, but would like to? (e.g., church, rotary club, book club, astrology club)

Resources

☑ Have there been important people in your life (e.g., friends/family) that you have felt supported by in the past but currently do not spend time with? Who?

☑ Are there places you used to hang out/people you used to hang out with that you do not currently? Describe who and where.

☑ In the past, did you belong to any groups, clubs, and/or organizations? What were they? Did you enjoy them? What did you enjoy about them?

Health

Current Status

Psychiatric	*Physical*
• Psychiatrist currently seeing	• Medical doctor currently seeing
• Medications	• Dentist

• Do you experience symptoms of your illness? What are they like? What kinds of things do you do to cope with or manage your symptoms? • What produces stress for you? What do you do to manage stress?	• Description of physical health • Diet and eating habits • Do you exercise? What type? • Pharmacy and pharmacist • Use of over-the-counter medications. • Birth control • Smoking habits

Desires/Aspirations

☑ Are there things you are working on or would like to work on with regard to your physical or mental health? (e.g., losing weight, managing symptoms, smoking less, drinking less)

☑ What is important to you in this area? Is there anything you would like to learn more about, improve or change in this area?

Resources

☑ Address resources used in the past for any of the areas mentioned in current status.

☑ Patterns of hospitalization: When was your last hospitalization? Was it state or private? How often do you typically go into the hospital? What happens before you go in (precipitating factors)? Are the hospitalizations usually voluntary or involuntary?

☑ Were any of the resources used in the past (DR's, hospitals, exercise activities, medications, diets, symptom management techniques) particularly helpful?

Leisure/Recreation

Current Status

☑ What do you do for fun?

☑ What are your hobbies?

☑ What do you do to relax and enjoy yourself?

Example: Areas of Leisure/Recreational Activities

Sports activities • Basketball, football, softball, tennis, swimming	Outdoor— Nature Activities • Hiking, fishing, canoeing, picnics, hunting, camping	Social pursuits • Parties, visiting, table games, talking on the phone, shopping
Individual entertainment • Listening to the radio, TV, people watching, listen to music	Intellectual pursuits • Reading, lectures, noncredit classes, going to library	Cultural/Artistic • Instruments, painting, crafts, visiting museums, art class, concerts, movies

• Meditative pursuits • Prayer, yoga, bible study	• Trips, excursions, vacations	• Shopping • Cooking/baking/knitting

☑ Do you ever go out and do things on weekends? If so, what do you usually do?

☑ Do you have a TV? Would you like one? What is your favorite TV show? Do you like movies? What kind? Who is your favorite actor?

☑ Do you like to read? Who is your favorite author? Do you go to the library?

☑ Do you like to cook? What is your favorite meal? Do you like to go out to eat?

☑ What talents do you have? What are your hobbies?

☑ If you could do anything you wanted for one day, what would you do?

☑ When do you get bored? What do you do when you get bored?

Desires/Aspirations

☑ What fun things do you like to do, but are not doing currently?

☑ Have you ever wanted to try something that sounded like fun, but you never have done?

☑ Explore desires listed in current status.

Resources

☑ Explore past involvements, interests, activities listed in current status. Where did the person do the activities? With whom?

☑ What activities did you most enjoy in the past? What was it about the activities you enjoyed?

Spirituality

Definition

Spirituality refers to any set of beliefs and/or practices that give a person a sense of hope, comfort, meaning, purpose in their life, or a connection to the greater universe.

For some people this may have to do with God and some type of organized religion, for others it may be an individual relationship with a higher power, for others it may not be specifically defined. Religion is not necessarily synonymous with spirituality.

Do not limit the definition to only an institution, church, or denomination. Also, do not impose your own thoughts or beliefs on the person.

Examples

• Meditation	• Music	• Nature
• Art	• Community Service	• Fellowship with others

• 12-step	• Organized religion	• Political justice
• Temple	• Rituals	• Altruism/giving

Possible Approaches to Talking About Spirituality
☑ Is there anything in your life that brings you a sense of comfort, meaning, or purpose in your life?
☑ What gives you the strength to carry on in times of difficulty?
☑ What do you believe in?
☑ What do you have faith in?

This topic can also come up within other life domains, such as social support. Often times, spirituality is linked with connection to others in a social context.

Culture
Culture is a symbolic system of values, beliefs, rituals and behaviors learned, shared, and transmitted between a particular group of people. Culture can come in many different forms and we all belong to more than one culture. Here we refer to culture(s) that the person identifies with most strongly.

Examples

• Baptist	• rural	• Irish
• Maori	• gypsy	• Lakota
• gay and lesbian	• Buddhist	• conservative
• feminist	• Deaf	• Wiccan

Possible Questions to Uncover Importance of Culture
Rituals
☑ Do you celebrate any special occasions such as Christmas, Easter, anniversaries or weddings?
☑ How are these celebrated?
☑ Can you remember your most special occasion?

Family
☑ As you were growing up, did you have much to do with your extended family or family friends?
☑ What was it like living with your family? What were your parents' roles?
☑ What would you do at gatherings of family and friends?

Language
☑ Do you speak any other languages? Have you ever wanted to learn another language?
☑ Do you or your family ever use phrases from other language?

Nationalism
- ☑ Do you like to watch any national events?
- ☑ What countries have you visited? What country would you most like to visit? Why?

Songs
- ☑ Do you have any songs that you really like?
- ☑ Did you ever sing/hear songs that brought back memories? Did your family teach you any songs?

Stories
- ☑ Are there any stories that have been around for years that you strongly connect with?
- ☑ Do you know any stories that your parents may have told you?

Dances
- ☑ What is your favorite style of dancing?
- ☑ Did you learn any dancing when you were younger? Do you want to learn any style of dancing?

Food
- ☑ Does your family have certain food they prepare for gatherings? (e.g., Christmas ham or taro)

Values and Beliefs
- ☑ Are there any strong beliefs that were held by your family? What do you think of this?
- ☑ Who is a person that represents your beliefs?
- ☑ What do you value most in life? Have you always felt that way?

Quality Review of
Strengths Assessment

Consumer's Name _____   Date Reviewed _____

Case Manager's Name _____

Yes   Somewhat   No   Complete and thorough—each life domain has rich
                       and detailed information.

Yes   Somewhat   No   Individualized and specific—gives a clear picture of
                       who this person is. (Here's a good test. Blank out
                       the name and make copies for everyone on the
                       team. Team members should be able to readily
                       identify this person by the information provided.)

Yes   Somewhat   No   Clear indication of the person's involvement in the
                       assessment—signature, personal comments,
                       information written by person, written in person's
                       own words

Yes   Somewhat   No   Used in an ongoing manner—updated regularly
                       upon meeting with person (weekly for first few
                       meetings, at least monthly after that)

Yes   Somewhat   No   Includes natural resources (as opposed to only
                       formal resources) in *each* area.

Yes   Somewhat   No   The individual's wants and desires are listed,
                       prioritized, and written in person's own language
                       (vs. unprofessional jargon).

Yes   Somewhat   No   Reflects cultural, spiritual, ethnic, and/or racial
                       information that holds meaning for the person.

Yes   Somewhat   No   Reflects consumer's skills, talents, accomplishments and abilities—what they know about, care about, have a passion for in each life domain.

Quality Review of Personal Plan

Consumer's Name _____   Date Reviewed _____

Case Manager's Name _____

Long-Term Goal

Yes   No   Goal is taken from the "wants" section of the strengths assessment, that is, long-term goal clearly reflects what person wants, what motivates him/her, not what others think they need to do.

Yes   No   Goal is written in person's own words.

Short-Term Goals (actions steps/tasks)

Yes   Sometimes   No   Date recorded that the action step is written.

Yes   Sometimes   No   Goals are measurable (outcomes oriented).

Yes   Sometimes   No   Goals are achievable (broken down into small steps).

Yes   Sometimes   No   Goals are positive (what *will* be done rather than what *will not* be done).

Yes   Sometimes   No   Dates to be achieved are recovered (no "ongoing").

Yes   Sometimes   No   Are tasks being achieved and target dates recorded?

Yes   Sometimes   No   Is goal progress reflected in comments section?

Yes   Sometimes   No   Resources/information from strengths assessment are reflected in goal plan.

Yes   No   The consumer has signed the plan.

Appendix V

Strengths Case–Management Fidelity Scale

	1	2	3	4	5
1. Case Manager Job Responsibilities: Case manager's job responsibilities are fully devoted to case management.	Case managers spend less than 70% of their time doing case-management related activities.	Case managers spend 70–79% of their time doing case-management related activities.	Case managers spend 80–89% of their time doing case-management related activities.	Case managers spend 90–99% of their time doing case-management related activities.	Case managers spend 100% of their time doing case-management related activities.
2. Caseload Ratios: Case managers have low caseload ratios (this varies depending on intensity of caseload, but no more than 20:1).	Case managers serve more than 30 clients.	Case managers serve 26–30 clients.	Case managers serve 21–25 clients.	Case managers serve 16–20 clients.	Case managers serve 15 or fewer clients.
3. Size of Team: Case managers are part of a small team (preferably no more than six) under a single supervisor.	Team consists of nine or more case managers.	Team consists of eight case managers.	Team consists of seven case managers.	Team consists of six case managers.	Team consists of five or less case managers.
4. Integrated Services: Supported Employment and Integrated Dual Diagnosis Treatment (IDDT) specialists are part of the case management team.	Program does not have supported employment or IDDT specialists.	Either supported employment or IDDT specialist are part of overall CSS program, but not part of team.	Supported employment and IDDT specialists are part of overall CSS program but not integrated on team.	Either a supported employment or IDDT specialist attend group supervision as part of team and accept referrals directly from case managers on team.	Supported employment and IDDT specialist attend group supervision as part of team and accept referrals directly from case managers on team.

5. Supervisor's Focus and Responsibilities: Majority of supervisor's time is spent engaged in activities directly supporting case managers.	Less than five hours per week.	6–10 hours per week.	11–15 hours per week.	16–20 hours per week.	21 or more hours per week.
6. Frequency and Length of Group Supervision: Team meets once per week for at least two hours.	Team does not meet on regular basis.	Team meets every other week for less than two hours.	Team meets every other week for at least two hours.	Team meets once per week for less than two hours.	Team meets once per week for at least two hours.
7. Focus and Quality of Group Supervision: Group supervision time is devoted to in-depth discussion of specific clients.	Less than 50%.	51–69% of time spent discussing specific clients in depth.	70–79% of time spent discussing specific clients in depth.	80–89% of time spent discussing specific clients in depth.	90–100% of time spent discussing specific clients in depth.
8. Strengths Assessment: The Strengths Assessment is a stand-alone tool used according to the Strengths Model of Case Management; not mixed with any other type of assessment tool.	Strengths assessment is not used or is mixed with other type of assessment tool.	Less than 50% of strengths assessments meet criteria.	51–69% of strengths assessments meet criteria.	70–89% of strengths assessments meet criteria.	90% or more of strengths assessments meet criteria.
9. Personal Plan: The personal plan is a stand-alone tool used according to the strengths model of case management; not mixed with any other type of goal planning document.	Personal plan is not used.	Less than 50% of personal plans meet criteria.	51–69% of personal plans meet criteria.	70–89% of personal plans meet criteria.	90% or more of personal plans meet criteria.

Strengths Case-Management Fidelity Scale

	1	2	3	4	5
10. Location of Client Contact: Majority of contact with clients occurs out in the community.	Less than 50% of case managers' time with clients occurs in the community.	50–64% of case managers' time with clients occurs in the community.	65–74% of case managers' time with clients occurs in the community.	75–84% of case managers' time with clients occurs in the community.	85% or more of case managers' time with clients occurs in the community.
11. Resources: Case managers use a higher proportion of naturally occurring resources rather than formal mental health services.	Less than 25% of resources used or accessed were naturally occurring resources.	26–39% of resources used or accessed were naturally occurring resources.	40–59% of resources used or accessed were naturally occurring resources.	60–74% of resources used or accessed were naturally occurring resources.	More than 75% of resources used or accessed were naturally occurring resources.
12. Hope-inducing Behaviors: Case managers exhibit hope-inducing behaviors when interacting with people receiving services or other staff.	None of the sources indicate a dominance of hope-inducing behaviors.	One source indicates a dominance of hope-inducing behaviors.	Two sources indicate a dominance of hope-inducing behaviors.	Three sources indicate a dominance of hope-inducing behaviors.	Four sources indicate a dominance of hope-inducing behaviors.

References

Altshuler, S. C., & Forward, J. (1978). The inverted hierarchy: A case manager approach to mental health. *Administration in Mental Health, 6*(1), 57–68.

American Psychological Association (APA). (1977). Ethical standards of psychologists. Washington, DC: American Psychological Association.

Anthony, W., & Farkas, M. (1990). Psychiatric rehabilitation. Boston: Boston University.

Anthony, W. & Unger, K. (1991). "Supported education: An additional program resource for young adults with long term mental illness." *Community Mental Health Journal, 27*(2), 145–156.

Anthony, W. A. (1979). *Principles of psychiatric rehabilitation.* Baltimore: University Park Press.

Anthony, W. A. (1994). Recovery from mental illness: The guiding vision of the mental health system in the 1990's. In IAPSRS (Eds.), *An introduction to psychiatric rehabilitation* (pp. 557–57). Boston: International Association of Psychosocial Rehabilitation Services.

Anthony, W. A. (1996, April). Managed care case management for people with serious mental illness. *Behavioral Healthcare Tomorrow,* 67–69.

Anthony, W. A., Cohen, M. R., & Farkas, M. D. (1990). *Psychiatric rehabilitation.* Boston: Boston University, Center for Psychiatric Rehabilitation.

Arns, P., & Linney, J. (1993). Work, self, and life satisfaction for persons with severe and persistent mental disorders. *Psychosocial Rehabilitation Journal, 17*(2), 63–79.

Aviram, U. & Segal, S. P. (1973). "Exclusion of the mentally ill. Reflection of an old problem in a new context." *Archives of General Psychiatry, 29,* 126–131.

Axelrod, S., & Wetzler, S. (1989). Factors associated with better compliance with psychiatric aftercare. *Hospital and Community Psychiatry, 40,* 397–401.

Axinn, J., & Levin, H. (1975). *Social welfare: A history of the American response to need.* New York: Harper & Row.

Bachrach, L. L. (1982). Young chronic patients: An analytic review of the literature. *Hospital and Community Psychiatry, 33,* 189–197.

Bachrach, L. L. (1992). Case management revisited. *Hospital and Community Psychiatry, 43*(3), 209–210.

Barker, R. (1968). *Ecological psychology*. Stanford, CA: Stanford University Press.

Barry, K. L., Zeber, J. E. et al. (2003). "Effect of strengths model versus assertive community treatment model on participant outcomes and utilization: two-year follow-up." *Psychiatric Rehabilitation Journal, 26*(3), 268–277.

Bartlett, H. M. (1958). Toward clarification and improvement of social work practice. *Social Work, 3*, 3–9.

Bateson, G. (1972). Steps to an ecology of mind. New York: Ballentine.

Bassuk, E. L. (1986). *The mental health needs of homeless persons*. San Francisco: Jossey-Bass.

Becker, D. R. & Bond, G. R. (2002). *Supported employment implementation resource kit: User's guide*. Rockville, MD: Center for Mental Health Services, SAMHSA.

Becker, D. R. & Drake, R. E. (2003). *A working life for people with severe mental illness*. New York: Oxford University Press.

Beisser, A. (1990). *Flying without wings: Personal reflections on loss, disability, and healing*. New York: Bantam.

Berg, I. K., & Miller, S. D. (1992). *Working with the problem drinker: A solution-focused approach*. New York: W. W. Norton.

Berlin, I. N. (1968). Resistance to change in mental health professionals. *American Journal of Orthopsychiatry, 69*, 109–115.

Bissonnette, D. (1994). *Beyond traditional job development. The art of creating opportunity*. Chatsworth, CA: Milt Wright and Associates.

Blanch, A., Carling, P. J. et al. (1988). "Normal housing with specialized supports: A psychiatric rehabilitation approach to living in the community." *Rehabilitation Psychology, 33*(1), 47–55.

Blanch, A., & Parrish, J. (1993). *Alternatives to involuntary treatment: Results of three roundtable discussions*. Bethesda, MD: Community Support Program, Center for Mental Health Services.

Bleach, A., & Ryan, P. (1995). *Community support for mental health: A handbook for the care programme approach and care management*. London: The Sainsbury Centre for Mental Health.

Bleuler, M. (1978). *The schizophrenic disorders* (p. 409). New Haven, CT: Yale University Press.

Bond, G. R. (1991). Variations in an assertive outreach model. *New Directions for Mental Health Services, 52*, 65–80.

Bond, G. R. (1998). "Principles of the individual placement and support model: Empirical support." *Psychiatric Rehabilitation Journal, 22*(1), 11–23.

Bond, G. R., & Dincin, J. (1986). Accelerating entry into transitional employment in a psychosocial agency. *Rehabilitation Psychology, 31*, 143–145.

Bond, G. R., Evans, L., Salyers, M. P., Williams, J. & Kim, H. (2000). Measurement of fidelity in psychiatric rehabilitation. *Mental Health Services Research, 2*(2), 75–87.

Bond, G. R., McDonel, E. C., & Miller, L. D. (1991). Assertive community treatment and reference groups: An evaluation of their effectiveness for young adults with serious mental illness and substance abuse problems. *Psychosocial Rehabilitation Journal, 15*(2), 31–43.

Bond, G. R., McGrew, J. H., & Fekete, D. M. (1995). Assertive outreach for frequent users of psychiatric hospitals: A meta-analysis. *Journal of Mental Health Administration, 22*(1), 4–16.

Bond, G. R., Salyers, M. P. et al. (2004). "How evidence-based practices contribute to community integration." *Community Mental Health Journal, 40*, 569–588.

Bond, G. R., Witheridge, T. F., Dincin, J., & Wasner, D. (1991). Assertive community treatment: Correcting some misconceptions. *American Journal of Community Psychology, 19*(1), 41–51.

Borland, A., McRae, J., & Lycan, C. (1989). Outcomes of five years of continuous intensive case management. *Hospital and Community Psychiatry, 40,* 369–76.

Boyer, S. L. (1991). *A comparison of three types of case management on burnout and job satisfaction.* Doctoral dissertation, Department of Psychology, Indiana University-Purdue University, Indianapolis.

Brehm, J. W. (1966). *A theory or psychological reactance.* New York: Academic.

Bright, J. R. (1964). *Research, development, and technological innovation: An introduction.* Homewood, IL: Irwin.

Brower, A. M. (1988). Can the ecological model guide social work practice? *Social Service Review, 62*(3), 411–429.

Bryer, J. B., Nelson, B. A., Miller, J. B., & Krol, P. A. (1987). Childhood sexual and physical abuse as a factor in adult psychiatric illness. *American Journal of Psychiatry, 144,* 1426–1430.

Bulham, H. A. (1985). *Frantz Fanon and the psychology of oppression.* New York: Plenum Press.

Burgess, E. (1939). Introduction. In R. Faris & H. W. Dunham (Eds). *Mental disorders in urban areas* (pp. 1–3). Chicago: University of Chicago Press.

Burns, M. (1958). *The historical development of the process of casework supervision as seen in the professional literature of social work.* Unpublished doctoral dissertation, University of Chicago.

Caboolture Adult Mental Health Services. (1995). *Community connections: The cornerstone of community services development for people with a psychiatric disability in Caboolture.* Caboolture, Queensland, Australia: Author.

Carling, P. J. (1995). *Return to community.* New York: Guilford Press.

Carling, P, J., & Ridgway, P. A. (1988). Overview of a psychiatric rehabilitation approach to housing. In W. A. Anthony & M. A. Farkus (Eds.), *Psychiatric rehabilitation: Turning theory into practice.* Baltimore: Johns Hopkins University Press.

Carlson, L., Gowdy, E. et al. (1998). *Best practice in reducing hospitalization.* Lawrence, KS: University of Kansas School of Social Welfare.

Carlson, L. S., Eichler, M. S., Huff, S. & Rapp, C. A. (2003). *A tale of two cities: Best practice in supported education.* Lawrence, KS: The University of Kansas School of Social Welfare.

Center for Mental Health Services. (1993). *Mental Health Statistics.* Rockville, MD: Author.

Chafetz, L., & Goldfinger, S. M. (1984). Residential instability in a psychiatric emergency setting. *Psychiatric Quarterly, 56,* 20–34.

Chamberlain, R., & Rapp, C. A. (1991). A decade of case management: A methodological review of outcome research. *Community Mental Health Journal, 27*(3), 171–188.

Chamberlain, R., Topp D., & Lee, R. (1995). *Kansas Mental Health Reform: Progress as Promised.* Lawrence, KS: The University of Kansas School of Social Welfare.

Chamberlin, J. (1978). *On our own: Patient-controlled alternatives to the mental health system.* New York: Hawthorn Books.

Chambers, D. (1993). *Social Policy & Social Programs.* New York: Macmillan.

Chapin, R. K. (1995). Social policy development: The strengths perspective. *Social Work, 40*(4), 506–514.

Ciompi, L. & Muller, C. (1976). *The life-course and aging of schizophrenics: A long-term follow-up study into old age.* Berlin, Germany: Springer.

Coleman, J. W., Katz, E., & Menzel, H. (1966). *Medical innovation: A diffusion study.* New York: Bobbs-Merrill.

Compton, B., & Galaway, B. (1984). *Social work process* (3rd ed.). Homewood, IL: Dorsey.

Cowger, C. (1989). Assessment guidelines for clinical practice: A strengths perspective. *University of Illinois School of Social Work Newsletter, 2*(2), 4–5.

Cowger, C. D. (1992). Assessment of client strengths. In D. Saleebey (Ed). The Strengths *Perspective in Social Work Practice*, (pp. 139–147). New York: Longman.

Crane-Ross, D., Roth, D. et al. (2000). "Consumers' and case managers' perceptions of mental health and community support service needs." *Community Mental Health Journal*, *36*(2), 161–178.

Crapanzano, V. (1982). The self, the third, and desire. In B. Lee, (Ed). *Psychosocial theories of the self*, (pp. 179–260). New York: Plenum Press.

Curtis, J. L., Millman, E. J., & Struening, E. (1992). Effect of case management on rehospitalization and utilization of ambulatory care services. *Hospital and Community Psychiatry*, *43*, 895–899.

Curtis, L. C., & Hodge, M. (1994). Old standards, new dilemmas: Ethics and boundaries in community support services. In The Publication Committee of IAPSRS (Eds). *An introduction to psychiatric rehabilitation.* (pp. 339–56). Boston: The International Association of Psychosocial Rehabilitation Services.

Davidson, W. S., & Rapp, C. A. (1976). Child advocacy in the justice system. *Social Work*, *21*, 225–232.

de Shazer, S. (1988). A requiem for power. *Contemporary Family Therapy*, *10*, 69–76.

Deci, E. L. & Ryan, R. M. (2000). "The "what" and "why" of goal pursuits: Human needs and the self-determination of behavior." *Psychological Inquiry*, *11*, 227–268.

Deegan, P. (1990). Spirit breaking: When the helping professions hurt. *Humanistic Psychologist*, *18*(3), 301–313.

Deegan, P. (1992). The independent living movement and people with psychiatric disabilities: Taking back control over our own lives. *Psychosocial Rehabilitation Journal*, *15*(3), 3–19.

Deegan, P. E. (1988). Recovery: The lived experience of rehabilitation. *Psychosocial Rehabilitation*, *11*(4), 11–19.

Deegan, P.E. (1996). Recovery as a journey of the heart. *Psychiatric Rehabilitation Journal*, *19*(3), 91–97.

Deegan, P. E. (2005). The Importance of Personal Medicine: A Quality Study of Resilience in People with Psychiatric Disabilities. *Scandinavian Journal of Public Health*, *66*, 1–7.

Degen, K., Cole, N., Tamayo, L., & Dzerovych, G. (1990). Intensive case management for the seriously mentally ill. *Administration and Policy in Mental Health*, *17*(4), 265–269.

Deitchman, W. S. (1980). How many case managers does it take to screw in a light bulb? *Hospital and Community Psychiatry*, *31*, 788–89.

DeJong, P., & Miller, S. D. (1995). How to interview for client strengths. *Social Work*, *40*(6), 721–864.

DeSisto, M. J., Harding, C. M., et al. (1995a). "The Maine Vermont three-decades studies of serious mental illness: I. Matched comparisons of cross-sectional outcome." British Journal of Psychiatry, 167, 331–338.

DeSisto, M.J., Harding, C.M., et al. (1995b). The Maine and Vermont three-decades studies of serious mental illness: II. Longitudinal course. *British Journal of Psychiatry*, 167, 338–342.

DiClemente, C. C., & Velasquez, M. W. (2002). Motivational interviewing and the stages of change. In W. R. Miller & S. Rollnick (Eds.), *Motivational interviewing: Preparing people for change* (2nd ed., pp. 217–250). New York: Guilford Press.

Dietzen, L. L., & Bond, G. R. (1993). Relationship between case manager contact and outcome for frequently hospitalized psychiatric clients. *Hospital and Community Psychiatry*, *44*(90), 839–43.

Dion, G., & Anthony, W.A. (1987). Research in psychiatric rehabilitation: A review of experimental and quasi-experimental studies. *Rehabilitation Counseling Bulletin*, *30*, 177–203.

Dodd, P., & Gutierrez, L. (1990). Preparing students for the future: A power perspective on community practice. *Administration in Social Work, 14*(2), 63–78.

Doll, W. (1976). Family coping with the mentally ill: An unanticipated problem of deinstitutionalization. *Hospital & Community Psychiatry, 27*(3), 183–185.

Drake, R. E., Goldman, H. H. et al. (2001). Implementing evidence-based practices in routine mental health service settings. *Psychiatric Services, 52*(2), 179–182.

Drake, R. E., Mercer-McFadden, C., Muesser, K. T., McHugo, G., & Bond, G. R. (1998). A review of integrated mental health and substance abuse treatment for patients with dual disorders. *Schizophrenia Bulletin, 24*(4), 589–608.

Drake, R. E., Merrens, M. R., & Lynde, D. W. (Eds.). (2005). *Evidence-based mental health practice: A textbook.* New York: W. W. Norton & Company.

Eichler, M. S., Gowdy, E. A., & Etzel-Wise, D. (2004). *I'm in my home and I'm happy: Effective supported housing practices in Kansas.* Lawrence, KS: The University of Kansas School of Social Welfare.

Elton, C. (1927). *Animal Ecology.* London: Sedgewick and Jackson.

Estroff, S. E. (1987). No more young adult chronic patients. *Hospital and Community Psychiatry, 38*(1), 5.

Estroff, S. E. (1989). Self, identity and subjective experiences of schizophrenia: In search of the subject. *Schizophrenia Bulletin, 15*(2), 189–96.

Ewalt, P. L., & Honeyfield, R. M. (1981). Needs of persons in long-term care. *Social Work, 25*, 223–231.

Fanon, F. (1968). *The wretched of the earth.* New York: Grove Press.

Faris, R., & Dunham, H. W. (1939). *Mental disorders in urban areas.* Chicago: University of Chicago Press.

Fast, B., & Chapin, R. (1996). The strengths model in long-term care: Linking cost containment and consumer empowerment. *Journal of Case Management, 5*(2), 51–57.

Fast, B., Chapin, R., & Rapp, C. (1994). *A model for strengths-based case management with older adults: Curriculum and training program.* Unpublished manuscript, School of Social Welfare, The University of Kansas, Lawrence, KS.

Fergeson, D. (1992). In the company of heroes. *The Journal, 3*(2), 29.

Fischer, J. (1978). *Effective casework practice.* New York: McGraw-Hill.

Franklin, J., Solovitz, B., Mason, M., Clemons, J., & Miller, G. (1987). An evaluation of case management. *American Journal of Public Health, 77*, 674.

Freire, P. (1970). *Pedagogy of the oppressed.* New York: Continuum.

Friedrich, R. M. (July, 1995). *Is there hope for those who require long-term care?* Paper presented at the National Alliance for the Mentally Ill Annual Convention, Washington, DC.

Gamson, W. A. (1968). *Power and discontent.* Homewood, IL: Dorsey.

Gehrs, M., & Goering, P. (1994). The relationship between working alliance and rehabilitative outcomes of schizophrenia. *Psychiatric Rehabilitation Journal, 18*, 43–54.

General Accounting Office (1996). *Practice guidelines: Managed care plans customize guidelines to local interests.* Washington, DC: General Accounting Office.

Germain, C., & Gitterman, A. (1980). *The life model of social work practice.* New York: Columbia University Press.

Germain, C. B. (1991). *Human behavior in the social environment: An ecological view.* New York: Columbia University Press.

Glaser, E. M., Abelson, H. H., & Garrison, K. N. (1983). *Putting knowledge to use.* San Francisco: Jossey-Bass.

Glater, S. I. (1992). The journey home. *The Journal, 3*(2), 21–22.

Goering, P., Wasylenki, D., Farkas, M., Lancee, W., & Ballantyne, R. (1988). What difference does case management make? *Hospital and Community Psychiatry, 39*, 272–76.

Goffman, E. (1961). *Asylums.* Garden City, NY: Anchor Books

Goldfinger, S. M., Dickey, B., Hellman, S., O'Bryan, M. O., Penk, W., Schutte, R. R., Seidman, L J., & Ware, N. (1994). The Boston project: Promoting housing stability and empowerment. In Center for Mental Health Services (Ed.), *Making a difference: Interim status report on the McKinney Research Demonstration Program for homeless mentally ill adults,* 39–56.

Goldstein, H. (1943). *Social practice: A unitary approach.* Columbia, SC: University of South Carolina.

Goldstein, H. (1992). Victors or victims: Contrasting views of clients in social work practice. In D. Saleebey (Ed.), *The strengths perspective in social work practice.* (pp. 27–38). New York: Longman.

Goscha, R. (2005). *Pawnee Mental Health Center strengths case management report.* Lawrence, KS: The University of Kansas School of Social Welfare.

Gowdy, E., & Rapp, C. A. (1989), Managerial behavior: The common denominators of effective community based programs. *Psychosocial Rehabilitation Journal, 13,* 31–51.

Grimmer, D. (1992). The invisible illness. *The Journal, 3*(2), 27–28.

Grimshaw, J. M., Shirran, L., Thomas, R., Mowatt, G., Fraser, C., & Bero, L., et al. (2001). Changing provider behavior: An overview of systematic reviews of interventions. *Med Care, 39,*(8, Suppl. 2), 11–45.

Grinnell, J. (1917). Field tests of theories concerning distribution control. *American Naturalist, 51,* 115–128.

Gutierrez, L. M., Parsons, R. J., & Cox, E. O. (1998). *Empowerment in social work practice: A sourcebook.* Pacific Grove, CA: Brooks/Cole.

Gutride, M. E., Goldstein, G. P., & Hunter, G. F. (1973). The use of modeling and role playing to increase social interaction among social psychiatric patients. *Journal of Consulting and Clinical Psychology, 40,* 408–415.

Hackney, H., & Cormier, L. S. (1973). *Counseling strategies and objectives.* Englewood Cliffs, NJ: Prentice-Hall.

Harding, C., Brooks, G., Takamaura, A., Strauss, J., & Brier, A. (1987b). The Vermont longitudinal study of persons with severe mental illness I: Methodology, study sample, and over all status 32 years later. *American Journal of Psychiatry, 144*(6), 718–26.

Harding, C., Zubin, J., & Strauss, J. (1987). Chronicity in schizophrenia: Fact, partial fact, or artifact? *Hospital and Community Psychiatry, 38*(5), 477–86.

Harding, C. M., Brooks, G., Ashikage, T., Strauss, J. S., & Brier, A. (1987a). The Vermont longitudinal study of persons with severe mental illness II: Long-term outcome of subjects who retrospectively met *DSM-III* criteria for schizophrenia. *American Journal of Psychiatry, 144*(6), 727–35.

Hatfield, A.B., & Lefley, H.P. (1993). *Surviving mental illness: Stress, coping and adaptation.* New York: Guilford Press.

Heider, F. (1958). *The psychology of interpersonal relations.* New York: Wiley.

Hepworth, D., & Larsen, J. A. (1986). *Direct social work practice.* Chicago: Dorsey.

Hogan, M. & Carling, P. J. (1992). "Normal housing: A key element of a supported housing approach for people with psychiatric disabilities." *Journal of Community Mental Health, 28,* 215–226.

Holingshead, A.B., & Redlick, F.C. (1958). *Social class and mental illness.* New York: Wiley & Sons.

Hornstra, R. K., Bruce-Wolfe, V., Sagduyu, K., & Riffle, D. W. (1993). The effect of intensive case management on hospitalization of patients with schizophrenia. *The Journal of Hospital and Community Psychiatry, 44*(9), 844–53.

Hough, R., Harmon, S., Tarke, H., Yamashiro, S., Quinlivan, R., Laudau-Cox, P., Malone, R., Renker, V., & Morris, B. (1994). The San Diego Project: Providing independent housing and supported services. In Center for Mental Health Services (Ed.), *Making a difference: Interim status report on the McKinney Research Demonstration Program for homeless mentally ill adults*, 91–110.

Huber, G., Gross, G. et al. (1975). "A long-term follow-up study of schizophrenia: Psychiatric course and prognosis." *Acta Psychiatrica Scandinavica, 52*(1), 49–57.

Huxley, P., & Warner, R. (1992). Case management, quality of life, and satisfaction with services of long-term psychiatric patients. *Hospital and Community Psychiatry, 43*(8), 799–802.

Jacobson, A., & Richardson, B. (1987). Assault experiences of 100 psychiatric inpatients: Evidence of the need for routine inquiry. *American Journal of Psychiatry, 144*, 908–13.

Jaffe, P. G., & Carlson, P. M. (1976). Relative efficacy of modeling and instructions in eliciting social behavior from chronic psychiatric patients. *Journal of Consulting and Clinical Psychology, 44*, 200–207.

Jansson, B. (1990). *Social Welfare Policy*. Belmont, CA: Wadsworth.

Kadushin, A. (1974). Supervisor-supervisee: A survey. *Social Work, 19*(3), 288–97.

Kagle, J. D., & Cowger, C. D. (1984). Blaming the client: Implicit agenda in practice research. *Social Work, 29*(4), 347–352.

Kaplan, L., & Girard, J. (1994). *Strengthening high-risk families*. New York: Lexington Books.

Karger, H. J. (1981). Burnout as alienation. *Social Service Review, 55*(2), 270–83.

Kaufman, J., & Zigler, E. (1987). Do Abused Children Become Abusive Parents? *American Journal of Orthopsychiatry, 57*, 186–92.

Keil, J. (1992). The mountain of my mental illness. *The Journal, 3*(2), 5–6.

Kieffer, C.H. (1984). Citizen empowerment: A developmental perspective. In *Studies in empowerment* (pp 9–36). New York: The Haworth Press.

King, R., Le Bas, J. et al. (2000). "The impact of caseload on the personal efficacy of mental health case managers." *Psychiatric Services, 51*(3), 364–368.

Kirk, S., & Kutchins, H. J. (1988). Deliberate misdiagnosis in mental health practice. *Social Service Review, 62*, 225–37.

Kisthardt, W. (1992). A strengths model of case management: The principles and functioning of helping partnerships with persons with persistent mental illness. In D. Saleebey (Ed.), *The strengths model of social work* (pp. 59–83). New York: Longman.

Kisthardt, W. (1993). The impact of the strengths model of case management from the consumer perspective. In M. Harris & H. Bergman (Eds.), *Case management: Theory and practice* (pp. 165–82). Washington, DC: American Psychiatric Association.

Kisthardt, W. E., & Rapp, C. A. (1992). Bridging the gap between principles and practice: Implementing a strengths perspective in case management. In S. M. Rose (Ed.), *Case management and social work practice.* (pp. 112–25). New York: Longman.

Kisthardt, W. E., & Rapp, C. A. (1996). *Reconsidering Social Isolation from a Strengths Perspective*. Lawrence, KS: The University of Kansas School of Social Welfare.

Kretzmann, J. B., & McKnight, J. L. (1993). *Building Communities from the Inside Out*. Evanston, IL: Northwestern University.

Lamb, H. R., & Goetzel, V. (1971). Discharged mental patients—Are they really in the community? *Archives of General Psychiatry, 24*, 29–34.

Lamb, R. H. (1980). Therapist-case managers: More than brokers of service. *Hospital and Community Psychiatry, 31*, 762–64.

Lambert, M. (1992). Psychotherapy outcome research. In J. C. Norcross and M. R. Goldfried (Eds.), Handbook of psychotherapy integration (pp. 94–129). New York: Basic Books.

Larson, C. U. (1983). *Persuasion: Reception and responsibility* (3rd ed.). Belmont, CA: Wadsworth.

Lee, J. A. B. (1994). *The empowerment approach to social work practice*. New York: Columbia University Press.

Leete, E. (1988). A consumer perspective on psychosocial treatment. *Psychosocial Rehabilitation, 12*(2), 45–62.

Leete, E. (1989). How I perceive and manage my illness. *Schizophrenia Bulletin, 15,* 197–200.

Leete, E. (1993). The interpersonal environment: A consumer's personal recollection. In A. B. Hatfield & H. P. Lefley (Eds.) *Surviving mental illness,* (pp. 114–28). New York: Guilford Press.

Lehman, A. F., Postrado, L. T. et al. (1994). Continuity of care and client outcomes in the Robert Wood Johnson Foundation program on chronic mental illness. *Milbank Quarterly, 72,* 105–122.

Leiby, J. (1978). *A history of social welfare and social work in the United States.* New York: Columbia University Press.

Leventhal, H. (1970). Findings and theory in the study of fear communication. In L. Berkowitz (Ed.), *Advances in Experimental Social Psychology, 5.* (pp. 119–86). New York: Academic.

Levine, I. S., & Fleming, M. (undated). *Human resource development: Issues in Case Management.* Baltimore: University of Maryland Center of Rehabilitation and Manpower Services.

Levstek, D. A., & Bond, G. R. (1993). Housing cost, quality, and satisfaction among formerly homeless persons with serious mental illness in two cities. *Innovations and Research, 2*(3), 1–8.

Liberman, R. P. (1992). *Handbook of psychiatric rehabilitation.* New York: Macmillan.

Liberman, R. P., Massel, H. K., Mosk, M. D., & Wong, S. E. (1985). Social skills training for chronic mental patients. *Hospital and Community Psychiatry, 36,* 396–403.

Locke, E., Shaw, K., Saari, L., & Latham, G. (1981). Goal setting and task performance: 1969–1980. *Psychological Bulletin, 90*(1), 125–52.

Locke, E. A., & Latham, G. P. (1990). *A theory of goal setting and task performance.* Englewood Cliffs, New Jersey: Prentice-Hall.

Macias, C., Farley, O. W. et al. (1997). Case management in the context of capitation financing: An evaluation of the strengths model. *Administration and Policy in Mental Health, 24*(6), 535–543.

Macias, C., Kinney, R., Farley, O. W., Jackson, R., & Vos, B. (1994). The role of case management within a community support system: Partnership with psychosocial rehabilitation. *Community Mental Health Journal, 30*(4), 323–39.

Maluccio, A. (1979). *Learning from clients: Interpersonal helping as viewed by clients and social workers.* New York: The Free Press.

Maluccio, A. N. (1981). *Promoting Competence in Clients.* New York: Free Press.

Martin, P. Y. (1980). Multiple constituencies, dominant social values, and the human services administrator: Implications for service solving. *Administration in Social Work, 4*(2), 15–27.

McClelland, D.C., Atkinson, J.W., Clark, R.W., & Lowell, E.L. (1953). *The achievement motive.* New York: Appleton-Century-Crofts.

McCrory, D. (1991). The rehabilitation alliance. *Journal of Vocational Rehabilitation, 1*(3), 58–66.

McCrory, D., Connoly, P., Hanson-Mayer, T., Sheridan-Landolfi, J., Borone, F., Blood, A., & Gilson, A. (1980). The rehabilitation crisis: The impact of growth. *Journal of Applied Rehabilitation Counseling, 11*(3), 136–39.

McGrew, J. H., & Bond, G. R. (1995). Critical ingredients of assertive community treatment: Judgments of the experts. *The Journal of Mental Health Administration, 22*(2), 113–25.

McGrew, J. H., Bond, G. R., Dietzen, L., & Salyers, M. (1994). Measuring the fidelity of implementation of a mental health program model. *Journal of Consulting and Clinical Psychology, 62*(4), 670–78.

McKnight, J.L. (undated). *Beyond community services.* Evanston, IL: Northwestern University Center for Urban Affairs.

McQuilken, M., Zahniser, J. H. et al. (2003). "The work project survey: Consumer perspectives on work." *Journal of Vocational Rehabilitation, 18,* 59–68.

Mills, R. C., & Kelly, J. G. (1972). Cultural adaptation and ecological analogies: Analysis of three Mexican villages. In S. E. Golann & C. Eisdorfer (Eds.) *Handbook of community mental health.* (pp. 61–75). New York: Appleton-Century-Crofts.

Mintzberg, H. (1979). *The nature of managerial work.* Englewood Cliffs, NJ: Prentice-Hall.

Miringoff, M. L. (1980). *Management in human service organizations.* New York: Macmillan.

Modrcin, M., Rapp, C., & Chamberlain, R. (1985). *Case management with psychiatrically disabled individuals: Curriculum & Training Program.* Lawrence, KS: University of Kansas School of Social Welfare.

Modrcin, M., Rapp, C., & Poertner, J. (1988). The evaluation of case management services with the chronically mentally ill. *Evaluation and Program Planning, 11,* 307–14.

Moore-Kirkland, J. (1981). Mobilizing motivation: From theory to practice. In A. Maluccio (Ed.), *Promoting competence in clients.* (pp. 27–54). New York: Free Press.

Muesser, K. T., Salyers, M. P. et al. (2001). "A prospective analysis of work in schizophrenia." *Schizophrenia Bulletin, 27*(2), 281–296.

Munson, C. (1979). An empirical study of structure and authority in social work supervision. In C. Munson, (Ed.), *Social work supervision,* (pp. 286–96). New York: Free Press.

Murphy, L. B. (1962). *The widening world of childhood.* New York: Basic Books.

National Association of State Mental Health Program Directors. (1987). *Position statement on housing and support for people with long-term mental illness.* Alexandria, VA: NASMHPD.

National Institute of Mental Health. (1987). *Guidelines for meeting the housing needs of people with psychiatric disabilities.* Rockville, MD: NIMH.

Naylor, J., & Ilgen, D. (1984). Goal setting: A theoretical analysis of a motivational technology. In B. Staw & L. L. Cummings (Eds.), *Research in organizational behavior,* (Vol. 6, pp. 95–140). Greenwich, CT: Jai Press.

Neale, M., & Rosenheck, R. (1995). Therapeutic alliance and outcome in a VA intensive case management program. *Psychiatric Services, 46,* 719–721.

Neugeboren, B. (1985). *Organization, Policy, and Practice in the Human Services.* New York: Longman.

Noble, J., Hornberg, R., Hall, L. L., & Flynn, L. M. (1997). *A legacy of failure: The inability of the federal-state vocational rehabilitation system to serve people with severe mental illness.* Washington, DC: National Alliance for the Mentally Ill.

Ogawa, K., Miya, M. et al. (1987). "A long-term follow-up study of schizophrenia in Japan, with special reference to the course of social adjustment." *British Journal of Psychiatry, 151,* 758–765.

Olmstead, J., & Christensen, H. (1974). *Research report no. 2—Effects of agency work contexts: An intensive field study* (SRS No. 74–05416). Washington, DC: U.S. Government Printing Office.

Onken, S. J., Dumont, J. M. et al. (2002). *Mental health recovery: What helps and what hinders?* Washington, DC: National Technical Assistance Center for State Mental Health Planning, National Association of State Mental Health Program Directors.

Park, R. (1952). *Human communities.* Glencoe, IL: Free Press.

Patti, R. (1977, Spring). Patterns of management activity in social welfare agencies. *Administration in Social Work, 1*(1), 548.

Patti, R. (1985, Fall). In search of purpose for social welfare administration. *Administration in Social Work, 9*(3), 1–14.

Peele, S., & Brodsky, A. (1991). *The truth about addiction and recovery.* New York: Simon & Schuster/Fireside.

Pierce, C. (1970). Offensive mechanisms. In F. B. Barbour (Ed.) *The Black 70's* (pp. 265–282). Boston: Porter Sargent Publishers.

Peters, T. J., & Waterman, R. H. (1982). *In search of excellence.* New York: Harper & Row.

Peterson, C., Maier, S., & Seligman, M.E.P. (1993). *Learned helplessness: A theory for the age of personal control.* New York: Oxford.

Pincus, A., & Minahan, A. (1973). *Social work practice: Model and method.* Itasca, IL: F. E. Peacock Publishers.

Porter, M., & Sherman, P. S. (1988). *The Denver case management project.* Denver: Colorado Division of Mental Health.

Prochaska, J. O., Norcross, J. C., & DiClemente, C. C. (1994). *Changing for good: The revolutionary program that explains the six stages of change and teaches you how to free yourself from bad habits.* New York: W. Morrow.

Quinlivan, R., Hough, R., Crowell, A., Beach, C., Hofstetter, & Kenworthy, K. (1995). Service utilization and costs of care for severely mentally ill clients in an intensive case management program. *Psychiatric Services, 46*(4), 365–75.

Rapp, C. A. (1992). The strengths perspective of case management with persons suffering from severe mental illness. In D. Saleebey (Ed.), *The strength perspectives in social work* (pp. 45–58). New York: Longman.

Rapp, C. A. (1993). Client-centered performance management for rehabilitation and mental health services. In R. W. Flexer & P. L. Solomon (Eds.), *Psychiatric rehabilitation in practice.* (pp. 173–92). Boston: Andover Medical Publishers.

Rapp, C. A. (1993). Theory, principles, and methods of strengths model of case management. In M. Harris & H. Bergman (Eds.), *Case management: Theory and practice.* (pp. 143–64). Washington, DC: American Psychiatric Association.

Rapp, C. A. (1995). The active ingredients of effective case management: A research synthesis. In L. Giesler (Ed.), *Case management for behavioral managed care.* (pp. 5–45). Washington, DC: Center for Mental Health Services.

Rapp, C. A., & Chamberlain, R. (1985). Case management services to the chronically mentally ill. *Social Work, 30*(5), 417–22.

Rapp, C. A., & Poertner, J. (1992). *Social administration: A client-centered approach.* New York: Longman.

Rapp, C. A., & Wintersteen, R. (1989). The strengths model of case management: Results from twelve demonstrations. *Psychosocial Rehabilitation Journal, 13*(1), 23–32.

Rappaport, J. (1977). *Community psychology.* New York: Holt, Rinehart & Winston.

Rappaport, J. (1985). The power of empowerment language. *Social policy, 16,* 15–21.

Rappaport, J. (1990). Research methods and the empowerment social agenda. In P. Tolan, C. Keys, F. Chertok, & L. Jason (Eds.), *Researching community psychology.* Washington, DC: American Psychological Association.

Rappaport, J., Davidson, W., Mitchell, A., & Wilson, M. N. (1975). Alternatives to blaming the victim or the environment: Our places to stand have not moved the earth. *American Psychologist, 30,* 525–28.

Reilly, S. (1992). Breaking loose. *The Journal, 3*(2), 20.

Richmond, M. (1922). *What is social casework?* New York: Russell Sage.

Ridgway, P. (2000). *Resilience and recovery for psychiatric disability: Linko in concepts and research: Draft.* Washington, DC: Center for Mental Health Service.

Ridgway, P. (2001). "Re-storying psychiatric disability: Learning from first person narrative accounts of recovery." *Psychiatric Rehabilitation Journal, 24*(4), 335–343.

Ridgway, P., & Zipple, A. M. (1990). The paradigm shift in residential services: From the linear continuum to supported housing approaches. *Psychosocial Rehabilitation Journal, 13,* 11–31.

Rife, J. C., Greenlee, R. W., Miller, L. D., & Feichter, M. A. (1991). Case management with homeless mentally ill people. *Health and Social Work, 16*(1), 58–67.

Risser, P., A. (1992). An empowering journey. *The Journal, 3*(2), 38–39.

Robinson, G., & Bergman, G. T. (1989). *Choices in case management.* Washington, DC: Policy-Resources Incorporated.

Rog, D. (2004). "The evidence on supported housing." *Psychiatric Rehabilitation Journal, 27*(4), 334–343.

Rogers, C. R. (1959). A theory of therapy, personality and interpersonal relationships as developed in the client-centered framework. In S. Koch (Ed.), *Psychology: A study of a science, vol. II.* New York: McGraw-Hill.

Rogers, E. M. (1968). *Diffusion of innovations* (3rd ed.). New York: Free Press.

Rogers, E. M. (1983). The communication of innovations in a complex institution. *Educational Records, 48,* 67–77.

Rogers, E. M., & Svenning, L. (1969). *Managing change.* Washington, DC: U.S. Office of Education.

Rogers, E. S., Walsh, D. et al. (1991). *Massachusetts survey of client preferences for community support services: Final report.* Boston: Center for Psychiatric Rehabilitation.

Rose, S.M. (1991). Acknowledging abuse backgrounds of intensive case management clients. *Community Mental Health Journal, 27*(4), 255–63.

Rose, S.M., & Black, B.L. (1985). *Advocacy and empowerment: Mental health care in the community.* Boston: Routledge & Kegan, Paul.

Rose, S. M., Peabody, C. G., & Stratigeas, B. (1991). Responding to hidden abuse: A role for social work in reforming mental health systems. *Social Work, 36*(5), 408–13.

Rothman, D. (1971). *The discovery of the asylum.* Boston: Little, Brown.

Russinova, Z. (1999). Providers' hope-inspiring competence as a factor optimizing psychiatric rehabilitation outcomes. *Journal of Rehabilitation, 65*(4), 50–57.

Ryan, C. S., Sherman, P. S., & Judd, C. M. (1994). Accounting for case management effects in the evaluation of mental health services. *Journal of Consulting and Clinical Psychology, 62*(5), 965–74.

Ryan, W. (1971). *Blaming the Victim.* New York: Random House.

Rydman, R. J. (1990). More hospital or more community? *Administration and Policy in Mental Health Services, 17*(4), 215–34.

Saleebey, D. (1996). The strengths perspective in social work practice: Extensions and cautions. *Social Work, 41*(3), 296–305.

Salyers, M. P., Masterton, T. W. et al. (1998). "Transferring clients from intensive case management: Impact on client functioning." *American Journal of Orthopsychiatry, 68,* 233–245.

Sanders, J. T., & Reppucci, N. D. (1977, October). Learning network among administrators of human service institutions. *American Journal of Community Psychology, 5,* 269–76.

Sands, R. G., & Cnaan, R. A. (1994). Two modes of case management: Assessing their impact. *Community Mental Health Journal, 30*(5), 441–57.

Santos, A. B., Doci, P. A., Lachanace, K. R., Dias, J. K., Sloop, T. B., Hiers, T. G., & Belvilacqua, J. J. (1993). Providing assertive community treatment for severely mentally ill patients in a rural area. *The Journal of Hospital and Community Psychiatry, 44*(1), 34–39.

Scheie-Lurie, M. (1992). Recovery: It takes more than finding the right pill. *The Journal, 3*(2), 36.

Sheafor, B. W., Horejsi, C. R., & Horejsi, G. A. (1991). *Techniques and guidelines for social work practice* (2nd ed.). Boston: Allyn & Bacon.

Sheldon, K. M. & Kasser, T. (1998). "Persuing personal goal: Skills enable progress but not all progress is beneficial." *Personality and Social Psychology Bulletin, 24,* 1319–1331.

Shern, D L., Lovell, A. M., Tsemberis, S., Anthony, W., LaComb, C., Richmond, L., Winarski, J., & Choen, M. (1994). The New York City Street Outreach Project: Serving a hard-to-reach population. In Center for Mental Health Services (Ed.), *Making a difference: Interim status report on the McKinney Research Demonstration Program for homeless mentally ill adults,* 57–73.

Shulman, L. (1979). *The skills of helping individuals and groups.* Itasca, IL: F. E. Peacock.

Shulman, L. (1992). *The skills of helping* (3rd ed.). Itasca, IL: F. E. Peacock.

Shulman, L., Robinson, E., & Lucky, A. (1981). *A study of the content context and skills of supervision.* Vancouver, Canada: University of British Columbia.

Simon, B. L. (1994). *The empowerment tradition in American social work.* New York: Columbia University Press.

Simons, R. L. (1982). Strategies for exercising influence. *Social Work Journal, 27*(3), 268–74.

Simons, R. L. (1985). Inducement as an approval to exercising influence. *Social Work, 30*(1), 56–68.

Simons, R. L. (1987). The skill of persuasion: An essential component of human services administration. *Administration in Social Work, 11*(3/4), 241–54.

Smalley, R. E. (1967). *Theory for social work practice.* New York: Columbia University Press.

Snyder, C. R. (1994). *The Psychology of Hope.* New York: Free Press.

Solomon, P. (1992). The efficacy of case management services for severely mentally disabled clients. *Community Mental Health Journal, 28,* 163–80.

Solomon, P., & Draine, J. (1994). Satisfaction with mental health treatment in a randomized trial of consumer case management. *Journal of Nervous and Mental Disease, 182,* 179–84.

Solomon, P., Draine, J., & Delaney, M. (1995). The working alliance and consumer case management. *Journal of Mental Health Administration, 22,* 126–134.

Srebnik, D., Livingston, J., Gordon, L., & King, D. (1995). Housing choice and community success for individuals with serious and persistent mental illness. *Community Mental Health Journal, 31*(2), 139–52.

Stanard, R. P. (1999). The effect of training in a strengths model of case management on outcomes in a community mental health center. *Community Mental Health Journal 35*(2), 169–179.

Stanley, R. (1992). Welcome to reality-Not a facsimile. *The Journal 3*(2), 25–26.

Steele, K. & C. Berman (2001). *The day the voices stopped: a memoir of madness and hope.* New York: Basic Books.

Stein, L., & Test, M. A. (1980). Alternative to mental hospital treatment 1 conceptual model: Treatment program, and clinical evaluation. *Archives of General Psychiatry, 37,* 392–97.

Strauss, J. B., Hafey, H., Lieberman, P., & Harding, C. M. (1985). The course of psychiatric disorder, III: Longitudinal principles. *American Journal of Psychiatry, 142,* 289–96.

Strauss, J. S. (1989). Subjective experiences of schizophrenia: Toward a new dynamic psychiatry. *Schizophrenia Bulletin, 15,* 177–78.

Strickberger, M.W. (1990). *Evolution.* Boston: Jones & Bartlett.

Sullivan, A. P., Nicolellis, D. L., Danley, K. S., & MacDonald-Wilson, K. (1994). Choose-Get-Keep: A psychiatric rehabilitation approach to supported education. In IAPSRS (Eds.), *An introduction to psychiatric rehabilitation* (pp. 230–40). Boston: International Association of Psychosocial Rehabilitation Services.

Sullivan, W. P. (1989). Community support programs in rural areas: Developing programs without walls. *Human Services in the Rural Environment, 12*(4), 19–24.

Sullivan, W. P. (1992). Reconsidering the environment as a helping resource. In D. Saleebey (Ed.) *The strengths perspective in social work.* (pp. 148–57). New York: Longman.

Sullivan, W. P. (1994a). A long and winding road: The process of recovery from severe mental illness. *Innovations and Research, 3,* 19–27.

Sullivan, W. P. (1994b). Recovery from schizophrenia: What we can learn from the developing nations. *Innovations and Research, 3*(2), 6–7.

Sullivan, W. P., & Rapp, C. A. (2002). Environmental Context, Opportunity and the Process of Recovery: The Role of Strengths Based Practice and Policy. In D. Saleeby (Ed.) *The Strengths Perspective in Social Work* (3rd ed.). New York: Longman.

Sullivan, W. P., & Rapp, C. A. (1991). Improving client outcomes: The Kansas technical assistance consultation project. *Community Mental Health Journal, 27*(5), 327–36.

Syx, C. (1995). The mental health service system: How we've created a make-believe world. *Psychiatric Rehabilitation Journal, 19*(1), 83–85.

Szasz, T. S. (1970). *The manufacture of madness: A comparative study of the inquisition and the mental health movement.* New York: Harper & Row.

Talbott, J. A. (1979). Deinstitutionalization: Avoiding the disasters of the past. *Hospital and Community Psychiatry, 30*(9), 621–24.

Talbott, J. A. (1988). The chronically mentally ill: What do we now know, and why aren't we implementing what we know? In J. A. Talbott (Ed.), *The perspective of John Talbott. New directions for mental health services, No. 37.* (pp. 43–58). San Francisco: Jossey-Bass.

Tanzman, B. (1993). An overview of surveys of mental health consumers' preferences for housing and support services. *Hospital and Community Psychiatry, 44,* 450–55.

Taylor, J. (1997). Niches and practice: Extending the ecological perspective. In D. Saleebey, (Ed.), *The strengths perspective in social work practice* (2nd ed.). New York: Longman.

Tedeschi, J. T., & Lindskold, S. (1976). *Social psychology: Interdependence, interaction and influence.* New York: Wiley.

Test, M. A. (1979). Continuity of care in community treatment. In L. I. Stein (Ed.), *Community support systems for the long-term patient.* New Directions for Mental Health Services, 2 (pp. 15–23). San Francisco: Jossey-Bass.

Test, M. A. (1992). Training in community living. In R. P. Lieberman (Ed.), *Handbook of psychiatric rehabilitation,* (Vol. 166, pp. 153–70). Needham Heights, MA: Allyn & Bacon.

Trickett, E. J., Kelly, J. G., & Todd, D. M. (1972). The social environment of the high school: Guidelines for individual change and organizational redevelopment. In S. E. Golann & C. Eisdorfer (Eds.), *Handbook of community mental health.* (pp. 98–115). New York: Appleton-Century-Crofts.

Truax, C. B., & Carkhuff, R. R. (1967). *Toward effective counseling and psychotherapy.* Chicago: Aldine.

Truax, C. B., & Mitchell, K. (1971). Research on certain therapist interpersonal skills in relation to process and outcome. In A. Bergin and S. Garfield (Eds.), *Handbook of psychotherapy and behavior change.* (pp. 299–344). New York: Wiley.

Tsuang, M. T., Woolson, R. F. et al. (1979). Long-term outcome of major psychosis. *Archives of General Psychiatry, 36,* 1295–1301.

Turner, J. C. (1977). Comprehensive community support systems for mentally disabled adults: Definitions, components, guiding principles. *Psychosocial Rehabilitation Journal, 1*(3), 39–47.

Turner, J. E., & Shifren, I. (1979). Community support system: How comprehensive? *New Directions for Mental Health Services, 2,* 1–13.

U.S. Department of Health and Human Services. (1983). *Statistical profile.* Washington, DC: U.S. Government Printing Office.

Unger, K. (1990). "Supported education for young adults with psychiatric disabilities." *Community Support Network News, 6*(3), 1–11.

Wasow, M. (1982). *Coping with schizophrenia: A survival manual for parents, relatives, and friends.* Palo Alto, CA: Science and Behavior Books.

Watzlawick, P., Weakland, J., & Fisch, R. (1974). *Change: Principles of problem formation and problem resolution.* New York: W. Norton.

Webster's Third New International Dictionary. (1976). Springfield, MA: G.C. Merriam.

Weick, A., & Chamberlain, R. (1997). Putting problems in their place: Further explorations in the strengths perspective. In D. Saleebey (Ed.), *The strengths perspective in social work practice* (2nd ed.). New York: Longman.

Weick, A., & Pope, L. (1988). Knowing what's best: A new look at self-determination. *Social Casework, 69*(1), 10–16.

Weick, A., Rapp, C. A., Sullivan, W. P., & Kisthardt, W. (1989, July). A strengths perspective for social work practice. *Social Work, 89,* 350–54.

Wells, C., & Masch, M. (1986). *Social work ethics: Guidelines for professional practice.* New York: Longman.

Werner, E., & Smith, R. (1982). *Vulnerable but invincible.* New York: Adams, Bannister, Cox.

Werner, E., & Smith, R. (1992). *Overcoming the odds.* Ithaca, NY: Cornell University Press.

White, R.W. (1959). Motivation reconsidered: The concept of competence. *Psychological Review, 66,* 297–333.

Wicklund, R. A. (1974). *Freedom and reactance.* Hillsdale, NJ: Erlbaum.

Wilson, W.J. (1987). *The truly disadvantaged: The inner city, the underclass, and public policy.* Chicago: The University of Chicago Press.

Wirth, L. (1964). *On cities and social life.* Selected papers edited by A. Reiss. Chicago: University of Chicago Press.

Witheridge, T. F. (1991). The "active ingredients" of assertive outreach. *New directions for mental health services, 52,* 47–64.

Wolfensberger, W. & Tullman, S. (1982). "A brief overview of the principle of normalization." *Rehabilitation Psychology, 27*(3), 131–145.

Wolin, S. J., & Wolin, S. (1993). *The resilient self.* New York: Villard Books.

Woolfolk, A. E., Woolfolk, R. L., & Wilson, G. T. (1977). A rose by any other name: Labeling bias and attitudes toward behavior modification. *Journal of Consulting and Clinical Psychology, 45,* 184–91.

Zaltman, G. (1973). *Processes and phenomena of social change.* New York: Wiley.

Zaltman, G., & Duncan, R. (1977). *Strategies for planned change.* New York: Wiley.

Index

Page numbers in bold indicate figures or tables